MW01687058

# SHIPPING BUSINESS

INSTITUTE OF
CHARTERED
SHIPBROKERS

Published by the

Institute of Chartered Shipbrokers

85 Gracechurch Street

London

EC3V 0AA

United Kingdom

Telephone: +44 20 7623 1111

Email: books@ics.org.uk

www.ics.org.uk

First published 2015
Reprinted 2018
ISBN 978-1-908833-65-5



Printed and bound in the UK by Cambrian Printers

Design and book production by Mark Clubb (design@theclubb.co.uk)

Front cover image: Port Pictures NL

# Foreword by
# HE Sultan Ahmed Bin Sulayem
# Chairman, DP World

The study of shipping, intrinsically brings with it the knowledge and understanding of the components of the fascinating and complex world of maritime transport and the role it plays in supporting and facilitating international trade. To place this education in a 21st Century context is even more crucial in view of the technological undercurrents that are rapidly changing the way the entire supply chain industry, including shipping, works.

As one of the original drivers of human civilisation and commerce, maritime transport has seen many transformational developments over the ages. From the simple oar to sail and steam engines, to electric and nuclear power, it has been a long journey in search of efficiency and excellence. Today we are on the cusp of another paradigm shift in the efficient management and seamless running of the supply chain across borders and around the world. This change is powered by information technology and the internet.

In today's technological age, as we know, information is power. The flow of information that supports the efficient management and smooth running of the maritime transport and logistics sectors is defining the way the industry functions, with far-reaching impacts on global trade and national economies. New generation container liners and marine terminals are already using IT-driven solutions such as gate automation, RFID tags to track container units, and sophisticated control tower operations that integrate everything from berthing ships to matching men and machines in the port area.

Increasingly too we are seeing road, rail and air connections linked to ports, with business parks springing up close by, making the port very much a hub and a gateway for trade. A prime example of this model is in Dubai with the Dubai Logistics Corridor, which opened in 2010. Jebel Ali port, which handles more than 15m teu a year, and the connected Jebel Ali Free Zone, now also under the DP World umbrella, home to more than 7000 international companies, is directly linked to Al Maktoum International Airport. Cargo from the seaport can move to the airport in just 20 minutes. Meanwhile, sophisticated and interlinked IT eliminates paperwork, provides visibility of shipments, monitors carrier and supply performance, automates customs entry and gate exits, and maximises yard space on wharves and slot space on ships. The platform is accessed by supply chain operators through Dubai Trade, an e-service provider that has won praise from the World Bank for enabling trading across borders, globalisation's core mantra.

The same integrated model was replicated at our new development, DP World London Gateway, where we built a brand new port on the Thames, with an adjacent business park, both connected with efficient road and rail links directly to the UK's biggest market, London, and empowered by IT.

As a global connector and facilitator of trade, the maritime shipping business enjoys influence that often extends beyond ships and terminals. DP World's experience is that efficient infrastructure stimulates trade by reducing supply chain complexity and cost, which has a knock on benefit for local communities – and of course for those involved in supply chain management. This means that increasingly, marine terminal operators are being seen as long term strategic innovation partners.

The rise of sustainability as an issue is linked directly to this trend. Demands for greater reliability, agility, and lower costs are exerting positive pressure on the industry's operating model. Superior sustainability performance is no longer an option, but a necessity for stakeholders across the supply chain.

In this context, the effective and efficient management of risks and opportunities demands strategies that can deliver continuous improvement in baseline business, social and environmental performance that validate sustainability. Tactical investments in innovation, technology and collaboration will define the way the industry progresses in the future.

Shipping is one of the oldest commercial activities in the world and it continues to be a major force in global trade. The world's merchant fleet still carries 90% of international trade by volume; accounts for more than a third of the value of global trade and generates millions of jobs.

As the world becomes more competitive, professional and personal development assumes greater importance as a career growth engine. This text published by the Institute of Chartered Shipbrokers opens the door to a world of possibilities and opportunities in the truly global business of shipping.

HE Sultan Ahmed Bin Sulayem

Chairman, DP World

# ACKNOWLEDGEMENTS

First and foremost we would like to thank HE Sultan Ahmed Bin Sulayem for his inspirational support in the revision of this book. We must also acknowledge the contribution of several industry professionals, among them Paul Wright, TRACE International and TRACE Incorporated who have shared their wealth of knowledge and experience with the Institute.

Special thanks are due to YK Chan, Michalis Taliotis and Xanthos Kyriacou for their efforts in the review of this book. Acknowledgement must also go to Andrew Lansdale and Costas Lambrou for their assistance in the updating of this book and to Paul Ridgway and Dinah Bromwich for their efforts in improving the quality of the text.

The illustrations have been sourced from across the industry but particular thanks go to Danny Cornelissen of Port Pictures NL. The artistry of these images raises the stakes in the appearance and presentation of our maritime text books.

# CONTRIBUTING EDITORS

## Paul Wright

Paul Wright has been involved in the international shipping industry for over 50 years. At the age of 13 he entered HMS *Conway* Merchant Navy Training School. He joined Alfred Holt and Company (later Ocean Fleets) of Liverpool as an apprentice deck Officer in 1966.

On completion of his apprenticeship he served as a deck officer on a variety of ships of the company, including general cargo vessels, car ferries and passenger liners with service between Europe and the Far East and West Africa. He also served for a short time on research vessels of the Natural Environmental Research Council. In 1976 and for the next three years he served with Overseas Containers Ltd on their Far East container ships.

During his time with Ocean Fleets he completed a Degree in Maritime Studies at the University of Wales, Institute of Science and Technology.

In 1979 he joined Plymouth School of Maritime Studies as a Lecturer and embarked on an academic career. For the first 12 years he was involved with the training of cadets and deck officers for the Merchant Navy. With the decline of UK Merchant Navy training he broadened his interests, taking a Master's degree in International Shipping. On the ending of officer training at Plymouth he joined the International Shipping and Logistics Group, of what had become Plymouth University, taking on the responsibility as Head of Group between 2000 and 2006. His area of teaching focussed on Maritime and Business, including Shipping Practice, Port Operations and Maritime Geography. In 2006 he was asked to support the development of the newly constituted Plymouth University Marine Institute as Associate Director, Marketing and Outreach.

After 35 years in marine and maritime education in July 2014 Paul retired from Plymouth University. He retains links as a Visiting Fellow of the Plymouth University Marine Institute. He further maintains his interests in the field of nautical matters through involvement with various organisations, including the Maritime Foundation and Western Maritime Training.

Paul is a Council Member of the Nautical Institute and has served as Honorary Secretary and Chairman of the South West of England Branch.

## TRACE International and TRACE Incorporated

TRACE International and TRACE Incorporated are two distinct entities with a common mission to advance commercial transparency worldwide by supporting the compliance efforts of multinational companies and their third party intermediaries. TRACE International is a non-profit business association that pools resources to provide members with anti-bribery compliance support while TRACE Incorporated offers both members and non-members customizable risk-based due diligence, anti-bribery training and advisory services. Working alongside one another, TRACE International and TRACE Incorporated offer an end-to-end, cost-effective and innovative solution for anti-bribery and third party compliance.

TRACE recently launched a Shipping and Maritime Initiative to help vessel owners, shipping agents and freight forwarders tackle bribery and address extortionate demands at ports. TRACE contributes to the compliance efforts of this industry with cost effective tools and though developing best practices and advocating for international standards. As part of this initiative, TRACE is working with leading stakeholders to offer TRACEcertification, a due diligence review and compliance credential, to shipowners, charterers, shipmanagers and port agents. To learn more, visit www.traceinternational.org.

## Alexandra Wrage President and Founder, TRACE International

Alexandra Wrage is president and founder of TRACE International, the world's leading anti-bribery business organization. She is the author of *Bribery and Extortion: Undermining Business, Governments and Security*, co-editor of *How to Pay a Bribe: Thinking Like a Criminal to Thwart Bribery Schemes* and the host of the training DVD *Toxic Transactions: Bribery, Extortion and the High Price of Bad Business*, produced by NBC. Ms. Wrage has written three compliance guidebooks and is a guest blogger for Corporate Counsel. She speaks frequently on topics of international law, anti-corruption initiatives and the hidden costs of corruption.

Ms. Wrage is a member of the 2015 B20 Taskforce on Anti-Corruption, which will draft recommendations to G20 leaders for consideration in their global economic policies. She has held numerous committee positions, including Chair of the Anti-Corruption Committee of the ABA's International Section and Chair of the International Legal Affairs Committee of the Association of Corporate Counsel, and has participated in anti-bribery working groups with the OECD and UN Global Compact.

Ms. Wrage was named one of the Canadians Changing the World by the and received the 2014 Women in Compliance Lifetime Achievement Award for Service to the Compliance Industry. Prior to founding TRACE, Ms. Wrage was international counsel at Northrop Grumman. Ms. Wrage, a Canadian, studied law at King's College, Cambridge University.

## Jake Storey, Vice Chairman of the Maritime Anti-Corruption Network (MACN)

Jake has been Vice Chairman of the Maritime Anti-Corruption Network (MACN) and has sat on its steering committee since 2012.

He has over 25 years' experience of the shipping industry. Most recently he worked at ship owning and operating group Gearbulk as their Chief Risk Officer. Prior to joining Gearbulk, Jake was the CFO for Inchcape Shipping services UK a global port agency group, and before that he worked for Hill Samuel Merchant Bank, where he was first introduced to the maritime industry; working for Wallems, Escombe Lambert, Lambert Brothers, Lavino Shipping and the Wescol group.

Jake holds a MBA from Manchester Business School, as well as being a chartered accountant and a qualified corporate treasurer. He also holds a BA Hons in History and Politics from Keele University.

# CONTENTS


| | | |
|---|---|---|
| | Foreword | iii |
| | Acknowledgements | v |
| | Contributing Editors | vi |
| **Chapter 1** | **THE BUSINESS ENTITY AND COMMUNICATIONS IN THE SHIPPING BUSINESS** | **1** |
| 1.1 | Introduction | 2 |
| 1.2 | The sole trader | 2 |
| 1.3 | Partnerships | 2 |
| 1.4 | Limited liability companies | 3 |
| 1.5 | Company horizontal and vertical integration | 7 |
| 1.6 | Company organisation and management | 7 |
| 1.7 | Statutory accounts | 9 |
| 1.8 | Profit and loss account | 10 |
| 1.9 | Balance sheet | 10 |
| 1.10 | Company shares | 12 |
| 1.11 | Quality management | 13 |
| 1.12 | Communications in the shipping business | 15 |
| 1.13 | Methods of business communication | 15 |
| 1.14 | Data storage and retrieval | 18 |
| 1.15 | The internet and e-commerce | 18 |
| 1.16 | Ship-to-shore connectivity | 18 |
| 1.17 | Conclusion | 19 |
| **Chapter 2** | **BUSINESS ETHICS** | **21** |
| 2.1 | What are ethics? | 22 |
| 2.2 | Ethics in shipping business | 22 |
| 2.3 | Maritime fraud | 24 |
| 2.4 | Insurance fraud | 24 |
| 2.5 | Documentary fraud | 24 |
| 2.6 | Other areas of fraud | 25 |
| 2.7 | Other criminal activities | 25 |
| 2.8 | Detecting and avoiding fraud | 26 |
| 2.9 | Bribery | 27 |
| 2.10 | Baltic Exchange Guidance on Required Standards of Members | 27 |
| **Chapter 3** | **ANTI-BRIBERY COMPLIANCE – CHALLENGES IN SHIPPING** | **31** |
| 3.1 | Introduction | 32 |
| 3.2 | Significant anti-bribery legislation | 32 |
| 3.3 | Key national anti-bribery legislation | 33 |
| 3.4 | Extraterritorial jurisdiction of leading anti-bribery legislation | 34 |
| 3.5 | Current anti-bribery enforcement trends | 35 |
| 3.6 | Exceptions to anti-bribery laws | 36 |
| 3.7 | Anti-bribery compliance best practices for the shipping industry | 37 |
| 3.8 | Collective action to fight corruption in the shipping industry | 43 |
| 3.9 | Conclusion | 44 |

## Chapter 4 THE SHIP 47

| | | |
|---|---|---|
| 4.1 | Introduction | 48 |
| 4.2 | Dimensions | 48 |
| 4.3 | Capacity | 50 |
| 4.4 | Tonnage | 51 |
| 4.5 | Ship types | 52 |
| 4.6 | Liquid bulk ships (tankers) | 53 |
| 4.7 | Dry bulk ships | 60 |
| 4.8 | Container ships | 67 |

## Chapter 5 The Geography of Trade 73

| | | |
|---|---|---|
| 5.1 | Seaborne trade | 74 |
| 5.2 | Crude oil | 74 |
| 5.3 | Coal | 77 |
| 5.4 | Iron ore | 77 |
| 5.5 | Grain | 77 |
| 5.6 | Other dry bulk cargoes | 80 |
| 5.7 | Unitised cargo | 80 |
| 5.8 | Ports | 82 |
| 5.9 | Abbreviations and expressions used in communication with ports | 84 |
| 5.10 | Physical restrictions to port entry | 85 |
| 5.11 | Waterways | 85 |
| 5.12 | Political restrictions | 86 |
| 5.13 | Choke points | 87 |
| 5.14 | Impact of union disputes | 87 |
| 5.15 | Natural phenomena | 87 |
| 5.16 | Weather routeing | 92 |
| 5.17 | Salinity of the oceans | 92 |
| 5.18 | Navigational seasonal zones | 93 |

## Chapter 6 Chartering, Markets and Practice 95

| | | |
|---|---|---|
| 6.1 | Introduction | 96 |
| 6.2 | The merchant | 96 |
| 6.3 | The broker | 96 |
| 6.4 | The chartering market | 97 |
| 6.5 | Charter parties | 100 |
| 6.6 | Forms of charter party 1: the voyage charter party | 102 |
| 6.7 | Forms of charter party 2: the time charter party | 106 |
| 6.8 | Forms of charter party 3: the demise charter party (bareboat charter party) | 109 |
| 6.9 | Tanker charter parties | 110 |
| 6.10 | Bills of lading | 112 |
| 6.11 | Conclusion | 113 |

## Chapter 7 Purchase, sale and ship management 115

| | | |
|---|---|---|
| 7.1 | Ship sale and purchase | 116 |
| 7.2 | New buildings | 116 |
| 7.3 | Secondhand ships | 117 |

| | | |
|---|---|---|
| 7.4 | Process of selling a ship | 118 |
| 7.5 | Drydocking a ship prior to sale | 120 |
| 7.6 | Demolition | 123 |
| 7.7 | Financing the purchase | 124 |
| 7.8 | Valuations | 124 |
| 7.9 | Ship managers | 125 |
| 7.10 | Full management | 125 |
| 7.11 | The ship management contract | 128 |
| **Chapter 8** | **Port and liner agency** | **129** |
| 8.1 | Port agents | 130 |
| 8.2 | The charterer's agents | 131 |
| 8.3 | The agent's fee | 132 |
| 8.4 | The agent's duties | 133 |
| 8.5 | Liner agency | 135 |
| 8.6 | Liner agent remote from the port | 139 |
| 8.7 | Agency contract | 140 |
| **Chapter 9** | **International trade and finance: International terms of sale** | **141** |
| 9.1 | Introduction | 142 |
| 9.2 | The basic contract | 142 |
| 9.3 | Goods | 143 |
| 9.4 | Property | 143 |
| 9.5 | Risk | 144 |
| 9.6 | International contracts of sale and Incoterms 2010 | 144 |
| 9.7 | Incoterms relating to sea and inland waterways | 146 |
| 9.8 | Non-maritime Incoterms | 148 |
| 9.9 | The use of terms in international trade | 150 |
| 9.10 | Remedies for breach of contract | 151 |
| 9.11 | Law and jurisdiction | 153 |
| 9.12 | Postscript | 153 |
| **Chapter 10** | **Finance and insurance in international trade** | **155** |
| 10.1 | Introduction | 156 |
| 10.2 | Methods of payment | 156 |
| 10.3 | Documents associated with the letter of credit | 158 |
| 10.4 | Confirming houses | 159 |
| 10.5 | Risks in international trading | 159 |
| 10.6 | Foreign exchange | 160 |
| 10.7 | Transaction costs in international trade | 164 |
| 10.8 | Insurance | 165 |
| 10.9 | Trade terms in export sales | 167 |
| 10.10 | Warranties | 167 |
| 10.11 | Types of cargo policies | 168 |
| 10.12 | Effecting insurance | 169 |

| | | |
|---|---|---|
| 10.13 | Conditions of insurance | 171 |
| 10.14 | Marine cargo insurance policies | 171 |
| 10.15 | Premiums | 173 |
| 10.16 | Claims procedure | 174 |
| 10.17 | The principle of average | 174 |

## Chapter 11 International shipping organisations 177

| | | |
|---|---|---|
| 11.1 | Introduction | 178 |
| 11.2 | Shipowners' organisations | 178 |
| 11.3 | Brokers' and agents' organisations | 181 |
| 11.4 | United Nations bodies | 185 |
| 11.5 | International Ship Classification | 187 |
| 11.6 | International seafarer support organisations | 189 |
| 11.7 | Maritime insurance | 191 |
| 11.8 | Other shipping-related international bodies | 193 |

## Appendices 195

| | | |
|---|---|---|
| Appendix 1 | Gencon 94 | 197 |
| Appendix 2 | NYPE 93 | 200 |
| Appendix 3 | Shellvoy 6 | 214 |
| Appendix 4 | Shelltime 4 | 234 |
| Appendix 5 | Loadline map | 243 |
| Appendix 6 | S & P particulars sheet | 244 |
| Appendix 7 | Norwegian Saleform 93 | 245 |
| Appendix 8 | Norwegian Saleform 2012 | 251 |
| Appendix 9 | Shipman 2009 | 259 |
| Appendix 10 | Statement of Facts | 280 |
| Appendix 11 | Disbursement account | 282 |
| Appendix 12 | Fonasba Agency aggreement | 283 |
| Appendix 13 | Certificate of cargo insurance | 288 |
| Appendix 14 | Institute Cargo Clauses (A) | 289 |
| Appendix 15 | Institute Cargo Clauses (B) | 292 |
| Appendix 16 | Institute Cargo Clauses (C) | 295 |
| Appendix 17 | Congen Bill of Lading | 298 |
| Appendix 18 | Letter of Credit | 300 |
| Appendix 19 | UCP600 | 302 |

Chapter 1

# The business entity and communications in the shipping business

*The world's oldest financial exchange, the Belgian bourse of Antwerp began trading in 1460 and closed its doors in 1997*

## 1.1 INTRODUCTION

The business of shipping is an exciting and dynamic activity involving many different tasks, skills and sectors. The basic functions which underpin all business activities are common to companies involved in the shipping business. It is important that persons involved in shipping have a basic understanding of the business functions which affect their work.

The shipping business is concerned with operating ships and meeting the demand for transport by sea. Demand for ships is described by economists as a derived demand. A *derived demand* can be defined as the *'need for a service which occurs due to the want of another service'*. In the shipping business, the demand for ships is created by businesses needing the services of ships to transport goods for trading. The only exception to derived demand in the shipping business is found in the cruise sector, where demand is created for the service which is offered.

Functions undertaken in any business are broadly the same. They include sales, accounting, marketing, and human resource management. The difference in size of company will result in different structures to undertake the different functions. Large companies will have separate functional departments whereas in smaller companies, such as partnerships, the business functions will be undertaken by a small staff. In the case of a sole trader they will be undertaken by a single individual.

## 1.2 THE SOLE TRADER

A sole trader is a person who enters business on his or her own account, contributing the capital to start the business, working in it with or without the assistance of employees, and receiving the profits or proceeds as a reward.

No formal procedure is required to set up such a business, though the trading name may have to be registered and some businesses may require a licence to operate.

The sole trader is completely independent and can make his or her own decisions and put them into effect quickly. Personal attention to customers' and clients' requirements and low overhead costs make this a basic organisation and provides an effective business unit in a specialist area such as shipping business. Marine surveyors, consultants, small port agencies and brokers' businesses can operate as sole traders.

A sole trader is not required to reveal the details of the business to anyone, apart from confidential disclosures required for tax purposes. The sole trader's status carries with it a number of disadvantages, which includes unlimited liability. Unlimited liability means that the sole trader is personally liable to the full extent of his or her private wealth for the debts of the business. If the business is made insolvent the sole trader may lose all possessions to satisfy the business creditors. It can be difficult for the sole trader to regulate working hours and to take time off for holidays. If the sole trader becomes ill and unable to work, the business can quickly get into difficulties. Due to limited resources, a sole trader may have problems if wanting to expand the business without loss of independence.

## 1.3 PARTNERSHIPS

An alternative available to a sole trader who wishes to expand his or her business is to take one or more partners. A partnership, sometimes known as a firm, will be owned by the partners. The additional partners will often bring wide experience to the firm. A partnership will benefit from increased capital, allowing the firm to expand. As the former owner, a sole trader will share responsibility for control of the firm with the additional partner(s). In a partnership arrangement, the private nature of the business is preserved with the partners being jointly responsible for the debts of the partnership. Within a partnership, all business decisions must be taken with the full agreement of all the partners. Disagreement can lead to the break-up of the partnership. The death of a partner can also make it difficult for a partnership to continue if the deceased partner's share of the business has to be withdrawn to settle their estate. In practice, partnership agreements usually make provision for the firm to continue even after a partner has died or retired.

Some countries sanction a limited partnership. A limited partnership is a partnership designed to protect non-executive partners, that is, partners who only provide capital for the partnership. Protection is in the form of limiting their liability to the extent of their financial participation.

## 1.4 LIMITED LIABILITY COMPANIES

The most significant difference between the sole trader, partnership and larger businesses is the concept of limited liability. In the United Kingdom a limited liability company can be identified by the abbreviation following the company's name. *Ltd* means a private company limited by shares, and *plc* means a public limited company. A private company limited by shares and a public limited company will be distinguishable wherever in the world they are established.

A **private company limited** by shares, Ltd, will not offer shares for sale to the general public. Such a company could be a small business rather like a partnership, but one where the owners have decided to incorporate the company with their liability limited. Exceptionally, there are some large private limited companies where the shareholders have managed to keep the shareholding within the family.

Another situation for the establishment of a private limited company is where the company is a subsidiary of a parent company which owns all the shares in its daughter.

A **public limited company**, plc, will allow its shares to be freely offered for sale. In the UK, the value of shares of a public limited company is quoted on the stock exchange. Many countries make it obligatory for anyone acquiring an interest of more than a certain percentage of a public limited company to disclose the fact. In the UK, the percentage for disclosure is set at 5%.

A private company limited by shares and a public limited company are owned by shareholders. An individual shareholder is only liable for the company's debts up to the value of the shares he or she holds. If the company becomes insolvent the shareholders may find their shares are worthless. They are not required to provide additional funds to pay the balance of the company's indebtedness. A creditor to a failed company would only receive a proportion of the amount owed to them.

It may appear that a public limited liability company provides a license for the company directors to use other people's money without responsibility. This is not the case as company law gives protection to the shareholders in general and in particular to minority shareholders against majority shareholders. Protection is also afforded to the creditors by the legal requirement for limited companies to have their accounts audited by an independent qualified accountant or accounting firm.

Following a satisfactory audit, a profit and loss account, which sets out the company's income and expenditure for the previous year, and a balance sheet which shows the assets and liabilities the company at the end of that year, are distributed to every shareholder and lodged with a government agency. In the UK, the government agency is Companies House which is overseen by the Registrar of Companies. For a small fee, anyone may obtain details of a limited company's structure and copies of its annual accounts.

**In the UK, corporate records are kept at Companies House in Cardiff, South Wales**

It has been said that *'what a company's annual accounts reveal is interesting, but what they conceal is vital'*. There is no substitute for care (prudence) when dealing with a limited liability company because companies of whatever size can become insolvent.

## Capital

Capital in book-keeping terms is the total value of all the company's fixed assets, investments and cash. Assets are divided into fixed assets and current assets.

Capital is the money required to start a commercial enterprise. More may be required from time to time to maintain its momentum or to increase the range of its activities.

Capital is needed for two basic purposes: to purchase machinery or equipment or anything that will become a fixed asset such as a ship; and also to run the company, to pay wages, salaries and rent. The latter is known as working capital.

Whatever it is used for, capital has to be raised. One method is by letting other people become part-owners of the company. Capital may also be raised by borrowing the money from a bank or other financial institution; this is often referred to as loan capital. The borrower has to pay the lender interest at an agreed percentage per year in addition to repaying the loan in agreed instalments.

Interest is the percentage of the capital sum that the borrower pays the lender for the use of the money borrowed. Borrowing and lending are essential elements of commercial life. A company may find it has more cash than it needs for its immediate purposes. It will deposit this with a bank so that it earns interest instead of lying idle. On another occasion it may have a temporary shortage of ready cash, which will require a short-term loan from the bank known as an overdraft. A well-managed company can usually negotiate a substantial overdraft facility.

A special type of borrowing, often used for buying large capital items such as ships, is by means of a mortgage. This is the name of the deed or agreement signed by the owner of the ship. In exchange for the loan of a substantial amount of its cost, the shipowner pledges the ship as security for the loan. If the owner cannot meet the loan repayments and interest charges, the lender may foreclose on the mortgage, allowing the lender to take possession of the ship. Note that it is the borrower who gives the mortgage to the lender, so the borrower (the shipowner in this example) is called the mortgagor. The bank or finance house that accepts the mortgage becomes the mortgagee.

A ship, a building or a piece of machinery is capital and is classified as a fixed asset. Many companies invest in associated businesses. For example, a shipping company might invest in part of a terminal operating company. Such an investment, indeed any long-term investment, will also be classified as a fixed asset.

## Incorporation of a company

When a company is incorporated, the owners create a legal person, an entity in its own right. The company will continue even after the death of the original founder. It will remain in existence until formally wound up.

In a limited company, any shareholder can theoretically sell all or part of their shares to a third party. Unlike a partnership, a major shareholder need not be on the board of directors but may have a voice in deciding who should be on the board. Conversely, a member of the board of directors is not, by English law, bound to be a shareholder.

The qualification theoretically was used at the beginning of the previous paragraph because, in the case of some private companies, the founders will want to pick and choose who should be a part of their venture. They can protect themselves by writing specific clauses into the two documents which create the company known as the memorandum of association and the articles of association. The clause, called the pre-emption clause, sets out the procedure to be followed upon the death of a shareholder or should a shareholder wish to sell his or her shares. The pre-emption clause will insist on the shares being first offered to other existing shareholders, with details as to how their value should be calculated.

## A partnership or a limited liability company?

What determines whether a small group should form a partnership or incorporate themselves into a limited liability company? Being able to limit one's liabilities could be one reason, but it is possible to start a limited company with only two £1 shares being issued. The working capital in such a company could be provided by loans from a bank, with the directors, friends and relatives who have invested in the company to be paid back as soon as profit allows.

A company with a small asset base would not be attractive to anyone expected to grant extended credit. If a company goes to a bank for a loan, the bank will want some sort of security. The security will usually be in the form of personal guarantees from the shareholders. It means that the directors are placed in a similar position as if they were partners. As a result, the shareholders may decide to dispense with the expense and formalities of incorporation and simply form a partnership. In many cases, the decision to form a partnership or a limited company will be affected by whichever produces the smaller income or liability to corporation tax.

## Subsidiary and conglomerate companies

A company organisation chart may show several divisions which are subordinate to the parent company. The main function of the parent company is to control the capital of the subordinate company. Each of the subordinate companies, often known as subsidiary companies, are required to convince the parent board of directors of the financial viability of any enterprise requiring capital investment. Where economies of scale can be achieved, the parent company may run common central services such as human resources, training and information technology.

A conglomerate is a company in which separate divisions are engaged in activities which are apparently unrelated.

In some large companies, divisions may consist of more than one subsidiary company; for example, in the shipping division where there is a shipowning company which is managed quite separately from a company dealing with shipping services. On some occasions, there may be a need for sub-subsidiaries to be created. The establishment of a sub-subsidiary may be required in the situation where it is more convenient, or obligatory, for an overseas branch to be separately incorporated into a country.

## Attractiveness to the investing public

Why should an already established limited liability company be concerned about being attractive to the investing public? Three reasons are given in answer to the question:

- A company belongs to its shareholders. Shareholders have the right to attend the company's annual general meeting. At the annual general meeting, the shareholders have the right to dismiss members of the board of directors if the company's performance is not as expected;

- If a company wants to expand and needs capital beyond its own resources, it could turn to a bank to raise the additional capital. A company needs to have a mix of debt and equity to ensure that it does not become unable to repay its debt in case of a downturn in business. It is therefore prudent to seek additional capital through a mixture of borrowing and by offering new shares on the market. The more efficient and profitable the company, the easier it will be to raise the additional money;

- Directors of any company need an external measure of their success, or otherwise. One measure is what the stock market thinks and is shown by the price being offered for the company's shares.

A discussion on how stock markets operate is outside the scope of this book. It is, however, useful to study the financial pages of the press. Take a look at familiar companies and observe the daily movement of the share price. It is not unusual to find shares that have been established over a long period of time to have a low par value, being traded at several times that price. A study of a company's share price over a period of time compared to the trend of a general index, such as the FTSE 100 index, will provide an assessment of what the market thinks about how the particular company is being run. Several websites provide graphs showing the change of price of the particular share over time.

The **value of a share** is a measure of the expectation of the size of the dividend that a company will pay. However, the measure can be masked by the daily fluctuation of the price resulting from investors seeking profits from buying and selling shares.

## 1.5 COMPANY HORIZONTAL AND VERTICAL INTEGRATION

As previously noted, conglomerates consist of a number of different divisions operating in a variety of sectors. A conglomerate will have grown from a small, single activity company which has acquired other businesses. The other businesses may have been attractive private limited companies that could not develop further without the resources of a larger organisation, or struggling enterprises that were bought cheaply with the potential of turning them into profitable business through careful management.

Whatever the original reason for their acquisition, the component divisions of a conglomerate provide a good example of horizontal integration. The diverse and seemingly unrelated nature of their activities provides the parent company and group with a broad base of operation in a number of different businesses, industries, countries and even continents.

At the present time, conglomerates are not favoured as generally investors prefer companies to focus on a core business. Diverse companies can suffer from a conglomerate discount which means that the aggregate value of the individual businesses on a stand-alone basis is higher than for the conglomerate as a whole.

The opposite of a conglomerate is a vertically integrated company. A vertically integrated company is one which controls all activities within a particular industry from source of the raw product to the consumer, including transport needs. The major international oil companies are a good example of complex vertical integration.

## 1.6 COMPANY ORGANISATION AND MANAGEMENT

The organisation of a shipping services company within the shipping division provides an opportunity to consider not only the various operational departments, including chartering, ship operations and technical management, but also the service departments. The service departments of a company include the secretariat, human resources and accounts.

The functions of the service departments are present in all companies, regardless of size. The difference between a small and a large company is that in a large company, separate departments will undertake the specific functions whereas in a small company, the same functions will be undertaken by individual partners or delegated to staff members as part of their duties.

### The secretariat

The secretariat is a vital role in any company. The company secretary is the only member of a company recognised by law. The company secretary is responsible for the company complying with all the legal requirements imposed on a limited company. The company secretary is subordinate to the company directors who are the directing mind of the company. However, the position of the company secretary is permanent and is the point of contact between the company and the authorities, such as the tax collectors and registrar of companies. Company directors can be dismissed by shareholders at the annual general meeting of the company.

## Human resources department

The human resources or personnel department plays a critical role in a company and the importance of its function cannot be overstated. The human resources department is concerned with the recruitment, selection, training, employment, dismissal and promotion of staff. Most countries have laws relating to employment covering many aspects including employment protection, redundancy payment and discrimination.

In the shipping business, work of the human resources department will cover shore-based personnel and ship crewing. Ship crewing, if not undertaken in-house, will be outsourced to a specialist ship management group. Whilst the shore-based side of a shipping business generally uses available national labour, ship crewing is undertaken within a global labour market.

## The accounts department

The accounts department is a non-operational section within a company. It is involved with all aspects of finance. The department concerns itself with financial accounting, management accounting, and credit control. Finance is a resource and its proper management can be a significant factor in the profitability of the enterprise. The failure of many companies occurs not due to the adverse difference between income and expenditure, but of poor cash flow, that is, the company simply running out of money. Cash flow can be managed.

## Financial accounting

Financial accounting is the process of recording, summarising and reporting business transactions so that an accurate picture of a company's financial position and performance can be established. Financial accounting leads to the preparation of financial statements, including the profit and loss account, balance sheet, and cash flow statement.

## Management accounting

Apart from accounts which a company is obliged to maintain in order to satisfy the auditors, the other role of the accounts department is to produce management accounts. Management accounts are defined as *'the provision of financial data and advice to a company for use in the organisation and development of its business'*.

The formality and complexity of management accounts will vary depending upon the size of the company. The purpose of management accounting is to inform operational members of the company about their contribution to the business, advise managers about the financial implications of present and future projects, and explain the financial consequences of business decisions. Management accountants are skilled in the analysis of financial information and the formulation of strategy. They have an understanding of risk, good communication skills to help explain finance to non-financial managers and expertise in budgetary planning.

## Credit control

Credit control is an important business function, particularly in times of high interest rates. Good control of credit contributes to a company's survival. The credit controller's duties go beyond the task of debt chasing. Deciding who should be granted credit, how much and for how long is the constructive side of the controller's work. Dispatching final demands or issuing writs to recover debt is looked on as a failure in credit control.

The Royal Courts of Justice, London

Credit control is only one side of controlling cash flow. Debit control is equally as important. It is not desirable for a company to acquire the reputation of being a bad payer. Suppliers may build into their price structure an element based upon the fact that their customers will not settle invoices until they have received a statement, usually at the end of the month. Some suppliers offer discounts for early payment. Taking advantage of discounts and/or not settling before the appropriate date are essential parts of cash-flow control.

For a company to have large sums of money in the bank for long periods of time earning low levels of interest is inefficient. A company will require a financial policy concerning investment of its cash resources for the short and longer term.

### Budgetary control

Budgetary control is defined as a system of control management in which actual income and expenditure are compared with planned income and expenditure. Budgetary control allows management to identify the difference between the planned and actual budget and make appropriate adjustments. Experience enables a reasonable estimate to be made of the more volatile elements of expenditure and income. With a budget in place for comparison, it is possible for management to see where **variances** arise and whether they are due to the vagaries of the market or can be controlled by remedial measures.

## 1.7 STATUTORY ACCOUNTS

It is important to be able to read and understand the published accounts of a limited company. All limited companies are required to publish annual accounts which show a true and fair view of the company's financial position. The published accounts must be audited and made available to the public. A great deal can be learned about a company from reading the accounts, including its activities, size and financial health. Whilst the law may differ from country to country regarding the precise form that published accounts must take, the basic pattern is similar.

The statutory accounts, known as the financial statements are the

- profit and loss account, also known as a trading account or income statement;
- balance sheet, sometimes referred to as a statement of financial position;
- cash flow statement.

In brief, the profit and loss account shows the income, expenditure and profits of a company over a period of time, the balance sheet describes the company's assets, liabilities and equity at a given point in time, and the cash flow statement reports on the company's cash flow activities Whilst the information required in published accounts is limited, many companies append notes explaining certain items in the further detail. Current company law in the UK requires some specific statements to be included in the notes, for example, details of salaries to higher paid directors and employees.

## 1.8 PROFIT AND LOSS ACCOUNT

The profit and loss account is a record of the company's trading activities during the preceding year and its title usually includes the words 'For the year ended…' The profit and loss account shows the total income, also known as turnover of the company over the preceding year.

In addition, the profit and loss account shows the income from trading and overhead expenses. Taking one from the other will show a trading profit or loss. It is usual to deduct interest paid on bank loans, or other borrowed money, separately from trading expenses. The resulting figure is the company's profit before tax. Company's profit before tax, sometimes known as pre-tax profit, is a useful figure to use when comparing the year-on-year performance of a company, or when comparing the performance of different companies.

In the profit and loss account, tax, sometimes known as taxation on profit, corporation tax, profit tax or similar name, is shown. The company's profit before tax will be adjusted by tax payable to establish the company's net profit figure.

Theoretically, the company's profit before tax could be shared out among the shareholders of the company, but this seldom happens. The normal procedure is for some profit to be retained. The profit and loss account will show the amount of profit retained and the amount that has been distributed to shareholders as a dividend.

## 1.9 BALANCE SHEET

The balance sheet has the following words in its title: 'As at...' The balance sheet gives a snapshot of what is owned, and what is owed to and by a company, on a particular date. What is owned by a company is known as its assets. What is owed by a company is known as its liabilities.

## Assets

A company will own assets to enable it to undertake its business. There are two types of assets, fixed assets and current assets.

## Fixed assets

Fixed assets are concerned with the company's tangible assets and investments. The word 'fixed' speaks for itself. The word 'tangible' literally means assets that can be touched and is sometimes used to describe a subdivision of fixed assets. To a shipowner, a fixed asset would be a ship. Simply anything of a permanent nature which can be sold to raise money were the company to cease trading is described as a fixed asset. Unfortunately, fixed assets depreciate over time and the balance sheet will need adjustment. Depreciation, the reduction of value of a fixed asset with time, can be established by different methods. Depreciation methods include straight line depreciation and the declining balance method. Straight line depreciation is commonly used by shipowners. Straight line depreciation allows an asset's value to be reduced by a stated percentage each year. For example, a ship written down over a 20 year period will be depreciated at 5% per year. The amount and time by which an asset is depreciated is agreed with the auditors pursuant to the relevant laws. Auditors look after the shareholders' interests and will ensure the correction valuation of a company. The amounts by which assets are depreciated become an expense in the profit and loss account.

Some fixed tangible assets, including freehold land or buildings, can increase rather than decrease in value with time. These assets will have to be re-valued periodically. Re-valuation requires care because one yardstick for measuring a company's health is its return on capital employed. If fixed assets are overvalued, the return on capital employed will be poor. Conversely, if fixed assets are undervalued, the return on capital will appear to be greater. An undervalued company might be attractive to predatory takeover bids.

Company investments are also recognised as fixed assets. As already stated, a prudent company will put money into reserves. Reserves are invested and kept working, even though not being used for the company's own business. A parent of a group of companies will show the value of its subsidiaries as investments.

## Current assets

Current assets including cash, stock, and debtors are assets which can be consumed or exhausted in the operation of the company during a period of time, normally the accounting year. Cash includes company money held in its bank accounts. Stock, although tangible, is not fixed. Stock includes raw materials, work in progress or finished goods in inventory. If the company is a going concern, stock has a fairly clearly defined value. If the company were to cease trading, it is unlikely that stock could be sold at the same price as its value to the active company. Debtors are recorded in the list of current assets. Debt is value owed to a company. Company accountants will study details of outstanding debts and decide what proportion of these may never be paid. Provision will have to be made in a reserve fund for bad debt. The remaining debt will be paid to the company over time and represents part of the company's value.

## Liabilities

Opposite assets on the balance sheet are liabilities. Current liabilities are a company's debts or obligations to others that are due within a period of time, normally one year. Liabilities include loan capital, creditors and contingencies. Liabilities will be settled over time through the transfer of money goods or services.

Loan capital is the value of what is owed to people who have lent the company money at an agreed rate of interest. A company may decide to borrow money rather than sell shares. While selling shares will provide capital it will dilute the ownership of the company. A large company may borrow money from a bank rather than go to the financial market to raise capital through the issue of shares. As long as profits are made, the loan debt can be paid. Lenders, particularly the banks, will normally insist on a security against loans. If a company fails, the banks will have first claim against the residual value of its assets.

When considering the financial stability of a company, the relationship between loans and share capital is a factor to be considered. The relationship is referred to as gearing. If a company is too highly geared, a company will be at risk if there is a downturn in trading conditions. High gearing is not necessarily a sign of poor company health. Those who provide loans will not normally lend without reasonable assurance that they will get their money back should the company fail. Under current liabilities is a statement of what the company owes to its creditors.

As well as the current liabilities of loan capital and creditors, many companies will have further amounts to take away from the assets, such as a provision for contingent liabilities. For example, if a company was defending a legal claim, no matter how confident it might feel about the outcome, the dispute would not exist without the other side being hopeful of winning. Under such circumstances, the auditors would insist on an amount of money being set aside against the possibility of an adverse decision by the court.

A study of a company's liabilities to its debtors will provide recognition of how well a company is managing its cash flow. Cash flow is defined as *'the movement of cash in and out of a company, in the form of payments to suppliers and collections from customers'*. If customers who owe cash to a company take longer to pay than the company takes to pay its suppliers, the company will eventually run out of cash. No matter how profitable a company appears, if it has no cash it will fail.

It is not easy to assess how a company is managing its cash flow from the sparse information given in published accounts but, as a general rule, the current assets should be greater than the current liabilities that are within the detail of the accounts; it will be a healthy sign if the creditors are greater than the debtors.

The description of the balance sheet above has shown a substantial net figure of total assets minus current liabilities. It appears that there is an imbalance. The liability which establishes balance is the money shareholders put up as owners of the company, known as shareholders' funds.

## 1.10 COMPANY SHARES

Shareholders are persons who provide the capital for a company and are known as the owners of the company. A company must be provided with finance when it is established. It will continue to need further funds throughout its life. Shareholders supply finance in the expectation of receiving income through the payment of dividends. It is anticipated that income achieved by owning shares will be greater than that achieved by placing money on deposit with a bank. There is also the hope that, as the company continues to develop, the value of the shares will grow.

There are three different types of shareholdings in a company, namely ordinary shares, preference shares and debentures.

**Ordinary shares** represent equity ownership in a company. If the company has had a difficult financial year the directors may decide not to pay a dividend to the owners of ordinary shares.

**Preference shares** give their holders prior claim on any profits available for the dividend. Preference shareholders are entitled to a fixed dividend. Whilst ordinary shareholders have voting rights in the running of a company, it is unusual for the same right to be given to owners of preference shares.

Another form of share is **debentures**. A debenture is a medium to long-term debt instrument used by large companies to borrow money at a fixed rate of interest. A debenture is normally related to the company's fixed assets. In the case of a company being dissolved, the debenture holder has first claim on the proceeds when sold. Interest on debentures is paid before any dividends are considered. Interest payable to debenture holders, to mortgagees and on bank loans is usually shown separately from the trading figures in the profit and loss account.

### Retained profits and reserves

In good years some of a company's profits may be retained. Retained profits can be used by a company wishing to expand and make use of its own money to do so. A company may wish to create a reserve. Sensibly invested, a reserve may enable a company to survive a temporary recession in trade, provide a source from which to pay a dividend in a poor trading year, provide a source of available capital in the event of an unexpected opportunity and provide funds for an expense that only happens at irregular intervals. For example, a shipowner might place money into a reserve to cover the costs associated with the five-yearly ship survey.

Companies might also create a bad debt reserve to meet the failing of customers unable to pay their debts. Experience will be used to decide how much should be put in the bad debt reserve.

## 1.11 QUALITY MANAGEMENT

The needs of customers will only be met if a company has control of the human administrative and technical factors that affect the quality of its service. The quality of the service will only be controlled if tasks, equipment and procedures are used in the same way every time. Methods of control can be documented and used to assess the operation. Regular audits can be carried out to check that procedures are being followed and targets being met. Quality audits and reviews can lead to suggestions for improvements in the way work is carried out which will benefit the company's clients and thus the business itself.

Companies may choose to demonstrate their commitment to quality by registering with a national or internationally recognised independent assessment body. The body will testify that the company's systems have achieved a certain international standard for quality assurance. The process is known as accreditation and serves as evidence to the company's customers, and to the world at large, that the company meets certain quality criteria.

Ship management companies were among the first shipping businesses to embrace the concept of quality assurance as the services they provide to shipowners in a highly competitive field lend themselves to documented processes. In recent years, the International Safety Management (ISM) Code has adopted a number of documentary procedures relating to safety at sea and in effect turned these into a mandatory quality management system.

ISO 9001 is a series of international standards used for measuring quality systems. Companies who are registered and have achieved the required benchmarks can display the standard designation symbol.

**Most classification societies provide independent confirmation of quality systems**

To register for accreditation a company will have to document its business procedures, prepare a quality manual, and assess its quality management systems. It is then assessed by an independent body, which will measure its performance against internationally defined standards. The process lends itself to skills and expertise of organisations such as classification societies, whose work in the shipping business routinely requires them to provide independent confirmation of the seaworthiness of ships. Many businesses, both within and outside shipping, can be seen to display accreditation of their quality systems by classifications societies such as Lloyd's Register (LR), Bureau Veritas (BV) American Bureau of Shipping (ABS) and Det Norske Veritas Germanicsher Lloyd (DNV GL).

After the initial assessment and award, a company will be visited at regular intervals by the accrediting body to ensure ongoing compliance. It is necessary that everyone in the organisation follows the procedures outlined in the quality manual.

The concept of quality is continually developing. What may be of acceptable quality today may not be so in the future as customers' perceptions change. Although most companies benefit from introducing quality initiatives, there can be problems associated with implementation, such as:

- costs of inspection, training and material;
- time required by both management and staff to make the system work;
- different viewpoints on short-term costs and long term results. Quality initiatives require a long-term view and benefits can be difficult to measure;
- changes in cultures are not easy and may be resisted.

Therefore, a company and its personnel must be absolutely committed to the concept of quality management if its introduction is to be a success. Likewise, the system will need to be reviewed at regular intervals in order to ensure that it is still serving its purpose.

## 1.12 COMMUNICATIONS IN THE SHIPPING BUSINESS

Communication is the successful exchange of information between a minimum of two parties. It deals with the transmitting and receiving of information in various formats.

Communication is an essential part of human interaction. The benefits of effective communication are many and obvious as they enhance all aspects of personal and professional lives. Ineffective or misunderstood communications in personal lives may give rise to problems or embarrassment, but in professional lives the results of misunderstandings can be significant for the business or community.

Shipping is a communication intensive industry and communication skills are a vital element of management.

Shipping, like many other industries, uses terminology and abbreviations unique to itself. To communicate effectively, it is important to be sure that corresponding parties are familiar with the terms being used. The customary language used in the international shipping industry is English, which may not be the native language of either of the parties involved in communicating with each other.

Due to the international nature of the shipping industry, the recipient of a communication may be separated by time zones. Although the use of mobile communication devices allows people to be contactable without limit, they may not be readily available to receive a message or respond immediately to its contents.

## 1.13 METHODS OF BUSINESS COMMUNICATION

The communication culture has changed immeasurably in recent years. Until relatively recently, communication with colleagues, principals, agents, shippers, cargo receivers and other parties was completed by three primary methods: the landline telephone, the fax and the written or typed letter.

Today, the primary methods of communication have been largely superseded by the use of mobile telephones, email, instant messaging, the internet and PDA (personal digital assistant). A PDA is defined as a handheld device combining computing, telephone, internet and networking features. It can function as a cellular phone, web browser and personal organiser. Since 2010, the PDA has been replaced by the smartphone.

### Letters, reports and memoranda

The written letter is still regarded as an excellent communicative tool, especially for contractual and complex communications. In some instances, hard copy paper documents are required in business to meet legal and or audit requirements.

### Face-to-face

Even in times where other communication tools are available, face-to-face meetings are an essential way of establishing sound business relationships. The technicalities of contractual negotiations can be more easily overcome during face-to-face meetings.

### Landline telephone

The landline telephone is a reliable and cost effective method of communication. The telephone is a personal tool but, like all phones, has the disadvantage that the nuances conveyed by facial expression and body language are not accessible.

### Mobile phone

The mobile phone is more than just a convenience and is now regarded as a vital business tool.

### Smartphone

The smartphone is described as *'a mobile phone with an advanced mobile operating system'*. The smartphone combines the features of a mobile phone with other mobile devices, including a PDA, media player and GPS navigation system. The smartphone has a touch screen interface and camera. It can run third party apps. The smartphone is a significant business communication tool, allowing great mobility and worldwide connectivity. It allows those involved in the shipping industry, which at times relies on quick decisions, to be readily available from almost any location.

**Video conferencing can often replace business travel.**

### Tele or video conferencing

Tele or video conferencing is a form of communication which allows some of the benefits of meeting in person without the inconvenience and cost of travel. Video conferencing uses phone lines to transmit video, as well as sound, between two or more locations. Due to the fact that cameras, microphones, audio playback, special software and high-bandwidth networks are required, video conferencing is generally only available from appropriately equipped facilities. As networks become more powerful and the hardware components less expensive, a lower quality version of this function is available on many personal computers.

## Skype

Skype is a telecommunications software product that provides the opportunity, at low or zero cost, for video chat and conference calls using computers, tablets and mobile devices via the internet.

## Short message service (SMS) & Multimedia messaging service (MMS)

SMS is a communication method that allows the interchange of short text messages between mobile phones. It is estimated that, globally, there are 2.5 billion active SMS users accounting for 75% of all mobile phone subscribers. MMS is a telecommunications standard, again by mobile phone or smartphone, for sending messages that includes multimedia objects such as images, audio and video.

## Electronic Mail (email)

Email is a standard form of business communication offering a cost-effective, efficient and more-or-less instantaneous service. It allows the same message to be sent to a number of addresses simultaneously and the recipient can forward the message to other contacts. Attachments, such as documents, spreadsheets, digital photographs and scanned images can be sent with the message and arrive in a form which can be manipulated by the receiver without any further processing. Email is commonly used for internal communications in large organisations and between those who maintain their own secure networks. The use of email has made the telex system largely redundant.

A side effect of the general adoption of email by the business community as a means of communication has been the acceptance of a relatively informal style of written communication that did not exist in the media formally used. Emails are generally written in casual style, reflecting the informality that has become acceptable in the business world.

## Facsimile

The facsimile (or fax) is a convenient and universally accepted method of transmitting a document via a standard telephone connection. Along with scanned email documents it has immediate advantages of permitting, for example, a copy of a charter party complete with alterations and additions to be sent to the recipient. Diagrams, handwritten messages can also be transmitted over this system.

## Electronic data interchange (EDI)

Many large organisations and government departments now make use of electronic means of transmitting data between computers to remove the need for slow and labour intensive paper documentation or re-entering data. This saves time, money and resources in the routine submission of statistical data, customs entries and other information.

In the shipping business, most multi-modal transport systems now rely on electronic methods of document transmission. In recent years, the introduction of new technology has allowed the standardisation of these systems and the ongoing improvement in information technology techniques makes this practice increasingly standard.

## 1.14 DATA STORAGE AND RETRIEVAL

A vital advantage of business computer systems is the ability to store and retrieve large volumes of information rapidly, and to collate and sort data at speeds unachievable by any other means. The facility enables, for example, a sale and purchase broker to interrogate a database applying the criteria of a range of ships required by a potential buyer, and to select only those which may be of interest. Information can then be transmitted instantly to the client without further need for processing. Similarly, subscribers to organisations whose role is to provide information can use their own computer terminals to access real-time online data stored by the organisation itself. For example, subscribers to Lloyd's Register of Ships can, by using their own confidential log-in details, access up-to-date information on new additions or alterations to the Register. The facility is extremely valuable in the shipping business which depends on fast access to accurate data.

## 1.15 THE INTERNET AND E-COMMERCE

Whilst the internet provides a medium for the transmission of email and remote access to the databases of large organisations, it also provides, through the World Wide Web, a resource for business in terms of access to information. Few organisations involved in shipping, whatever their size, do not maintain their own website. A website acts as a showcase for their business, a valuable source of information to their customers and potential customers, and access to conducting business electronically.

Internet purchasing is now an established and accepted part of commercial life. A properly maintained website can display information and illustrations of articles or services for sale.

Chartering a ship or booking cargo space is not quite such a simple transaction, although it is now possible, through a number of organisations, to carry out such business transactions using the internet.

### Intranet

An intranet uses the same technology as the internet but operates within the confines of a single organisation. The principal constraint is the bandwidth (capacity) of the organisation's network. An intranet allows internal information to be distributed and maintained at low cost.

## 1.16 SHIP-TO-SHORE CONNECTIVITY

A ship is a mobile platform which may operate in remote areas of the world. Today, except within limited range of the shore, ships depend on communication satellites for connectivity with the shore. The lack of satellite capacity has limited the development of broadband services such as access to data and information associated with the internet to the ship. This omission is being redressed. By 2016 a new series of Inmarsat communication satellites operating the Inmarsat Global Xpress service will be in orbit. The completion of the satellite configuration will greatly improve ship-to-shore communication. Business and commercial opportunities will be enhanced, crew welfare will be helped by improved connection between ship and home, and safety-related communication, beyond the statutory minimum required for Global Maritime Distress Satellite System (GMDSS), will be possible. Companies, including Inmarsat, provide specialist communication packages for merchant ships, coastal merchant ships, the fishing community and leisure craft.

Satellite communication has replaced Morse code at sea

### Inmarsat

Inmarsat (International Maritime Satellite) was set up through the International Maritime Organization (IMO) in 1979 as a not-for-profit intergovernmental agency, to operate a satellite communication network for the maritime community. Twenty years later, due to political pressure and commercial opportunity, it was decided to modify Inmarsat's activities as an intergovernmental agency by splitting its commercial activity from its public safety obligations. Today, Inmarsat is a public limited company, listed on the London stock exchange. The public safety role is undertaken by the International Mobile Satellite Organisation (IMSO).

## 1.17 CONCLUSION

Modern communication methods have transformed the way in which all business, including the shipping business, is conducted. Without the advances in communication technology, the scale of international trade would not have developed as it has. While technological advances in communication methods have facilitated the efficient flow of information, e-commerce is vulnerable to risk. All organisations have to adopt rigorous risk management procedures to ensure the integrity and security of their systems.

Chapter 2

# Business ethics

*The Dutch East India Company undertook the first Initial Public Offering in 1602 and thus became the first public company to issue stock*

## 2.1 WHAT ARE ETHICS?

Everyone knows what ethics are until you ask them to define them. The word itself comes from the Greek language and translates almost exactly into the Latin word for morals. Philosophers have been writing learned theses on these subjects since the written word emerged. Some equate ethics to the difference between good and evil or right and wrong or virtue and vice, but ethics are not exactly any of these.

Ethical behaviour is tricky to define and ethics change with time. We are prepared to accept some business practices today that would have been considered quite unethical a hundred years ago. In some parts of the world, the practice of unofficial payments made to individuals to obtain preferential treatment is accepted, if not entirely approved of. In other countries this would be utterly condemned.

An understanding of ethics is gained from the working environment, colleagues and competitors, and from the business community in which an individual is involved.

## 2.2 ETHICS IN SHIPPING BUSINESS

The law looks after the problems of crime, tort or breaches of contract but one needs the mutual trust of the unwritten law in order to keep the wheels of our particular industry turning.

Examples are probably the easiest way to look at the subject. Take a chartering situation where several brokers are competing with one another to get a charterer to work through them. The sure way for this to come about is if a suitable owner opens the bidding with a firm offer. One way of achieving this would be for a broker to present a fabricated offer to the owner pretending that this emanated from the charterer. They would, of course, ensure that the pseudo offer was not one where there was any risk of the owner accepting 'clean' but attractive enough for the owner to make a counter offer which the deceitful broker can then carry to the charterer as if the owner had started the negotiations. That sort of procedure is clearly unethical.

That example also shows the clear division between what is unlawful and what is unethical. If the fabricated offer had indeed been accepted clean, the charterer whose name had been used would almost certainly repudiate the contract, and the owner would then have had a clear legal case against the errant broker for 'breach of warranty of authority'. As, however, the unethical broker was cunning enough to make sure their offer would not be acceptable, there is no contract to repudiate, no damages to claim so no legal case to bring against them.

Ethics in shipping go much further than this one example because principals must be able to trust their agents and brokers and vice versa, and brokers have to be able to trust each other.

A bill of lading is evidence of a contract, the contract itself often being discussed in a telephone conversation between the two parties involved.

Ethics demand that temptation is resisted to take the easy way out and use lies to explain away situations where one knows that no contrary proof is possible. That sort of temptation, not to exert oneself to do the best possible, can occur in any aspect of shipping business.

The Baltic Exchange, in London, has always been especially particular about ethical behaviour. It is perhaps in a fortunate position because of the examples set in the days of daily, face-to-face contact among those using that marketplace. It is much more difficult to play a dirty trick on a fellow broker when you are likely to meet them and/or their friends the very next day.

Furthermore, the Baltic's attitude to ethical behaviour enabled its governing board to discipline members for a breach of ethics. It did not have to wait until a law had been broken or a contract breached.

The Baltic, pictured below, is one of the few organisations to have produced a written code of ethical behaviour, which members must adopt in order to be accepted. The *'Baltic Code of Ethics and Market Practice'* concerns itself with standards of behavior which are expected of shipbrokers and lists practices which are not acceptable. To flout any of the guidance given is to risk expulsion and loss of reputation.

**Shipbrokers are expected to comply with unwritten laws of behaviour**

While the world outside the Baltic Exchange does not have the same ability to exert discipline, the shipping world is fortunately a fairly tight-knit community and persistent breakers of the unwritten laws eventually become known and find they either have to mend their ways or risk isolation. It is fair to say that self-regulation in ethical behaviour throughout the shipping business depends as much on the fear of loss of reputation and loss of livelihood as on the altruistic observance of business ethics for the good of the profession.

The one definition of ethics is that which is summed up so succinctly in the motto of the Institute of Chartered Shipbrokers: Our Word Our Bond.

## 2.3 MARITIME FRAUD

Fraudulent practice in one form or another is common to many areas of commerce, and imposes a considerable cost on the law-abiding community in terms of losses directly attributable to fraud and the price of precautionary measures taken to try to prevent it.

The shipping business is the perfect vehicle for a number of fraudulent practices that tend to take advantage of the high degree of trust upon which the industry depends.

## 2.4 INSURANCE FRAUD

Unscrupulous shipowners, in league with dishonest merchants, have been known to over-insure a ship and its cargo and subsequently arrange for it to sink in bad weather in a remote location, claiming far more than the ship or its contents were worth.

The celebrated case of the tanker *Salem* illustrates a large-scale fraud that almost succeeded. Under the name *South Sun*, it loaded 195,000 tonnes of crude oil in Kuwait for an innocent Italian charterer in Genoa. On passage through the Indian Ocean the vessel's name was quietly changed to *'Lema'*. It anchored off Durban and discharged its cargo (which had since been sold to another oil company for $56 million) illegally, refilling its tanks with seawater to give the impression of being still fully laden.

Continuing on its illicit voyage, now under the name *Salem*, it mysteriously sank after an explosion off the coast of Senegal. Had it not been for the fact that the officers and crew, when picked up from their lifeboats by the rescue services, had their suitcases with them, the intended claim for the loss of the ship and its now non-existent cargo might well have been met.

Insurance companies have their own investigators to make enquiries into any suspicious losses, but even though they may save their underwriters from fraudulent claims, it may be difficult to track down and prosecute the perpetrators. Insurance frauds are not, as some dishonest parties might claim, 'victimless' crimes. The insurance companies and their underwriters may eventually recover their losses through the premiums paid, but the burden is borne at the end of the day by all those honest parties who take out insurance and pay their premiums in the first place.

## 2.5 DOCUMENTARY FRAUD

All parties in shipping business will be aware of what a bill of lading looks like and the important role it plays in international trade as proof that goods have been loaded on a ship as a document of title to those goods, and as a form of security.

In shipping company offices, there may be drawers full of blank B/L forms of various types. Any one could be typed up, signed, stamped ORIGINAL and would be indistinguishable to the unpractised eye from a genuine bill representing real cargo. There is a problem of recognising a genuine B/L and the signatures of the ship's master or his authorised agent. Forgery and fraud associated with B/L are not unknown.

The ease with which documents in shipping business can be forged, altered, fabricated or otherwise adulterated is not lost upon the criminal fraternity, giving rise to a series of fraudulent documents presented to banks in support of letters of credit or to shipping companies for release of cargo or to innocent individuals as documents of title, all of which are calculated to obtain funds or goods by deception.

## 2.6 OTHER AREAS OF FRAUD

Major incidents of fraud tend to make the headlines, but there are far more frequent incidents that may never be detected. Even though the figures involved for each individual may be small, they are nonetheless damaging to the business of shipping and collectively amount to millions of lost dollars a year.

As many liner operators are aware, shippers are frequently tempted, when booking cargo, to 'under-measure', reducing the volume of their cargo upon which they will eventually pay freight. In some cases, this will only be discovered by sharp-eyed deck officers during loading operations, or if the company carries out spot checks on the dimensions of cargo delivered to the port in advance of shipment. Such fraudsters are trading on the fact that their under-declaration will not be noticed, and that, even if it is, they will simply claim that this was an innocent error. The cost to the carrier of carrying out such checks of course eventually rebounds upon the innocent as well as the guilty. In this way it can be seen that the victims of fraud are not simply those who are the prime target of dishonest behaviour but the wider shipping community.

Another example in which parties may collude quite innocently, is the so-called 'letter of indemnity' or 'back letter' issued by a disreputable shipper of cargo to a master or his owners in exchange for a clean bill of lading. For example, if a cargo of chemicals in drums on pallets is loaded, and the chief officer of the ship notices that many of the drums are secondhand, rusty, dented and leaking, the master is unlikely to sign a bill of lading without insisting that it should bear a clause to this effect. If he does not, he and his owners can be held responsible for the condition of the drums upon discharge. In order to secure a 'clean' bill of lading to obtain full payment from the consignee (whether through a letter of credit or otherwise), the shippers may offer to indemnify the master and owners against any claim for damaged cargo, issuing them a letter accordingly. This may indeed protect the owners from any subsequent claim, but it has the effect of giving the shippers a bill of lading which misrepresents the condition of the cargo. The bank, the consignee, or an innocent third party may then be induced to part with payment for the cargo as described in the bill of lading. Had they been aware that the cargo was contained in leaky, rusted, dented and secondhand drums, they may well have decided not to do so. They are the victims of a fraud.

## 2.7 OTHER CRIMINAL ACTIVITIES

The range of criminal activities involving shipping business goes beyond fraud. Whilst not classified as fraud, other activities include smuggling, where contraband goods, arms or drugs are concealed in the cargo or ship – often without the knowledge of the cargo – or shipowners. Illegal immigrants are also frequently smuggled by sea with or without the complicity of the carrier. There have been cases where bogus crewing agencies have attempted to obtain entry permits for illegal migrants by pretending that the migrants are seafarers due to join a ship in the intended country of destination. All criminal activities are a threat to the reputation and integrity of the shipping community.

**Smuggling is a centuries-old scourge of governments, who commissioned revenue cutters**

## 2.8 DETECTING AND AVOIDING FRAUD

International fraud connected with shipping business is a major problem, not simply for the victims but for the business as a whole. The difficulties of detecting and preventing fraud are considerable as it is frequently very sophisticated. In cases where such activity has been discovered it has often been found that the fraud has been perpetrated over a long period of time without the victims realising it has taken place.

Even when companies discover that they have been the victims of a fraud, they are frequently reluctant to admit the fact, as it does not reflect well upon their reputation or their security systems. In one case, a key staff member of a liner agency was found to have taken bookings from a number of shippers on a freight prepaid basis. He put the bookings through the system as freight collect, issued his own receipt on company letterheads to the shippers and pocketed the freight. He then made out duplicate bills of lading on the line's form, but stamped 'freight paid' which he issued to the shippers, who were none the wiser. It was inevitable, of course, that rather irate consignees would demand to know why they should have to pay the freight twice to obtain the goods and they would quickly alert the shipping company. Not surprisingly, subsequent investigations revealed that the employee had left with the proceeds of the deceit.

Without the assistance of the law-enforcement agencies, victims are unlikely to be able to track down the offenders and so the criminal can go unpunished and the criminals are able to perpetrate the same fraud on another unsuspecting party.

Sophisticated criminals will frequently use to their advantage the protection of different jurisdictions worldwide, especially those where freedom of information is highly restricted, and from which extradition is difficult. This makes the pursuit of criminals both expensive and time-consuming, and is calculated to put off even the most determined victims.

There are, fortunately, a number of measures that companies and individuals can take to avoid becoming victims of fraud. Checking the '*bona-fides*' of customers and clients is a straightforward precaution. Limited liability companies have their details filed in the public domain and credit checks can be carried out by a number of private agencies very speedily. Enquiries can also be made within the trade or profession, and names crosschecked in directories, or with chambers of commerce and other institutions. Education and training are powerful weapons in the fight against fraud, and information is readily supplied by organisations such as the International Maritime Bureau (IMB), Baltic and International Maritime Council (BIMCO), insurance companies, banks and others to alert likely victims to the dangers which are posed by fraudsters and criminals. Customs, police and revenue authorities worldwide are also committed to preventing fraud and can be of great assistance in pursuing and prosecuting criminals in the public interest.

## 2.9 BRIBERY

The recent UK Bribery Act defines bribery as *'giving someone a financial or other advantage to encourage that person to perform their functions or activities improperly or to reward that person for having already done so'*. There are particular risks for individuals and companies involved in international business activity where different countries have different ethical standards. Bribery is an illegal act and can have severe ramifications for those involved. The subject of bribery is such a large one that the next chapter is devoted to it.

## 2.10 BALTIC EXCHANGE 'GUIDANCE ON REQUIRED STANDARDS OF MEMBERS'

The motto of the Baltic Exchange and the Institute of Chartered Shipbrokers is Our Word Our Bond. It captures the importance of trust in shipping and relates to the importance of ethical business practice in shipping. Terms of contracts established by members of the Baltic, whether written or oral, are sacrosanct and members rely on such commitment. In addition, the directors of the board governing the Baltic Exchange have provided guidance on required standards of its members. Guidance includes:

- all market participants are required to honour their contractual obligations in a timely manner;
- in the conduct of their profession members must exercise reasonable care to avoid misrepresentation and shall be guided by the principles of honest and fair dealing;
- a broker must only offer or bid a ship or cargo when duly authorised by a principal or by a broker acting on the instructions and authority of the principal;
- an owner or owner's broker may only offer his/her vessel 'firm' for one cargo at a time. Similarly, a charterer or charterer's broker may only offer his/her cargo 'firm' to one vessel at a time ('firm' means that an enforceable contract has been formed and the offer is unconditionally accepted by the party to whom it is made);

- a principal may receive multiple firm offers for a vessel or cargo, but must always make it clear at the time if he/she is already out firm elsewhere;
- an unsolicited offer or proposal does not necessarily establish the channel of negotiation;
- prior to quoting business from a principal previously unknown to him, a broker should take reasonable steps to obtain his/her background and reputation of the principal concerned;
- all parties must ensure there is absolute clarity regarding the payment of broker commissions;
- brokers who act as Baltic panellists must apply impeccable standards of honesty and integrity to the role.

The importance of ethical behaviour and its relationship to the motto which enshrines the behaviour of members of the Baltic Exchange, 'Our Word Our Bond' influences the behaviour of many involved in the shipping business.

The Baltic Exchange is not the only body which sets out an ethical code for its members. All persons involved in business may at times be tempted to take actions which are dishonest or against the public interest. Other organisations within the shipping business set out codes of conduct to guide the ethical behavior of their members.

## The Baltic Code 2014 Ethics and Market Practice

The Baltic Exchange — The Baltic Code

### Unacceptable Practices

The Directors have highlighted, from time to time, certain practices, which they consider unacceptable from brokers accredited to the Baltic Exchange.

These include:

1. Organisations operating as Freight Contractors/Freight Speculators offering named tonnage against tenders without the authority of owners/disponent owners.
2. Agents/brokers implying that they hold a ship/cargo firm or exclusively when they do not, in order to secure a response from another party.
3. Off-setting against hire or freight payment(s), amounts representing unspecified or vague claims.
4. Withholding payment of commissions in respect of hire/freight/deadfreight/ demurrage earned and paid.
5. Using information obtained from Exchange members for business transacted directly with or between non-Baltic members. This practice involves the use of market-sensitive information given by another member, but being used outside the Baltic market.
6. Passing market-sensitive information gained through the Exchange to non-Baltic brokers or agents so that they can deal directly with Baltic members' principals or their brokers. This has the effect of diluting the value of the market and runs the risk of an agreement being concluded with someone who may not be fully familiar with the practices of the market and may not observe the same standards of business ethics.
7. Owners offering their vessel firm for business when they hold a firm offer from another charterer. The unwanted offer should be declined before the owner makes another offer
8. Charterers fixing two vessels for one cargo and then holding both vessels over a period of time on "subjects".
9. The distribution of route or index rates, produced by the Exchange from its panel reporting companies, for the purpose of pricing charters or contracts without an appropriate commission to a Baltic broker.

If a member of the Exchange fails to comply with any of the above terms or practices he may be disciplined by the Directors under the Rules. The Directors have power to censure, suspend or expel a member from the Exchange in these circumstances.

The Exchange has arrangements for investigating disputes between members, and between members and non-members, which arise from the breach of these basic principles or the employment of unacceptable practices and market ethics generally. These are set out below. Members are encouraged to bring such instances to the attention of the Exchange in writing so that they can be investigated.

Our word **our bond**

The Baltic Code

The Baltic Exchange

## CHARTERING

### Knowledge Required

Trading members are expected to have a reasonable knowledge of world port geography, and principal trading areas, including main types of ships and cargoes.

### Main Types Of Vessels

Modern cargo vessels range from small coasters to very large bulk carriers and ultra large tankers, but generally fall into a number of groups types.

**Bulk Carriers (Dry Cargo)**

All these vessels are single deckers with a varying number of holds for the carriage of bulk cargoes such as grain, ore, coal, steel etc.

**Handysize**

About 20/35,000 dwt, 4 holds/hatches or 5 holds/hatches

Geared with 25-35 ton cranes

**Handymax**

About 36/49,000 dwt, 5 holds/hatches

Geared with 25-35 ton cranes

**Supramax**

About 50/58,000 dwt, 5 holds/hatches

Geared with 25-35 ton cranes

**Panamax/Kamsarmax**

About 65/82,000 dwt, 7 holds/hatches

Usually gearless

**Capesize**

About 120/200,000 dwt, 9 holds/hatches

Gearless

**Very large Ore/Bulk**

About 220/360,000 dwt, 9 holds/hatches

Gearless

The above are only a guidance of general groups, as the sizes of such types of vessel and their performance varies and evolves over time.

Our word **our bond**

Chapter 3

# Anti-bribery compliance – challenges in shipping

*Queen Isabella of Spain was featured on a commemorative coin in 1893 – the first lady to be cast on a US coin*

## 3.1 INTRODUCTION

Bribery is widely recognised as a global problem that adversely affects national economies, local communities and businesses. The cost to the business community includes greater risks, unpredictable expenses, wasted time and overall uncertainty. Local communities suffer from theft, sub-standard products and loss of confidence in governments.

To address this complex problem, many governments have strengthened their anti-bribery legislation and, slowly, their pace of enforcement. Many have realised that fighting bribery requires a co-ordinated, international effort.

For the shipping industry, which is inherently multijurisdictional, a co-ordinated anti-bribery strategy is particularly promising. Such a strategy can tackle pervasive bribery in ports around the world. It also brings more certainty to the multiple, layered business partnerships by both demanding and providing greater transparency regarding the beneficial ownership of vessels, as well as the identity of other players in the shipping supply chain. It is much easier to build trust, which is fundamental to the maritime industry, when one is confident in one's counterparts. Sailors' lives, the safety of vessels, the security of cargo, and the 90% of world trade that is transported by ships are at stake.

## 3.2 SIGNIFICANT ANTI-BRIBERY LEGISLATION

### International anti-bribery conventions

The Inter-American Convention against Corruption (IACAC), adopted by the Organization of American States (OAS) in 1996, was the first major international judicial instrument dedicated to fighting corruption. The IACAC requires that its signatory states incorporate into their judicial systems mechanisms to prosecute active, passive and transnational bribery, among other illegal practices. Currently, 33 states have ratified the IACAC.

One year later, in 1997, in a global effort to address the 'supply side' of bribery, the Organisation for Economic Co-operation and Development (OECD) adopted the Convention on Combating Bribery of Foreign Public Officials in International Business Transactions (OECD Anti-Bribery Convention). The OECD Anti-Bribery Convention requires signatory countries to criminalise bribing foreign officials, as well as aiding, abetting and authorising such an act. All of the OECD 34 member countries and seven non-member countries – Argentina, Brazil, Bulgaria, Colombia, Latvia, Russia, and South Africa – have adopted the OECD Anti-Bribery Convention as of April 2015.

A rigorous peer-review monitoring system was established to ensure countries' implementation and enforcement of the OECD Anti-Bribery Convention. The OECD Working Group on Bribery oversees the monitoring process which is conducted in three phases:

- the evaluation of a country's legislation to adequately implement the OECD Anti-Bribery Convention;
- the assessment of a country's effectiveness to apply the legislation; and
- the review of a country's enforcement of the Convention and its compliance with previous recommendations.

In 2003, in another significant global anti-bribery effort, the United Nations Convention against Corruption (UNCAC) was adopted; it entered into force in 2005. The UNCAC requires parties to criminalise a wide range of corrupt acts, including domestic and foreign bribery. It also established guidelines for the creation of enhanced accounting and auditing standards for the private sector. By April 2015, 175 entities, including 172 UN member states, the Cook Islands, the State of Palestine, and the European Union, had ratified the UNCAC. The United Nations Office on Drugs and Crime (UNODC) serves as a Secretariat of the Conference of the States Parties, established to ensure UNCAC's implementation and review.

The African Union Convention on Preventing and Combating Corruption (AU Convention) was also adopted in 2003, the same year as UNCAC, and by 2014, 35 out of 53 member states of the African Union had ratified it. The AU Convention covers a range of criminal offences including domestic and foreign bribery, as well as public and private sector corruption on both supply and demand sides. It is unique in containing mandatory provisions with respect to private-to-private corruption.

## 3.3 KEY NATIONAL ANTI-BRIBERY LEGISLATION

### The United States Foreign Corrupt Practices Act (FCPA)

The 1977 enactment of the US Foreign Corrupt Practices Act (FCPA) was among the first significant anti-bribery legislative actions taken by a country. The FCPA has two primary components: anti-bribery provision and accounting provisions. Under the FCPA's anti-bribery provisions, US companies or persons, or those with a connection to the United States of America, are prohibited from corruptly giving or promising to give money or anything of value to a foreign government official with the intent of obtaining business or other improper advantage. Under the FCPA's accounting provisions, there are requirements to record accurately in a company's books and records all payments, including permissible facilitation payments and payments made under duress, and to have adequate internal controls. The FCPA is jointly enforced by the US Department of Justice (DOJ) and the US Securities and Exchange Commission (SEC). Notably, the FCPA does not explicitly criminalise commercial sector – as opposed to public sector – bribery.

### The United Kingdom's Bribery Act

The United Kingdom moved anti-bribery legislative efforts forward once more through its enactment in 2011 of the United Kingdom's Bribery Act (UK Bribery Act). The UK Bribery Act, which is enforced by the Serious Fraud Office (SFO), marked a significant broadening of domestic anti-bribery laws. The UK Bribery Act makes it a crime both to bribe and to receive bribes from another person, and criminalises both public and commercial sector bribes. There are three primary provisions in the UK Bribery Act:

- Section 1 prohibits offering an advantage to anyone with the intent of inducing that person to improperly perform a relevant function;
- Section 6 specifically creates an offence for the bribery of a foreign official to obtain a business advantage; and,
- Section 7 imposes liability on a commercial organisation for failing to prevent an associated person (who can be an employee, agent or subsidiary) from bribing another person (whether a UK official, foreign official, or private citizen) on behalf of the company.

The UK Bribery Act also contains an 'adequate procedures' defence, under which companies can defend themselves against certain bribery-related allegations if they have in place a robust anti-bribery compliance programme.

Key differences exist between the FCPA and UK Bribery Act, as illustrated in the table below:

| US FCPA | UK Bribery Act |
|---|---|
| Prohibits only public bribery | Prohibits public and commercial bribery |
| No statutory defence for businesses that have adequate procedures to prevent bribery | Statutory defence for businesses that have adequate procedures to prevent bribery |
| Permits facilitating payments, but narrowly interpreted | Prohibits facilitating payments |
| Prohibits only outbound bribery | Prohibits outbound and inbound bribery |

### Brazil's Corporate Anti-Bribery Statute

Developing countries have also increasingly started to take notice of the need for robust anti-bribery legislation, particularly to spur investment in their countries. Brazil's Corporate Anti-Bribery Statute (Brazilian Anti-Bribery Law) entered into force in January 2014. The Brazilian Anti-Bribery Law provides strong incentives for companies that have their headquarters, branches or subsidiaries in Brazil, to detect and prevent potential instances of bribery, or be fined up to 20% of the gross income of the company in the year prior to the start of the investigation. Under the law, companies may receive credit if they successfully demonstrate that they have an effective compliance programme in place and for co-operating with investigative authorities.

## 3.4 EXTRATERRITORIAL JURISDICTION OF LEADING ANTI-BRIBERY LEGISLATION

The OECD Anti-Bribery Convention calls for a broad interpretation of territorial jurisdiction to avoid requirements of 'extensive physical connection to the bribery act'. Article 4 of the OECD Anti-Bribery Convention states that signatories ought to take measures to establish jurisdiction over the bribery of a foreign public official when the offence is committed in whole or in part in the signatory's territory. It also instructs countries to prosecute their own nationals for bribery occurring abroad where a country's laws allow for such extraterritorial jurisdiction.

Certain anti-bribery regulations, such as the FCPA and the UK Bribery Act, can apply to both domestic and foreign nationals or entities, even if they act outside of national borders. The FCPA applies to:

- Issuers – Publicly-traded US companies and foreign companies traded on US exchanges;
- Domestic Concerns – Non-public US businesses, US citizens and US residents;
- Foreign companies to the extent that they engage in conduct that violates the FCPA either (1) 'while in the territory of the United States' or (2) by employing use of 'an instrumentality of interstate commerce.'

The US government takes a broad jurisdictional approach in terms of FCPA enforcement. The US government has indicated that simply sending an email from one foreign office to another through a server located in the United States of America, or sending money from one foreign location to another via a US bank, would establish US jurisdiction for FCPA enforcement.

In comparison, the UK Bribery Act applies to offences committed in the United Kingdom, as well as offences committed by UK citizens, residents, and corporations outside the UK. Corporate liability extends to all organisations incorporated in the UK or carrying on a business or part of a business in the UK, regardless of whether the UK has jurisdiction over the individual who committed the offence. However, the Ministry of Justice's Guidance to the UK Bribery Act clarifies that, unlike US enforcement of the FCPA, the UK government would not consider a company as 'carrying on a business in the United Kingdom' solely because the company's securities are listed on the London stock exchange. Similarly, a parent company may not qualify as having a business in the UK, based on the mere fact that it has a UK subsidiary.

## 3.5 CURRENT ANTI-BRIBERY ENFORCEMENT TRENDS

As countries continue to adopt more robust anti-bribery legislation, the possibility of prosecution of both companies and individuals for violating anti-bribery laws is no longer remote. Operating through the 'customs of the port', as opposed to relevant anti-bribery laws, is no longer an acceptable way of conducting business. Anti-bribery law violations levied against corporations are resulting in increasingly higher fines. For example, the average FCPA fine has doubled over the last five years, reaching an unprecedented $160m in 2014.

As a result of US regulators' expansive interpretation of the jurisdictional application of the FCPA, as mentioned above, almost one-third of all FCPA cases have been brought against non-US companies. Non-US firms have paid more than four times the FCPA fines and settlements paid by US firms. Eight out of 10 companies that paid the highest FCPA penalties are non-US companies, including Siemens (Germany) with $800m in fines, Alstom (France) with $772m in fines, Total (France) with $398.2m in fines, Snamprogetti (The Netherlands) with $365m in fines, and Technip (France) with $338m in fines.

In addition, more individuals are being targeted in bribery-related matters. Penalties for individuals violating the FCPA include up to five years in prison, a maximum criminal fine of $100,000 per violation, or both. Under the UK Bribery Act, individuals may face up to ten years imprisonment in addition to unlimited fines. The 2014 OECD Foreign Bribery Report stated that over half of the 427 cases completed and analysed for the report involved corporate management or CEOs.

The shipping, transportation and logistics industries have seen the impact of growing international anti-bribery enforcement. For example, in 2010, Swiss global logistics firm Panalpina World Transport (Holding) Ltd and its US subsidiary Panalpina Inc. admitted to bribing customs officials on behalf of their customers to clear equipment and goods in at least seven countries, including Angola, Azerbaijan, Brazil, Kazakhstan, Nigeria, Russia and Turkmenistan. As a result of this bribery scheme, the company settled with the US Government for approximately $82m. But the U.S. Government did not stop there. Instead, it went after several of Panalpina's clients, charging them in relation to Panalpina's actions. These clients, including Royal Dutch Shell PLC, Pride International, Tidewater Inc, Transocean Inc, GlobalSantaFe Corp. and Noble Corp, paid a total of about $237m in fines for paying bribes to foreign officials in several countries to expedite customs services, avoid required inspections, and obtain false paperwork.

The shipping and transportation industry has also faced significant bribery-related fines from non-US jurisdictions. For example, SBM Offshore, a Dutch manufacturer of floating production systems for the oil and gas industry, paid US$240m to the Dutch Public Prosecutor's Office to resolve allegations related to bribes allegedly paid in Angola, Brazil and Equatorial Guinea.

While some companies in the shipping and transportation industry have faced anti-bribery enforcement actions, the industry has not yet been targeted as part of a so-called industry sweep, in which the government targets a particular industry and uses information gained from one co-operating company to pursue other companies in the same industry. Such industry-focused enforcement has been conducted by the United States of America, the United Kingdom and China. Given that logistics and shipping are often components of a regular supply chain, the shipping and transportation industries could predictably end up in the regulators' spotlight as a result of investigations initiated against other companies in the supply chain.

## 3.6 EXCEPTIONS TO ANTI-BRIBERY LAWS

### Facilitation payments

While facilitation payments are permitted under the US FCPA and the laws of Australia, New Zealand and South Korea, they are illegal in almost every country in which they are paid. These small bribes are usually paid to facilitate some government action. For example, in Taiwan there is an expectation from the local government officials, via the port agents, to be paid under the table about US$100 for an 'in / out' charge. In India, similar demands are made and labelled 'for the smooth passage of the vessel'. In the Suez Canal – often called the 'Marlboro Canal' – gifts of whisky and cigarettes are expected to ease the transit of the vessel through the canal.

Under the FCPA, facilitation payments are payments to expedite routine government actions, such as loading and unloading cargo, or scheduling inspections related to transit of goods across country. The DOJ and SEC clarify in a 2012 Resource Guide to the FCPA that such a payment is usually a 'one-time, small payment to obtain a routine, non-discretionary government service that a company is entitled to receive'. Despite the narrow facilitation payments exception to the FCPA, the US government regularly encourages companies to prohibit or discourage facilitation payments 'in view of the corrosive effect of small facilitation payments, particularly on sustainable economic development and the rule of law', following the recommendations of the OECD's Working Group on Bribery. Moreover, the Resource Guide to the FCPA emphasises that *'even when the payment may qualify as an exception to the FCPA's anti-bribery provisions, it may still violate domestic laws, specific contractual terms, and, if not accurately recorded, the FCPA's books and records provisions'.*

Despite this limited exception for facilitation payments under US law and a handful of other national laws, facilitation payments are illegal under the UK Bribery Act and most national anti-bribery laws. The Guidance to the UK Bribery Act states clearly that 'facilitation payments, which are payments to induce officials to perform routine functions they are otherwise obligated to perform, are bribes', and therefore are not allowed.

A worldwide campaign to abolish facilitation payments is driven by the desire of the international compliance community to eradicate a culture of corruption, reduce distortion and uncertainty in business operations, and strengthen public service, particularly in countries where the poor bear the greatest burden of small bribes. A report by TRACE International, *'The High Cost of Small Bribes'* points to the inherent illegality of facilitation payments and describes the accounting dilemma that those paying them face: companies must choose between falsifying their records in violation of their own laws or recording the payment accurately and documenting a violation of local law. Opponents of elimination of the exception for facilitation payments argue that instead of punishing the suppliers of facilitation payments, governments should first attempt to reduce the demand for such payments by addressing the root causes of bribery.

### Payments made in response to extortion (duress) vs. commercial coercion

Shipowners and ship masters face numerous illegal demands for bribes in many parts of the world. These demands often involve some kind of coercion, and ship masters are confronted with the difficult choice of either acquiescing to illegal demands and making themselves vulnerable to potential liability, or refusing these demands and incurring operational costs for extra waiting time spent in ports or damaged cargo. Coercion on the part of port, customs and other officials also often involves intimidation of the crew. Because of the prevalence of this problem, it is important to understand the legal difference between payments made voluntarily versus in response to extortion or commercial coercion.

The DOJ and SEC explain that a payment – any payment, not necessarily a facilitation payment made in response to true extortionate demands under imminent threat of physical harm' cannot be seen as made with corrupt intent or for the purpose of obtaining or retaining business. According to the 2003 Eleventh Circuit Pattern Jury Instructions, to establish duress or coercion, a defendant must generally demonstrate that he or she (i) was under unlawful, present, immediate and impending threat of death or serious bodily injury; (ii) did not negligently or recklessly create a situation where he/she would be forced to engage in criminal conduct (for example, had been making payments as part of an ongoing bribery scheme); (iii) had no reasonable legal alternative to violating the law; and (iv) there was a direct causal relationship between the criminal action and the avoidance of the threatened harm.' According to the UK Ministry of Justice's clarifications to the UK Bribery Act, 'the common law defence of duress is very likely to be available in such circumstances as well'.

One example of extortion, given by the US Congress, is a payment to an official to keep an oil rig from being dynamited. Under the FCPA, such payments must be accurately recorded, so that the company and its management are informed of the payments and can establish that the payments were appropriate under the circumstances.

Commercial coercion, or threats to property, on the other hand, is different from extortion. A payment made in this situation can be considered a bribe. Mere commercial coercion does not involve an immediate threat of death or serious bodily injury, such as in the case of extortion. Instead, this is usually 'a demand on a part of a government official for a payment as a price for gaining entry into a market or to obtain contracts', according to the Resource Guide to the FCPA. The practice has been that, as long as a bribe payer can safely walk away without making a payment, it is more likely to be a situation involving commercial coercion, as opposed to extortion *(US v Kozeny)*. As Congress noted when it enacted the FCPA, the fact that the payment was *'first proposed by the recipient… does not alter the corrupt purpose on the part of the person paying the bribe'.*

## 3.7 ANTI-BRIBERY COMPLIANCE BEST PRACTICES FOR THE SHIPPING INDUSTRY

As international anti-bribery enforcement gains momentum, so does the need for individuals to be aware of anti-bribery laws and for companies to have robust anti-bribery compliance programmes in place. Anti-bribery compliance procedures should include a clear and concise anti-bribery policy, strong contractual anti-bribery clauses, rigorous risk assessment, a thorough third- party due diligence, regular training, and periodic reviews and audits, among other elements.

## Anti-bribery policy

Companies should have a succinct anti-bribery policy that is easily understood by all employees and includes clear industry-specific examples of what constitutes bribery. Policies should include details on employees' responsibilities when encountering a demand for a bribe, including who should be contacted, how the employee should document an incident, and how they should respond to a demand.

It is not unusual for companies in the shipping industry to have a zero tolerance policy towards bribery. Given the safety issues and related responsibilities that a vessel master has towards his vessel and the crew, companies' anti-bribery policies have to ensure that the master and the vessel's superintendent or operator have the authority to respond to situations that give rise to life-threatening issues, as long as they are reported and documented.

The role of ship managers is critical in the effective performance and operation of a vessel. Often the master's first call in an emergency will be to the vessel's superintendent. Therefore it is important that the ship manager is aware of, fully understands, and acts in accordance with the shipowner's anti-bribery policies.

## Anti-bribery risk assessments

A company's anti-bribery risk assessment is critical for understanding overall bribery risks faced by the company. For companies in the shipping and transportation industry, factors to consider in this general anti-bribery risk assessment include the company's business model, trading patterns and strategies, and other shipping related factors, such as the type of vessel, cargo, port, experience of the master, and the type of services required in the port.

In addition to a general company risk assessment, companies in the shipping industry should also consider undertaking a port-level anti-bribery risk assessment. The port-level risk assessment should ideally be built into the normal operational planning that occurs when preparing for a port call. Given the different bribery risk posed by each port, preparation has to be flexible enough to adapt to the relevant level of risk and the nature of the shipping operation. All key players, such as a vessel's master, superintendent, operator, as well as the relevant port agents, should take part in the formal planning. This will ensure that the shipmaster is prepared to respond adequately to various risks, including demands for bribes in particular ports or in handling particular shipping operations.

Where applicable, a rigorous port-level risk assessment should include the following:

- understanding of the various authorities and other parties the vessel will need to engage with, such as Port State Control inspectors, immigration, customs, pilots, tug master, and stevedores;

- information regarding government officials with whom a company has regular contact, such as port, customs and immigration, as well as the employees of local maritime bodies and certain suppliers in the port who may also be government officials;

- information regarding whether there are any unusual requirements that have to be complied with;

- the company's own direct or secondhand knowledge of situations which have previously occurred at the port;

- intelligence and other information from a company's own port agent about potential bribery risk areas, what to expect on arrival and what to expect during the port call;
- the terms and conditions of related freight contracts, in particular the anti-bribery clauses that the company has agreed to;
- understanding applicable local laws, as opposed to local customs and regulations;
- assurances that the vessel and crew have all of their relevant permits and documents in order;
- assurances that the port agent is familiar with the company's anti-bribery policy.

Completing a port-level risk assessment will not necessarily guarantee a trouble-free port call, but it will help to ensure that the company has adopted a defensible process and has made reasonable and adequate preparations. The Maritime Anti-Corruption Network (MACN) collates information for its members on port corruption hotspots, the types of demands being made, and by whom, together with an assessment of the consequences of resisting the demands. This tool can be immensely helpful when planning a port call.

MACN is an industry- and member-led group that was established in 2012 to help support companies that operate in the maritime supply chain to develop and maintain robust and appropriate anti-bribery compliance programmes. MACN does this through member 'benchmarking' meetings, the provision of anti-bribery training programmes and webinars to support members' compliance programmes, as well as the sharing of intelligence on where bribes are being demanded and vessels are being disrupted. MACN membership is comprised of shipowners from all the main sectors: tankers (oil and gas), dry bulk, offshore, car carriers and containers, as well as port agents, ship managers, forwarders, and leading trading, oil and mining companies.

## Anti-bribery clauses

A company's compliance efforts will benefit significantly from robust anti-bribery clauses included in its supplier agreements, as well as freight contracts. It is important that the company ensures that all of its business partners are familiar with and understand the company's anti-bribery policy. The latter can be detailed in the company's standard supplier agreements with port agents, ship management, and stevedores.

Leading charterers now frequently include robust anti-bribery clauses in their freight contracts. Some of the terms can be more onerous than international anti-bribery legislation, such as no gifts or facilitation payments. That means that a vessel master sailing through the Suez Canal is not allowed to hand out cigarettes or other gratuities to ensure the smooth transit of the vessel, except for situations that involve the safety of the crew or the vessel. A failure to comply with these contractual terms can result in the contract being terminated, the freight being withheld, and the loss of future business opportunities. Therefore it is critical to be aware of anti-bribery clauses during the voyage and during port call planning. These clauses often extend the liability for anti-bribery compliance to the contracting parties' supply chain; for a vessel owner, that would include their port agents and ship managers.

Currently, there is no standard anti-bribery clause but the Baltic and International Maritime Council (BIMCO), as mentioned above, is preparing to publish a clause, which will help charterers and owners to manage the bribery challenges arising in their global operations. In addition, TRACE has developed standardised anti-bribery clauses for low, medium and high-risk relationships.

## Anti-bribery training

It is becoming commonplace within the maritime supply chain for companies to provide their customers with copies of their anti-bribery policies and confirmation that their employees have been trained adequately to implement those policies. Anti-bribery training should address the company's policies, procedures and relevant legislation, and be provided to all levels of the shore-based staff along with the vessels' masters and senior officers. Some associations of shipowners have published training materials for their members that cover training for seafarers. In addition, MACN has an online anti-bribery training platform, which is free for its members, that covers both shore-based staff and seafarers.

Training for seafarers should include what a master should do and who in the organisation they should contact when an illegal demand is made. Likewise, the reporting lines for vessel operators and vessel superintendents should be detailed. If a ship-owning company employs a third-party technical ship manager, for example, clear instructions should be given to the ship manager with regard to anti-bribery training for the officers who will sail on its vessel.

A vessel-owning company should also provide anti-bribery training to its time charterers (i.e. time chartered vessel owners), shipbrokers, or port agents, with whom long-term or important relationships have been established. A company should periodically update training materials to ensure that all employees remain aware of their obligations and responsibilities under current legislation, while keeping records of training completion by each employee.

## Due diligence

Under most anti-bribery laws, companies can be liable for the improper payments made by their third parties, such as subcontractors, vendors, brokers, sales agents, consultants and contractors. Under the FCPA, companies can be held responsible if they were aware, or had a reason to believe, that the third party would use its compensation in a way that violates the law. Actual knowledge is not required and wilful ignorance is not a defence.

The use of third parties to convey bribes is commonplace. About 90% of recently concluded FCPA cases involved a third party. This corresponds to the trend identified in the OECD 2014 Foreign Bribery report that 75% of all 427 resolved anti-bribery cases since 1999 involved payments through intermediaries - either agents or 'corporate vehicles', such as subsidiary companies, local consulting firms, companies located in offshore financial centres or tax havens, or companies under the beneficial ownership of the public official who received the bribes.

The role of third parties in many bribe schemes illustrates the need for all companies to know their third parties. Conducting due diligence on third parties is an important risk mitigation measure. Under the UK Bribery Act, a company may escape liability for failing to prevent bribery by showing that it had adequate procedures in place to prevent and detect bribery. To reduce liability, companies are required to

- conduct due diligence on their third-party intermediaries, such as port agents, suppliers and consultants;
- perform regular risk assessments, internal reviews and audits; as well as

- include anti-bribery clauses in their contracts with third parties.

With a strong compliance program, companies may demonstrate that any deviations from policy or law were not authorised, and therefore avoid penalties. Similarly, under the FCPA, companies can receive lowered fines as a result of having a robust anti-bribery compliance programme, including conducting due diligence on their third parties.

Ultimately, companies that adopt effective anti-bribery compliance programmes and invest in meaningful due diligence can have a legal and competitive advantage over their competitors. They will learn not only about the past corporate governance of their partners, but about prior misconduct, bankruptcies, ties to the government, and demonstrate a willingness to embrace international anti-bribery standards.

Given the relatively opaque nature of the shipping industry, performing the appropriate level of due diligence can be time-consuming and expensive. Determining the appropriate level of due diligence will depend on a variety of factors, such as the type of service provided by intermediaries, a country's corruption rating, the degree of interaction with government officials, and the amounts of money involved. The era of long-term business relationships based on trust in the maritime industry is being increasingly replaced by more commercialised and fluid relationships. Furthermore, legal obligations and commercial expectations have also changed; now it is necessary to be able to document clearly that you know who you are doing business with, and have identified and addressed any relevant reputational issues. This due diligence should include identifying the beneficial shareholders, as well as the senior management of the suppliers or joint venture partners. The challenge is that this information must be regularly updated to account for frequent changes.

The four key players in the maritime industry that should be subject to due diligence are shipbrokers, port agents, shipowners, and ship managers. Shipbrokers have been a part of the industry for centuries, and their commission levels are market-based and generally clearly understood by other players. Nevertheless, there have been accusations that broker fees were used to pay bribes to obtain contracts on behalf of their principals. This demonstrates the need for a principal to perform the appropriate level of due diligence on its brokers, agents and managers, as well as to make sure that they are aware of a principal's anti-bribery policy.

The use of port agents is integral for the majority of global operations in the shipping industry. Some of these relationships have been established over many years. Nevertheless, an appropriate level of screening is required, including confirming that port agents are aware of the principal company's anti-bribery policy. Often the most challenging ports for the principal are those that are least familiar, with no established relationships with a local port agent. It is not uncommon that 'the customs of the port', as opposed to the local laws, are the perceived means of operation in such ports. Therefore it is necessary to provide port agents with clear instructions on appropriate conduct and undertake adequate port call planning ahead of time.

As for due diligence on shipowners, it is important that the true beneficial owner of the vessel is known, as well the identity of shareholders and senior management. The screening of a vessel should ensure that it has not been used in violation of any sanctions regime. The challenge is that the fixing of a vessel can be a rushed process with only hours available to make a deal. Nevertheless, the appropriate level of due diligence must be performed. In reality, many companies that charter vessels limit their checks to the review of a rather generic Baltic Exchange style fixing questionnaire, without verifying key information, such as confirming the beneficiary shipowners, as well as screening the vessel, the company's shareholders and the senior management. But it is important to keep in mind that, if a shipowner makes an illegal payment, the time charterer can be held liable for the violation. The charterer can also be in breach of an anti-bribery clause of its freight agreement or sub charter party.

An Australian entity, RightShip, offers a ship vetting information system to charterers and shippers to assist with due diligence. TRACE has partnered with RightShip to create an additional anti-bribery compliance component within an existing global database and system for rating ships. The new component seeks to substantially decrease corruption at ports and will be developed based on, among other elements, identification of beneficial ownership and screening of individual shipowners against international watch lists and media databases. The launch of the new compliance rating is scheduled later this year.

## Reporting

For a company to have an effective compliance policy, all of its employees must know what to do when they encounter an incident of bribery and corruption. This could be on a vessel or in the office. Clear reporting lines need to be established, documented and communicated to employees. Explaining how the reporting mechanism works should be detailed in the company's anti-bribery training.

It is common that a designated point of contact for a ship master is his or her vessel superintendent, who must be given clear instructions and training on how to handle a bribery-related incident. Such instructions should address:

- whether the incident affects the safety of the crew and/or the vessel;
- who they should contact ashore;
- what level of authority they have; and
- how and where the incident should be documented.

Shore-based personnel may also encounter incidents of bribery, and therefore need to be trained to be able to identify and properly handle those incidents.

Some companies have an independently managed and hosted telephone and web-based functionality (hot-line) where individuals can anonymously report incidents of bribery. Properly reporting and documenting any bribery incident is a company's first step in addressing a potential problem. Due to the systemic nature of bribery, there may be little that a company can do on its own, but it can share this information with its shipowners' association, port agents or shipbrokers' association, BIMCO, Intercargo, Intertanko, and an industry group, such as MACN.

The key to proper anti-bribery reporting is obtaining and retaining required documentation, which is often an official receipt or invoice for the cost incurred. Port agents and others who provide services to the vessels, including port authorities and pilots, should always be asked to provide receipts for all payments. Requests for payment in cash should be resisted whenever possible, and at least documented when they cannot be avoided. In cases when proper documentation cannot be obtained, a company can use its accounting system as an effective low-cost means for recording such incidents. A company can set up an account code for un-receipted transactions, for example, so that management is aware of potential bribery risks and can address them appropriately.

Data collected through the internal reporting processes, including companies' accounting systems, can improve risk assessment at a voyage and port call planning, as well as training. For example, a vessel-owning company can record a vessel-related incident on the vessel's incident management system that should already be in place as part of IMO regulations.

### Review and audit

Some form of review and audit is required to ensure that a company's anti-bribery compliance program is in fact effective. An audit in the shipping industry should include a review of port disbursement accounts to make sure that the cost charged is clearly identified and has a legitimate purpose. Some companies use third-party companies, such as DA-Desk, to review their disbursement accounts. Such a review can also be used to screen port disbursement accounts for suspicious items. If an organisation has an 'un-receipted transactions' account code, the audit should focus on those transactions and use the results to improve the anti-bribery compliance programme.

Additionally, it is prudent for a principal to have an audit clause in contracts with its suppliers. Depending on the assessed level of risk, the principal may need to periodically exercise that audit right to strengthen its anti-bribery compliance programme. An audit right that is triggered by a credible suspicion of misconduct and is used strategically is generally considered preferable to blanket audit rights that are rarely, if ever, exercised.

### Tone at the top

Finally, a company's senior management and board should carefully review the effectiveness of the company's anti-bribery compliance programme. It is not sufficient just to implement an anti-corruption programme without regular oversight, review and commentary from the board and senior management. Many in the industry believe that it is the tone set by the board and senior management that has the strongest impact on the adequacy of a company's anti-bribery compliance procedures and actual conduct.

## 3.8 COLLECTIVE ACTION TO FIGHT CORRUPTION IN THE SHIPPING INDUSTRY

There is a growing demand for collective action in the shipping industry, particularly from trade associations, shipping agents, shipping principals, and service providers. All stakeholders have common objectives to:

- avoid delays and extortionate demands at ports;
- increase commercial transparency;
- eliminate expensive and duplicative paperwork; and
- spend more time on core business.

Collaborative compliance is gaining traction in the industry. There are a number of organisations that offer a range of cost-effective and collaborative solutions to compliance. DA-Desk, the organisation that was founded to increase transparency in the disbursement account process, works to reduce cost and improve efficiency for over 140,000 port calls annually and has recently added an optional anti-bribery certification to its listing for port agents. This gives port agents an opportunity to embrace greater transparency and to demonstrate their shared commitment to the business ethics of their larger partners. Similarly, the RightShip platform can display a shipowner's completed compliance certification along with more than 50 risk factors that they already consider for the 60,000 commercial vessels they assess online.

It would also be beneficial for everyone in the industry to include government officials in their compliance efforts. MACN is ready to assist with that effort through its recent initiative to provide local port officials with compliance toolkits that include anti-bribery training modules designed specifically for the shipping industry.

At the same time, TRACE works together with global partners to provide anti-bribery compliance certification to shipping and port agents, as well as service providers. Stakeholders are increasingly realising that it is beneficial to select partners that have a TRACEcertification: shipping principals acquire assurance in their agents, while agents choose to work with reputable principals. Both, agents and service providers, seek TRACEcertification to demonstrate their commitment to transparency.

TRACEcertification turns third-party compliance into a reality for shipping companies with multiple agents and service providers at ports. A TRACEcertification report is prepared as a result of a thorough questionnaire based on the best practices of hundreds of multinationals, including questions about beneficial ownership, related entities, ties to the government, and past misconduct. The certification process includes analysis of résumés for key personnel, audited financials or a financial reference, as well as whether a code of conduct has been adopted, and training for employees conducted.

## 3.9 CONCLUSION

While the pace of change in the shipping and transportation industry can be slow, anti-bribery enforcement is moving ahead at a very fast pace on an international scale. As a result, the shipping industry has to rapidly and meaningfully respond to the growing need for anti-bribery compliance. The anti-bribery strategy of wilful blindness, and accepting that making illegal payments or payments that breach contractual obligations are the costs of doing business, are not appropriate. Unlike in the recent past, collaborative tools and networks now exist that can support companies who want to operate globally and remain compliant.

CASE STUDY: Dealing with Economic Coercion in the Shipping Industry.

Ship masters are often required to make decisions regarding whether to meet bribery demands based on extremely challenging circumstances. For example, in one challenging situation faced by a ship master, multiple government officials came on board a ship at the same time and demanded a full search of the vessel, referring to some vague irregularities. They had no clear documentation verifying the need for a full search. Moreover, the officials implied that they might not need to do a full search if they received a small payment. This type of search could require disrupting the crew, who were resting after a long day at sea. Under the working hours directive stipulated in the International Convention for the Safety of Life at Sea (SOLAS), the crew must have uninterrupted rest for at least six hours a day to make sure that the vessel is operated safely. Would a payment made in response to the officials' demands be permissible under these circumstances? Would the master be able to claim the defence of duress?

Strictly speaking, the situation described does not involve a direct threat of death or serious bodily injury, and instead is an egregious example of frequently used commercial coercion. In this example, the government officials might be using the pretext of the need to search the vessel. If they are successful in their demands, and the ship master gives in, the circle of extortion could continue. The demand for bribes often leads to even more bribery demands, uncertainty and entrenched impunity.

The Baltic and International Maritime Council's (BIMCO) anti-bribery clause can be valuable in these situations. It seeks to bring more certainty into situations involving requests for bribes. The clause is jurisdiction-blind, meaning that parties still have to comply with relevant anti-bribery legislation, but it provides them with an opportunity to contractually negotiate the consequences of either making or refusing bribes, depending on applicable laws. Thus, shipowners will be able to communicate their concerns regarding potential retaliatory actions against vessels or crew in case of the refusal to make payments, and charterers would have to agree to the extra costs resulting from laytime and other unfavourable consequences.

Chapter 4

# The Ship

*A dollar bill usually lasts for about 18 months of use before it wears out*

## 4.1 INTRODUCTION

Anyone intending to pursue a career in the shipping business, or understand how it operates, needs some basic knowledge of the vehicle used to carry the cargo at sea – the ship. Ships have advanced throughout the ages and are integral with today's commercial activity.

Between the turn of the 21st century and the end of 2013, cargo carried by sea increased from 5 billion tonnes to 9.5 billion tonnes. Of the 50,000 cargo-carrying ships responsible for international seaborne trade in 2013 there were 10,000 dry bulk carriers, 7,500 oil and chemical tankers, 5,000 container ships and 300 gas carriers.

## 4.2 DIMENSIONS

**Length Overall (LOA):** the extreme length of the ship measured from bow to stern. When the overall length is followed by the notation (BB) it indicates that the ship has a bulbous bow and the LOA will include the length of the bow.

**Length Between Perpendiculars (LBP):** the length between the forward perpendicular (FP) and the after perpendicular (AP) measured on the summer loadline.

The FP is defined as 'a perpendicular drawn to the waterline at the point where the foreside of the stem meets the summer loadline. The AP is defined as 'a perpendicular drawn to the waterline at the point where the aft side of the rudder post meets the summer loadline, or, where no rudder post is fitted, it is taken to the centre of the rudder stock'.

**Length on Water Line (LWL):** is the length of the ship on the summer loadline.

**Moulded Breadth:** sometimes referred to as the moulded beam, is the greatest breadth amidships from heel of frame to heel of frame.

**Extreme Breadth:** is the maximum breadth to the extremities of the ship's structure.

**Moulded Depth:** is described as the vertical distance amidships from the top of the keel to the top of the upper deck beam at the side.

**Draught:** is the vertical distance between the ship's waterline and the keel.

**Light Draught:** the vessel's draught at light displacement is called its light draught.

**Draught Marks:** draught marks are marks carved at the bow and stern on each side of the ship to measure the draught of the ship. Metric or impirical units may be used. On longer vessels, draught marks will be carved at the point amidships. The draught mark readings are recorded prior to and on completion of loading or discharge. They will be used if a draught survey is undertaken.

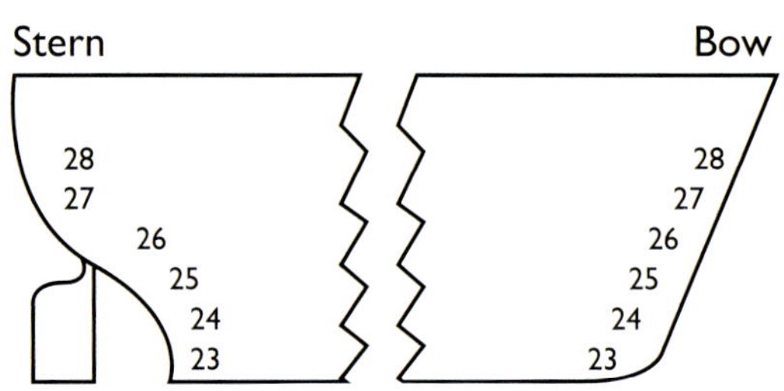


**Stern (aft) and Bow (foward) draught marks**

**Trim:** trim is the difference between the draught read at the bow and the draught read at the stern. For best seakeeping qualities, a ship will be trimmed by the stern.

**Variation of draught:** for the same mass, a ship will have a greater draught in fresh water than in sea water because of the difference in the specific gravity (SG), sometimes referred to as the density of the water. Fresh water has a SG of 1.000. Sea water has a SG of 1.025. The SG of brackish water will lie somewhere between the two. As well as reading the draught marks on arrival and before departure, the ship's officers will also measure the specific gravity (density) of the water. The instrument used to find SG is a hydrometer. For the same mass of cargo loaded a ship will have a deeper draught in fresh water than it will in salt water.

Other abbreviations associated with draught:

**SWAD** is the abbreviation for Salt Water Arrival Draught. It is the maximum draught that a vessel in a loaded condition should draw upon arrival at a port of discharge. SWAD required will vary according to the port.

**FWAD** is the abbreviation for Fresh Water Arrival Draught. It is used for upriver ports where there is fresh water rather than salt water.

**BWAD** is the abbreviation for Brackish Water Arrival Draught. Brackish water occurs where a river meets the sea. The water in which the ship floats will be neither fresh water nor salt water but a mixture of the two.

**Bar Draught** is the limiting draught required to pass over a bar at the entrance to a river.

**Air Draught** is the vertical distance from the waterline to the ship's highest point, usually the top of the tallest mast.

**Freeboard:** The vertical distance between the waterline and the uppermost continuous deck equipped with permanent means of closing all openings which are exposed to the elements. The waterline is that which is dictated by the loadline.

**Loadline:** By international convention, all merchant ships must be marked with a loadline. The distance from the upper edge of the loadline to the upper edge of the deck line indicates the minimum permissible freeboard. The loadline used will vary depending upon the time of year, density of water at the port and loadline zone through which the ship will pass. The loadline passing through the Plimsoll mark is the summer loadline. The Plimsoll mark and loadline are carved into the ship's hull amidships on both sides of the hull. The summer freeboard is based on the length of the ship.

**Loadline zones:** The reason for the different loadlines is the need to establish reserve buoyancy for the ship. In areas of the world where severe weather is expected, the Northern Atlantic in winter (Winter North Atlantic), a greater freeboard is required than where the weather is more benign as in the tropical areas (T).

**Scantlings:** All structural parts such as frames, beams, shell plating and bulkheads used in the construction of ships are covered under this heading and it refers to their size or thickness. The classification societies have fixed rules and tables for the construction of steel ships, which must be observed by shipbuilders in order to obtain the required certificates.

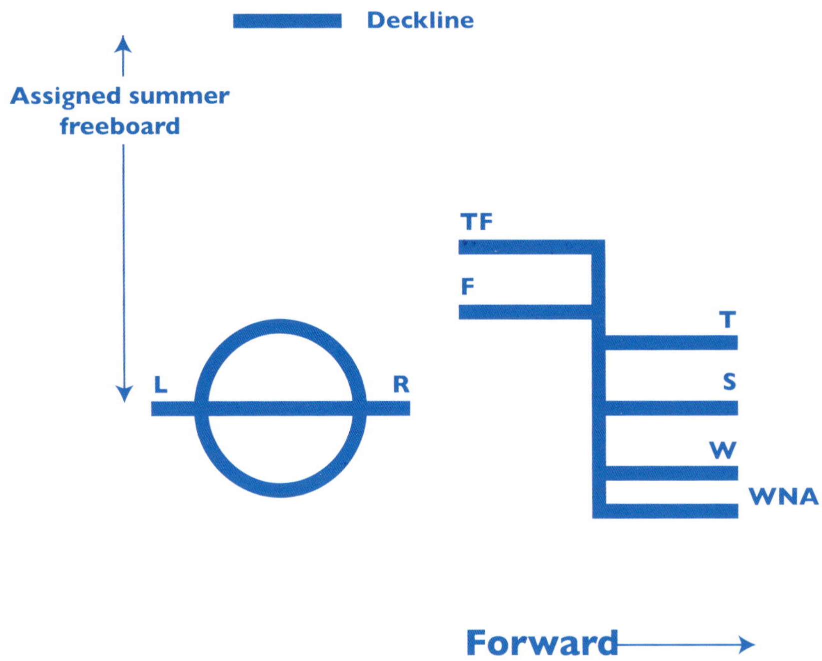


| | |
|---|---|
| **TF** | **Tropical fresh water** |
| **F** | **Fresh water** |
| **T** | **Tropical sea water** |
| **S** | **Summer, sea water** |
| **W** | **Winter, sea water** |
| **WNA** | **Winter, North Atlantic for vessels <100m in length** |
| **LR** | **Letters indicating the registration authority (here, Lloyd's Register)** |

**Typical ship loadlines**

## 4.3 CAPACITY

Another important measurement of merchant ships is that of the actual volume of the holds. This is because many cargoes are so light that the ship can be physically full before being loaded down to its permissible freeboard. There are two such measurements, grain capacity and bale capacity which can be expressed in cubic metres or cubic feet.

**Grain capacity** is the cubic capacity of a cargo space where the breadth is measured from the inside of the shell plating, the tank-top to the top of the beams and length from forward to aft bulkhead. Grain capacity includes hatchways. Insulated spaces are not included. (Ceiling in maritime terms means the bottom of the hold, not the part overhead.)

**Bale capacity** is the cubic capacity of a space measured from the inside of cargo battens (permanent dunnage) and from the ceiling to the underside of the beams.

The names become self-explanatory when one considers the fact that a bulk cargo such as grain can flow around beams and frames and fill every part of the hold, whereas cargo which comprises individual pieces (such as bales) will not be able to flow into spaces between frames, but gaps will be left between each piece.

**Teu** is the method of expressing the carrying capacity of a container ship. Teu stands for Twenty Foot Equivalent Units. Despite widespread standardisation of metric measurements in the maritime world, because containerisation began in the USA, which still retains imperial standards of measurement, freight containers are referred to in feet and inches. Except for specialist units, containers are either 20ft or 40ft long by 8ft wide and 8ft6in high. A 20ft container is one teu. A 40ft container is two teus. Occasionally one may encounter reference to the feu, a Forty Foot Equivalent Unit.

**Lane metres (LM)** is used by ships which are designed to carry wheeled cargo. As the name implies, it is the measure of the length of the lanes in the cargo decks. It is commonly used to express the size of roll-on roll-off (ro-ro) ships and car carriers (CACA). In the case of car carriers, one would also need to know the headroom to get a meaningful measure of the ship's carrying capacity.

## 4.4 TONNAGE

There are different measurements of tonnage. When comparing one vessel with another, the same tonnage measurement needs to be used. Most of the following measurements can be found on the ship's plans.

The tonnage of a ship is an expression of weight (mass) stated in long tons, where one ton is equal to 2,240lbs, or metric tonnes, where one tonne equals 1,000kg.

The word ton is also used as a close approximation to volume under the International Convention on Tonnage Measurement of Ships 1969. Prior to the Convention, one ton related to a volume measurement of 100 cubic feet.

**Deadweight (DWT)** is described as the weight (mass) of cargo, stores, fuel, passengers and crew carried by the ship when loaded to its minimum permissible freeboard in salt water. The term is usually used to describe a ship loaded to its summer marks.

**DWAT** is an abbreviation which expanded means 'deadweight all told'.

**DWCC** is an abbreviation which refers to 'deadweight cargo or carrying capacity'.

**Displacement** is the total weight (mass) of the ship and everything on board. The volume of water displaced varies according to whether a ship is floating in salt or fresh water, but the weight (mass) of water displaced will be the same in each situation. Displacement tonnage is rarely used to describe the size of a merchant ship, but is used as a measure of warship and cruise ship size.

**Light displacement Ton (LDT)** is the actual weight of a ship measured in long tons or tonnes and includes full equipment plus the weight of the machinery and boilers. Bunkers, cargo, dunnage, provisions, water and other consumables are excluded.

**Gross tonnage (GT):** The use of the word tonnage here is really a misnomer as gross tonnage is essentially a measure of volume. The International Convention on Tonnage Measurement of Ships 1969, which came into force in 1982 defines gross tonnage as *'the capacity in cubic metres of all the spaces within the hull, and of the enclosed spaces above the deck available for cargo, stores, fuel, passengers and crew with certain exceptions'.* The gross tonnage of a ship is found by a formula based on the total volume of all the enclosed spaces in cubic metres. Gross tonnage is a measurement of the size of a ship and forms the basis for manning regulations, safety rules and registration fees.

**Net tonnage (NT):** net tonnage is also established by formula, based upon the gross tonnage, moulded depth, moulded mean draught at summer loadline and the number of passengers (if any) carried. Essentially, net tonnage is the internal volume of the ship, less deductions for crew, engine, propelling and navigating spaces, and is a crude measurement of the ship's revenue-earning capacity. Net tonnage, as well as gross tonnage, is used to calculate port fees. The terms gross registered tonnage (GRT) and net registered tonnage (NRT) may be met but are not in common use having been respectively replaced by gross tons (GT) and net tons (NT).

**Suez and Panama Canal tonnage:** Both the Suez Canal Authority and the Panama Canal Authority have their own rules for the measurement of tonnage used to establish the toll charged for a ship to pass through the canal. The Panama Canal uses a unit, following the 1969 International Convention on Tonnage Measurement for ships, known as the Panama Canal Universal Measurement System (PC/UMS). The Suez Canal Authority uses the Suez Canal Net Tonnage (SCNT) as the basis for its tolls. The SCNT is derived with modifications from the net register tonnage system established in 1873.

## 4.5 SHIP TYPES

Over the last 50 years specialisation in the carriage of cargoes by sea has seen an increasing number of ship types, each having their own specific design features. .

This section looks at the three of the most common types of cargo-carrying ships involved in international trade:

- tankers
- bulk carriers
- container ships.

The aim of this section is to provide sufficient knowledge of specific ship types for practitioners in the shipping business to be able to appreciate the ship's layout, structure and essential dimensions.

For practitioners in the shipping business, for example, agents, charterers or brokers, undertaking transactions associated with a ship it is invaluable to have a clear mental picture of the ship type concerned. It is useful to be able to sketch the ship in plan, profile and transverse cross section, and recognise the salient features such as hold layout, hatch covers, position of the engine room, bridge and accommodation, layout of bunker, water ballast and fresh water tanks.

Ship descriptions covered in this section include:

### Liquid bulk ships

- Crude oil tanker
  - Ultra-large crude carrier (ULCC)
  - Very large crude carrier (VLCC)
  - Suezmax tanker
  - Panamax tanker
  - Aframax tanker
- Product tanker
- Chemical tanker
- Parcel tanker

- Liquefied natural gas carrier (LNG)
- Liquefied petroleum gas carrier (LPG)

### Dry bulk ships

- General purpose bulk carrier
  - Very large bulk carrier
  - Capesize bulk carrier
  - Panamax bulk carrier
  - Handysize bulk carrier
- Ore carrier
- Open bulk carrier
- Combination carrier

### Container ships

- Fully cellular container ship
  - Panamax
  - post-Panamax
  - new Panamax
  - post new Panamax
- Multipurpose/container ship
- Feeder container ship

## 4.6 LIQUID BULK SHIPS (TANKERS)

Tankers are designed for the carriage of liquid bulk cargoes including crude oil, oil product oil, chemicals, liquefied gases, vegetable oils, molasses, wine and orange juice. Tankers are generally described in terms of deadweight tonnage (dwt) because this is the basis on which they are chartered. The cargo-handling mode for tankers is pump on and pump off. Shore pumps and gravity are used for loading and ship's own pumps for discharging. This is because pumps are far less efficient at sucking liquid than they are at pushing it. The ship's pumps have only to lift the cargo a short height from the tank bottom, but then pump it through a long pipeline to a shore tank.

### Crude oil tanker

The crude oil tanker is used for the carriage of crude oil. The pattern of the oil trade is for the crude oil to be loaded near the point of production and taken to refineries near the areas of consumption. Oil companies have been able to take full advantage of economies of scale in connection with the size of crude carriers. Sale and purchase (S&P) brokers will encounter different terms relating to the size of the crude oil tanker such as the very large crude carrier (VLCC) and, occasionally, the ultra-large crude carrier (ULCC).

A typical large modern tanker will be double-skinned, have all machinery and accommodation aft, a small crane amidships at the ship's manifold to handle the hoses used for loading and discharging. The cargo space is divided transversely into five or six compartments, each of which is in turn divided by two longitudinal bulkheads running the length of the ship. This provides either 15 or 18 separate tanks, viz a centre tank, and port and starboard wing tanks. Smaller tankers may have a single longitudinal bulkhead providing 10 or 12 separate tanks, viz port and starboard tanks. The tanks are connected by bottom pipelines and valves to the tanker's pump room and then through drop and deck lines to the manifold, enabling the cargo to be safely loaded and discharged. It is important that the loading and discharging sequence of the crude oil cargo is undertaken to ensure that bending stresses to the hull do not exceed the permitted maximum levels, otherwise there is a risk of hull failure with consequent oil spillage. In addition to the cargo tanks, there are port and starboard slop tanks used, when required, to segregate an oily water mixture and eliminate risk of pollution.

Double hulled tankers carry ballast water in the bottom tanks and side tanks of the double hull structure. Tankers in ballast transiting between destinations require ballast water for additional weight to improve stability while at sea. Double hulled tankers use the space between the outer and inner hulls as a segregated ballast tank for the ballast water. The common name for this ballast is segregated ballast because it is isolated from the cargo system and the cargo tanks.

Ballast water is loaded and discharged in such a way as to avoid undue stress to the ship's hull. Ballast water is essential on the ballast voyage without cargo to ensure that the ship has a draught sufficient to allow good seakeeping abilities and maintain a submerged propeller.

In the hull structure, separating the cargo tanks from the machinery space and accommodation, is a cofferdam. The cofferdam is a space which ensures complete separation of the cargo from the engine room and provides a space for the cargo pumps, known as the pump room.

Many tankers are equipped with heating coils, heated by steam from the ship's boiler, to ensure that the cargo does not become too viscous to be pumped.

Because crude oil has all the different fractions from light unstable gases to thick tarry material, any empty space in a tank would soon be filled with a mixture of gas and air, an explosive combination. The same risk applies when the cargo has been discharged but oily residues remain. To obviate such a risk, the empty space is filled with an inert gas which is usually generated from the engine exhaust, suitably treated. The treatment device and the pipeline system is called the inert gas system (IGS).

After normal discharge, the sides and bottoms of the tanks are coated with oil residues which, in the past, were cleaned with water sprayed around the tank by a device rather like a giant lawn sprinkler, called a Butterworth system. This produced an oily water emulsion which had to be separately dealt with by the refinery. More recently, it was discovered that by using some of the ship's own oil cargo under pressure, a satisfactory cleaning result could be obtained. Therefore, crude carriers today are equipped with a crude oil washing (COW) system.

## Classification in terms of size - Tankers

**Ultra-large crude carriers (ULCC):** A ULCC is a tanker which has a deadweight in excess of 320,000 dwt. The world's largest tanker, *Seawise Giant* of 564,700 dwt was built in 1979. It had a length of 458 metres and a maximum draught of 24 metres. It was scrapped in 2009 having spent the last years of its life as a floating storage tank. Presently the largest operational ULCCs are two TI class supertankers which were built in 2002 and have a capacity of 442,585 dwt. TI refers to the VLCC Tanker Pool operator Tankers International LLC.

**Very large crude carriers (VLCC):** The size of a VLCC ranges from 200,000 to 319,999 dwt. They are the workhorses of the crude oil trade and are designed to carry a parcel of two million barrels of cargo. A barrel is 42 US gallons or about 162 litres. It is confusing but traditionally oil has been traded and priced in barrels. It is a measure of volume rather than one of weight.

Typical dimensions of a VLCC are: length overall (LOA) – 330-340 metres, beam 58 metres, draught – 20-21 metres; deadweight 310,000 tonnes. They will have a service speed of 14-15 knots with a fuel consumption of about 50-55 tonnes per day.

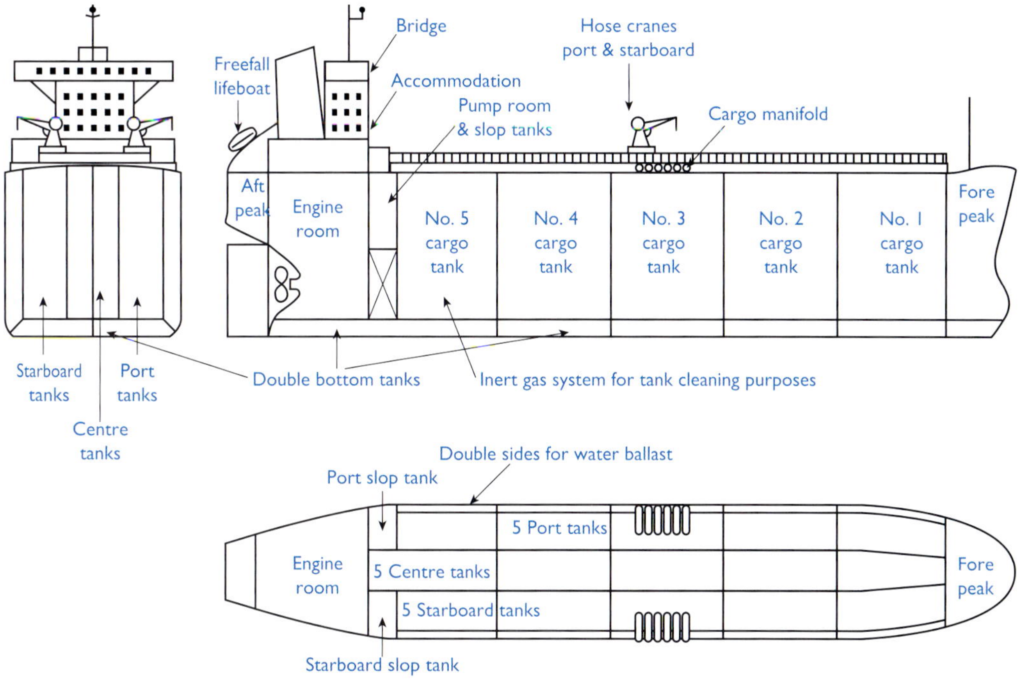


**A typical VLCC tanker**

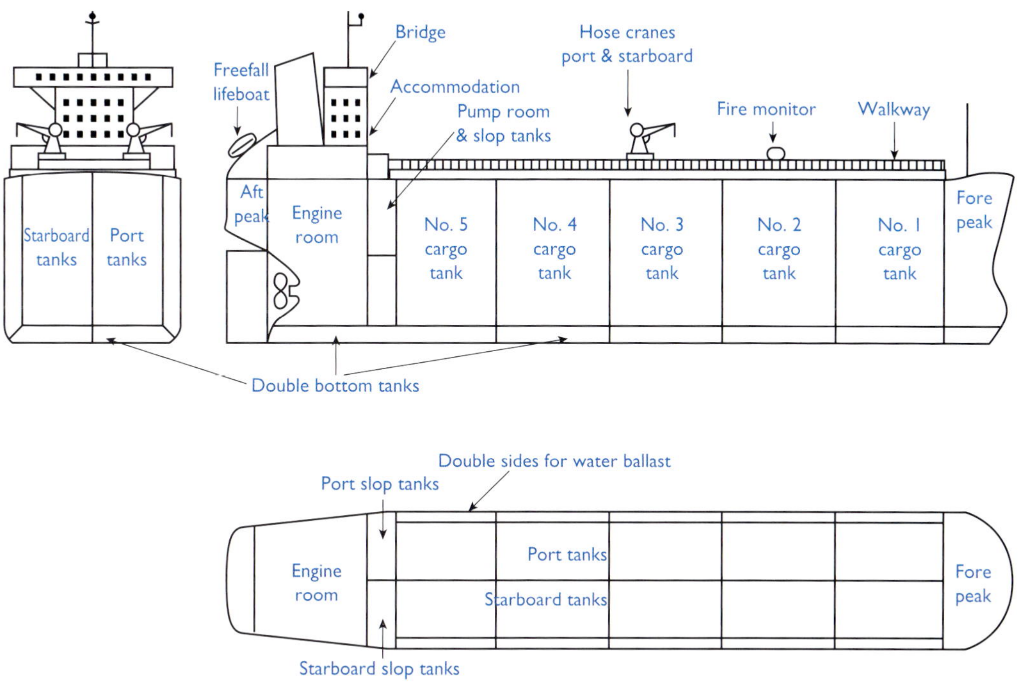


**A typical Suezmax tanker**

**Suezmax:** a Suezmax tanker is a tanker of between 120,000 dwt and 199,999 dwt with dimensions which enables it to transit the Suez Canal fully laden. Since the tankers' inception, the canal has been deepened and widened, but the name, Suezmax, is still used. The Suezmax tanker is also referred to as a million barrel tanker. A Suezmax tanker will be limited by the depth of the canal which allows a maximum 20.1 metres draught. There is also an air draught limit, due to the Suez Canal Bridge, of 68 metres. To achieve economies of scale, tankers larger than Suezmax will have to make passage around South Africa or tranship part of the cargo prior to passing through the Suez Canal. The length of a Suezmax tanker is unlimited. The maximum draught allowed depends on the beam of the tanker. Draught is assessed using a table of wetted cross sectional area.

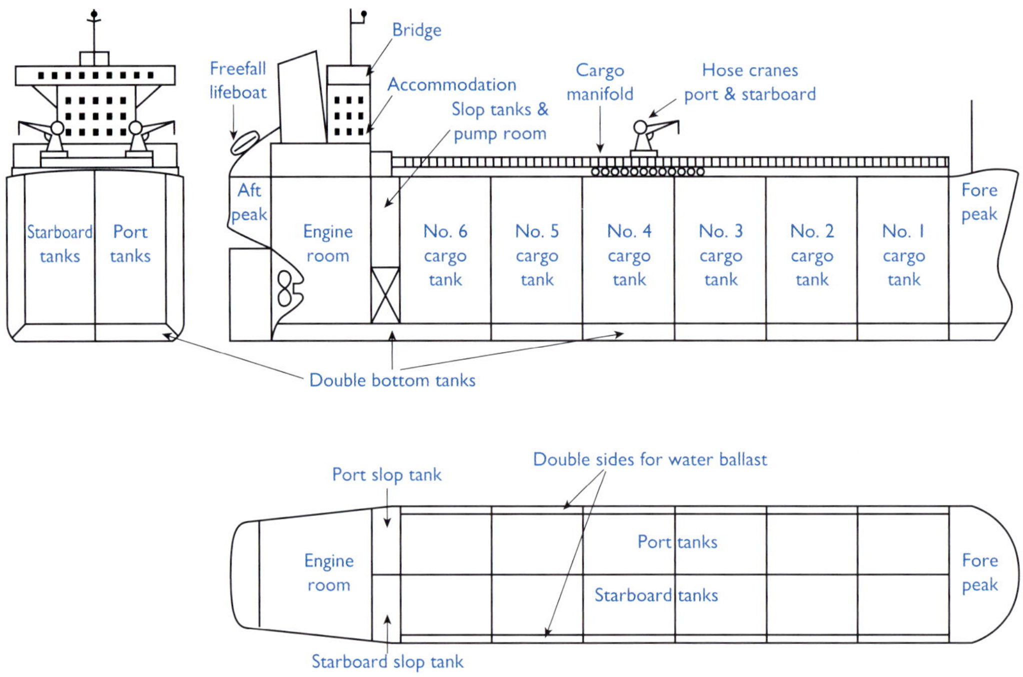


**A typical Aframax tanker**

**Aframax/Large Range 2 (LR2) Tanker:** AFRA is the acronym for Average Freight Rate Assessment. These are rates assessed periodically by the London Tanker Brokers' Panel at the behest of the major oil companies. The major oil companies use AFRA as a source of unbiased market rates when they buy oil from each other. The size of an Aframax tanker is in the range of 80,000 dwt to 119,999 dwt. The size of the Aframax tanker means that they can use most ports in the world and are useful for short to medium hauls. Typical dimensions of an Aframax tanker are: length overall (LOA) 245 metres; beam 40 metres; draught 14 metres. The Aframax tanker will be powered by a single low speed diesel engine providing a service speed of between 15 and 16 knots at a daily fuel consumption of about 50 tonnes. Although Aframax ships have been included in the crude oil tanker section, the term refers to size and tankers of Aframax size may be found in the products trade.

**Panamax/Large Range 1 tanker:** There are just over 400 Panamax tankers. The Panama Canal is a locked canal, the lock basins restricting the dimensions of tankers which can use the Canal. The present lock dimensions are 320 metres in length, 33.5 metres in width and a depth of 12.5 metres. A Panamax tanker of 70,000 dwt has dimensions which allow it to pass through the Canal although it may be draught restricted. The dimensions of a Panamax tanker are typically: LOA 227 m, breadth 32.3 metres, draught 14 metres. Service speed 15 knots. The opening of the new Panama Canal system in 2016 will influence the size of the maximum size transiting the canal and hence the definition of the Panamax tanker.

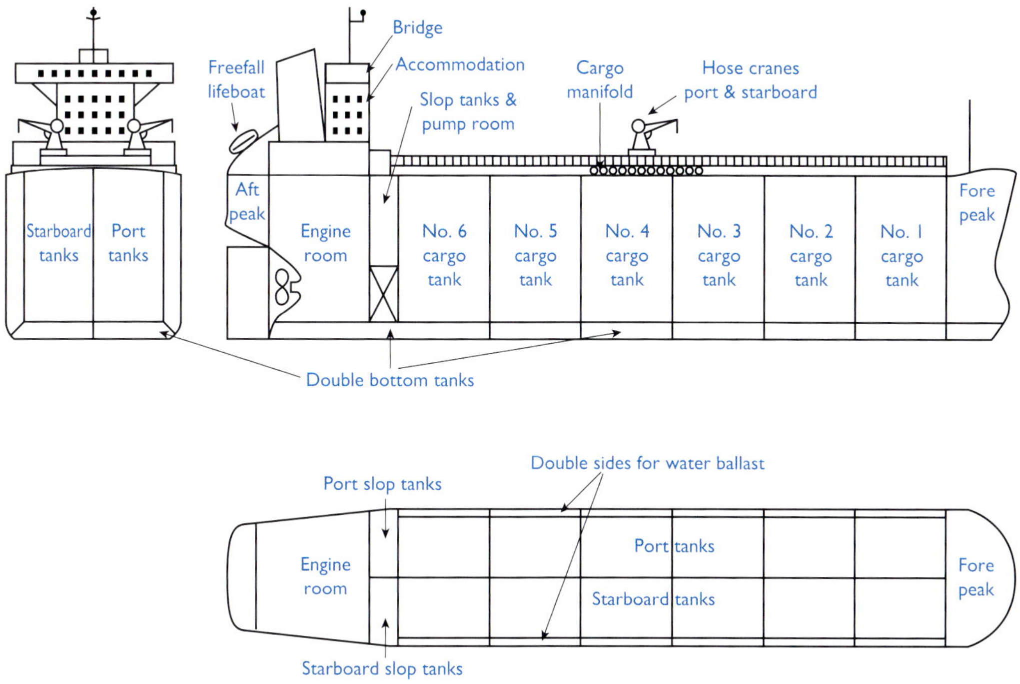


**A typical Panamax tanker**

## Product tanker

Product tankers are double-hulled tankers designed for carrying refined petroleum products from the oil refinery to another refinery or the end user. Product carriers carry clean or dirty products. The size of a product carrier varies widely depending upon the trade for which it is intended. Coastal product tankers about the coast of the UK range between 3,500 dwt and 15,000 dwt. The size of deepsea product tankers ranges between 45,000 dwt and 100,000 dwt. Clean products refer to light refined products including jet fuel, gasoline and, petroleum products. Dirty products include heavy oils such as fuel oil, diesel and bunkers. Tankers which regularly work in the dirty trades have heating coils in the tanks to maintain the viscosity of the oil.

Almost all the cargoes carried in product tankers are intended for use without further refining, thus cleanliness and avoidance of contamination are important. For this reason, it is obligatory to have the tanks coated with an epoxy or similar inert plastic coating to avoid any cargo contact with bare steel and to make cleaning easier. Tank cleaning in product carriers is by high pressure washing with water. There is no equivalent of COW in product carriers. Changing from a dirty to a clean product will require the ship's tanks to be cleaned, an expensive operation.

Product carriers, especially those in the clean trades, are able to segregate grades of cargoes; the ability to carry four or more separate grades is not uncommon.

## Chemical tanker

A chemical tanker is a sophisticated double-hulled ship designed for the carriage of liquid chemical cargoes listed in the IMO's Bulk Chemical Code. The size of chemical carriers varies from small tankers less than 10,000 dwt to those in the Panamax range. Cargoes carried by a chemical tanker include by-products of the oil refining process which can exhibit flammable, reactive corrosive or toxic properties. In addition, a chemical carrier is required to carry other sensitive cargoes, such as vegetable oils, tallow and methanol. The parcel size of a typical cargo varies between 2,000 tonnes and 6,000 tonnes. The individual parcels are accommodated in the ship's cargo containment system which typically consists of 30 variable sized tanks. Individual tanks are made of stainless steel, or, if of mild steel, are treated with a coating of zinc or epoxy paint to prevent cargo coming into contact with the mild steel of the tank structure. The transverse stiffeners of the tanks are external allowing the internal tank walls to be smooth and easy to clean. Each tank is served by an individual deep well pump and associated piping which prevents contamination between different cargo types. Tanks may have a heating system to maintain the viscosity of certain cargoes. The pumping capacity of each of the deep well pumps will be between 200 and 400 tonnes per hour.

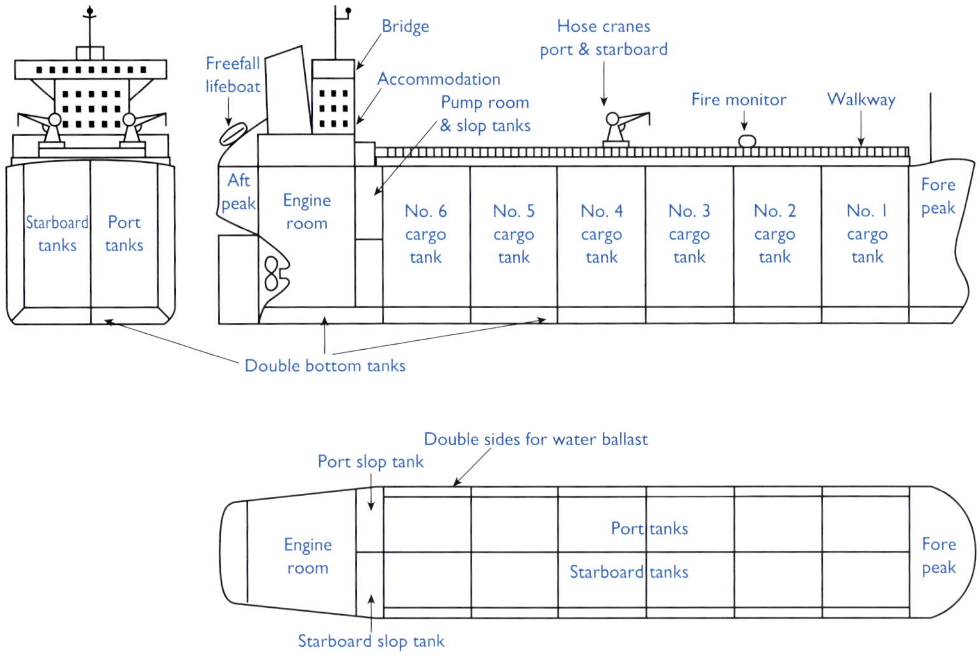


**A typical chemical tanker**

The term parcel tanker is sometimes used to define a tanker, normally a product chemical carrier. It refers to the fact that liquid chemicals and petroleum products are regularly carried in small parcel sizes and the tanker is required to have a number of separate tanks to meet the need. A parcel tanker is not a specific ship type.

## Gas Carriers

### Liquefied natural gas (LNG) carrier

Natural gas is a ready source of fuel. Natural gas can be pumped directly from the gas wells through gas pipeline for home and industrial heating. However, it is uneconomic to transport gas by sea in its gaseous state. If the gas can be made liquid, liquefied natural gas (LNG), its volume will be only 1/600 of when in the gaseous state, and economic transport by sea is viable. To reduce natural gas to its liquid form the temperature of the natural gas has to be reduced to minus 160° C and maintained at that temperature during the sea voyage and during storage. An LNG tanker is a specialised vessel which has special tanks, either of a spherical standalone or membrane-integrated design to maintain the very low cargo temperature. In both systems, the tank is separated and insulated from the ship's hull. Insulation is necessary to prevent the mild steel of the ship's hull becoming brittle at such low temperatures. The largest class of LNG tankers are known as Q-Max, where Q refers to Qatar and Max, the maximum size of tanker able to berth at Qatar's LNG terminals. The Q-Max tankers have a carrying capacity of 266,000 cubic metres of liquefied natural gas. The dimensions of the Q-Max are: length overall (LOA) 345m, beam 54m and draught 12m. The Q-Max LNG tanker has five separate cargo tanks. Its primary power system consists of two slow speed diesel engines able to achieve a service speed of 19.5 knots. At the end of 2013 there were almost 385 LNG tankers in the world fleet.

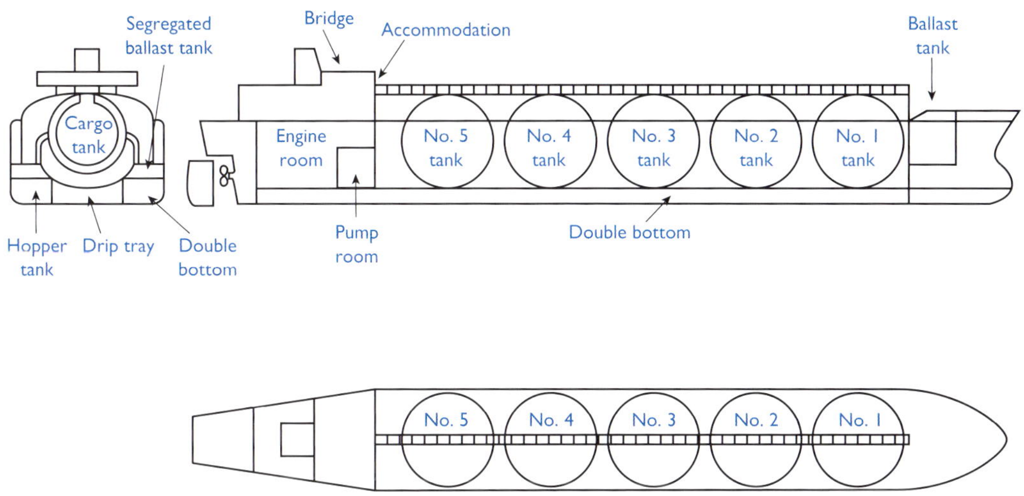


**A typical LNG sperical (moss) tanker**

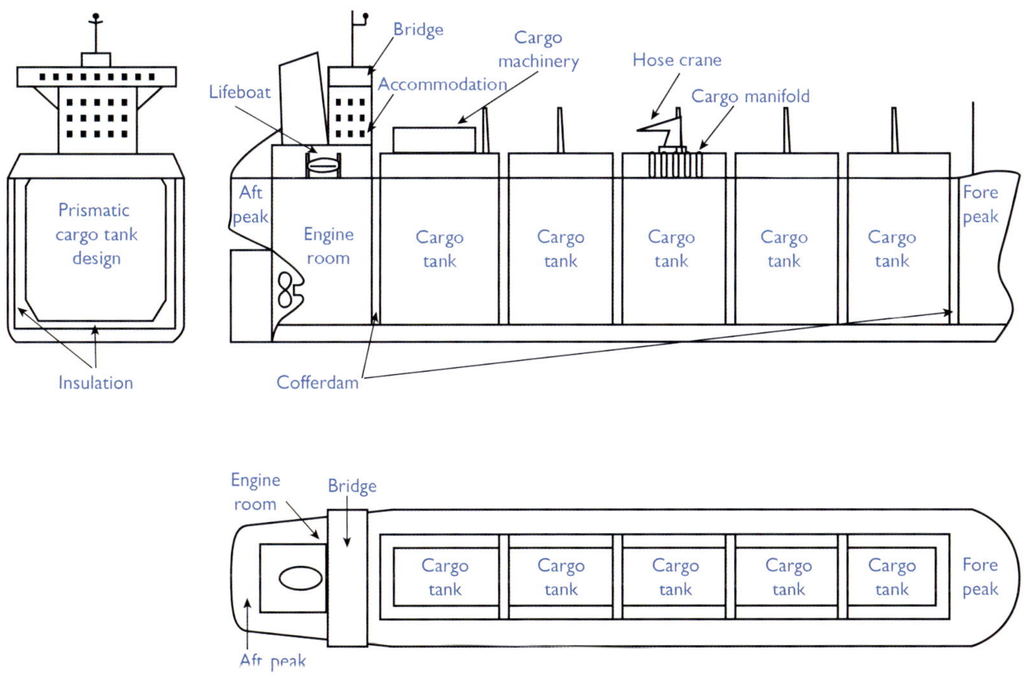


**A typical LNG membrane (prism) tanker**

## Liquefied petroleum gas (LPG) tanker

Petroleum gas is a by-product of the refining process of crude oil, and its domestic use as propane and butane is well known. It is also used within industrial processes such as the production of fertiliser. As liquid, petroleum gas (LPG) is carried in specialist vessels. At the end of 2014 there were almost 1300 LPG tankers worldwide.

The LPG tankers have between 10,000 and 100,000 cubic metres cargo capacity and are divided into different subgroups based on size. The largest group are referred to as very large gas carriers (VLGC) and have a capacity of between 60,000 and 100,000 cubic metres. Other groups include large gas carriers (LGC) - 40,000 to 59,999 cubic metres, mid-size LPG carriers, 20,000 to 39,999 cubic metres and handysize LPG carriers with a capacity of between 10,000 and 19,999 cubic metres. Transport of gas is only economic if the gas is reduced to a liquid state. Change of state between a gas and a liquid can be achieved by reducing the temperature in the containment tank, or by an increase in pressure or by a combination of temperature reduction and increase in pressure. There are various forms of cargo systems used to maintain liquefied petroleum gas (LPG) whilst on passage at sea, namely fully pressurised, semi-pressurised and fully refrigerated systems.

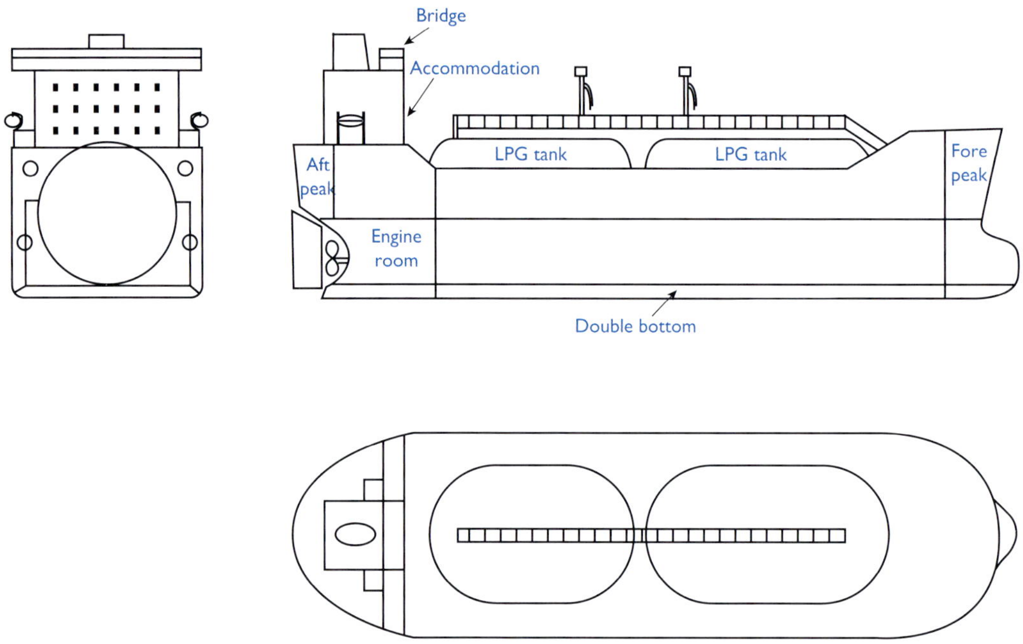


**A typical LPG tanker**

The VLGC are fully refrigerated, carrying LPG at low temperature and atmospheric pressure. The VLGC incorporate membrane tanks into the ship's structure. In addition to carrying LPG, the VLGCs transport ammonia and vinyl chloride. Fully pressurised LPG tankers are found in the handy and mid-sized group. The containment system comprises of two or three horizontal or vertical tanks, placed independently within the hull structure. Each tank will have a capacity of between 3,500 and 7,500 cubic metres. The semi-pressurised LPG tankers provide the greatest flexibility in cargo handling.

Other bulk liquid carriers are designed for specific tasks including the carriage of fruit juice and wine in which the containment system does not form part of the hull structure.

## 4.7 DRY BULK SHIPS

Dry bulk ships are designed specifically for the bulk carriage of loose dry cargo of a homogeneous nature, such as coal and grain. There are different structural types of dry bulk ships including the general purpose dry bulk carrier, the ore carrier, the open type and the combination carriers, including the ore/oil carrier (OO), oil/bulk/ore (OBO) and the product/oil/bulk/ore carrier (PROBO).

All ships within the bulk carrier category are single-decked with machinery and accommodation aft. They typically have 5-8 cargo holds with wide hatches, up to 60% the breadth of the ship to allow direct vertical loading without the need for trimming due to the design of the vessels with wingtanks. Dry bulk carriers have double bottom tanks for the carriage of bunkers and ballast water. Unlike tankers, most dry bulk ships do not have a double hull structure. The interior of the cargo holds are unobstructed to allow free use of grabs for discharging.

## General purpose bulk carrier

Each hold of the general purpose bulk carrier will have upper and lower hopper tanks, which provide self–trimming characteristics and aids easy discharge. The upper and lower hopper tanks can be used to hold ballast water when required. Ballast water is necessary to ensure that the seakeeping qualities of the ship, including immersion of the propeller, are maintained when the ship is not carrying cargo. The ballast tanks are also used to ensure stability and prevent excessive bending stresses being created in the ship's hull. The ship's hull will be stressed during loading, discharge and carriage of the cargo. Ballast water will be moved into the hopper tanks using high capacity ballast pumps and the ballast pipe-line system.

A general purpose bulk carrier, depending on its size, will be either geared or gearless. A geared bulk carrier is one which has cargo loading and discharging equipment installed. A gearless bulk carrier will not be equipped with its own loading or discharging equipment and will rely on the terminal's loading and discharging equipment. Non-geared bulk carriers will be loaded by a conveyor system and gravity. This is a high speed operation where loading rates in iron ore terminals can exceed 14,000 tonnes per hour. Discharge is generally be shoreside gantry and grab.

Different cargoes have different characteristics which need to be understood prior to loading. For example, the carriage of grain can be dangerous, as grain can flow during the movement of the ship in a seaway. Hopper-shaped holds reduce the cargo's movement at sea.

Dry cargo bulkers have not until recently reached the exceptionally large sizes common in the tanker trades. Very large bulk/ore carriers and ore carriers between 250,000 dwt and 400,000 dwt are now in service on the long distance routes.

## Ore carrier

The ore carrier design differs from that of the general purpose bulk carrier. The ore carrier is designed with a relatively small centre hold above a deep double bottom. The aim of the structure is to minimise hull stress by reducing stiffness created by a large metacentric height (a measure of stability). Either side of the cargo hold are wing tanks which are used for ballast water. The ore carrier will have between seven and nine holds in which to carry the ore cargo. Ore carriers are gearless. Access to the holds is by means of sliding weather deck hatch covers. Because of the density of metallic ores, the cubic capacity of the cargo containment space is small. The structure of the ore carrier is robust due to the rough treatment that grab discharge can inflict.

## The open hatch bulk carrier (OHBC)

Generally a smaller bulk carrier which has a double hull structure and wide hatchways, up to 90% the ship's breadth. While able to carry dry bulk cargoes they can also be used in the container and timber trades where the ability to spot load through the unobstructed hatchways provides ease of the cargo operation. OHBC are geared having deck gantry or deck slewing cranes.

### Combination carriers (OO) (OBO) (PROBO)

There are three acknowledged forms of combination carrier, the ore oil (OO) carrier, the ore/bulk/ore carrier (OBO) and the product/ore/bulk/oil carrier (PROBO). The aim of the combination carrier was to create a design of ship which could serve two or more markets so that, in the event of one cargo market failing, opportunity might be found elsewhere. The combination carrier has common cargo compartments with specific cargo-handling systems. The combination carrier will be double hulled. Classification society rules only allow the carriage of one cargo type at a time. Combination carriers are few in number due to the high cost associated with readying the ship to operate in the different trades.

### Self-discharging bulk carriers

Self-discharging bulk carriers are used for the unloading of their own bulk at ports such as those in the Great Lakes of North America where intensive use of the expensive, specialised discharge equipment is justified. There are a small number of self-discharging bulk carriers used for the movement of iron ore in medium and short haul inter-regional trades.

### Classification in terms of size - dry bulk carriers

### Very large ore carriers (VLOC) Very large bulk carriers (VLBC)

The bulk carrier fleet includes ships which have a deadweight capacity in excess of 200,000 dwt which are known as the very large ore carrier (VLOC) or the very large bulk carriers (VLBC). The Chinamax (Valemax) VLOC was developed by Vale to improve the economic efficiency of moving iron ore between Brazil and China. Of 400,000 dwt, they are among the world's largest ships. They are able to carry twice the cargo carried by a Capesize bulk carrier at a capital cost

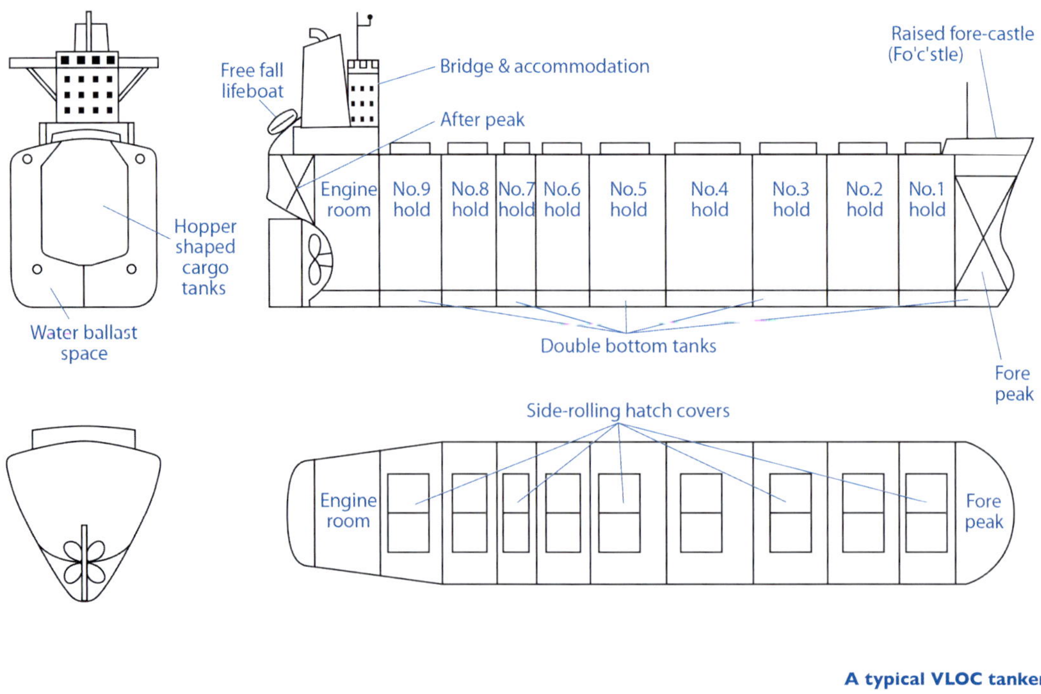


**A typical VLOC tanker**

of only one third more. The dimensions of the Chinamax is LOA 362m, beam 65m and moulded draft 23m. They are powered by a single low speed diesel engine which provides a service speed of 14 knots on a daily fuel consumption of 97 tonnes. The VLOC is gearless and depends on shoreside terminals for loading and discharging.

### Capesize bulk carriers

The Capesize dry bulk carrier is a ship which is unable to transit the Suez Canal or Panama Canal and therefore has to use the Cape of Good Hope or Cape Horn route. Deepening of the Suez Canal will have affected the category of the ship size. A Capesize bulk carrier typically has a deadweight in excess of 150,000 dwt and dimensions; LOA 290m, breadth 45m and draught 18m. The deep draught restricts the number of terminals which the Capesize vessel can use. A Capesize bulk carrier will typically have nine cargo holds. It will be gearless depending on cargo loading and unloading on shore terminal facilities.

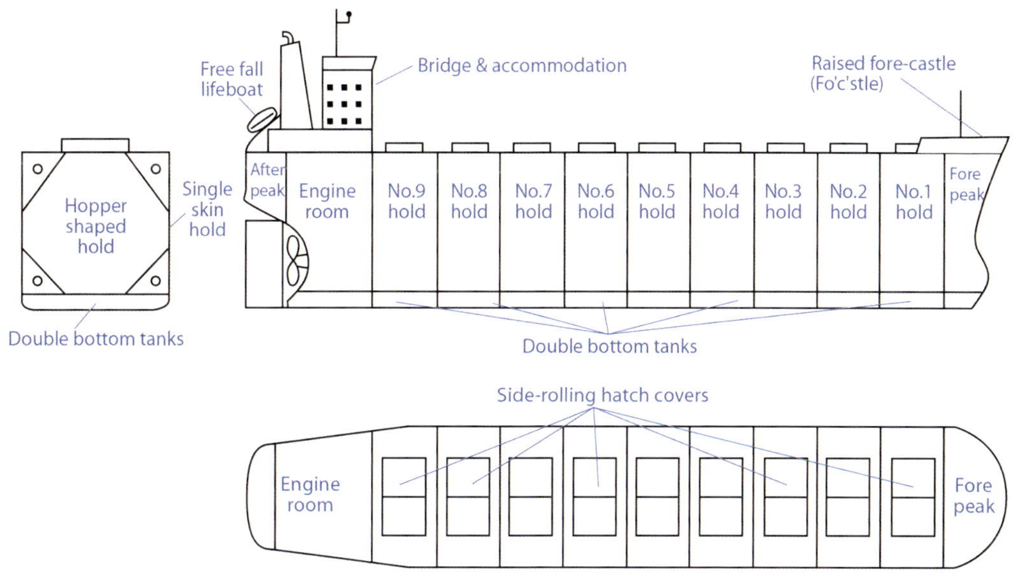


**A typical Capesize tanker**

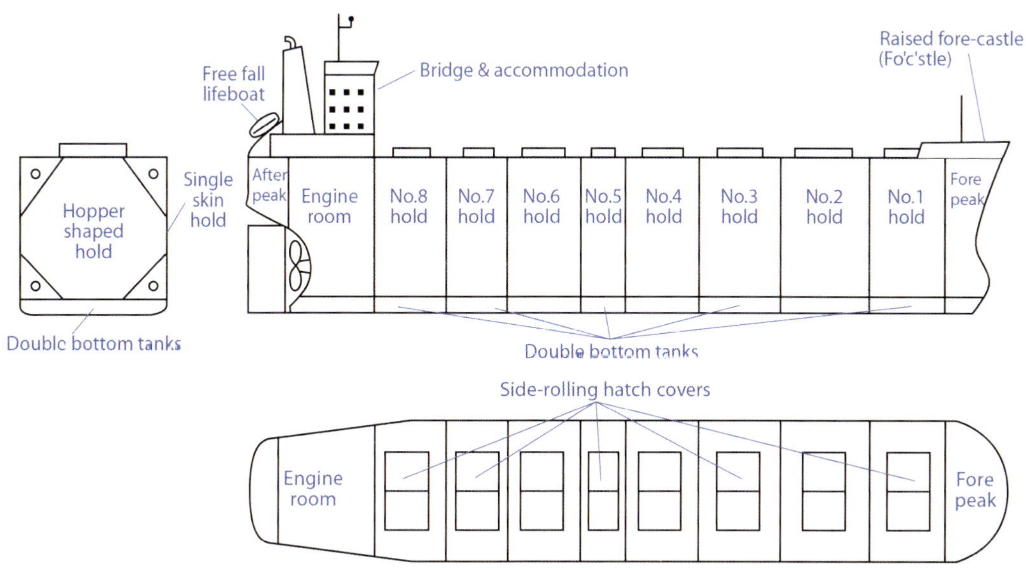


**A typical Mini-Capesize tanker**

### Post-Panamax/mini Cape bulk carriers

Post-Panamax/mini Cape bulk carriers are a class of ship which have a carrying capacity of between 87,000 dwt and 115,000 dwt, a higher cargo capacity than the Panamax bulk carrier. The post-Panamax/mini Cape bulk carrier has a shallower draught and larger beam than the Panamax bulk carrier, being designed to load bulk cargoes from draught-restricted ports. The wider beam restricts this class of ship from transiting the present Panama Canal. The layout of the post-Panamax/mini Cape is similar to the Panamax bulk carrier having seven holds. They are usually non-geared.

### Panamax bulk carrier

A Panamax bulk carrier has a deadweight of between 60,000 and 79,999 dwt and is able to use the present Panama Canal. The Panamax bulk carrier is designed to carry the maximum amount of cargo within the constraints imposed by the locks of the Panama Canal. A Panamax bulk carrier may be geared or gearless. It will have up to seven separate cargo holds and will be of single hull construction. The dimensions of a typical 70,000 dwt Panamax bulk carrier will be overall length 225m, breadth 32m and draught 12.04m.

The Panama Canal is a locked canal, the lock basins restricting the dimensions of bulk carriers which can use the Canal. The present lock dimensions of 320m in length, 33.5m in breadth and depth of 12.56m limiting the dimensions of the Panamax bulk carrier to an overall length of 227m and 32.3m breadth. The draught is restricted and varies with the amount of rainfall which falls in Lake Gatun. The opening of the new Panama Canal system in 2016 will influence the size of the maximum size transiting the canal and hence the definition of the Panama bulk carrier.

### New Panamax bulk carrier

The new Panama Canal lock system will have lock basins 427m long, 55m wide and a depth of 18m. The system will be able to accommodate bulk carriers with larger dimensions than at present. The dimensions of the new Panamax bulk carrier of 120,000 dwt will be an overall length of 266m, a beam of 49m and draught of 15.5m.

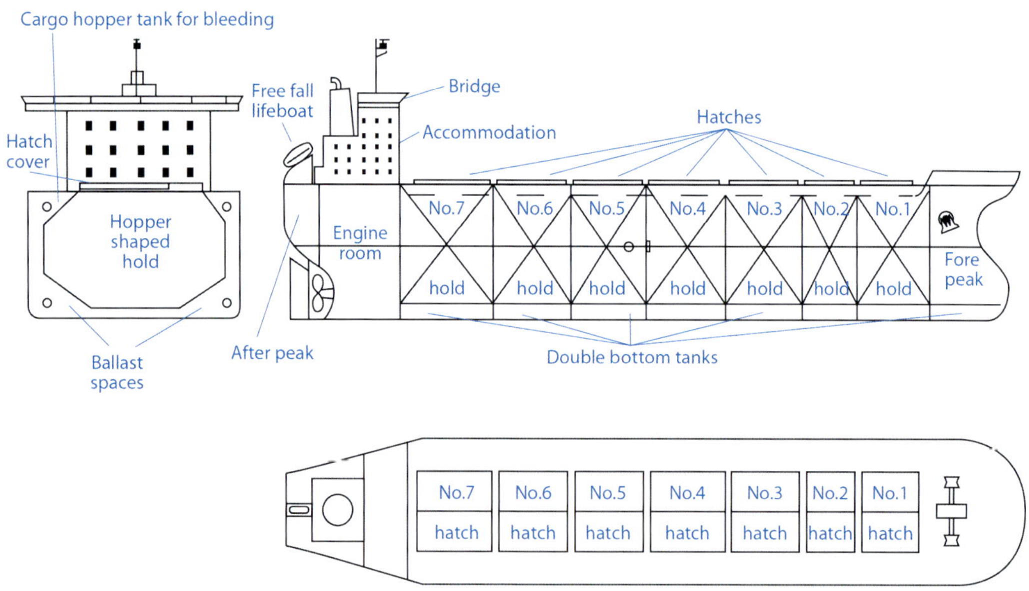


**A typical Panamax bulk carrier**

**Supramax bulk carriers** are bulk carriers between 50,000 dwt and 59,999 dwt, a cargo-carrying capacity approaching that of the conventional Panamax bulk carrier. The supramax bulk carrier operates on geographically dispersed trade routes, generally carrying grains and minor bulks. The dimensions of a typical 55,000 dwt supramax bulk carrier will have the following dimensions:

LOA 190m breadth 33m and draught 11.5m. The supramax bulk carrier has a single deck, and has five cargo holds of conventional bulk carrier design. It is a geared ship with four cranes serving the five holds. The crane capacity will be between 25 and 35 tonnes.

**Handymax bulk carrier.** The handymax bulk carrier has a carrying capacity of between 40,000 dwt and 49,999 dwt. The dimensions of a typical 45,000 dwt handymax bulk carrier will have the following dimensions: LOA 180 metres breadth 32m and draught 11m. The handymax bulk carrier is single decked, has five cargo holds of conventional bulk carrier design and is geared. Four deck cranes are provided for cargo loading and discharging. A typical service speed is 15 knots, using 30 tonnes of fuel oil per day.

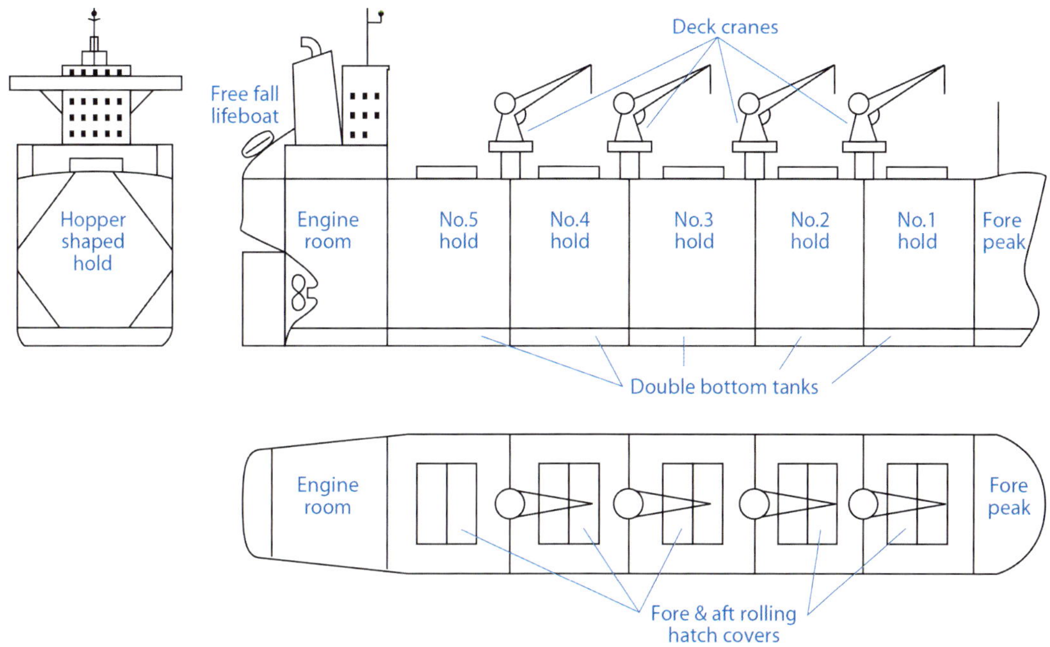


**A typical Supramax/Handymax**

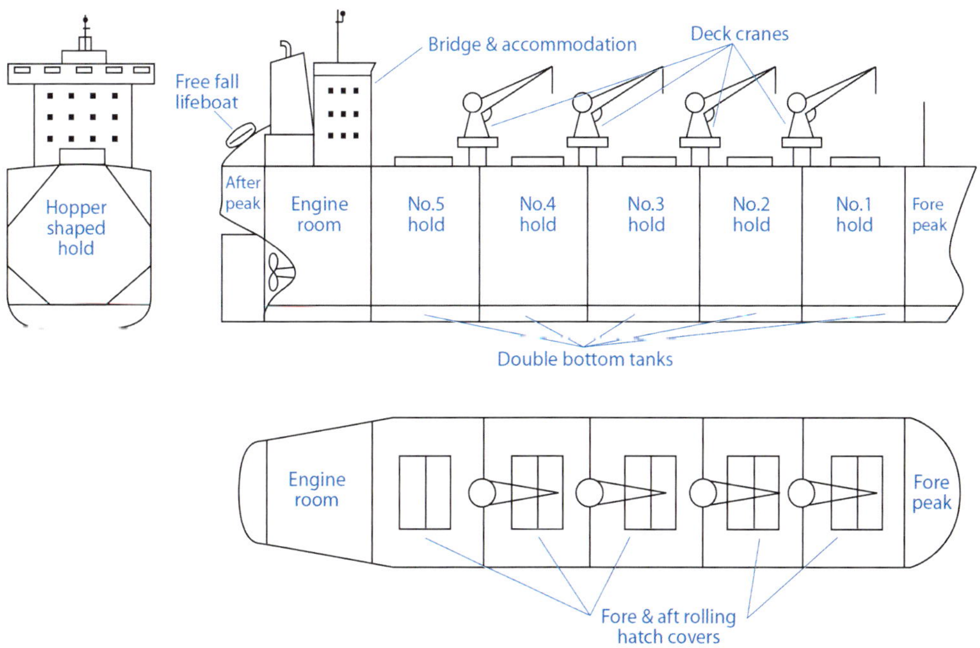


**A typical Handysize bulk carrier**

**Handysize bulk carrier.** A handysize bulk carrier is a bulker which has a carrying capacity between 10,000 dwt and 39,999 dwt. A handysize bulk carrier will have four holds of conventional bulk carrier design, served by onboard deck cranes for cargo operation. The dimensions of a typical vessel under the classification will be capacity 28,000 dwt, overall length 170m, breadth 27m and draught 9m. A typical service speed is about 14 knots using 23 tonnes of fuel oil per day. Bulk carriers of the handy size are involved in carrying minor bulk cargoes and are well suited to using small ports with length and draft restrictions. Their cargo gear enables them to service ports lacking cargo loading and unloading infrastructure.

GENERAL BULK CARRIER SIZES

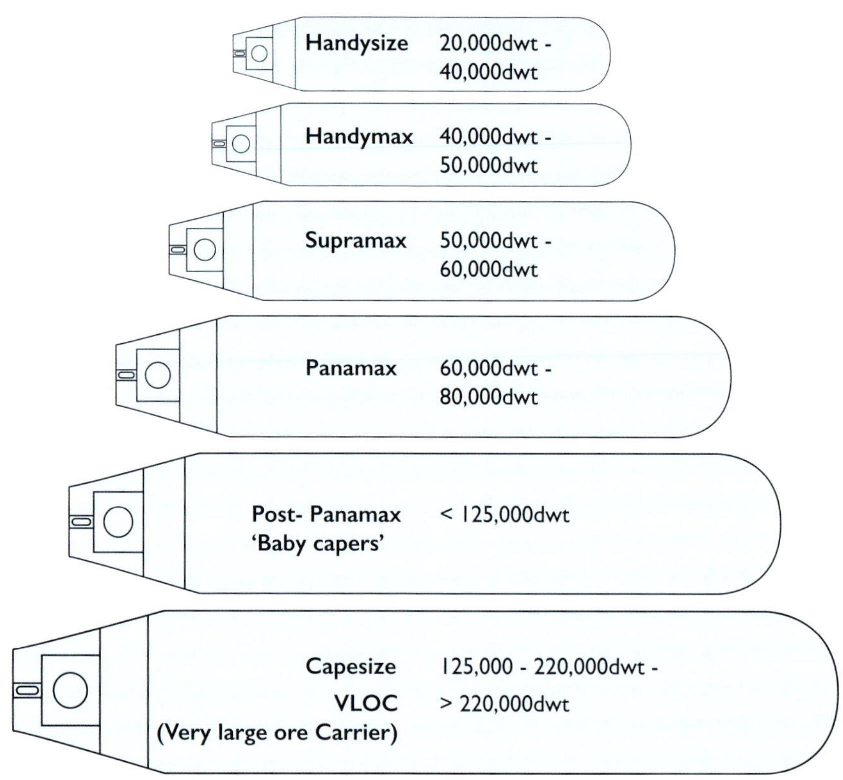


## Regional Classifications

Bulk carriers may be classified by the region they serve which in turn provides an approximation of their size.

**Chinamax /Valemax.** The Chinamax class are the largest ore carriers in the world having LOA of 362m and a deadweight of 400,000 dwt. The ore carriers operate between Brazil and China.

**Kamsarmax** bulk carriers which have a maximum length of 229m and are suitable for berthing at the port of Kamsar in the Republic of Guinea to load bauxite.

**Newcastlemax** refers to the maximum size of the bulk carrier able to enter the port of Newcastle in Australia, namely LOA of 300m and breadth of 50metres.

**Setouchmax** is a bulk carrier of 230,000 dwt, the maximum size able to navigate the Setouch Sea in Japan.

**Seawaymax.** The canal lock basins restrict the size of bulk carriers using the St Lawrence Seaway. The limiting dimensions are LOA 226m and a maximum draught of 8m.

**Malaccamax.** The largest size of bulk carrier which can pass through the Straits of Malacca. Dimension limits are LOA 330m, draught 20m and capacity of 300,000 dwt.

**Dunkirkmax.** The maximum size of bulk carrier able to use the lock system into the port of Dunkirk. The key maximum dimensions are LOA 289m, breadth 45m relating to a capacity of 175,000 dwt.

## 4.8 CONTAINER SHIPS

The first specialised oceangoing containerships were developed in the mid-1960s and over time replaced the traditional general cargo ships on the major liner routes. The container ship was designed around the ISO standard freight container which are of 20 or 40 ft in length. The capacity of a containership is referred to in teus (twenty-foot equivalent units), that is the number of 20ft containers which can theoretically be carried by the ship. A 40ft container is the equivalent of 2 x 20ft containers and occasionally container ship size may be referred to by the maximum the number of 40ft containers it could theoretically carry, that is feus (forty-foot equivalent units). Presently (2015) there are about 5,000 container ships in the world fleet having a combined capacity of 19 million teu.

The container ship carries containers in cellular guides within its holds, referred to as underdeck (UD) containers. The cellular guide system aids loading and discharge and eliminates the need for lashing the containers. Specialised container ships carry containers on deck (OD). OD containers have to be lashed in position in accordance with the ships lashing plan. Container-lashing equipment is maintained on board.

The **fully cellular container ship** is non-geared and relies on terminal loading and unloading systems for cargo operations. The number of holds varies with the size of the container ship. The holds are subdivided lengthwise (longitudinally) into 20ft and 40ft bays for container stowage. The number of rows of containers carried across the ship (transversely) varies with the ship's breadth. The number of tiers of containers, that is, the height of the container stack, will depend on the position of the stow and whether OD or UD.

There have been designs for a hatch-less container ship but they met with limited success due to the inflexibility they provide for loading patterns.

All container ships will have a complex water ballast system to ensure that the ship is upright during loading, that the trim of the ship is appropriate and that stress in the ship's hull are minimised. The specialised container ship also has special location for the carriage of reefer containers.

Since the introduction of cellular container ships there has been a continuing growth in ship size and container capacity. The first deepsea fully cellular container ships entered service on the Europe to Australasia trades in 1969 had a capacity for 1500 teu. The largest container ship which entered service in 2015 has a capacity exceeding 19,000 teu. The growth in container ship size has been the result of the use of containers for transportation and the increased efficiency which can be realised with larger ships. It is anticipated that growth in container ship size will grow still further.

Containers can be carried on general cargo ships which serve trades that demand flexibility of the ship's capacity in terms of cargo types carried. The general cargo ships can also be used to supplement mainline trade routes.

Containers destined for smaller ports are transhipped into feeder ships which have a capacity from 200 teu to 2,000 teu depending on the service requirement. The smaller feeder container ships which serve unsophisticated ports without terminal loading and discharging equipment will be equipped with their own lifting gear.

## Classification of container ships in terms of size

Container ships are classed according to their carrying capacity and dimensions. The classification refers to generation of build or limits imposed by the Panama Canal. The latter classification has been complicated by the development of the new lock basins in the Panama Canal.

**Post-new Panamax.** The post-new Panamax container ships, which commenced delivery in 2014, have a capacity of more than 18,000 teu. The ship's length overall is 400m, its breadth 55m which exceeds the maximum breadth of the new Panama lock basins by 4m. Ships of this class typically carry 10 tiers of containers on deck and 10 tiers high underdeck (UD). Twenty-three rows of containers can be placed across the ship's breadth. The post-new Panamax ships will be involved in the Europe to Asia trade. The design of ships of this size is recognised by the separation of the accommodation from the engine room casing and funnels. The design provides additional transverse strength and enhanced carrying capacity compared to the accommodation and engine room in the two-thirds position from for'd. The post-new Panamax container ships may have two engines each turning a separate propeller, or a single engine and propeller. A maximum speed of 22 knots is achievable but a slow service speed is 10.5 knots.

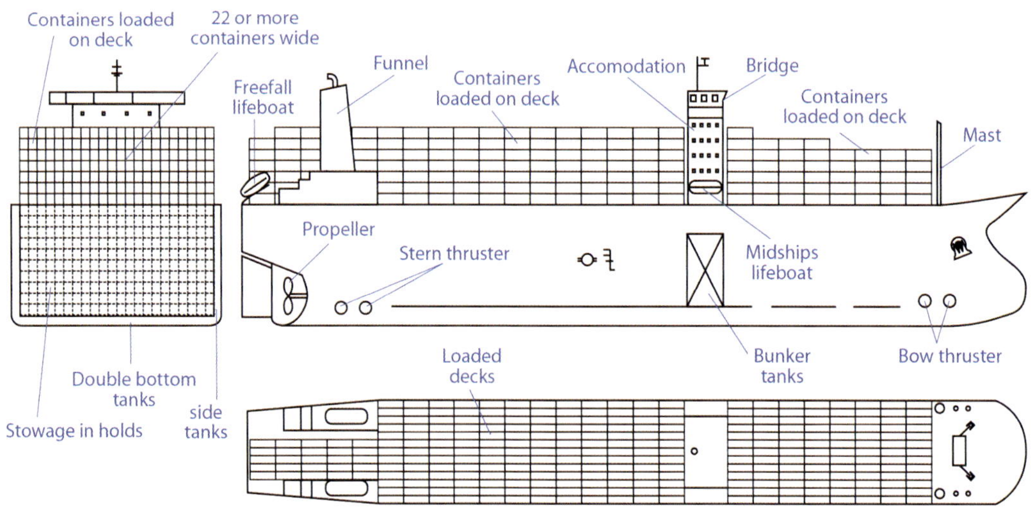


**A typical post-new Panamax container ship**

**New-Panamax** container ship dimensions are limited to the maximum size of the new Panama lock basins. The new-Panamax container ships carry between 10,000 and 14,500 teus and have dimensions of 366m overall length, 48m breadth and a maximum draught of 15m. Container ships of this class carry 20 containers across the breadth of the ship. They typically carry containers eight tiers high on deck (OD) and 10 tiers high underdeck (UD).

The **ultra-large container vessel (ULCV)** is a container ship having a capacity greater than 14,000 teu.

**Post-Panamax** container ships are ships which have dimensions too large to pass through the present Panama Canal lock basins. The first post-Panama containerships came into service in 1988 and are involved in the Pacific Ocean trades. The post-Panamax class has the capacity of between 4,000 and 5,000 teu.

A subcategory **post-Panamax Plus** class was defined in the year 2000 and refers to container ships with a capacity of between 6,000 and 10,000 teu. The post-Panamax container ships have a breadth of 15 rows compared to the 17 rows of the post-Panamax Plus container ships. The number of container rows impact on the size of the shoreside container gantry needed to service the ship.

Typical dimensions of the post-Panamax container ship are: overall length 285m, breadth 40m and draught of 13m. By comparison, dimensions of the post-Panamax Plus container ship are: overall length 300m, breadth 43m and draught of 14.5m.

**Panamax container ship.** The third generation container ships completed in the early 1970s were required to transit the Panama Canal as passage through the Suez Canal was denied due to its closure between 1967 and 1973. The Panamax container ships had an overall length of 294m, a breadth of 32m and a draught of 12m. The breadth of the containership allowed up to 13 rows of containers. A deep freeboard allowed for nine tiers of containers to be carried UD and three tiers OD. The capacity of the Panamax container ship varied between 3,000 and 4,500 containers depending on design.

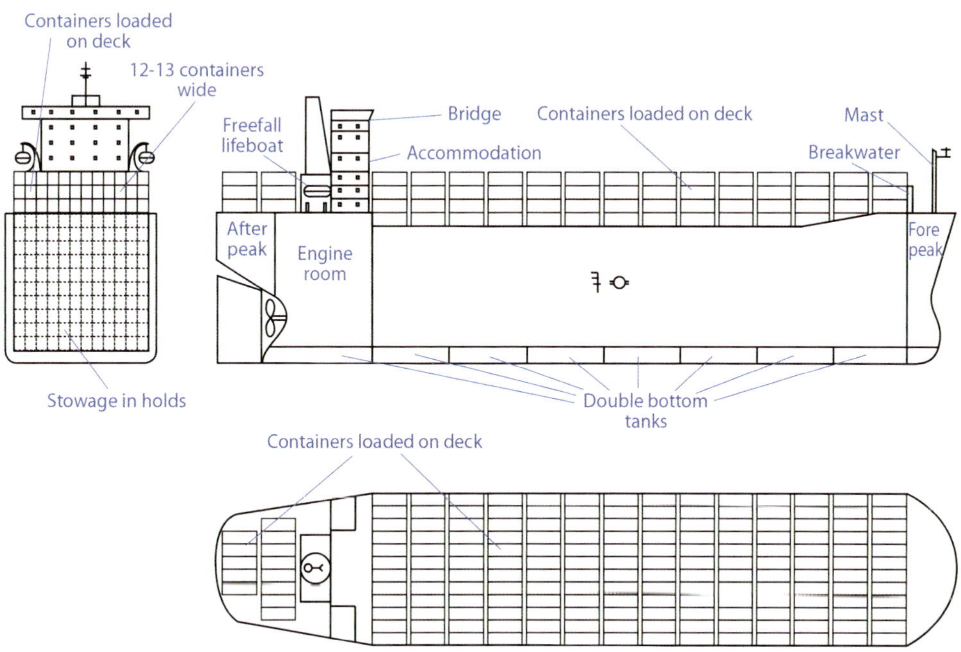


**A typical Panamax container ship**

**Multipurpose ships (MPP)** continue to be used for the carriage of containers. They are geared ships with the flexibility to carry general, bulk and heavy lifts in addition to containers. The nominal container capacity of a 31,000 dwt MPP would be in excess of 2,000 teu, with space for 120 UD and 800 OD. Multipurpose containership will have up to six holds.

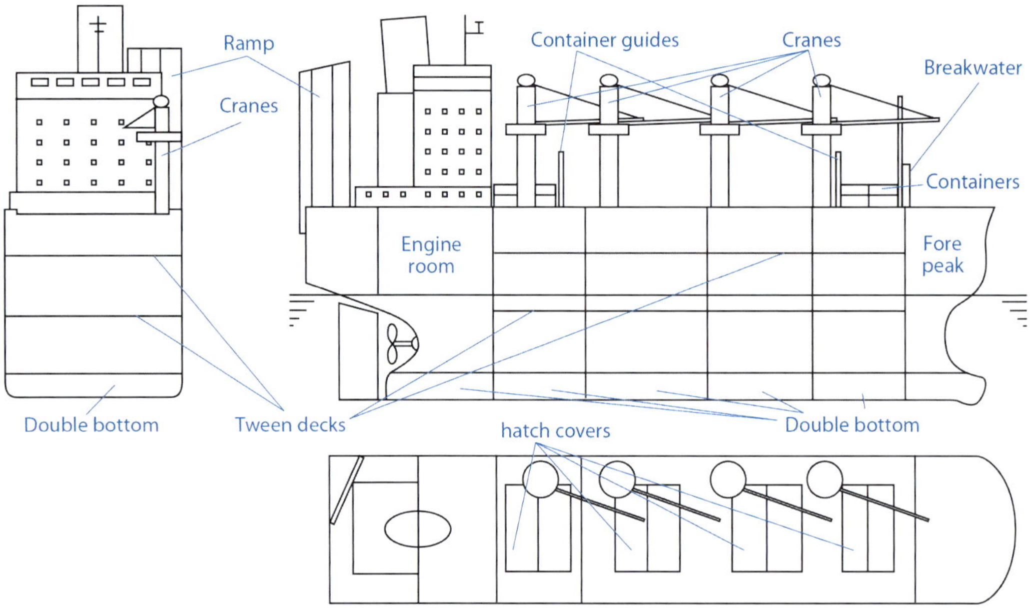


**A typical multi-purpose vessel**

Feeder container ships are used to distribute containers from hub ports to regional ports. There are three classes of feeder ships, ranging from the small-Feeder with a capacity up to 1,000 teu, the Feeder with a capacity of between 1,000 and 2,000 teu and the Feeder-max with a capacity of 2,000 to 3,000 teu. The dimensions of the feeder ships will vary with capacity. Feeder container ships are gearless, the small-Feeders having a speed of about 15 knots, the Feeder and Feeder-max a speed of up to 20 knots.

## Generation nomenclature

Container ship size has changed with time. It has been convenient to group container ships by the generation in which they were built. This has approximately related to size. The table below states the seven generations of container ships and the dates they came into service. The Triple E Class of 18,000 teu + have not a formal generational title, but could be considered the 8th Generation.

| Generation | | Class | Size (teu) |
|---|---|---|---|
| First Generation | 1956 - | Converted cargo ships/ tankers | 500 - 800 |
| Second Generation | 1960 - | Fully Cellular containership | 1,000 - 2,500 |
| Third Generation | 1970 - | Panamax | 3,000 - 4,500 |
| Fourth Generation | 1988 - | Post-Panamax | 4,000 - 5,000 |
| Fifth Generation | 2000 - | Post-Panamax Plus | 6,000 - 10,000 |
| Sixth Generation | 2014 - | New-Panamax | 10,500 - 15,000 |
| Seventh Generation | 2006 - | Post-New-Panamax (ULCV) | 14,000 + |

## CONTAINERSHIP EVOLUTION

TEU: twenty-foot equivalent units, length x width x depth below water in metres

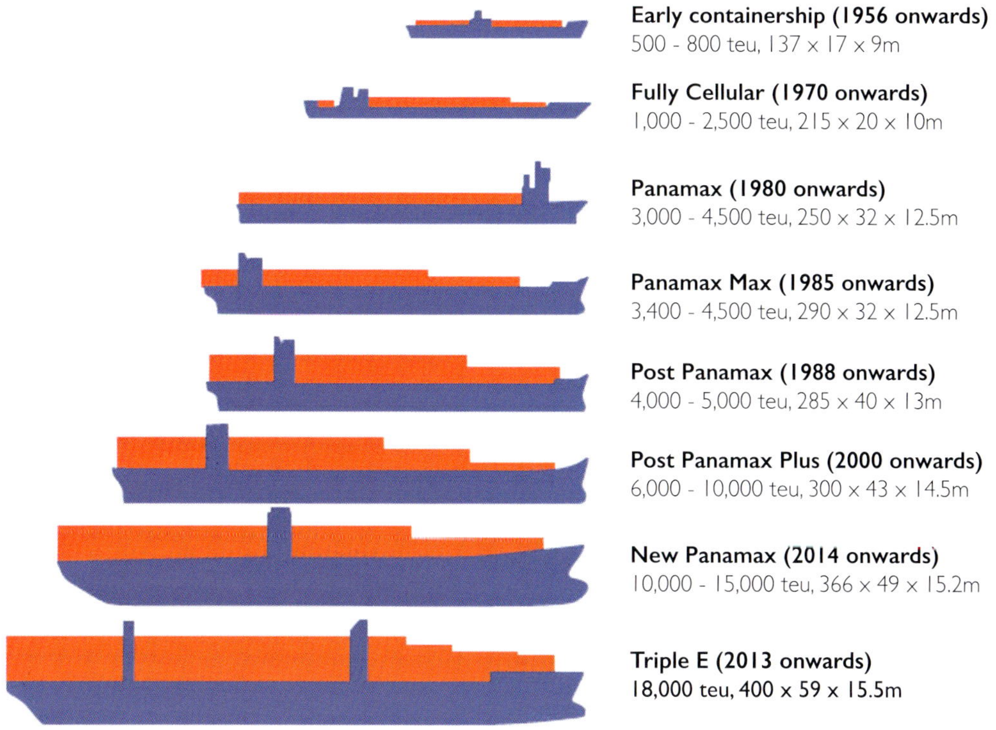


*Source: Jean Paul Rodrigue*

Chapter 5

# The geography of trade

*The sea carries 95% of world trade, representing the most economic means per tonne conveyed*

## 5.1 SEABORNE TRADE

Moving goods by sea or waterways is by far the most economic method of transport in terms of cost per tonne carried. It is estimated that over 95% of the world's trade is carried by sea. Shipping is a global business. Shipowners, operators, brokers, managers, agents and other specialists are involved with transporting materials, equipment and people from one part of the world to another. For all involved in shipping a good knowledge of maritime geography, concerning the location of nations, oceans, seas, ports and waterways is important. Spatial awareness, in particular, distance and time relationships between the world's major ports is of value. Access to a maritime atlas such as *Lloyd's Maritime Atlas* or *The Ship's Atlas* helps the shipbroker appreciate maritime geography.

Sea transport plays a crucial part in international trade. The continual improvement and development of ship types and cargo-handling systems has led to a reduction in the cost of sea transport. The cost of sea transport is no longer the barrier to trade it once was. Improvements have encouraged international trade ensuring a steady increase in the amount of cargo moved. In 2013 a total of 9.5 billion tonnes of cargo was moved in international trade by sea.

Of the many raw commodities moved in international trade by sea, four are dominant, namely, crude oil, coal, iron ore and grain. The movement of semi-processed commodities and manufactured goods involves the container shipping industry. These five important trades will be briefly considered.

## 5.2 CRUDE OIL

Crude oil is the single most important commodity traded in the world today. World demand for crude oil in 2013 was over 4,100 million tonnes, of which more than 1,800 million tonnes were carried by sea transport. Crude oil is a natural product. Significant oilfields have been discovered and exploited in various parts of the world – principally in the areas of the Middle East, the Caspian Sea, equatorial West Africa, the Caribbean and US Gulf, north and east of South America and in the North Sea.

Economics dictate that the most cost-effective structure for the crude oil industry is to transport crude oil from areas of production to refineries located in the areas of consumption, close to the end-user.

Crude oil tankers, which make use of the economies of scale, are among the largest ships in the world. Crude oil tankers are specifically designed for the carriage of crude oil and are rarely used in other trades. The size of a crude oil tanker is limited by the restrictions imposed at the principal loading and discharging locations. The locations are not necessarily conventional ports as loading and discharge terminals may be located offshore. An example is LOOP, the Louisiana Offshore Oil Port, located in the Gulf of Mexico. LOOP has been developed because it allows tankers with deep draughts to discharge their cargo in an area where the conventional ports are draught-restricted.

Consumers depend on **oil products**, derived from crude oil to power transport vehicles, for heating, power generation and as a feedstock for many industries. In 2013 in excess of 850 million tonnes of oil products were carried by sea. Petroleum, diesel and heating oils are among the many products of the refining process.

## Oil Trade / By Tanker Type

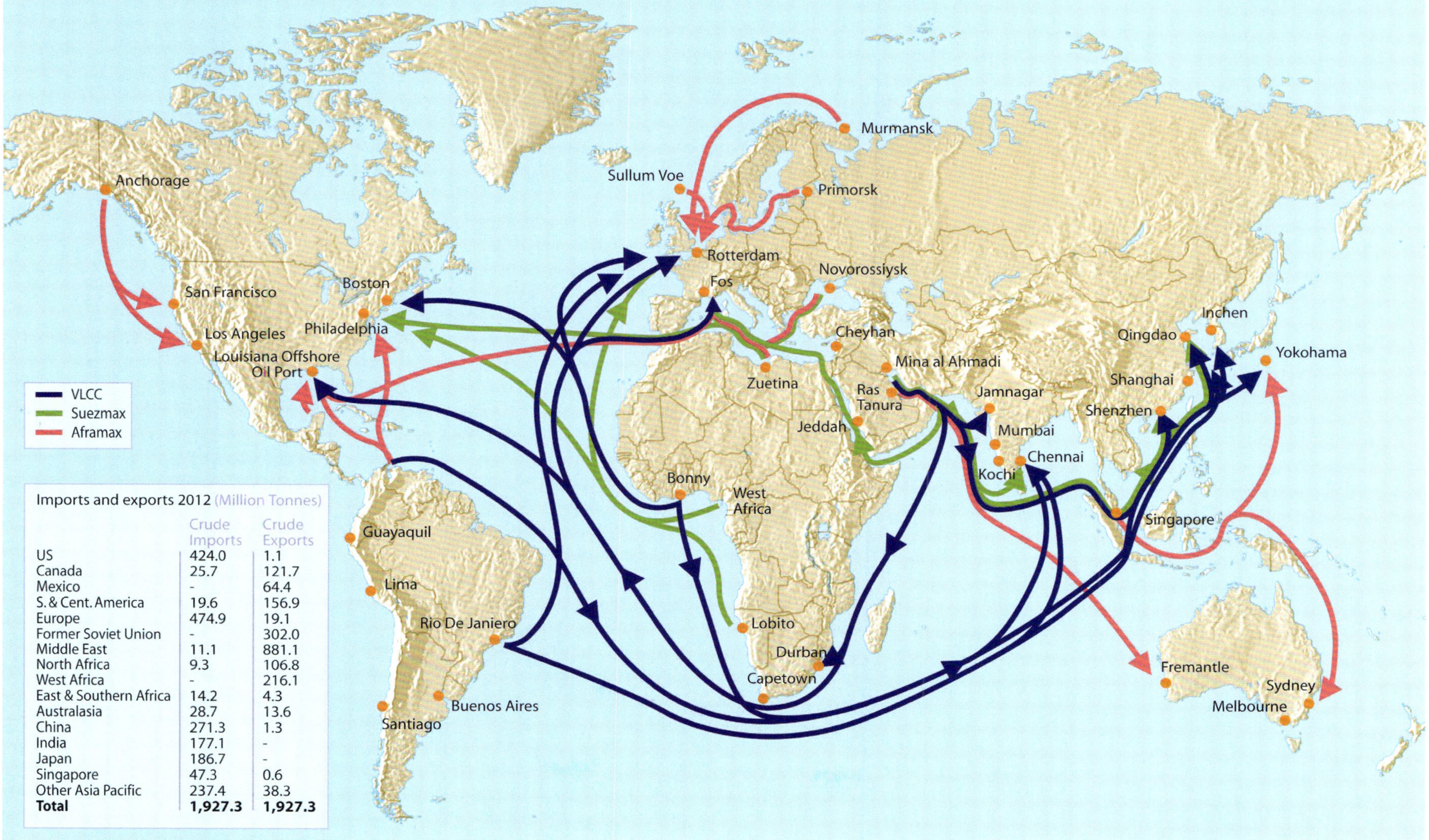


Imports and exports 2012 (Million Tonnes)

| | Crude Imports | Crude Exports |
|---|---|---|
| US | 424.0 | 1.1 |
| Canada | 25.7 | 121.7 |
| Mexico | - | 64.4 |
| S. & Cent. America | 19.6 | 156.9 |
| Europe | 474.9 | 19.1 |
| Former Soviet Union | - | 302.0 |
| Middle East | 11.1 | 881.1 |
| North Africa | 9.3 | 106.8 |
| West Africa | - | 216.1 |
| East & Southern Africa | 14.2 | 4.3 |
| Australasia | 28.7 | 13.6 |
| China | 271.3 | 1.3 |
| India | 177.1 | - |
| Japan | 186.7 | - |
| Singapore | 47.3 | 0.6 |
| Other Asia Pacific | 237.4 | 38.3 |
| **Total** | **1,927.3** | **1,927.3** |

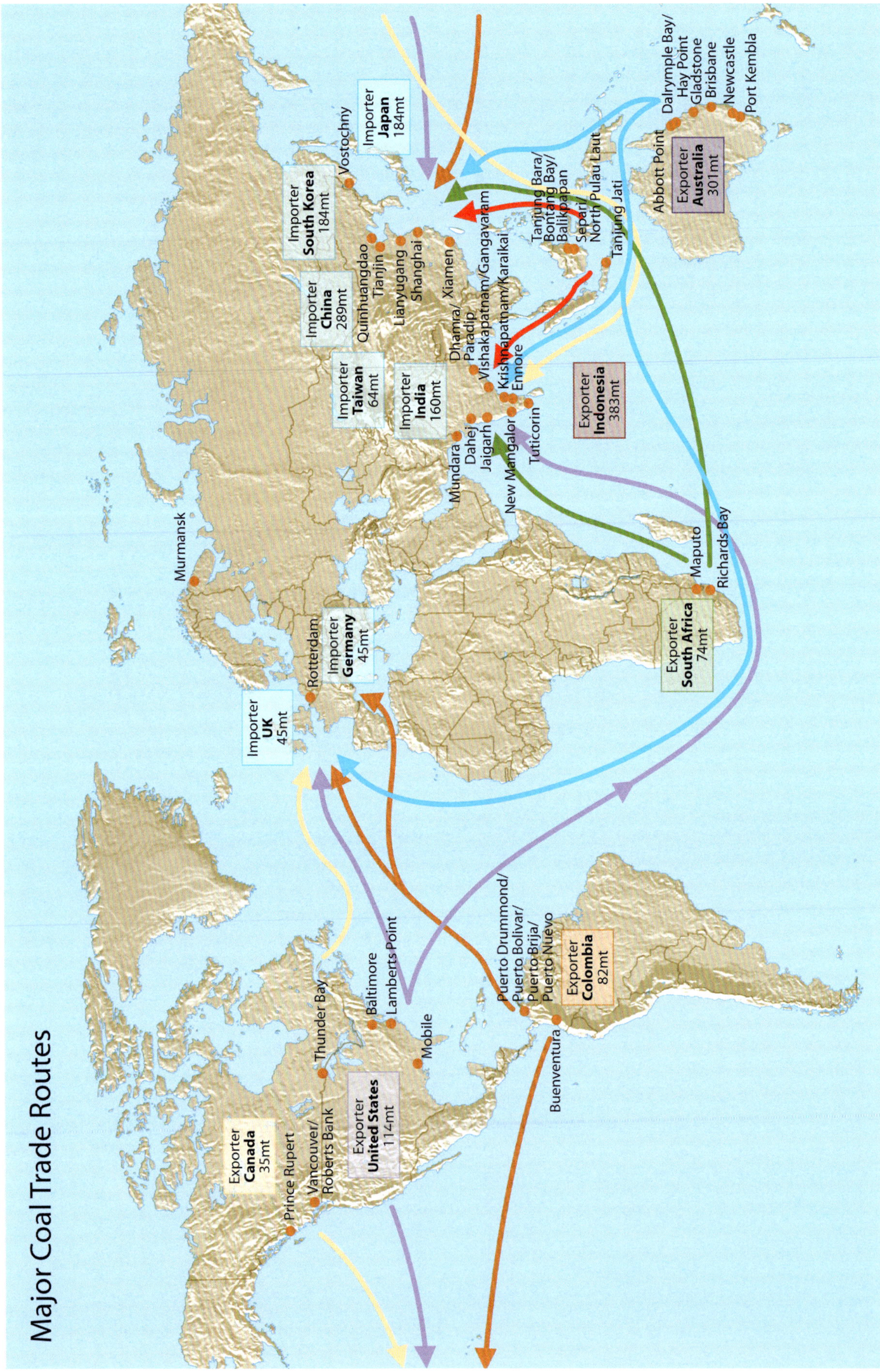
Major Coal Trade Routes
Exporter
Canada
35mt
Prince Rupert
Vancouver/
Roberts Bank
Exporter
United States
114mt
Thunder Bay
Baltimore
Lamberts Point
Mobile
Buenventura
Puerto Drummond/
Puerto Bolivar/
Puerto Brija/
Puerto Nuevo
Exporter
Colombia
82mt
Importer
UK
45mt
Rotterdam
Importer
Germany
45mt
Murmansk
Exporter
South Africa
74mt
Maputo
Richards Bay
Mundara
Dahej
Jaigarh
New Mangalor
Tuticorin
Importer
India
160mt
Importer
Taiwan
64mt
Importer
China
289mt
Importer
South Korea
184mt
Importer
Japan
184mt
Vostochny
Quinhuangdao
Tianjin
Lianyugang
Shanghai
Xiamen
Dhamra/
Paradip
Vishakapatnam/Gangavaram
Krishnapatnam/Karaikal
Ennore
Exporter
Indonesia
383mt
Tanjung Bara/
Bontang Bay/
Balikpapan
Separi
North Pulau Laut
Tanjung Jati
Abbott Point
Dalrymple Bay/
Hay Point
Gladstone
Brisbane
Newcastle
Port Kembla
Exporter
Australia
301mt

## 5.3 COAL

Coal is an energy source. **Steam coal** is used for power generation and coking coal as a heat source in industrial processes, particularly steel making. In 2013 about 7,800 million tons of coal were mined and consumed. Of this amount about 1,300 million tonnes were transported by sea from the sources of production to the industrial centres of the world where steel is made and power consumed. In spite of the fact that burning coal is not a very environmentally friendly process, it is still used to generate around 40% of the world's electricity.

Coal has a stowage factor (SF) of about 1.4m$^3$ per tonne. The SF of a dry cargo is defined as the ratio of the volume of a cargo to its weight, the units being cu - m$^3$ per tonne or cubic feet per ton.

Coal is transported by bulk carriers, which may or may not be equipped with discharging gear. Loading is usually by conveyor from shoreside. Where deep water is available at both loading and discharging ports, Capesize bulk carriers of over 80,000 dwt can be used to take advantage of economies of scale. Where restrictions dictate smaller parcels of bulk cargo, Panamax bulk carriers of 60,000-80,000 dwt or the smaller handymax bulkers are employed. Coal may be discharged by cranes with grabs at specialised terminals that serve steelworks or power stations.

## 5.4 IRON ORE

Most of the world's metals are produced from smelting mineral ores, such as iron ore which produces steel, or bauxite which produces aluminum. In most cases, the process is carried out some considerable distance from where the ore is mined.

Iron ore is used for the production of iron and steel and is the single largest dry bulk cargo traded. In 2013, about 1.3 billion tons of iron ore were moved by bulk carrier. China was the largest importer of iron ore receiving more than 730 million tonnes. Australia was the largest exporter exporting in excess of 524m tonnes.

Iron ore is a dense cargo. Concentrated iron ore typically has an SF of about 0.3m$^3$ per tonne compared to coal which has an SF of 1.4m$^3$ per tonne.

Iron ore is carried in specialist bulk carriers which have relatively small holds on top of deep double-bottom tanks. The structural arrangement provides strength whilst reducing stress caused by a large metacentric height, a measure of stability. The largest bulk carriers are of 400,000 dwt and require a draught of 23m. They are known as Valemax or Chinamax ships and are designed to carry iron ore between Brazil and China.

Iron ore is loaded and discharged at specialised terminals. An iron ore-loading terminal will have deepwater alongside, a specialist ship-to-shore loading gantry and extensive stock areas which feed the cargo to the ship by using a reclaimer and a series of high volume conveyors. Discharge is usually carried out using gantry-type grab fitted cranes, with the iron ore being moved from the quayside by conveyor belts through a stacker to the storage stack.

## 5.5 GRAIN

Most grains traded in bulk are destined for human or animal consumption. They include wheat, sorghum, soya, rice and the seeds of crops such as rape, sunflower, flax and cotton. Some grains are processed into pellets or meal prior to shipment.

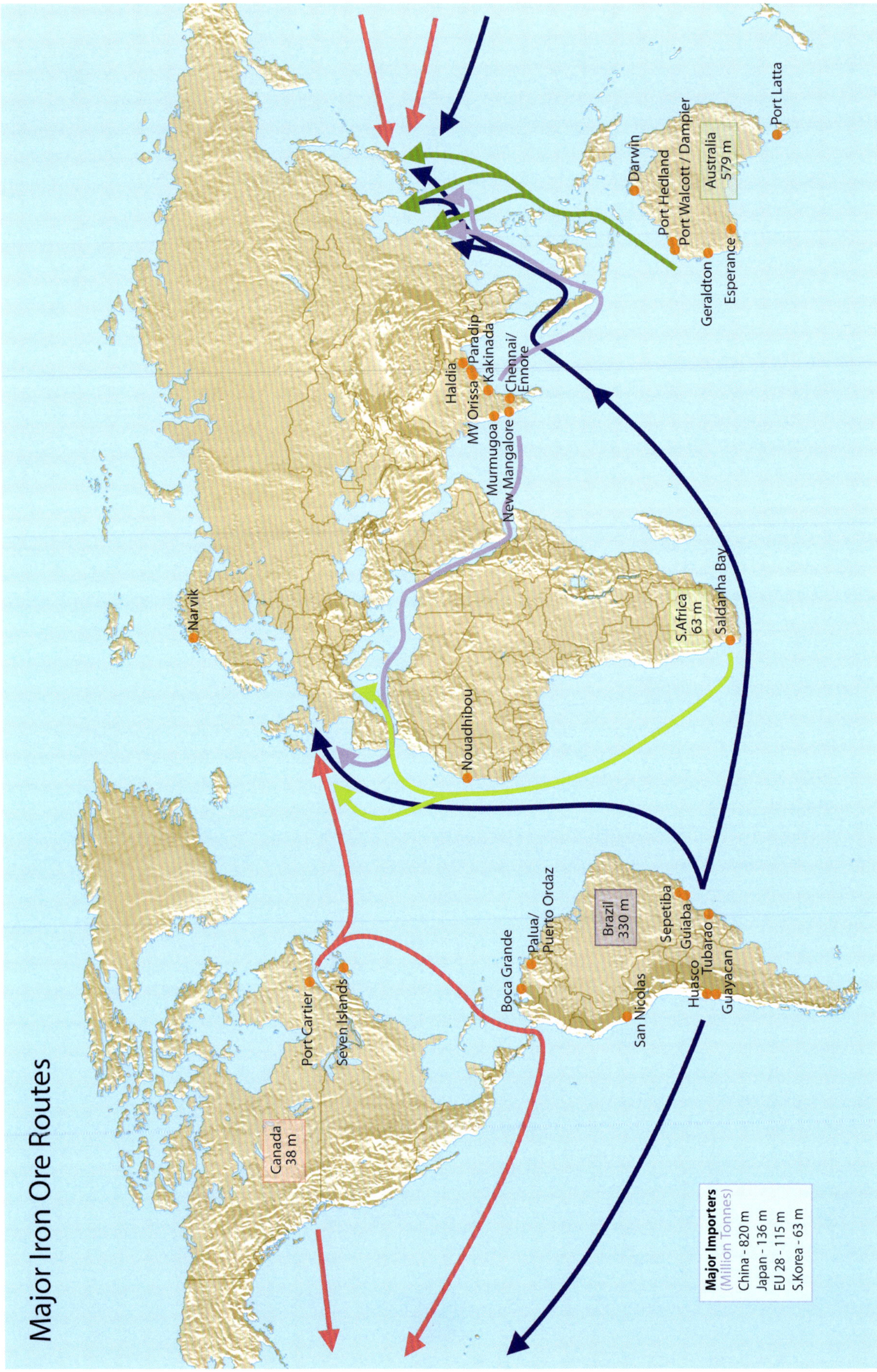
Major Iron Ore Routes
Canada
38 m
Port Cartier
Seven Islands
Boca Grande
Palua/
Puerto Ordaz
Brazil
330 m
San Nicolas
Huasco
Tubarão
Guayacan
Guiaba
Sepetiba
Narvik
Nouadhibou
S.Africa
63 m
Saldanha Bay
Murmugoa
New Mangalore
MV Orissa
Haldia
Paradip
Kakinada
Chennai/
Ennore
Darwin
Port Hedland
Port Walcott / Dampier
Australia
579 m
Geraldton
Esperance
Port Latta
Major Importers
(Million Tonnes)
China - 820 m
Japan - 136 m
EU 28 - 115 m
S.Korea - 63 m

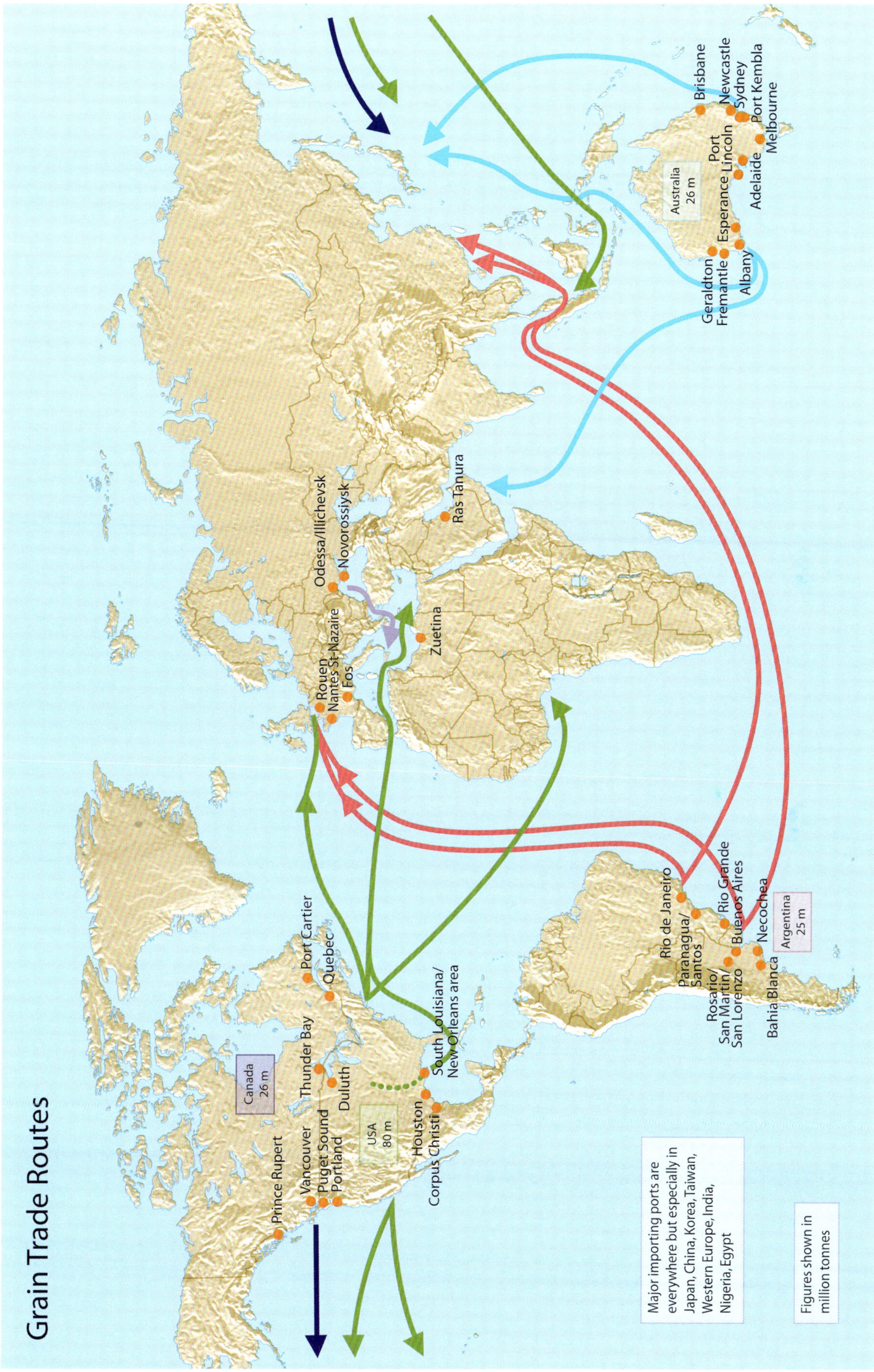
Grain Trade Routes
Prince Rupert
Vancouver
Puget Sound
Portland
Canada
26 m
Thunder Bay
Duluth
USA
80 m
Houston
Corpus Christi
South Louisiana/
New Orleans area
Quebec
Port Cartier
Rio de Janeiro
Paranagua/
Santos
Rosario/
San Martin/
San Lorenzo
Rio Grande
Buenos Aires
Necochea
Bahia Blanca
Argentina
25 m
Rouen
Nantes St-Nazaire
Fos
Zuetina
Odessa/Illichevsk
Novorossiysk
Ras Tanura
Geraldton
Fremantle
Albany
Esperance
Port
Lincoln
Adelaide
Melbourne
Port Kembla
Sydney
Newcastle
Brisbane
Australia
26 m
Major importing ports are everywhere but especially in Japan, China, Korea, Taiwan, Western Europe, India, Nigeria, Egypt
Figures shown in million tonnes

Demand and supply for grain varies each year, depending on the quality of the harvest and climatic events, such as floods and drought. The changes affect volumes, prices, availability and ultimately, trading patterns. In 2013, the movement of grain by sea amounted to 384 million tonnes. General purpose bulk carriers are used for the carriage of grain cargoes.

In reported fixtures of the grain market the abbreviation **HSS** is sometimes used to describe a grain cargo. HSS is a shipping term referring to heavy grains, soya beans and sorghums. The heavy grains have a SF of about 1.3$m^3$ per tonne, which is not dissimilar to coal.

There is a danger in carrying grains and seeds in bulk, namely that of cargo shift. In extreme cases, cargo shift can lead to capsize of the ship. To avoid this problem, bulk carriers have self-trimming holds or special wing tanks that bleed cargo into the main hold. This ensures that space created above the cargo of grain as it settles is filled. There are alternatives to preventing the shift of cargo including the use of shifting boards or over-stowing the bulk grain cargo with bagged grain.

Loading of grain is usually undertaken from shore silos by loading chute. As with all cargo handling, time is money. Grain-loading equipment is capable of loading ships at a rate exceeding 30,000 tonnes per day. Discharging facilities vary considerably, the fastest and most efficient being the pneumatic suction systems in use at most of the world's major grain-importing ports. Other methods of discharge include mechanical bucket or screw elevators or the use of grabs.

Production of grain for export is concentrated in the fertile agricultural areas of the world including the Canadian and North American grain belt, Argentina, Uruguay and Brazil in South America, Australia, New Zealand, Thailand and its neighbours in the Far East, and Russia. Grains and seeds are purchased by the highly populated industrial areas of the world and are shipped to third world countries as seed for planting, human or animal consumption or, in some cases, for famine relief.

## 5.6 OTHER DRY BULK CARGOES

In addition to the coal, iron ore and grains described above, a further 2.25billion tonnes of dry bulk cargoes are moved by sea each year. Included are bauxite and phosphate which, together with coal, iron ore and grain, are known as the five major bulks. Other dry bulk cargoes include copper, manganese and lead ores, steel products including beams and plate, minerals such as granite and clays, fertilisers including nitrates and potash, building materials, timber and scrap. Normally dry bulk cargoes will be carried by bulk carrier, the size of which varies with the parcel size.

Specialist ships are used for the specific carriage of large quantities of similar cargo. For example, refrigerated or reefer ships are designed to carry fruit, dairy products and meat at controlled temperatures in bulk. Refrigerated ships have insulated holds and are equipped with refrigeration equipment to keep the high-value cargoes at exactly the right temperature. The ships have high speed capability enabling the cargo to be delivered quickly and in good condition. Other types of dry cargoes carried and in what some consider to be bulk form include livestock and motor vehicles.

## 5.7 UNITISED CARGO

Quite separate from the bulk dry and liquid trades described above, is the shipping sector associated with unitised and containerised cargo. In its wider sense, unitised cargo includes

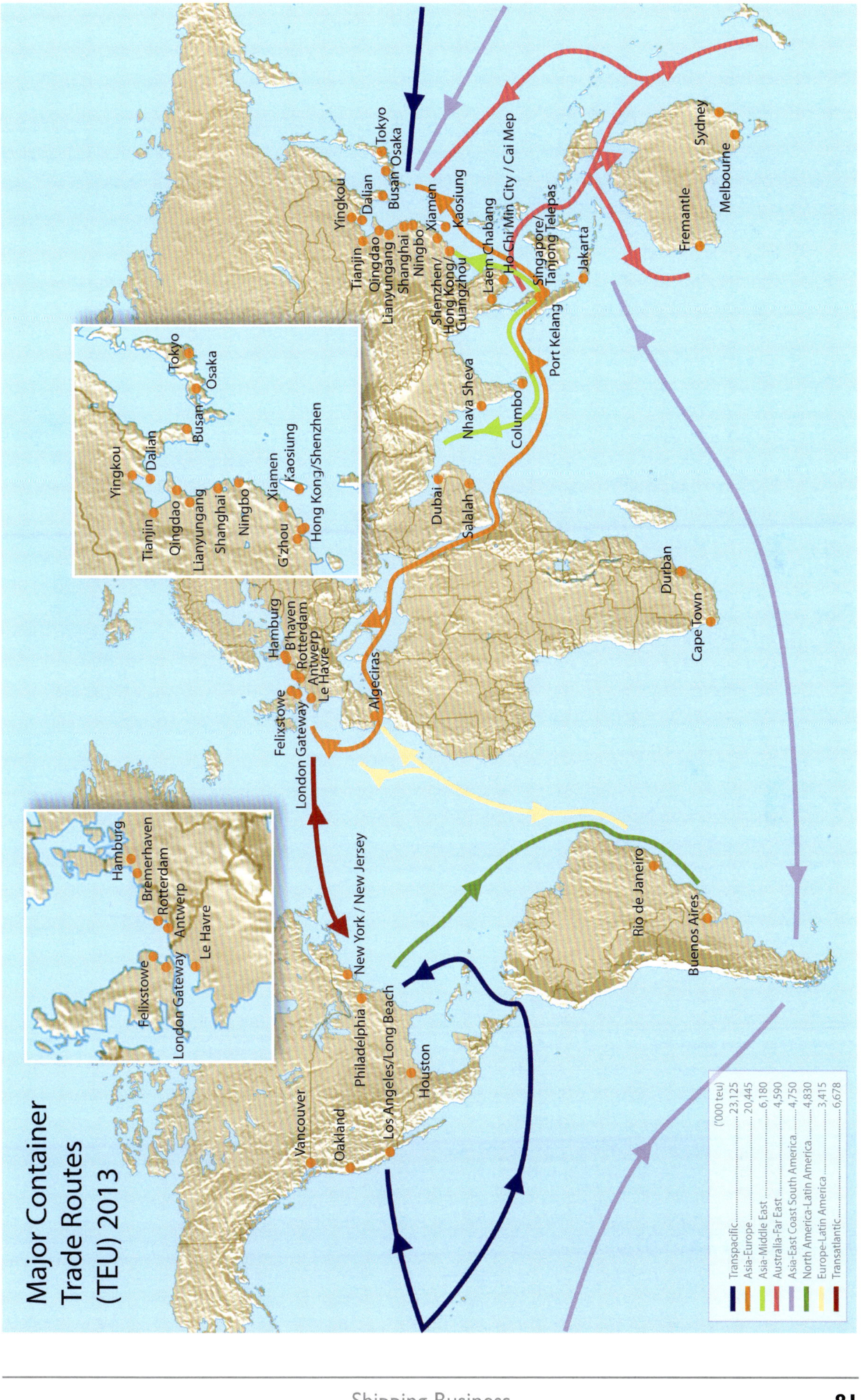
Major Container Trade Routes (TEU) 2013
('000 teu)
Transpacific 23,125
Asia-Europe 20,445
Asia-Middle East 6,180
Australia-Far East 4,590
Asia-East Coast South America 4,750
North America-Latin America 4,830
Europe-Latin America 3,415
Transatlantic 6,678
Vancouver
Oakland
Los Angeles/Long Beach
Philadelphia
Houston
New York / New Jersey
Rio de Janeiro
Buenos Aires
Felixstowe
London Gateway
Hamburg
B'haven
Rotterdam
Antwerp
Le Havre
Algeciras
Cape Town
Durban
Dubai
Salalah
Nhava Sheva
Columbo
Port Kelang
Singapore/Tanjong Telepas
Jakarta
Laem Chabang
Ho Chi Min City / Cai Mep
Shenzhen/Hong Kong/Guangzhou
Kaosiung
Xiamen
Ningbo
Shanghai
Lianyungang
Qingdao
Tianjin
Yingkou
Dalian
Busan
Osaka
Tokyo
Fremantle
Melbourne
Sydney
Bremerhaven
G'zhou
Hong Kong/Shenzhen

palletised goods, packaged timber, 'jumbo' bags and pre-slung cargo. It also includes specially designed lighters and barges used by lighter aboard ship (LASH) systems.

It is the international freight container that over the last 50 years has revolutionised the general cargo trades. Advances in technology, ship design and cargo-handling equipment, combined with heavy investment in terminal development and the adaptation of road, rail and inland waterway systems, have allowed a multi-modal transport system to develop. The common feature being the international standard 20 and 40 foot containers. Advances still continue as exemplified by the growth in the size of the container ship.

The ability to fill and empty containers at points remote from ports and terminals, the reduction in theft and damage and the use of multiple transport modes to allow a true door-to-door service are among the benefits that the use of container systems have provided to goods' manufacturers. Fierce competition on the major container trade routes led to reduced freight and improved efficiency.

Establishing a fully integrated container service requires a large capital investment in specialist ships, berth facilities, terminals and depots, handling equipment, road, rail and waterway connections, and containers. Container services involve deepsea container ships which trade between the world's major port terminals and feeder ships which link the major ports to smaller ports within the same area. The hub and spoke system which has developed provides fast and reliable transit times for the container. There are few parts of the world to and from which door-to-door container services cannot be offered.

## 5.8 PORTS

Traditional ports around the world have developed in step with the communities they serve. In many cases, it was the presence of a natural harbour that encouraged people to settle in a particular area. Thereafter, with growth in the population, the port grew. Some ports owe their existence to the exploitation of a bulk commodity which has been exported. Grain ports in North and South America are typical examples while, more recently, terminals in otherwise largely uninhabited regions of the world have been built to allow for the export of minerals, such as coal and iron ore.

The extent to which a port will develop, stagnate or even fail depends on many factors including:

- depth of water;
- protection from adverse weather;
- space for cargo storage;
- infrastructure, including road, rail and inland waterway connections;
- availability of labour.

Port location will dictate the extent to which a port will grow or contract. Many examples could be given but a contrast between the two United Kingdom (UK) ports of Liverpool and Southampton is illustrative.

Liverpool developed from being a small coastal port in the seventeenth century to becoming the second port of the British Empire at the turn of the 20th century. Liverpool's enclosed dock system was established to ensure that ships could remain afloat whilst their cargoes were loaded and discharged. Entry into the enclosed docks system was through locks which created limits to the size of ships which could enter the docks. The hinterland of Liverpool was densely populated and highly industrialised. The container revolution of the early 1970s, combined with the decline of the UK's industrial base, encouraged new thinking by shipowners regarding port and terminal location. The desire to use a non-enclosed port and a port which was located close to north-western European ports with the minimum deviation, led to the relocation of one of Liverpool's main international trades, the UK to Far East trade, to the south coast port of Southampton. Further opportunities in serving the trade route were later taken up by the development of the port of Felixstowe, presently the UK's largest container port. The result of the change was a serious decline in the role of Liverpool as a port. Developments in the second decade of the 21st century, including the building of a new riverside container terminal capable of serving two 380m mega post-Panamax container ships, are among the maritime activities seeing a renewal of the port of Liverpool.

It is sometimes difficult to classify a port into a single category. Generally, ports have many facilities for numerous traffic activities. The listing below shows some of the key categories for which a port is used:

**Entrepot port:**
A port where goods are transferred from one ship to another. For example, a port such as Rotterdam acts as an entrepot port where cargo arrives in large ships and is transferred to smaller coastal ships and/or barges for onwards transit.

**Naval port:**
A home port for a national navy. Ports such as Plymouth and Portsmouth in the UK were chosen for their strategic locations.

**Ferry port:**
A port used for short sea routes usually connecting two countries. Dover and Calais are ferry ports from which ferries cross the English Channel between England and France.

**Outport:**
An outport is the name given for a subsidiary port built in deeper water than the original port. London Gateway is an outport of the port of London.

**Fishing port:**
A smaller port which is the home port for a fishing fleet, usually located near recognised fishing grounds. A fishing port will have good inland transport facilities for quick despatch of the fishing catch.

**Cargo port:**
The large majority of ports deal with cargo imports and or exports. Cargoes will be varied in nature. All forms of cargo pass through a cargo port including dry and wet bulk, containers and cars. Cargo ports provide the facilities for the transfer of cargo between ship and shore and storing cargo prior to or after discharge. Good examples of cargo ports are Rotterdam and Antwerp.

**Free port:**
A free port is a port in which a free zone is established. A free zone is an area of land that is considered for customs purposes to be outside the territory of its host country. Goods may be brought into the zone without import duties being paid. Duty is paid only if the goods are imported from the zone to the territory of the host country. Enterprises in the zone are able to hold stock without adding the duty element to their working capital. In addition to having a suspended customs regime, some free zones within a free port will offer incentives such as tax

concessions or grants designed to encourage business. Zones may also be exempt from the operation of certain laws or regulations which apply to the national state. The variety of concession offered by different countries makes it difficult to generalise about the potential benefits of free zones. The opportunities for a particular zone will depend upon the exact nature of the regulations applying to the zone and how these compare with conditions in the host and neighbouring countries.

Port Information:
Major maritime publishers produce annual information, both in hard copy and digital format, about the capability of ports. *The Guide to Port Entry* is an example. Port information is also provided by port authorities. The port agent is able to confirm the accuracy of published information.

## 5.9 ABBREVIATIONS AND EXPRESSIONS USED IN COMMUNICATION WITH PORTS

Communications about port restrictions inevitably use abbreviations or expressions. Included are abbreviations associated with length, breadth and draught of the ship. Ports will have restrictions on the size of ship which can be accommodated. The general comments below add to those already made and relate to their use in port communications. The geographical limitations are self-explanatory.

**Length Overall (LOA):** it is important for a port to know the LOA of a ship. LOA, the maximum length of the ship, can be restrictive. In some cases, a ship will not be able to enter the port because of its length. This may be due to the meander of the river system, (for example, on the Seine) or because the actual berth is too short (for example, port information states Alexandria 620ft LOA max).

**Breadth (beam):** the breadth of a ship is important as it may restrict the passage of the ship. Restriction will be imposed by the width of the channel or lock basins which have to be negotiated to reach the designated terminal. The breadth of the ship will also concern the terminal operators where the outreach of the shore-based loading or discharge equipment may be a limiting factor. In the latter circumstance, shipowners may be requested to give additional information about the ship such as the distance between ship's rail (side) and the hatch coaming (side of hatch). This is for the purpose of confirming that the shore cargo installation has sufficient reach.

**Draught:** if no draught restriction is stipulated and the load or discharge port is named in the charter party, it is the shipowner's responsibility to ensure that the vessel can meet the draught restrictions. If the ship is fixed to a range of discharge ports, the responsibility remains with the charterers to ensure that the vessel is safe to enter the port(s) with its draught and that a safe berth is to be nominated.

The charterers may require further information, such as the height from the waterline to the top of the hatch coaming in fully ballasted condition. This is to ensure that the vessel can remain beneath the shore load/discharge facility during the entire cargo operation.

**Bar draught:** where a river meets the sea, the velocity of the river water will reduce. Silt in suspension will fall out and a bar will be formed. Ships loading upriver will load to a draught at which they are able to pass safely over the bar. In some areas of the world, the ship may be able to top off in other ports with sufficient depth prior to making its deepsea passage. Examples include the Martin Garcia Bar where ships load to a bar draught up the River Parana, topping-off at Buenos Aires. Similarly, loading in Bangkok requires completion at Ko Sichang.

In some ports, there may be a combination of factors that the shipowner must consider. For example, in Buenaventura, Colombia, there is a wharf which is divided into imports and exports. The depth of water at low tide is 8m and consequently charterers of the ship and receivers of the cargo always need the vessel to agree to the term 'not always afloat but safely aground' abbreviated as NAABSA. For additional protection, the shipowner may add the words 'where it is customary for vessels of similar size to lie aground'. An additional problem at Buenaventura is the bar at the entrance to the port can only be crossed by ships with a maximum draught of 9m and sufficient water is only available from one hour before to one hour after high water.

## 5.10 PHYSICAL RESTRICTIONS TO PORT ENTRY

In addition to draught, further physical restrictions to port entry include:

- weather conditions;
- ice, which will be discussed later in this section;
- swell;
- war zones;
- piracy.

Where ship size has increased beyond the physical capability of the original port, if an economic business case is made, the port authority will develop capability downstream or in a new location. Over time, the focus of shipping in London has moved 20 miles downstream from London Pool to London Gateway, a new container port and logistics centre on the north bank of the river Thames. The new development is capable of handling container ships of up to 18,000 teu allowing the economies of scale to be exploited.

## 5.11 WATERWAYS

There are several important man-made waterways available to the international shipping community including the St Lawrence Seaway, the Panama Canal and the Suez Canal. Whilst the waterways were sufficiently large at the time of building, increase of ship size can make the waterways obsolete or restrictive to modern ships.

### St Lawrence Seaway

The St Lawrence Seaway is a series of canals linking the North American Great Lakes to the Gulf of St Lawrence and the Atlantic Ocean. Whilst the lakes are deep, when the canals were built, a decision had to be taken on the dimensions of the canal locks. The building of 15 locks which raise ships from sea level to Lake Ontario and Lake Erie, 150m above sea level, was a large undertaking. An agreement between the ship's requirements and civil engineering constraints resulted in a limitation of ship size to a maximum length of 225m, a maximum beam of 24m and a fresh water maximum draught of 8.1m.

Physical limitations restrict the largest ships that the St. Lawrence Seaway can accept to 30,000 deadweight. The ships can load 18,000 tonnes of cargo on the Seaway draught of 8.1m. Outward bound a ship will top off at Montreal. Ships operating in the Seaway have special equipment including additional fairleads for mooring lines, onboard sewage systems and extra lighting.

Despite the restrictions of size and the almost complete shutdown of the Great Lakes during three of the northern hemisphere winter months due to ice, the St. Lawrence Seaway is a valuable link to the grain and industrial heartlands of the USA and Canada.

### The Panama Canal

The Panama Canal, which opened in 1914 is a 48 mile long canal which links the Atlantic and the Pacific Oceans, saving 8,000 miles on the shortest sea distance between New York and San Francisco. The Panama Canal has a series of locks which lift ships across the Isthmus of Panama. The canal is presently being widened, deepened and new locks built to allow larger ships to transit.

The locks in the present canal can accept ships up to 274.3m long with a maximum breadth of 32.3m. The maximum draught depends on rainfall but a draught of about 12m fresh water is generally accommodated. Many shipowners consider the Panama Canal restrictions when ordering ships, and the description Panamax to describe a design incorporating the maximum dimensions the canal can accept is now firmly implanted in the shipping vocabulary.

The development of the Panama Canal, planned for completion in 2016, will create a further classification of ship size, the new Panamax. The new Panamax ship, will be a ship having the following maximum dimensions; a length of 427m, a maximum breadth of 55m and a draught up to 15m. Container ships with a capacity of 15,000 teu will be able to use the canal. The development when complete will have cost in excess of $5.5 billion.

### The Suez Canal

The Suez Canal was completed in 1869 and links the Mediterranean to the Red Sea. The canal provides an important route from Europe to the Middle East and Asia, with savings of almost 5,000 miles over the shortest sea route. The canal has a length of 86 miles and was cut through an isthmus of land and shallow lakes. It is a sea level canal and has no locks. Because it has no locks, the dimensions of the Suez Canal have developed as the size of ships has increased.

At present, the limiting dimensions for ships transiting the Suez Canal are a draught of 20.1m and air draught of 68m. The maximum length of a ship transiting the Suez Canal is unlimited. The Suez Canal Authority produces a table of maximum width which is related to draught. The deadweight of a Suezmax tanker is between 120,000 dwt and 200,000 dwt and will have a 50m beam. Tankers in ballast as large as 370,000 dwt can be accommodated in the Suez Canal. There are plans for further development of the Suez Canal.

## 5.12 POLITICAL RESTRICTIONS

Physical restrictions and climate are not the only constraints on where a ship may trade. For example, a ship on time charter shall not be required without the consent of its owners to enter into a port or zone which is involved in a state of war or where the ship's cargo or crew might expect to be subject to arrest. Trade between certain ports and countries maybe restricted due to a political boycott or sanctions. Problems in this respect include countries such as Israel that is blacklisted by some Arab countries, and vessels that are known to have traded to Israeli ports maybe banned from entering the ports of certain Arab countries. Similarly, owners and operators of ships that have called at Cyprus ports under Turkish control can expect to be prevented from calling at Greek Cypriot ports as a result of government policy.

## 5.13 CHOKE POINTS

Choke points are narrow channels along widely-used global routes which can restrict the movement of large ships and can be of political concern regarding security. Recognised choke points include the Hormuz Strait, the Malacca Strait, the Bab el-Mandeb Strait into the Red Sea, the Skagerrak and Kattegat, into the Baltic Sea and the Dardenelles leading into the Black Sea.

## 5.14 IMPACT OF UNION DISPUTES

If there is a dispute about the terms of a crew contract of employment, the ITF (International Transport Workers' Federation) can black a ship. The ITF tends to concentrate its efforts in certain areas of the world where shore labour such as stevedores or tug crews will support seafarers in dispute and possibly prevent ships from entering ports or from sailing.

The working of ports can be influenced by strikes or lock-outs which occur when port workers are in dispute with employers. The result can be the effective closure of the port requiring alternative arrangements influencing the ship's schedule to be made.

Political exclusions will be encountered in time charter parties where the owner does not want to risk its ship being blacked. The shipowner will seek to exclude places where there is political risk from the list of ports or countries to which the ship may be traded by the time charterer. Voyage charter parties carry clauses relating to strikes and lock-outs as well aspolitically-motivated blockades and warlike actions.

## 5.15 NATURAL PHENOMENA

The operation of a ship is influenced by natural phenomena, including tides, ocean currents, ice and weather.

### Tides

Tides have an effect on merchant shipping. The vertical rise and fall of tide will impact on the depth of water and the maximum draught a ship can be loaded to in order to arrive safely at a port. The tide will also influence the length of time that a ship will be able to stay in a port. The length of time will determine whether the cargo can be discharged and the ship always remains afloat. In some ports it may not be possible for the ship to remain always afloat and the term 'Not always afloat but safely aground' (NAABSA), may need to be negotiated.

Information regarding times and heights of high and low water are found in tide tables. Tidal streams will influence the time a ship will need to make good a distance between two places. A tidal stream atlas will provide details of the strength and direction of tidal streams. Tides are caused by the gravitational attraction of the sun and the moon on the earth. While the moon is smaller than the sun, its closeness to the earth means that it has over twice the tidal effect of the sun.

The height and times of high and low water differ each day depending on the position of the sun in relation to the moon. When the sun and moon are in conjunction or opposition, the highest tides occur. They are known as the spring tides. At times of half moon, the two more equal gravitational pulls cancel out to give neap tides.

## Weather and navigation

A merchant ship is exposed to the weather which can be defined as the state of the atmosphere at a particular place and time. Weather is described by pressure, pressure change, temperature, cloud, precipitation, wind direction and force and sunshine. Weather is studied by meteorologists and climatologists. Ships' officers have supported the meteorologists in their understanding of how the weather works, by providing observations of the weather since the mid-nineteenth century.

Various practical books help provide information about meteorology at sea, including *Meteorology for Mariners* and the *Mariners' Handbook.* While there is great value in understanding the general circulation of the atmosphere, including trade winds, intertropical convergence zones, and middle latitude depressions, the following section will consider four areas related to global weather which impact on navigation, namely, depressions and tropical storms, monsoons, ice and ocean currents.

## Depressions and tropical storms

Depressions and tropical storms are regions of low atmospheric pressure around which winds circulate in an anticlockwise direction in the northern hemisphere and clockwise in the southern hemisphere.

A depression occurs in the temperate region at the boundary between two air masses, usually cold polar air and warm subtropical air. A small disturbance occurring at the frontal boundary will trigger the development of a depression. The path of a depression is east or north-east in the northern hemisphere, and east or south-east in the southern hemisphere. Depressions and their associated warm, cold and occluded fronts are large-scale physical events and usually occur in a family of up to five successive events. Wind speeds in excess of 64 knots can be experienced in a deep depression.

A tropical storm is a more violent phenomena covering a smaller area on the earth's surface. Tropical storms are experienced at latitudes 20 degrees north or south of the equator on the east coastlines of the Pacific, Atlantic and Indian oceans. The characteristic path of a tropical storm is westwards, recurving to the north in the northern hemisphere and to the south in the southern hemisphere. Within the storm area, winds in excess of 135 knots can be experienced. In addition to the wind, torrential rain, high seas and tidal surges are experienced within a tropical storm. There is a great risk to ships and port infrastructure and severe damage can be caused.

Tropical storms are known as cyclones in the Indian Ocean, hurricanes in the North Atlantic, North East Pacific, west and north-west coasts of Australia, and New Zealand and typhoons in the north-west Pacific, including the China Sea. Some tropical storms have local names, such as Willy Willies in Australia. The greatest period of activity of tropical storms occurs between July and October in the northern hemisphere and between December and March in the southern hemisphere.

## Monsoons

The term monsoon comes from the Arabic word *mausim* meaning season. The monsoon is caused by the relative change of pressure over land compared to the oceans and is created by the heating and cooling of the land mass. The most important monsoon regions at sea are the north Indian Ocean and China Seas in the northern hemisphere, and the north and north-west Australian waters in the southern hemisphere.

In the northern hemisphere summer a deep low pressure region occurs over the Asian continent creating an anticlockwise air circulation which results in winds of a south-westerly direction. The South-West Monsoon of the north Indian Ocean lasts from May until September and is characterised by strong and humid south-westerly winds, giving a significant amount of cloud and rain on windward coasts.

In the northern hemisphere winter, a high pressure region occurs over the Asian land mass creating a clockwise air circulation which results in winds from a north-east direction. The North-East Monsoon of the north Indian Ocean lasts from November to March and is characterised by moderate and dry north easterly winds with clear skies.

Regular seasonal changes of limited scale in other parts of the world are known as monsoons.

## Roaring Forties

In the southern hemisphere, between latitudes 40°S and 60°S the oceanic winds are not inhibited by land and consequently have unrestricted movement around the globe. The winds generated in the region are very strong and regular and are known as the Roaring Forties. The consistency of the winds creates a large ocean swell.

## Beaufort scale

The Beaufort scale is a numerical scale devised by Admiral Sir Francis Beaufort at the beginning of the nineteenth century to differentiate between various wind strengths. The number 0 on the Beaufort Scale represents calm, the air being practically motionless, whilst the number 12 represents a surface wind speed exceeding 64 knots and above. Between the two extremes, the

**The Beaufort scale**

numbers indicate intervening wind speeds. The Beaufort wind scale has been internationally agreed. Deepsea, the force of wind is referred by photographic comparison with the state of the sea. Force 0 represents a sea like a mirror with Force 12 being described as 'the air filled with foam and spray; sea completely white with driving spray; visibility severely affected'.

Within the terms of a time charter, the performance speed of the ship is related to a number on the Beaufort scale, usually Force 3 or 4. The object is that the vessel should perform at the prescribed speed with prevailing winds up to a maximum wind speed of Force 3 or 4. Should the ship not perform as stated, the charterers may make a speed claim against the shipowners for non-performance.

Another scale used for reporting conditions at sea, and sometimes used for vessel performance descriptions, is the Douglas Sea State Scale, also called the International Sea and Swell Scale. It was devised to estimate the roughness of the sea for navigational purposes. The scale has two codes; one is used for estimating the sea state and the other for describing the swell.

## Ocean currents

Ocean currents may be divided into the following types:

- those caused by the wind;
- those due to distribution of water masses of varying temperature, salinity and density;
- tidal currents.

Currents flow at all depths in all the oceans. Mariners and shipbrokers are interested in surface currents and the effect they have on the passage of a ship. The main cause of currents in the ocean is the direction of wind blowing on the sea surface.

Warm currents flowing from the tropics, such as the Gulf Stream, ensure a temperate climate for the British Isles and keep ports as far north as Narvik in Norway ice-free all the year round. Conversely, currents from the poles such as the Kamchatka current sweeping down to north of Japan can result in severe winters on Hokkaido even though it is several degrees of latitude further south than England.

## Sea fog

Sea fog, sometimes known as advection fog, occurs where warm moist winds blow over cold currents. The temperature of the air is cooled causing condensation creating fine water droplets producing fog. The principal areas where sea fog is experienced include the Grand Banks, off the coast of Newfoundland, where the warm North Atlantic Drift meets the cold Labrador current and in the north-west Pacific Ocean, where the warm north Pacific current meets the cold Kamchatka current. In both locations the maximum frequency of fog occurs during May to September, the northern hemisphere summer. Other areas where sea fog is experienced include the western seaboards of the continents lying within the Trade Wind Belts, for example, off the coasts of California, Peru, Chile, Namibia and Morocco. More locally, sea fog can be experienced in the Bering Strait, the Baltic Sea, Hudson Bay and in the south-west approaches to the English Channel.

There are other types of fog which affect shipping, namely frontal fog, Arctic sea smoke and radiation fog.

## Icebergs

Cold currents from the polar regions will also carry icebergs into the shipping lanes. This is particularly the case in the north-west Atlantic where icebergs calve from the glaciers of Greenland and are carried south on the Labrador current. Icebergs eventually melt when they meet the warmer seas. Icebergs can be found south of 48° North with the greatest number being seen between April and June. Icebergs represent a major navigational hazard to shipping with the longest iceberg measured south of Newfoundland being more than 500 m. The United States Ice Patrol, funded by international contribution, maintains observations and provides warnings to ships operating on the east coast of America and Canada.

In the Antarctic, icebergs are formed by breaking away from the Antarctic landmass. They are a hazard to the relatively few numbers of ships which operate in the Antarctic Ocean.

## Ice

In addition to the icebergs described in the above, ice can have an impact on the movement of ships. Certain ports freeze over for varying periods of time during winter. It is important to be aware of where ice conditions are found and the time of year the condition is prevalent.

Apart from Arctic/Antarctic regions, the main areas where ice affects shipping are;

- the Baltic Sea between 1 November and 31 March, impacting on the ports of St. Petersburg, Helsinki, Luleå, and Stockholm;

- the St. Lawrence River between 31 December and 31 March impacting on the ports of Montreal, Baie Comeau, and Port Cartie;

- the St. Lawrence Seaway between 15 December and 1 April (the opening and closing dates for vessels transiting the seaway vary from year to year depending upon the severity of the winter). In order to avoid vessels being trapped in the Great Lakes, the St Lawrence Seaway Authority publishes the proposed closing date in advance. Ships may be allowed to pass through the seaway after the official closing date, subject to weather conditions.

In addition to the areas referred to above, ice conditions are prevalent in Albany, situated on the Hudson River, NY. The port of Churchill situated on the west coast of the remote Hudson Bay is only open for navigation between the end of July and October.

Ice conditions also affect the west coast of British Columbia, the east coast of Russia, northern China, North Korea and the Black Sea ports of Russia and Romania between October and May

The term 'first open water' (FOW) means the first date when a ship can enter an area of ice in relative safety. Additional insurance premiums still have to be paid over and above normal rates.

The icebreaker is a specialist ship that has been designed to keep ice-restricted ports open during the winter, especially in the Baltic Sea and the Gulf of St. Lawrence. During severe winter conditions, the icebreaker may not be totally successful in maintaining ice-free channels. Finland and Russia lead the world in the development of icebreakers, some of which have nuclear power plants to provide propulsion.

Reports and forecasts concerning ice conditions in the northern hemisphere are produced every winter by BIMCO, covering NW Europe and Scandinavia. The Canadian government provides reports and forecast for its own waters.

The development of the North-West Passage and Northern Sea Route across the Arctic Sea for use by merchant ships has created interest in ice movement, ice navigation and the operation of ships in ice. It is anticipated that further development will occur in future years due to climate change. Using the North-West Passage and Northern Route will reduce the physical distance from Asia to northern Europe and North America, and provide access to Russia's northern ports and opportunities for the exploitation of the natural resources of the Arctic Sea.

Merchants whose usual ports and routes are closed by ice will need to use alternative means of transport and use ice-free ports. For example, Narvik can be used as an alternative to the northern Baltic ports, or the Atlantic seaboard ports of Canada can be an alternative to the northern Canadian ports.

Severe weather conditions do not merely interfere with safe navigation. Cargo-handling operations in ports and on interior transport routes may also face difficulties. In severe cold, for example, steel becomes more brittle and machinery can fail as a result. Diesel oil becomes waxy or freezes, and, of course, human beings cannot function properly for long in extremes of temperature. Monsoon rain is bound to disrupt cargo handling and may well cause delays to inland transport. Tropical storms can similarly wreak havoc with damage to port installations, warehouses, road and rail transport as well as ships in port.

## 5.16 WEATHER ROUTEING

Today's systems of weather reporting and forecasting have enabled specialist companies to offer a service to ships' masters. On contracting with a weather routeing company, the master is given information about the weather likely to prevail on the voyage with advice on the course to take to avoid the worst conditions. During the voyage, the ship keeps in touch with the routeing service both to report on the weather the ship is actually experiencing and to receive amendments to the suggested route as a result of the updated forecast. The service makes for safer and quicker passages but the data recorded by the routeing company can provide expert evidence when a dispute arises about the effect of weather on a voyage.

Satellite communication systems now enable ships to receive up-to-the-minute weather information including forecasts, charts and satellite images allowing the ship's command to exercise their responsibilities for selection of the route as an alternative to the use of a weather routing company. Despite the technical sophistication which can be employed, ships are still being lost without trace, presumably due to the stress of weather.

The insurance world also takes account of the increased risks caused by climatic conditions and requires shipowners to pay increased premiums if they intend to trade outside the International Navigating Conditions.

## 5.17 SALINITY OF THE OCEANS

The oceans cover 71% of the area of the earth's surface. All the world's oceans are saline, that is, composed of salt water. The concentration of salt, which affects the density of the water, is not uniform, the variation being caused by water evaporation rates, supplies of fresh water and changes due to mixing and circulation.

The highest salinity is found in the tropics due to the high evaporation although at the equator, it is lower due to heavy rain and lower evaporation. Towards the poles, melting ice supplies fresh water and therefore causes lower salinity levels.

## 5.18 NAVIGATIONAL SEASONAL ZONES

Climatic and weather conditions affect every ship. In the nineteenth century there was concern in the UK about the number of ships which were lost at sea. The reason for loss was the limited reserve buoyancy associated with the deep draughts at which they sailed. As a result of the campaigning of the social reformer Samuel Plimsoll, a system of marking the position of the minimum freeboard, the distance from the water line to the main deck on all British ships was introduced. In the early 1930s a refinement of this system became an international convention, known as the Load Line Regulations. The Plimsoll Mark took into account the difference in density between fresh water and salt water.

The **Load Line Regulations** prescribe zones of the world where severe weather is more prevalent and, for safety reasons where it is required, that a ship has greater freeboard, and increased reserve buoyancy. Some loadline zones are permanent whilst others are seasonal.

From a commercial consideration, the depth to which a ship is allowed to load determines the weight of cargo it can carry, which in turn affects the amount of freight it can earn. It is important that this factor is taken into account when calculating voyage estimates. During a voyage, a ship may cross from one loadline zone to another more than once. Its draught must not exceed the maximum limits for each zone. This is further complicated by the changing seasonal limits such that the time of crossing zones needs to be considered when determining the amount of cargo to be loaded.

Chapter 6

# Chartering, markets and practice

*In the United Kingdom, shipping accounts for about 2% of the GDP – more than restaurants, takeaway food, and civil engineering combined*

## 6.1 INTRODUCTION

The Institute of Chartered Shipbrokers recognises six disciplines involved in the shipping business: dry cargo chartering, tanker chartering, sale and purchase, ship management, port agency and the liner trades. There are interrelationships between the disciplines.

## 6.2 THE MERCHANT

A merchant is defined as *'someone who sells and buys goods'*. For each merchant who sells goods, there will be a merchant who buys goods. Price and arrangements for transferring the goods are agreed between the seller and the buyer. Transfer arrangements cover finance, insurance, customs clearance and transport. The amount of goods to be carried, the mode frequency and regularity of the merchant's transport needs vary. The shipping business has evolved to support the merchants, whether sellers or buyers, by providing an economical means of transport using ships.

The level of demand for shipping depends on the amount of cargo being moved. The demand for shipping is secondary to the demand created by merchants. The demand for shipping is known as a derived demand. Despite the world recession, which in 2009 saw a 370 million tonne reduction of goods moved by ships, the period between 2000 and 2013 saw a doubling of goods carried by ships. Matching the supply side of shipping to the demands of the merchant is difficult. If, for example, merchants reduce their level of business, the demand for ships and shipping services will reduce. An oversupply of shipping capacity will occur and transport costs (known as freight) will fall. The supply of ships cannot be quickly changed. Market adjustments on the supply side are slow as ships take time to build. Once built, they will have a life expectancy, depending on type, of between 25 and 40 years. Changes in the derived demand and supply of ship capacity are interactive and, in a free market economy, determine the value of freight.

The merchant will arrange for his/her goods to be transported by sea either using a liner shipping service or by arranging space associated with the tramp ship operator. Liner shipping provides a regular scheduled service at a tariff published in advance, with evidence of the contract of carriage being the bill of lading. Tramp shipping is mainly concerned with the movement of dry and liquid bulk cargoes. It is undertaken under free market conditions with a charter party being used as a contract between a shipowner and charterer.

## 6.3 THE BROKER

The broker is a person who acts as a negotiator between two parties, the shipowner and the charterer. He/she will act on behalf of one of the parties. There are three types of brokers:

- brokers who are staff members of the charterer's or shipowner's own business;
- brokers employed by companies who provide exclusive services to a principal;
- a competitive broker.

The broker who is a staff member of a major commodity house or shipowner will work within the organisation's own chartering department. He/she will provide the broking skills required to ensure that the company's needs are met. Chartering departments of major commodity houses or shipowners are located in the world's maritime centres such as London, New York, Piraeus, Hong Kong and Singapore.

An exclusive broker is a broker who is selected by a charterer or shipowner to look after all their business. An exclusive broker may have several clients. The exclusive broker will acquire a wide range of market intelligence allowing independent advice to be given to a principal, without conflict of interest.

In the last century, much of the world's shipping business was conducted by shipbrokers face-to-face on the floor of the Baltic Exchange, London

The third type of broking arrangement is the competitive broker. Some principals are confident of their own ability to assess the market and, instead of requiring advice from brokers, they need speed to 'fix' a ship or cargo. To achieve speed, the principal will place their business on the market through several brokers who are in competition with each other. The advantage of the system of having competitive brokers is the ability to cover the market in the shortest possible time. The disadvantage is human nature. Even the most ethical broker is likely to shy away from advising the principal to hold off while the market is moving in the principal's favour, recognising that a competitor may take on that business.

In addition to providing specialist ship brokers, the larger broking houses will provide other services to their clients including derivative products, financial services and research concerning the global shipping sector.

The work of the broker is to negotiate the details of an agreement between a shipowner and charterer which are embedded into a contract, known as the charter party.

## 6.4 THE CHARTERING MARKET

A charter party is a contract established between two parties, the shipowner and the charterer, for the use of a ship. The charter party is negotiated in a free market and is subject only to the laws of supply and demand associated with the current state of the market and the bargaining strengths of the two parties. The terms (clauses) in a charter party are free from statutory interference.

It is impractical to develop individual contracts for each transaction. In practice, the shipowner and charterer adopt a standard form of charter party that has been developed for a particular trade. The charter rate and any changes in the terms established in the standard form will be agreed during negotiation between the two parties. The amendments will ensure that the contract is acceptable to both parties.

## The dry cargo chartering market

The dry cargo market is concerned with the carriage of bulk raw materials, such as iron ore, grain and coal. Dry cargo chartering takes place in many cities throughout the world, with London holding a dominant position. London's position is due to its history and importantly, its geographical position which provides brokers and traders in London with opportunity to do business with Asia in the morning and with America in the afternoon.

The steady development in communication systems over recent years has meant that chartering is no longer carried out face-to-face through institutions such as the Baltic Exchange in London. Traditionally, brokers and traders would meet daily on the floor of the Baltic Exchange to do business. Intelligence which was once gathered by brokers on the floor is now reported through networked computer systems, internet-based information pages and from telephone conversations between brokers. Information networks are an important requirement within the shipbroking community.

Some shipbroking practitioners regret the disappearance of face-to-face contact as it reinforced the sense of a business community. Even though the role of the Baltic Exchange has changed and its position as a marketplace is no longer pre-eminent, its code of ethics, represented by its motto Our Word, Our Bond, has unsurpassed importance in today's shipping business. The code of ethics serves as a guarantee of high standards of commercial behaviour.

## The tanker chartering market

The tanker market is a specialist sector within the chartering business with its activities separating it from the dry cargo market. Tanker chartering subdivides into separate specialisms including crude oil, petroleum products, chemicals and liquefied gas. The tanker broker requires good negotiation skills, team-working abilities and market knowledge, including the availability of tankers which are available (open) for charter and cargoes coming into the market so that the right tankers can be placed before potential charterers. The tanker market is dominated by the oil majors including Shell, BP, ExxonMobil, Chevron and Total, by oil traders and by state-owned oil companies such as Saudi Aramco. At one time, the oil majors owned large fleets supplemented by many ships on long-term time charter. The recent trend has been for oil majors to reduce their owned fleets and depend on chartering ships from the independent tanker owners. Accommodating to new trends, the oil majors have developed their own chartering departments. Within the oil majors it is usual for only one broker to be involved between the owner and the charterer. Specialist shipbrokers have developed their own services.

The movement of **crude oil** has changed in recent years, affected by market globalisation and structural changes in trading patterns. Factors which drive demand for crude oil are economic growth and industrial production, environmental policies and conflicts between nations. Factors driving the supply of tankers include fleet capacity, the price and availability of new tankers and service structures. The general public tends to be made aware of the regular movement of crude oil only when there is potential disruption to supply or there is a crude oil tanker casualty. The crude oil market has seen the building of the world's largest ships, the ultra-large crude carriers (ULCCs). Growth in ship size has been halted for several reasons including the geographical limitation of tanker operations due to draught restriction, structural issues associated with shipbuilding, the impact of past recessions and the size of cargo parcel demanded. While there is an increase in ship size in other sectors of the shipping industry, the largest commercial trading ships afloat are the crude oil tankers represented by the 440,000 dwt Tanker International (TI) Class ULCCs.

One of the two largest tankers currently trading is *TI Europe*

The movement of **petroleum products** represents a separate tanker market. Crude oil, when refined, produces products ranging from petroleum gases, gasoline (petrol), jet fuel, diesel, heating oil and heavy fuel oils. The products are categorised as clean or dirty. Clean products include petrol and diesel and require particular care in handling to reduce the risk of contamination. Dirty products include heavy fuel oils which may need to be heated prior to pumping. Oil-consuming countries have traditionally moved crude oil from areas of production to refineries close to the market for economic and security reasons. The structure of the refining sector is changing. There is a development of export–orientated mega refineries, many situated close to areas of production. It is expected that the present day set up of regional refineries will reduce in number and product tankers will be required to link the producers of petroleum products and consumers. Seaborne trade in the sector has increased continuously over the last two decades. Aframax product tankers, of between 90,000 dwt and 120,000 dwt, provide the capacity and take advantage of economies of scale and flexibility in operation.

**Chemical and other products.** The fixing of chemical tankers is undertaken by specialist shipbrokers. Chemicals are among the most sophisticated by-products of the oil refining process. They involve a wide variety of substances including solvents, sulphuric acid, liquid ammonia and feedstock for manufacturing plastics. Chemical products can be volatile and highly toxic. In addition to carrying chemicals, chemical tankers are used to carry animal and vegetable oils. The chemical tanker is a complex ship with up to 40 cargo tanks of varying size and associated separate pipelines and pumping systems. One thing all chemical cargoes have in common is the need for absolute cleanliness of the containment system as chemicals and oils will be used without further refining. A cargo which is not up to specification, that is, 'off spec' is of limited value to a buyer. The majority of the world's fleet of 3,700 chemical carriers are of the handysize, that is, having a capacity of between 10,000 dwt and 60,000 dwt.

**Liquefied petroleum gas (LPG) and liquefied natural gas (LNG).** The most highly specialised tankers presently in use are those constructed for the carriage of liquefied natural gas (LNG) or liquefied petroleum gas (LPG). The sophistication of the tanker is concerned with its cargo containment system, pipelines and pumping arrangements which allow gas to be carried in a liquid form during transport. Initially, the LNG tanker was built for bespoke trade routes, but a spot market now exists. Presently (2015), the market for the LNG tanker is weak as slowing demand is clashing with rising output. Between 2015 and 2020 Australia's export capacity of LNG is expected to triple, putting it ahead of Qatar, the world's leading LNG exporting nation.

## 6.5 CHARTER PARTIES

A charter party is a contract established between a shipowner and a charterer for the use of the ship. There are three basic forms of charter party, namely:

- voyage charter party;
- time charter party;
- demise charter party (sometimes known as the bareboat charter).

The charter party contains written terms of agreement, known as clauses, between the shipowner and the charterer. A charter party is often of a standard form, sometimes with boxed layout allowing key information to be inserted in a logical and prescribed format. The clauses incorporated into a charter party state the rights, liabilities and obligations of the shipowner and the charterer. The clauses are separated from the boxed layout. Additional clauses and amendments to standard clauses can be agreed between the shipowner and the charterer. Standard charter parties have been established for different trades and different cargoes and are identified by specific code names. Charter parties are regularly revised and, when negotiating a fixture, the shipowner and charterer must work from the same edition.

Historically, most standard forms of charter party were developed by charterers who were also merchants. The charterer as a merchant needed a charter party to complement the contract of sale of the commodity. Charterers are static and are normally in a stronger position than an individual shipowner to establish the terms and conditions of the charter party. They found it possible to co-operate with other charterers, including competitors, to devise terms for the carriage of specific commodities to their advantage. In some trades, individual charterers have achieved a position of virtual monopoly.

Present day merchants do not have the power they once had. National bodies, such as the UK's Chamber of Shipping, and international organisations, including the Baltic and International Maritime Council (BIMCO), form rallying points for shipowners to fight the more unfair charterers' terms set out as clauses within a charter party. The result is greater mutual agreement between shipowners and charterers. In some cases, it is the shipowners in collaboration with BIMCO, which is renowned for its active and successful documentary committee, who have published standard form charter parties for a particular trade.

Modified charterers' clauses once accepted by shipowners, are adopted for general use as standard clauses. Despite best efforts, a standard clause will not suit everybody. Some of the convenience of having standard clauses is lost due to the need to make amendments and agree additional clauses to make the charter party fit the precise needs of the charterer or shipowner. In certain trades, the standard charter party form has become a framework on which to 'hang dozens of extra clauses'. But many printed clauses have stood the test of time with legal precedent ensuring that ambiguous wording is avoided.

# AMWELSH 93

Code Name: **"AMWELSH 93"**
**Recommended by**
**The Baltic and International Maritime Council (BIMCO)**
**The Federation of National Associations of**
**Ship Brokers and Agents (FONASBA)**

## AMERICANIZED WELSH COAL CHARTER©

*Issued by the Association of Ship Brokers and Agents (U.S.A), Inc.*

New York - 1953; Amended 1979; Revised 1993

THIS CHARTER PARTY, made and concluded in ..............................
this ............................ day of ............................ 19 ............................

Between ..............................

..............................

Owners of the ............................ (flag) Vessel ..............................
of ............................ built ............................ (year) at ............................ (where)
of ............................ tons of 1000 kilos total deadweight on summer freeboard, inclusive of bunkers, classed ............................ in ............................ and registered at ............................ under No ............................ The Vessel's length overall is ............................ and beam is ............................ The Vessel's fully laden draft on summer freeboard is ............................ now ............................ and

..............................

Charterers ..............................
of the city of ..............................

1. **Loading Port(s)/Discharging Port(s)**

That the said Vessel being tight, staunch and strong, and in every way fit for the voyage, shall, with all convenient speed, proceed to ..............................

..............................

............................ and there load, always afloat, and in the customary manner from the Charterers, in such safe berth as they shall direct, a full and complete cargo of coal ............................ tons of 2240 lbs/1000 kilos* ............................ % more or less in the Owners' option; and being so loaded, shall therefrom proceed, with all convenient speed, to ............................

............................ or so near thereunto as she can safely get, and there deliver her cargo, as ordered by the Charterers, where she can safely deliver it, always afloat, on having been paid freight at the rate of .. US $ per ton of 2240 lbs/1000 kilos* on bill of lading quantity.

**) Delete as appropriate*

2. **Freight Payment**

The FREIGHT shall be paid in ..............................

..............................

..............................

This is the first page of a typical charter party

## 6.6 FORMS OF CHARTER PARTY 1: THE VOYAGE CHARTER PARTY

There are many voyage charter forms. Some are specific to a particular trade. Like all charter parties, the voyage charter party is identified by a code which can relate specifically to a specific trade. Examples are shown below:

**AUSTWHEAT** Australian Wheat Board form voyage charter party

**GRAINVOY BIMCO** Grain voyage charter party

**NORGRAIN** North American Grain voyage charter party

**NUBALTWOOD** Baltic Timber trade voyage charter party

**OREVOY** Iron Ore voyage charter party

The GENCON voyage charter party is a general-purpose voyage charter party form intended for cargoes or trades for which no specific form exists. The GENCON voyage charter party is associated with a single voyage in which a shipowner agrees to load a specific quantity of a commodity cargo at port A and carry it to port B for agreed consideration known as the freight. As the GENCON voyage charter party is designed for non-specialised trades, both the shipowner and charterer may insist on certain additional clauses particular to their requirements being attached to the standard form. Shipowners and charterers are conservative and prefer to use a radically-amended GENCON charter party form than use the modern and more even-handed MULTIFORM charter published by the Federation of National Associations of Ship Brokers and Agents (FONASBA).

### GENCON 1994

The GENCON charter party form is the latest revision of a long series of GENCON charter parties dating back to the 1920s. GENCON consists of two parts. Part I, the front page, is in box format and requires specific information to be entered into each of the 26 individual boxes. The use of the box format helps ensure that salient details can be quickly seen. Numbers printed in each box refer to the clauses printed in Part II of the form. There are 19 Clauses in GENCON 1994. Cross-reference between Part I and Part II is made in the appropriate box with the abbreviation Cl and clause number following the box number and title. For example: 5. Vessel's name (Cl 1).

As a general rule, details inserted in the boxes of Part I are negotiable. Many will feature during negotiation when offers and counter offers are traded. Although the most fiercely contested area in negotiation is the level of freight, the dates and time allowed for cargo operation can also be crucial. Date and time impact on the profitability of the voyage for both shipowner and charterer.

In Part I of GENCON, boxes 1 to 12, refer to clause 1. Boxes 1 to 4 provide information about the shipbroker and the date and place where the fixture was made. Boxes 5, 6 and 7 require information about the name and address of the shipowner and charterer, and the name and basic details of the ship. Ship details required include gross tonnage, net tonnage and deadweight capacity.

Box 8 describes the geographical position of the ship relative to the charter and Box 9 states the date the ship will be 'expected ready to load'. Many factors can affect the ship's readiness to load and the term 'expected ready to load' is indicative of the ship's availability. But, if a shipowner states a date in Box 9 and takes on intervening business which causes the ship to miss the date, the shipowner will be guilty of misrepresentation. In extreme cases, misrepresentation can be grounds for the charterer to cancel the contract. The date when cancellation can be effected is shown in Box 21 entitled 'Cancelling date'.

Boxes 10, 11 and 12 address the loading and discharging ports and the type and quantity of cargo to be loaded. Clause 1 in Part II to which the details relate qualifies the port or place of loading and discharge by the phrase '… or so near thereto as she may safely get and lie always afloat'. Some loading or discharging berths, especially in tidal rivers, do not always have enough water alongside the berth for a ship. The berths are referred to as NAABSA berths '… not always afloat but safely aground'. If a ship is fixed for loading or discharging at a NAABSA berth, it must be specifically agreed in the charter party. If not, the shipowner has the right to refuse to put the ship there.

As far as the cargo is concerned, the charterers are expected to give full details of the cargo and, if they have fixed the ship for 'a full and complete cargo', they can expect the master and owners to demand sufficient cargo to bring the ship down to its loadline or to fill the cargo space. If the charterers fail to satisfy this request, they will be liable to pay dead freight on the shortfall as if it had been loaded.

Box 13 gives details of the freight payable, in amount per tonne ($/tonne) or a lump sum ($). It requests that the method of freight payment is stated; namely, prepaid freight or payment on delivery. Information regarding the currency used, method of payment, beneficiary and bank account are to be stated in Box 14. Options regarding payment of freight are stated in printed clause 4.

Details of responsibilities associated with the costs and risks of loading and discharging the cargo are covered in clause 5. The GENCON charter party envisages a situation where the shipper pays for the loading and the consignee for the discharging of the cargo. The term free in and out (FIO), recognises that the loading and discharging operations are free of expense to the shipowner.

There are some trades where it is customary for a shipowner to pay or contribute to the cost of loading and/or discharge. In such a case, when a GENCON 1994 form is used, a typed clause would have to replace clause 5 (a) which describes Costs and Risks. In the case of a ship having its own cargo handling gear, cranes or derricks, provision can be made to make use of it for loading or discharging cargo. Under clause 5 (b) Cargo Handling Gear, use of the ship's cargo handling equipment must be expressly agreed in advance and noted in Box 15. Clause (5c) recognises that shipowners expect charterers to be responsible for putting right any stevedore damage noted by the master during cargo handling operations.

Clause 6 referred to in Box 16, introduces laytime, a word that is exclusive to the world of chartering. Laytime refers to the time agreed by both parties for the loading or discharging of the cargo. Clause 6 may seem long, dealing with issues associated with the ship's readiness to load or discharge and the length of time required for the loading and discharging operation. Significant sections of maritime law are devoted to time-counting and disputes about the arrived ship. There are different ways in which laytime can be expressed including time (days, hours and minutes) or the tonnage to be loaded/discharged per day. Clause 6 covers separate laytime for loading and discharging, total laytime for loading and discharging and the commencement of laytime.

Disputes can also occur from a misunderstanding by the charterer and a shipowner about separate and total loading and discharging times, and the impact of bad weather. GENCON

Clause 6 has been refined over the years in the light of successive legal and commercial disputes but there is still scope for dispute. Boxes 17-19 require the name and place of business of the shipper and the identity of the charterer's agents at the loading and discharge port, all of relevance to the issue of laytime.

The compensation for exceeding the amount of time allowed for loading and discharging, is stated in Box 20, with details described in clause 7. The compensation is known as demurrage and is agreed during the charter party negotiations. As a ship only earns income when at sea, a shipowner will wish to minimise the time spent in loading and discharging the ship. If the charterer exceeds the agreed time, then the shipowner will expect compensation. A claim for demurrage may be made by the shipowner for every day or part of a day by which the agreed time is exceeded.

In some dry cargo trades, the converse may apply in which the charterer will earn a bonus if the load or discharge from the ship is in less time than agreed. The bonus is known as despatch and, if agreed, will be inserted as a typed clause in the GENCON form.

Clauses 5, 6 and 7 cover dispute-prone areas of a ship's time in port, namely loading and discharging, laytime and demurrage. Reference is made within the clauses to certain shipping words, the meanings of which are described below:

**Trimming:** The term trimming applies to bulk cargoes, such as grain, where the surface of the loaded cargo needs to be levelled out to make best use of the space available and to minimise the danger of the cargo shifting in the hold during the voyage.

**Dunnage:** Dunnage is timber or other material used to prevent contact between the cargo and the ship's hold. It allows drainage, ventilation and protection of the cargo as well as minimising movement.

**Tallying:** Tallying is the name given to the procedure of checking the number of packages as they are loaded on board or discharged from a ship.

**Stevedores unloading final cargo remnants**

**Stevedores:** Although technically the term stevedore refers to persons whose work involves the loading or discharge of the cargo on board a ship, it is often used to describe all labour involved with the loading or discharging operation.

**Agents:** The agents referred to in clause 6 (Boxes 18 and 19) are not the port agents appointed by the shipowner to look after the ship's interests, but are the charterer's agents who are responsible for co-ordinating the cargo operations at each end of the voyage. The appointment of port agents by the shipowner is dealt with in clause 14. The name of the port agent may be stated in a typed clause attached to the charter party.

The **Lien clause.** Clause 8 is designed to protect shipowners from non-payment of freight, demurrage and other such sums due to them. There is no reference to the clause in Part I.

Clause 9 concerns the cancelling date and is stated in Box 21. If the ship has not presented itself for loading by the cancelling date, the charterers have the option to cancel the charter party. Cancellation tends to be a last resort in most instances, as charterers are then faced with having to find another suitable vessel to carry the cargo. Similarly the shipowner will have to find other employment for the ship which may already be on its way to the expected loading port. Excessive delays may force the charterers to use this sanction.

**General Average** is covered by printed clause 12 and is referred to in Box 22. General average (GA) is the procedure where if a ship is involved in an extraordinary expenditure to avoid damage to the ship and her cargo, the cargo owners, as well as the shipowner, will contribute to that expenditure. The formal wording reads '.... preserving from peril the property involved in the common maritime venture'. General average has a long history and is covered by the York-Antwerp Rules. The York-Antwerp Rules lay down how the various parties' contributions will be calculated, a procedure known as Average Adjusting. All prudent merchants are careful to include general average in their insurance cover.

The parties responsible for paying taxes and dues on the vessel, cargo or freight are stated in clause 13. Taxes paid on freight are usually for the charterer's account, but if for the shipowner's account the fact must be stated in Box 23, Freight Tax.

**Brokerage commission** and to whom payable is stated in Box 24 with details covered in clause 15. The commission refers to that earned by the broker or brokers involved in the fixture and is their reward for bringing the negotiation between the shipowner and charterer to a satisfactory conclusion. The amount of brokerage involved is usually between 1.25% and 3.75% of the gross freight depending on whether one or more brokers are involved. Most charter parties, including GENCON, include brokerage on demurrage and dead freight. Dead freight is freight paid by the charterer of vessel for the contracted space, which is left partially unoccupied.

The remaining clauses in Part II, clause 11 and clauses 16-18 deal with eventualities which might be experienced during the voyage. Clause 11 covers collision between ships, clause 16, strikes and lockouts, clause 17, war risks, including hostilities and acts of piracy, and clause 18 is concerned with issues associated with ice at the port of loading or discharge.

The final printed clause, clause 19, concerns Law and Arbitration. It establishes the jurisdiction which will apply in the case of legal dispute or arbitration and is stated in Box 25 of Part I of the GENCON charter party form. This is an important consideration in international trading.

In summary, a voyage charter party form covers:

- date;
- names of the parties;
- name and description of the ship;
- loading port;
- nature and quantity of the cargo;
- discharge port; lay days/cancelling dates;
- rate of freight and manner of payment;
- loading/discharging costs;
- rates of loading and discharging (laytime);
- dispatch and demurrage rate;
- brokerage commissions.

Reading a fully copy of the GENCON voyage charter party is instructive and recommended.

### Consecutive voyages and contracts of affreightment (COA)

While a single voyage charter party is commonly used, many charterers will have more than one cargo to move. It may be convenient, particularly with an eye to fixing costs, for the contract between a charterer and shipowner to make a series of consecutive voyages. This procedure is helpful in trades where it is usual for the ship to make the passage to the loading port in ballast.

When the frequency of loading does not coincide with the consecutive voyages of a single ship, or in trades where returning in ballast is not normal, an alternative to consecutive voyages may be required. In such a situation, it is appropriate for the charterer and shipowner to agree parameters covering the frequency of loading, the range and size of ships available and the total quantity of the commodity to be moved within a given period. Under such arrangements the shipowner will have a degree of flexibility to maintain full employment of its ships and, if necessary, charter in other ships should they not have one of their own in the right position. The contract which is established is known as a contract of affreightment.

## 6.7 FORMS OF CHARTER PARTY 2: THE TIME CHARTER PARTY

Where the commodity is drawn from a number of different places and sold to several buyers in different locations, neither a voyage charter, consecutive voyage nor a contract of affreightment will give the charterer the flexibility required. This is especially the case if there are marked differences in the speed of loading or discharge at the different terminals involved. A resolution for the charterer is to move away from the contract of carriage based on a rate of freight per tonne of cargo carried and hire the ship on a contract based on time, known as a time charter.

Before the days of containerisation, the most prolific time charterers were the liner companies. Liner companies time chartered ships to supplement their fleets when demand in the general cargo market exceeded their own resources. BIMCO adopted the BALTIME charter party which proved to be popular. There are other time charter party forms including the New York Produce Exchange Form, known by the Code Name NYPE 93. NYPE 93 has been adopted by the documentary committee of BIMCO and the chartering and documentary committee of the Federation of National Associations of Shipbrokers and Agents (FONASBA). A joint working group from BIMCO, ASBA and the SMF are currently working on developing a modern NYPE Time Charter form.

Oil companies, for example, Shell, BP and Texaco produce individual time charters called BPTIME, SHELLTIME and TEXACOTIME.

**Oil companies own their own tankers, but always need to charter in extra tonnage**

The objective of a time charter is to transfer the commercial direction of the ship to the charterer while leaving the technical control, including employment of the ship's crew with its owners. The charterer decides where the ship will load and discharge and the time and expense of doing so. All the incidental expenses directly resulting from the commercial trading of the ship will be for the time charterer's account including port expenses. The biggest item of expenditure, after the hire payment, will be the cost of bunker fuel. One advantage of a time charter, unless excluded by a clause contained in the charter party, is that, if the charterer does not require the ship for any part of the period of hire, the ship can be sub-chartered to a third party on either a time or voyage charter basis. A charterer needing a ship for just one voyage but requiring the flexibility of a time charter will arrange a charter known as a trip time charter.

**Time charter party NYPE93:** Unlike GENCON, the NYPE93 charter party is of an open format. The wording of the NYPE 93 charter party covers the following key areas:

The names of the shipowner, charterer and the name of the ship will be stated. The details required of the ship under Description of the Vessel are more extensive than found in a voyage charter party. Of particular interest is detail of the ship's performance, including speed and fuel consumption. Wording states 'speed about...............knots, fully laden, in good weather conditions up to and including maximum Force ............on the Beaufort wind scale, on a consumption of about .....................long*/metric* tons of ..................'

Fuel consumption is of importance to the charterer as the cost of fuel is the largest item of expenditure after hire. Fuel consumption is a very important component of the agreement.

The duration of the time charter party is of importance and can be set out in terms of months or years. The time charter party will establish trading limits between safe ports.
Instead of the loading port stated in a voyage charter party, the time charter party will state the place of delivery along with the stipulation that the ship on delivery shall be tight, staunch and strong in every way.

While it is the intention that a time charter party will pass the commercial control of the ship and the risk of the voyage to the charterer, there are some dangerous or unpleasant commodities which the shipowner does not want his/her ship to carry. They will be noted under the Dangerous Cargo and Cargo Exclusion clauses. There may also be places which, for political reasons, the owner does not want the ship to visit and provision is made to prohibit these.

The responsibilities of the shipowner and the charterer will be clearly stated in the clauses Owners to Provide and Charterers to Provide. Essentially, the shipowners provide and pay for the capital and operating costs including crew and maintenance. The charterers provide and pay for voyage items including fuel, pilotage, and port charges.

Fuel, normally referred to as bunkers, is a major item of expenditure. Charterers pay for fuel on delivery of the ship and the shipowners will do so on redelivery under the clause Bunkers on Delivery and Bunkers on Redelivery. It is usual for the cost of fuel to be settled on the basis of current prices. In addition, the quality of fuel to be used by the charterer is agreed. Off specification fuel can cause serious damage to the main and auxiliary engines

The all-important clause, (10), Rate of Hire/Redelivery Areas and Notices, states the daily rate of hire (usually in US$) to be paid for the use of the ship by the charterer. The rate of hire is based on the ship's deadweight carrying capacity. There is a stipulation regarding the currency in which hire is to be paid and the time when hire payment is required, for example, semi-monthly in advance. To avoid recurring disputes on whether local time or GMT shall apply for the purpose of hire calculation or termination, Clause 10 solves this problem by providing that for this purpose the times of delivery/re-delivery or termination of charter shall be adjusted to GMT. If the payment of hire is not punctually made, the shipowner is given the right to withdraw the ship from the charterer's service. Shipowners have been known to take their ships away from the charterer, even if delay in payment is not caused by the charterer, in order to take advantage of an improved market elsewhere. A clause entitled Grace Period can be incorporated into the charter party to give the charterer some time to rectify a situation where delay in payment may occur.

The Hire Payment clause stipulates the time at which the charter commences. Time of hire is not the problem-prone area as it is with voyage charter parties, as the clause gives the charterer a limited time to take control of the ship. As with the voyage charter, there is a Laydays/Cancelling clause.

An important issue in a time charter is the suspension of hire payments for any time the vessel is not available to the charterer. Details are stated in the Off-Hire clause. The usual reason for a ship to go off-hire is a temporary technical break down. On a long time charter the ship may have to go off-hire in order to keep up-to-date with routine maintenance. The Off-Hire clause also concerns the consumption of bunker fuel during the period off-hire; '... all fuel used by the vessel while off hire shall be for the owners account'.

Other clauses in the NYPE93 charter party not mentioned above are interesting. Clause 8, entitled Performance of Voyages, describes the way in which the ship's master has to comply with the instructions of the charterer. 'The Master shall be conversant with the English language and (although appointed by the Owners) shall be under the orders and directions of the Charterers as regards employment and agency'.The ship's master has to balance the demands of the charterers without neglecting his/her primary responsibility to the shipowners regarding the safety of ship.

Further clauses within the NYPE93 charter party cover bills of lading, the appointment of a supercargo (cargo superintendent), provision of sailing orders and logs, general average, the payment of crew overtime, arbitration and brokers' commission.

A Rider of Suggested Additional Clauses, each which may or may not be incorporated into the NYPE93 charter party, are provided. Unless expressly agreed, they do not apply. Additional clauses include: the extension of cancelling clause, grace period, who pays for damage to cargo, what happens in the event of the outbreak of war, who conducts an on/off-hire survey, the responsibilities associated with damage committed by the stevedore's, and the charterer's privilege to fly its own house flag and paint the ship in its own colours and markings.

In summary, a time charter party form covers:

- date;
- names of the parties;
- ship's name and particulars;
- speed and fuel consumption;
- duration;
- places of delivery and redelivery;
- trading areas and limitations;
- rate of hire;
- laydays and cancelling;
- brokerage commissions.

Reading a fully copy of the NYPE93 charter party is instructive and recommended.

## 6.8 FORMS OF CHARTER PARTY 3: THE DEMISE CHARTER PARTY (BAREBOAT CHARTER PARTY)

A charterer may want a ship to be at its disposal for a long period of time, perhaps several years. The type of charter party which is arranged is called a demise charter party or bareboat charter party and the charterer is referred to as the disponent owner. The expression demise charter party is normally used because the word demise means transfer. A demise charter party transfers the complete operational role of the ship to the charterer. During the period of hire the demise charterer acts as if the ship is owned by them. It is quite usual for the demise charterer to change the ship's port of registry and flag for the period of the charter.

A demise charter party can be compared to a long-term lease of a house or office block. To all intents and purposes, the demise charterer acts as the owner and is seen as such by the outside world.

In many cases, a demise charter party can be used as an alternative way of financing a ship. The charterer may find it more convenient or beneficial to pay a monthly hire out of revenue than raise the capital to buy a ship.

## 6.9 TANKER CHARTER PARTIES

The tanker market uses single voyage and consecutive voyage charter parties as well as time charters and contracts of affreightment. The basic construction of a tanker charter party is similar as for dry cargo. While the broad areas of interest correspond with the charter party forms previously described, the details contained within a liquid cargo charter party differ. In some respects, the clauses are simpler, partly due to the fact that oil installations are almost invariably set well apart from port complexes so that readiness to load and time-counting clauses are far less complicated. Many charter parties have been compiled by the major oil companies, such as Shell, BP, Texaco and ExxonMobil, for their own use. Independent bodies such as the International Association of Independent Tanker Owners (INTERTANKO) and the Association of Shipbrokers and Agents (USA) Inc (ASBA) have developed standard charter party forms for others to use.

### Tanker voyage charter party

SHELLVOY 6 is the latest edition of Shell's tanker voyage charter party launched worldwide by Shell International Shipping and Trading Company Limited in 2005. SHELLVOY 6 consolidates the additional clauses and amendments used by Shell since the previous version of Shellvoy was published in 1987. It introduces some new provisions relevant to the current trading environment. The document, which is produced in open form, has three Parts:

- Part I concerns 15 lettered clauses (A-O) including description of the ship, position and readiness, load and discharge ports, cargo description and freight rate, described by Worldscale.

- Part II provides 56 numbered clauses covering the responsibilities and obligations of the shipowners and charterers including condition of the ship, cleanliness of the tanks, laytime, demurrage, heating of the cargo, bills of lading, war risks, drug and alcohol policy and arbitration.

- Part III covers geographic concerns, for example, the restriction of the ship not to transit the Great Barrier Reef Inner Passage, 'whether in ballast, en route to a loadport or laden' or, when in the United States of America, the ship 'will comply with all applicable United States Coast Guard (USCG) Regulations in effect'.

**Worldscale index:** A major difference between voyage charters for dry cargo and voyage charters for tankers is the way that freight is expressed. In dry cargo charter parties, freight is usually expressed in $/tonne of cargo carried. The oil industry uses a system known as Worldscale, referred to in clause G, Freight rate, of SHELLVOY 6. The Worldscale is described as 'an international freight index for tankers that provides a method of calculating the freight applicable for transporting oil by reference to a Standard Vessel engaged on a round trip voyage from one or several load ports to one or several discharge ports'.

The Worldscale organisation has calculated a nominal freight rate in US$/tonne for a standard tanker covering almost every conceivable voyage on which crude oil is carried. (Note: if a rate for a specific voyage has not been calculated, Worldscale will produce one.) The nominal freight rates are reviewed at regular intervals. Subscribers to the service can access the relevant rate at any time. Market levels of freight are expressed in terms of a percentage of the nominal freight rate. Worldscale 100 is the nominal freight rate for the specific voyage as calculated and issued by the Worldscale Association. Worldscale 150 means the freight on the voyage is 150% of the nominal freight rate, whereas Worldscale 50 means the freight achieved will be 50% of the nominal freight rate. By studying reported crude oil fixtures, it is straightforward to see how the crude oil freight market fluctuates and reacts to market forces.

**The Worldscale book, updated annually, is a popular way of calculating freight rates**

**Loading and Discharging:** Oil installations work 24 hours a day, 365 days a year. 72 hours is the total time allowed for loading or discharging because, regardless, tankers are equipped with pumps commensurate with their size. A loading and discharging clause in SHELLVOY 6 states that the cargo is loaded at the charterer's expense and risk to the ship's permanent hose connections, and is discharged to the ship's permanent hose connections at the shipowner's expense and risk.

**Demurrage:** Demurrage works in the same way in tanker charters as for dry cargo. The daily rate of demurrage as agreed following negotiations is stated in clause J of Part I of SHELLVOY 6 with a demurrage clause stated in Part II of the charter party.

## Tanker time charter party

SHELLTIME 4 is the latest edition of Shell's tanker voyage charter party. Initially issued in 1984, it was amended at the end of 2003. The charter party is produced in open format and comprises of 42 comprehensive and detailed clauses.

In addition, SHELLTIME 4 contains two appendices. Appendix A is the OCIMF Vessel Particulars Questionnaire. Appendix B is the Shell Safety and Environmental Monthly Reporting Template.

The OCIMF Vessel Particulars Questionnaire is a comprehensive 16 chapter listing of details concerning the tanker. It covers all aspects including operational history, certificates and documents carried on board, crew management, navigation equipment, safety equipment including inert gas systems, structural condition, pollution prevention arrangements, the cargo and ballast system including tank capacities, mooring and towing arrangements, the main propulsion system and structural condition.

The Monthly Reporting Template requires the ship to report any oil spill incident and any incident having potential for injury, damage or loss. It also requires a report on the ship's monthly consumption of fuel and diesel oil, and information on distance steamed. SHELLTIME 4 resides on BIMCO's online document system allowing it to be updated when required.

The quality standards required by Shell are emphasised in clause 1 of SHELLTIME 4 entitled Safety Management. The clause covers safety and environmental management systems and safe working procedures. The related clause 2 concerns Shipboard Personnel and their Duties and covers the number and quality of ship staff.

Reading a full copy of a tanker time and voyage charter party such as SHELLVOY 6 and SHELLTIME 4 is instructive and recommended.

## 6.10 BILLS OF LADING

A bill of lading is a document made out between the carrier and the merchant and which has three functions as follows:

- **receipt for the goods** the bill of lading provides evidence that the goods have been received by the carrier for shipment or received on board the ship. It gives certain details as to their condition on being received. If the goods are damaged on receipt, the bill of lading will be claused accordingly. If claused, the bill of lading will be regarded as a dirty bill of lading. Goods received undamaged will receive a clean bill of lading.

- **document of title** as a document of title, the carrier undertakes to deliver the goods against the surrender by a merchant of the original document. As a document of title, the bill of lading can be traded, and transfer of ownership of the goods described in the bill of lading can take place between the merchant named in the bill of lading to another. Trading of the cargo can occur while the ship is on passage. It is not unusual in certain trades for several transactions to take place between the loading port and discharging port.

- **evidence of a contract** between the shipper and carrier: the bill of lading is not a contract itself, but evidence that there is a verbal or written contract between the carrier and the merchant (exporter or importer).

The bill of lading is used in both the tramp and liner trades. It is of importance in international trade documentary procedures and is related to letters of credit. There are different forms of bills of lading available.

A long form bill of lading is typically used in the liner trades and incorporates an international convention which lays out the minimum terms and conditions concerning the carriage of goods. It also makes clear the carrier's obligations, exceptions from liability and the extent of the carrier's liability to the merchant. The merchant's responsibilities to the carrier are also set out as are the amounts recoverable from the carrier in cases of loss or damage. One of the following international conventions will be incorporated into the bill of lading: the Hague Rules, the Hague-Visby or Hamburg Rules. A new convention, the Rotterdam Rules established in 2009, is awaiting ratification by sufficient numbers of governments.

A short form bill of lading is used in conjunction with a charter party. It incorporates the 'terms and conditions, liberties and exceptions' of the charter party including the law and arbitration clause'. An example of a short form bill of lading is CONGENBILL 2007, published by BIMCO.

Bill of lading: CONGENBILL 2007 is a bill of lading designed to be used with charter parties. It is two pages in length.

Page 1 of CONGENBILL is in boxed form. It contains details under the following headings: a reference number, name and address of the shipper and consignee, the name of the ship, port of loading and port of discharge. Included is the shipper's description and statement of the gross weight of the goods and recognition that if goods are carried on deck they are carried at shipper's risk. Freight, payable as per charter party, and the amount of freight paid in advance are noted. Prior to the signatures of the master and agents a paragraph is provided which states: '[the cargo] shipped at the port of loading in apparent good order and condition on the vessel for carriage to the port of discharge or so near thereto as the vessel may safely get the goods. Weight measure, quality quantity condition, contents and value unknown'.

Page 2 of CONGENBILL lists the conditions of carriage and refers to the charter party. Clause 1 states that 'all terms and conditions. Liberties and exceptions of the charter party including the law and arbitration clauses and dispute resolution are incorporated'. Clause 2 is the General Paramount clause which applies the Hague or Hague-Visby Rules. Clause 3 is the General Average clause, which concerns where a general average is to be adjusted and settled. Clause 4 concerns the New Jason clause, used to protect owners against the possibility of US Lawsuits, and Clause 5, the Both to Blame Collisions Clause, designed to enable a carrier to preserve its defence in claims caused by collision between two ships.

In situations where a letter of credit is being used for the commercial transaction, the bill of lading along with the commercial invoice, packing list and insurance certificate will be provided to the seller's bank by the shipper which will be forwarded to the buyer against payment. Only clean bills of lading are normally accepted by the bank.

Reading a fully copy of the CONGENBILL 2007 bill of lading is instructive and recommended.

## 6.11 CONCLUSION

The role of the shipbroker in chartering is of great importance. The charter party is drawn up following negotiations and agreement. The shipbroker's focus will be on the successful completion of negotiations associated with the freight or hire and time of availability. Much of the detail established in the clauses of the charter party may not be immediate to the day-to-day activity of the broker. Information contained in this chapter is limited but provides an awareness of the complexities which are involved in fixing a ship. Reading a full copy of the time and voyage charter parties highlighted in the chapter is instructive and recommended.

Chapter 7

# Purchase, sale and ship management

*The world's first paper money was created in China over 1,400 years ago*

## 7.1 SHIP SALE AND PURCHASE

There are three distinct sectors of the sale and purchase market: new buildings, secondhand sales and demolition (scrapping).

New buildings provide opportunity for a shipowner to develop a fleet with ships built to the owner's specification. In 2013, about 1,800 new cargo-carrying ships of 140 million deadweight tons were built. However, the most active market is the sale and purchase of secondhand ships. It is rare for a ship to stay with the same owner from builder's yard to the demolition yard. A ship, depending on type, will have an active commercial life in excess of 20 years. In such a period, the requirements of a ship operator can change. Also, a depressed freight market can shorten a vessel's economic life as newer and more economical ships will be preferred by charterers. Demolition or scrapping takes tonnage out of the market. In 2013 more than 1,100 ships, accounting for 43 million deadweight tons, were scrapped.

Unlike the chartering markets, where the principals are clearly specialists in their respective fields of activity, any shipowner is at some time a buyer or a seller. Selling may be motivated by the need to dispose of ships made redundant by changing patterns of trade, or ships becoming obsolete in a particular owner's fleet and sold to make way for more modern additions, or simply as a way for the owner to make money through the buying and selling of the ship as assets.

## 7.2 NEW BUILDINGS

The purchase of a new ship is a complicated business. There are several stages which have to be considered before the ship is finally delivered to its owner.

Essential to a new build will be the contract between the shipyard and the prospective shipowner. The parties to the contract may agree to a contract based on a very general specification with clauses to take into consideration, variations of which come about as the detailed drawings are produced. As with charter parties, standard contract forms are available including the NEWBUILDCON adopted by BIMCO in 2007.

Often the builders produce models of the hull and try them out in testing tanks. After such tests, appreciable changes may be agreed. For example, the tank-test may prove that the ship will perform better if it is made longer than originally agreed. Improved performance could be a bonus for the buyer. If the ship's length is not critical, improved performance will enable extra cargo to be carried. The converse will be that the additional length of the ship may restrict its entry into some important ports.

In certain cases, where a shipowner employs their own naval architects, detailed drawings of the desired ship will be developed and then a number of different shipyards will be approached with a request to tender.

Most ships are built to a mainly bespoke design although some yards do offer standard designs. The trend towards a standard design philosophy was popular in the 1950s when shipowners were looking for a general-cargo ship to replace the World War Two Liberties. The SD14 (Standard Design 14 knot 14,000 tonner) built in the Sunderland yard of Austin & Pickersgill is an example of a standard design of that era. Today no standard designs carry a brand name but several yards have off-the-shelf designs for ships such as Panamax bulk carriers.

Among the advantages of using a standard design or accepting the design of a ship built for another owner, is a saving in the design cost element of the ship build. While naval architecture is a highly developed science, not all the problems of the forces of sea and weather can be simulated on the computer or tested in the tank. It is a combination of computer analysis, tank testing and experience which provide the present day ship designs.

Naval architects continue to develop ship structures of a size which takes advantage of the economies of scale, as seen in the development of iron ore carriers, mainline container ships and passenger vessels. Physical limitations and reduced flexibility of operation will be among the factors that will limit future development. The ability to build structures that float which are greater than any commercial ships presently afloat is possible as evidenced by the recent commissioning of the *Prelude*, a 600,000 dwt floating liquefied natural gas (FLNG) platform non-propelled vessel by Shell.

**Shell's dumb LNG ship, *Prelude***

## 7.3 SECONDHAND SHIPS

The majority of transactions in the sale and purchase market are for secondhand ships. It is in this sector where sale and purchase (S&P) brokers are most active. Brokers tend to build up connections with potential buyers and sellers as well as with other brokers. As with dry cargo chartering, it is more the rule than the exception for buyers and sellers to have their separate brokers.

S&P brokers produce and circulate information and broad details about ships they are trying to sell to brokers of potential buyers in an S&P particulars' sheet. The strength of any S&P broker's office lies in the maintenance of records of ships currently available for sale. An extensive database of vessels for sale can be a competitive advantage.

## 7.4 PROCESS OF SELLING A SHIP

The following comments refer to the activity of selling a ship.

Once the potential buyer's requirements are known, the broker will submit the S&P particulars' sheet of ships for sale that meet the criteria. The S&P particulars' sheet is forwarded by the broker to potential purchasers. Regardless of whether it is forwarded as hard copy or by electronic means, the broker supplying the details will state *'These particulars are believed correct but no guarantee is given of their accuracy'*. The particulars are compiled from information supplied by the owners (or their brokers) and augmented by details shown in Lloyd's Register or the books of other classification societies, such as Bureau Veritas, Det Norske Veritas – Germanischer Lloyd or the American Bureau of Shipping.

Among the most important particulars of the ship are: dead-weight, draught, year and place of build, dimensions, cubic capacities, cargo-handling appliances, arrangements of decks, water ballast capacities, numbers of holds and hatches, details of machinery and its builders, horsepower, speed and fuel consumption, bunker capacity, classification society and special survey position. Additional particulars will be needed for specialised ships. For example, the passenger capacity (usually lower berth) for passenger liners, details of refrigerating machinery for reefer ships, pumping capacities for tankers, container capacity expressed in twenty-foot equivalent units (teu) for container ships and lane length for roll-on/roll-off (ro-ro) vessels.

When a ship is to be sold for demolition it is normal to provide information regarding the ship's light displacement, the material of the propeller and spare propeller and whether a spare tail-shaft is retained on board.

Following the provision of the ship's particulars, two important features are required namely the purchase price and the position of the ship for inspection and delivery.

A buyer who is interested in a specific ship will usually request to see the ship's capacity plan. The ship's capacity plan provides details of the cargo-carrying arrangements. In addition, the buyer will also be interested in the ship's general arrangement plan. The ship's general arrangement plan gives details of the division and arrangement of the ship including a profile view of the ship, plan views of the most important decks, and transverse (cross-sectional) views at particular positions along the length of the ship. The individual profile plan and transverse views show the division of the ship into particular compartments (tanks, engine room and holds), the location of bulkheads and arrangements of the superstructure (including accommodation). Other information provided on the general arrangement plan will be significant items of the ship's equipment, including winches, cargo gear, bow thruster and lifeboats.

It is not the function of the broker to express an opinion regarding the condition of a ship unless they are factually aware of a specific concern. It is the buyer's superintendent or an independent firm of consulting surveyors appointed by the buyer who will undertake an inspection of the ship.

An initial inspection will involve a view of the classification society records which provide a history of the ship's structure from the commencement of build. In addition, the classification records will also provide details of damage and repairs which have been undertaken during the life of the ship and recommendations of the classification society surveyors following the periodical surveys. Possible areas of structural weakness will be identified which will demand careful inspection by the surveyor who carries out the physical inspection of the ship.

Sometimes the inspection takes place before the negotiations and sometimes offers are made subject to the examination of the ship. It rarely happens that the ship is drydocked at the time of the initial inspection.

The potential buyer will make a firm offer for a ship. A typical offer might read like this:

*Georgina*, On behalf of Moya Shipping of New City Court, London [the first offer may omit the prospective buyer's name and simply say something like 'first class buyers to be nominated'], we are authorised to offer firm for reply Tuesday July 7, 2013 17.00 BST London time basis details as set out in your email of July 3, 2013 timed 16.15 [or state time and date and type of whatever communication was used to give details of the ship]:

1. Price $19,750,000 – less 2% total commission this end.
2. Subject prompt inspection of the vessel with clean swept holds at Rotterdam within August 2013.
3. Subject approval of class records after inspection of same.
4. Buyer's reply on inspection of vessel and records within three working days after completion of vessel inspection.
5. Delivery of the vessel, charter free, at a port in Antwerp/Hamburg range at a safe anchorage or berth safely afloat within 30 days after signing of memorandum of agreement and deposit lodged with cancelling date in buyer's option.
6. Vessel to be delivered with class maintained, free of recommendations and free of average damage. All safety certificates to be up to date. Vessel to be delivered in substantially the same condition as when inspected.
7. National and international trading certificates to be unextended, clean and valid for a minimum period of six months from the time of delivery.

List of all certificates to be provided.

8. Dry docking as per NSF 1993 (Clause 6a to apply)
9. Vessel to be delivered with everything belonging to it on board, ashore and on order including all spare parts and spare equipment including spare propeller and tailshaft, radio/navaids not on hire (please itemise).
10. Purchase price to include bunkers and luboils as on board at time of delivery.
11. Vessel to be delivered free of all encumbrances/mortgages/maritime liens/taxes/claims and all debts whatsoever.
12. Buyer's right to place two men on board at buyer's risk and expense after contract signed, deposit lodged and buyer's signed indemnities provided.
13. Sellers to guarantee the vessel has not traded with/to Israel, Cuba, North Korea and is not blacklisted by the Central Boycott Office of the Arab League.
14. English law arbitration in London
15. Buyer's option to change flag and registration.

The term 'the ship's class at the time of delivery is to be maintained 'free of recommendations'' means that repairs which have been deferred for a specific period with the consent of the classification society, together with any further repairs that could be placed in the same category, are to be put right. Sometimes there is a concern about damage to the ship which is not within the province of the classification society. It is interesting that a ship can still be maintained in class even if its accommodation has been completely burned out or all its lifeboats washed overboard. Such a situation was dealt with by using the words 'free of average' but, the phrase has been replaced by 'free of damage recovering from underwriters'.

Other considerations to be aware of include payment for onboard stores and fuel, the validity of the ship's trading certificates at the time of delivery, including the possible need to insert a condition regarding government permission to buy or sell the ship and the inspection of the underwater hull, propeller and rudder by diver's inspection or drydocking.

A **memorandum of agreement (MoA)** between the buyer and the seller will be established. As a rule, agreement to purchase the ship will be made without seeing the condition of the hull below the waterline, the propeller and the rudder. A clause within the MoA, such as SALEFORM 2012 will build in adequate safeguards for the buyer. The clause entitled the 'Diver's Inspection/Drydocking Clause' will state:

*'The Buyers shall have the option at their cost and expense to arrange for an underwater inspection by a diver approved by the Classification Society prior to delivery of the Vessel ... the Sellers shall at their cost and expense make the vessel available for such inspection.'*

Alternatively the seller may be requested to:

*'...place the vessel in drydock at the port of delivery for inspection by the Classification Society of the Vessel's underwater parts... If the rudder, propeller, bottom or other underwater parts are found broken damaged or defective so as to affect the vessel's class such defects shall be made good at the Seller's cost and expense to the satisfaction of the classification society without condition.'*

While the vessel is in drydock and, if required by the buyer, the option may be taken to have the tail-shaft drawn and surveyed by the classification society. 'The drawing and refitting of the tailshaft shall be arranged by the Sellers. Should any part of the tailshaft system be condemned or found defective so as to affect the vessel's class, those parts shall be renewed or made good at the Sellers' cost and expense to the classification society's satisfaction.'

Unless the classification society requires a survey of the tail-shaft system to be carried out, or if parts of the system are condemned, found defective or broken 'the costs and expenses relating to the survey of the tailshaft system are borne by the Buyers.' The seller is required to make the ship available for either a diver's inspection or drydocking at their cost and expense.

## 7.5 DRYDOCKING A SHIP PRIOR TO SALE

Firstly, it is the responsibility of the sellers to bring the ship to the drydock ready for docking and subsequently from the drydock to the berth or place of delivery. The expenses involved in doing this, including tugs and pilot, if required, are for the sellers' account and these expenses should not be confused with those involved in the actually putting the vessel in and out of drydock and the drydock dues.

Once the ship is in the drydock, an inspection of the underwater parts will be carried out by the classification society's surveyors who are neutral referees and cannot be influenced by either sellers' or buyers' technical representatives, except to the extent that if a repair is called for the method of carrying it out may be discussed.

If the classification society's surveyor requires any work to be done on the underwater parts, the cost of putting the ship in and taking it out of drydock and the drydock dues will be paid by the sellers. On the other hand, if there are no repairs affecting the ship's class, these expenses are for the buyer's account.

Drydocking ships prior to sale is common

As a separate matter, buyers have the option of having the tail-end shaft drawn. This is the shaft that finally connects up the main engine with the propeller. If they elect to have it drawn for examination, it is done at the buyer's expense unless it is condemned or found defective so as to affect the ship's clean certificate of class. If it is condemned or defective, sellers would not only have to pay the cost of drawing and replacing the shaft plus the repairs thereto, but also the drydocking costs even though no other repairs were required on the other underwater parts.

Generally, there is a certain amount of negotiating in the matter of price and conditions, but when agreement has been reached it is the seller's broker's duty to draw up a memorandum of agreement (MoA).

A standard memorandum of agreement for the sale and purchase of ships has been developed within the industry. The Norwegian SALEFORM 2012 which has been adopted by BIMCO and the Norwegian Shipbrokers' Association is a recognised standard form. Other standard forms are the Nippon Sale Form 1999 and Singapore Ship sale form 2011.

Within SALEFORM 2012 are the following clauses:

- a preamble giving the names of the buyers and sellers, the name and brief description of the ship;
- definitions: including 'banking days', 'class', 'deposit';
- price: the price agreed given by amount and currency;
- payment: payment is normally made by a 10% deposit on signing the memorandum of agreement, the balance together with the release of the deposit is paid on delivery;
- inspections: refers to the buyer's inspection of the vessel's classification records and the availability of the ship for inspection by the buyer;

- time and place of delivery: states the place and time concerning where and when the ship will be delivered to the buyer;
- divers' inspections and drydocking;
- spares, bunkers and other items: states that the seller shall deliver the ship to the buyers with everything belonging to it on board and ashore describes how payments are to be made for bunkers remaining on board;
- documentation: lists the documentation the sellers should provide to the buyer including bills of sale, certificate of registry and declaration of class;
- encumbrances: a statement by the seller making clear that at the time of delivery the ship is free from all charters, encumbrances, mortgages, maritime liens and other debts;
- taxes, fees and expenses: covers the fees and expenses of the buyer and seller associated with the purchase and sale of the ship;
- condition on delivery: states that the ship shall be delivered to the buyer in the same condition as she was at inspection, fair wear and tear excepted;
- name/markings: buyers undertake to change the name and funnel markings following delivery;
- buyer's default: rights of cancellation by the seller of the agreement on the failure of the buyer to lodge the deposit or pay the purchase price;
- seller's default: if the seller fails to give notice of readiness or complete the legal transfer by the cancelling date the buyer is given the option of cancelling the agreement;
- buyers' representatives: gives the buyers the right to place two representatives on board the ship after the agreement has been signed and the deposit paid;
- law and arbitration: states the legal jurisdiction which governs the agreement and where, in case of dispute, arbitration should be undertaken;
- notices: states the recipients of notices for the sellers and buyers;
- entire agreement: confirms that the agreement consists of written terms relating to the sale and purchase of the ship.

When the time comes for delivery of the ship, this is carried out by the execution and delivery of documentation, including the bill of sale which, under English law, must be executed under seal. The bill of sale and other documents are handed over against a letter releasing the deposit and a banker's draft for the balance of the price. If extra payment for bunkers and spares is provided for, this is dealt with at the same time.

The following documents are handed over either on board or on shore:

- certificate of registry;
- loadline certificate;
- deratification certificate;

- safety construction certificate;
- safety radio certificate;
- safety equipment certificate;
- classification certificate;
- ship plans;
- bill of sale;
- declaration of ownership;
- articles of association;
- certificate of incorporation.

In many instances, the bill of sale must be legalised so that the document is authenticated in order for the buyer's flag to recognise the document's full legal effect.

Sales for demolition are, of course, much simpler with no problems about drydocking, registration or classification. Although the vessel can usually proceed to the port of destination in ballast under its own power, the arrangement of towage contracts or cargo voyages to the ultimate port of destination may be required.

## 7.6 DEMOLITION

The final incentive to sell is when a ship becomes uneconomic, obsolescent or fails to meet the regulatory demands required to keep it in trading condition. The only course left will be to sell the ship for demolition, scrap or recycling.

Ships are often run up on beaches to be demolished

Old age is not always the reason for scrapping, as has been seen on various occasions. The mismatch between the supply of ships and demand by shippers during the recession of the late 1970s and 1980s and the more recent world recession which commenced in 2008 can lead to modern ships being scrapped.

Prior to the recession of the 1970s and 1980s, there seemed to be no limit to the demand for crude oil carriers, and every yard which could build VLCCs or ULCCs had full berths and bulging order books. Then came the recession and with it an inevitable massive reduction in the demand for oil, resulting in some tankers going straight from the builder's slipway to a lay-up berth. In such a situation, many owners could find no prospect of trade for their ships and no funds to pay for mothballing them, so demolition was the only course left. Similarly, prior to the 2008 recession, ships were being ordered to be built in shipyards which had not been constructed. Then came the world recession, the oversupply of ships and busy demolition yards.

It is not unusual for a shipowner to sell an obsolescent ship for scrapping even though there may be buyers offering a better price wanting the ship for further trading. If a ship should be sold for trading to make room for a new addition to that owner's fleet, there would be two ships where there used to be only one. Ships naturally tend to be suitable for particular trades and so there is the risk that the seller would be providing a competitor with a ship with very low capital cost to amortise. Such an owner may decide that selling the redundant ship for trading rather than for scrap could risk increasing the amount of competition against the newly acquired ship.

## 7.7 FINANCING THE PURCHASE

In addition to the technical and commercial aspects of sale and purchase, the S&P broker is expected to understand the problems a buyer faces in finding the money to pay for a new ship.

Shipping companies can use their own reserves or will increase their share capital to raise finance for their new purchase.

Another method of financing the purchase of a ship is through the use of a bank loan secured by a mortgage. Prior to purchasing a ship, a prudent buyer will discuss the opportunity with the bank so that the general principles will have been covered. The discussion will involve the bank satisfying itself that the business plan is viable and that the ship to be purchased will be able to earn enough money to repay the loan and the interest.

In the case of new buildings, it is customary for progress payments to be made during the construction of the ship. There are usually five of these, the first on signing the contract, another when the keel is laid and at intervals until final payment is made. Final payment is made following successful sea trials when the ship is handed over to the ship owner. Payments' amounts and the time when due will be agreed between the shipbuilder and the buyer and stated in the new building contract such as NEWBUILDCON.

Up to 80% of the purchase price may be advanced through credit arrangements for new buildings, with the buyer providing the other 20% out of their own resources.

## 7.8 VALUATIONS

S&P brokers can be engaged to act as valuers. There are several reasons why an independent expert opinion of a ship's value at a specific time may be required. An independent valuation may be required for the following purposes:

- law cases and arbitration;
- general average (where the ship's value is needed to determine the owner's contribution to the average settlement);
- salvage awards;
- insurance claims;
- an independent check when the purchase is being made;
- revaluation of a company's assets for accounting purposes;
- loan to value covenants in bank financing.

Valuations establish the market value of the vessel at a particular time. The valuation given by an S&P broker will be given with the qualification that it is assumed 'the vessel is in good trading condition appropriate to its age'.

Valuation is not an easy task as, like the freight market, the S&P market fluctuates. It is also unusual for two vessels to be identical so the opportunity to benchmark is limited. A high degree of expertise is needed to provide a ship's value that can be substantiated if required.

## 7.9 SHIP MANAGERS

Ship managers include persons who manage the ships of an owner in-house, persons who in addition to providing in-house management offer their services to third parties. There are also independent ship managers who focus on third-party ship management. InterManager is the international trade association for the ship management industry. More than 35% of ships are managed through third-party managers.

The focus of this section is to appreciate the tasks undertaken by independent ship management companies.

The most complete management service is required where the ship has been bought as an investment and the shipowner does not want to play a role in running the ship. The complete management of the ship is placed under a ship management company. The manager will manage the ship as if it were their own, making all operational, technical and commercial decisions. This is referred to as full management.

Alternatively, the shipowner may subcontract one element of management to a third party, such as the technical management or crew management. Crew management is the most popular element subcontracted to a third party.

## 7.10 FULL MANAGEMENT

The task of providing a complete management service to a shipowner can be undertaken by a ship management company. Ship management has four principal elements: technical, operations, administration and crewing. The elements are similar whether undertaken in-house or for a third party.

## Technical management

The most important aspect of technical management is to ensure that ships are maintained to the standards set by the flag state and the classification society. It will include the development of planned maintenance systems, the monitoring and support to the hull and engine classification society surveys and ensuring the safety management of the ship.

Managers involved in technical management will include senior shore-based masters and chief engineers, often referred to as marine and engineering superintendents. In addition to the demands stated above they will have to ensure that ship's stores and spares are properly purchased and made available to the ship. The managers will also be involved should the ship be involved in an accident or have a technical failure, having to react quickly to resolve the problem. They will be mobile and will need to fly worldwide to oversee repairs.

## Operations management

Operations managers will be involved prior to the employment of the ship as they will be aware of the capabilities of the ship and the restrictions of its trading environment. Once a decision regarding the ship's employment has been made, it will be the operational managers who make it happen.

Operations departments in shipowners' offices may include the decision makers. The decision makers are those persons who determine what business will be negotiated and what rate of freight or hire will be accepted. They will authorise the brokers to make firm offers. To do this effectively, they will be skilled in voyage-estimating. A voyage estimate is a specialised form of budgeting which enables the value of different aspects of business on offer to be compared and related with the running costs of the ship concerned. Operations managers liaise closely with the technical department. For example, it would be ruinous if a drydocking were due at the same time that the operations managers had otherwise committed the ship.

Operations management also includes includes insurance and cargo claims.

## Administrative management

Essential administration among other things involves the all-important task of accounting. As technical and operations managers have to closely work together so do the accounts managers.

Of particular interest between technical, operations and administrative management is the comparison of the actual outcome of a particular voyage with the estimate which was made at the time it was fixed. If there are wide differences between the actual and the voyage estimate, an investigation will be required and data for future estimates adjusted.

## Crew management

Owners managing all other aspects of their ships may subcontract the supply and management of crew to a third party. There are a number of reasons for this practice.

Cost is one factor. The labour pool used to man ships is international. The practice of using a crew management company is adopted by many reputable owners, not just unscrupulous owners of substandard ships. Owners often flagout to other countries, enabling the ship to be managed from the original country and allowing it to be crewed in accordance with the laws of

Good crews are the key to a successfully-managed ship

the flag state. The benefits of this can include reduced tax on company earnings, lower registration fees, bilateral and multilateral trading agreements, limits on owner's liability, reduced ship survey fees and fewer restrictions within the flag requirements on ownership qualifications.

Shipping is involved in international trade. Ships of different nations compete in a common market, irrespective of the cost of living of individual countries. Salaries for jobs ashore will be higher in wealthier countries. To attract crews from that country, shipowners will have to match or exceed shore wages. The situation may be complicated by trade unions having negotiated higher wages. Going to sea is often no longer considered an attractive career option. Demographic patterns are creating difficulties for shipowners and managers trying to meet officer and crew needs from within the home country.

A typical situation may be an American owner with ships under a Liberian flag and crew supplied by contractors in the Philippines. British shipowners can enjoy the advantages of flagging out under an offshore but related flag. Under the Isle of Man registry, ships fly the British flag, but do not come under English law. Owners are not obliged to collect or contribute to social security payments or collect personal income tax from their employees.

Contracting overseas agencies for ships' crews is not a new practice and, for many developing nations, the supply of international crew has now become a significant invisible trade export.

Standard crew management agreements have been established by BIMCO under the code name CREWMAN 2009. The crew management agreement states that the crew managers 'shall provide suitably qualified crew who shall comply with the requirements of the Standards of Training, Certification and Watchkeeping Convention (STCW)'. The agreement reflects current crew management practice and recent legal developments. Clauses incorporated into the agreement are compatible with the standard BIMCO management agreement code named SHIPMAN 2009.

There are unscrupulous shipowners who wish to operate at an absolute minimum cost and level of conditions, regardless of the effect on welfare and safety. There are three forces acting to counter such practices:

- the natural reluctance among most charterers and shippers to entrust their goods to sub-standard operators;
- international memorandum of understanding (MoU) which support Port State Control which allows countries to detain unsafe ships in their ports;
- safeguards against undue exploitation of ships' crews exercised by the International Transport Workers' Federation (ITF).

Almost all transport unions throughout the world are affiliated to the ITF. The ITF is dedicated to ensure that seafarers receive adequate wages and conditions. Should the ITF decide that a contract regarding pay and conditions agreement, between employer and crew is abused it can call upon local transport unions to take action.

## 7.11 THE SHIP MANAGEMENT CONTRACT

Owners and managers can draw up individual contracts regarding ship management. BIMCO have produced a standard ship management agreement known as SHIPMAN 2009.

While it is rare for the agreement to be used without some amendment or addition, it serves as an excellent checklist to ensure that both parties cover all the necessary points.

The legal relationship between a shipbroker and their principal is defined by the law of agency. In ship management and within the same management contract there are areas of responsibility where the manager could be the principal while in others he will act as an agent. It is appropriate to be aware of the different relationships which are involved when reading the terms and conditions in the ship management contract form.

Chapter 8

# Port and liner agency

*Sea shells were once commonly used in many parts of the world as currency*

## 8.1 PORT AGENTS

A senior ship's captain once described the duties of his port agent in one sentence. Pointing along the length of this ship he said *'When I am at sea, all this is my responsibility; when I reach port I am looking for someone with whom to share that responsibility'.*

Regardless of the ship or service type, the need for an agent is the same. The agent agrees to look after all the needs of the ship and its personnel prior to and on arrival, during the stay in port and on and after following departure. The precise duties and services required to be undertaken by the port agent will vary depending on the ship, the cargo and locality.

An agent can be defined as *'a person or company that provides a service, typically one that involves organising transactions between two other parties'.* An agent is employed by one of those parties, namely the principal for whom he will act. Identifying the principal is a vital first step for the port agent as considerable amounts of money will be spent on behalf of the principal during the time the ship is in port.

In practice, the port agent will represent the ship through undertaking the services and duties agreed between itself and the principal. There will be a strong commitment to the role.

Is the agent's principal always the owner of the ship? In many cases this will be the case, but when a ship is bareboat chartered, the charterer will become the disponent owner. A disponent owner is described as a person or company which displaces or takes the place of the legal registered owner. The agent's principal will be the charterer. In a time charter party the clause 'Charterers to Provide' includes the following words, or similar: *'The Charterers, while the vessel is on hire, shall provide and pay for all the fuel, except as otherwise agreed, port charges, pilotages, towages, agencies, commission … '* confirming the relationship between the principal and the agent. The principal for whom the agent is acting is the one who pays the agency fee.

The relationship between the disponent owner, registered owner and port agent can present a dilemma. For example, the registered owner may need to undertake tasks for which the disponent owner (bareboat charterer), who is also the principal, has no responsibility, such as repairs or crew changes. The disponent owner as principal is expected to instruct the agent to act in all ways as if they were the shipowner, but the position of the agent as representing the ship is not always clear.

When a time charterer appoints a port agent, no contractual relationship between the agent and the legal owner is established. This may not be of importance when the services and duties carried out by the agent for the ship are routine and not of the time charterer's concern. It becomes rather different if such tasks are extensive and complex.

In extensive and complex cases, it may be appropriate to establish a direct contract stating the range of tasks to be undertaken and agreeing a fee between the legal owner and the agent appointed by the time charterer. Under the contract, the agent's expenditure on behalf of the legal owner can be paid without dispute.

If instructions from the registered owner create a conflict of interest with the time charterer, the agent will have to handle the situation without causing either party any distress. Both time charterer and legal owner must be made aware of the agent's position. It may on occasions be necessary for the port agent to revert to work exclusively for their principal (the time charterer) and the legal owner will have to appoint a separate agent.

## 8.2 THE CHARTERER'S AGENTS

Persons who have had dealings with charter parties may ask about the position of the charterer's agents. In some badly drafted voyage charter forms the words 'vessel to be consigned to charterer's agents at port of loading (or discharging)' may be encountered. More responsible compilers of charter party forms use the phrase *'Owners to appoint agents nominated by the charterers at the port of . . .'*

Legally, the agent represents the owner or disponent owner. There are cases where the charterers as the disponent owner stipulate that they should nominate the agents at the loading or discharging port, or both. There are several reasons why the charterer would wish to nominate an agent.

For example, in the tanker industry, charters will include a charterer's agents clause. Major refinery jetties are costly to operate. Refinery owners are keen to have the ships using the jetties represented by agents who understand the trade. By nominating an agent who has expertise in tanker agency, the refinery owners can be sure of receiving communications they can trust. Shipowners seldom resist such nominated appointments because they benefit by being represented by an agent who has trade expertise.

**Agents have to attend arriving or departing ships, whatever the time and date**

Another reason for a charterer wishing to nominate a charterer's agent might be the need to protect trade secrets. In the coal trade, agents in ports where coal is imported may have business connections with one of the importers. No charterer, as a disponent owner, would want to risk the legal owner appointing one of the charterer's competitors as the ship's agent. The charterer would, in this instance, insist on the right to nominate the appointment of the agent. While it would be normal for the legal owner to agree to this they would usually include an amendment to the charter party stating that they will accept the agent provided they are competitive. The amendment prevents the agent charging an exorbitant fee. Inevitably, the charterer expects a *quid pro quo* from the agent being nominated, which is usually in the form of keeping a supervisory eye on the charterer's interests.

There is seldom a contractual relationship between the charterer and the nominated agent prior to appointment. There are situations where a charterer has demanded a share of the agent's fee as an introductory commission.

An agent who is nominated by a charterer has to ensure there is no conflict of interest between itself, the legal owner and the charterer. In some cases, the registered owner may not be satisfied with the agent's ability to avoid favouring a nominating voyage charterer. In such a situation, the registered owner may appoint a supervisory or protecting agent to look after its interests. A supervisory or protecting agent would expect to deal with the domestic requirements of the ship, such as stores, cash and crew travel. They will also keep in close contact with the charterers' agents over matters such as working times and statements of fact to ensure the legal owner's interests are protected.

Except in specific trades such as tankers, where shipowners would be pleased to appoint the expert agent even if they were not nominated by the charterer, shipowners generally dislike the stipulation of charterer's agents. One of several reasons why shipowners dislike the charterers' agents clause is that they may have no opportunity to check on the financial strength of the nominated agent, but the owner is still expected to remit a substantial sum of money in advance of the ship's call.

## 8.3 THE AGENT'S FEE

Although it may seem strange to introduce the subject of remuneration before considering the agent's tasks, there is some logic to discussing the question of fees directly after having covered the subject of the methods of appointment.

In most countries, port agents have formed themselves into some sort of association. In Britain they did this in 1911 when an association that eventually became the Institute of Chartered Shipbrokers was formed. Most associations produce some sort of tariff of agency fees and, at one time, such a tariff or scale of minimum agency charges was mandatory upon all members of the association concerned. This is rarely the case today as the mandatory nature of such scales is now illegal in many countries. The USA has had its antitrust laws since the end of the last century. The United Kingdom extended its Restrictive Trade Practices Act to cover services during the latter part of the 1970s and this prohibition of mandatory scales of charges is reinforced by the free competition clauses in the Treaty of Rome, which created the European Community. The argument in support of outlawing mandatory scales is that they protect the sub-standard agent and deter the better ones from striving for greater efficiency. Those in favour of mandatory scales argue that keeping the fees the same but competing in quality of service provides protection for the consumer.

Owners still seem to welcome some sort of tariff for agency fees (just as much as they do for tugs and pilots) so that they can more quickly calculate their voyage estimates. Most tariffs, even when only advisory, tend to have some form of sliding scale based upon the size of the ship from which the basic fee is calculated with variations (usually additions) for non-standard tasks.

There is an argument that what agents are selling is their time and that the same amount of time is expended on a 50,000 dwt ship as on a ship of 150,000 dwt. The converse of this does not work. Using the same argument, the owner of the smaller ship would object to paying the fee appropriate to that involved in attending a ship several times larger. As a consequence, scales of agency fees are based on a balance of time, responsibility and ship size, the last being in reality a question of what the market will bear.

Under most competition laws, it is not an offence to base your charges on the scale. The offence would be for two or more agents to agree amongst themselves to charge the same, or for the institution publishing the scale to attempt to make it obligatory.

Whether a tariff is in existence or not, except in those few countries where there is a mandatory scale, it is important for the agent to agree the fee before the ship arrives. The fee does not include the agent's out-of-pocket expenses, such as the cost of communicating with the owner, the cost of travelling to and from the ship and similar items. These will be charged to the owner but will have to be justified in exactly the same way as any other items in the disbursement account.

Some ships require the expenditure of more time and effort than others, but except in the case of truly extraordinary circumstances, the same fee is charged for the same size and type of ship. Any differences mean the agent takes 'the rough with the smooth' in the expectation that expenditure will average out.

## 8.4 THE AGENT'S DUTIES

At the beginning of the chapter the agent's duties were referred to as looking after all the needs of the ship and its personnel before and on arrival, during the stay in port and on and after departure. The following sections give greater detail.

### Before arrival

Initially the agent must acknowledge the appointment. Two vital matters must be confirmed, namely (i) establishing whether the appointee is responsible for settling the disbursement account and (ii) providing the owner with a proforma disbursement account, including the intended agency fee.

A disbursement account is an account rendered by the port agent for all sums paid out in respect to the ship's call at the port including payment for pilotage, towage, cash advance to the ship's master, supply of provisions and stores and the agency fee.

Confirmation of responsibility for settling the disbursement account is not as elementary as it may sound. There have been cases where the appointment of an agent has been made by the ship's managers and the shipowner has fallen into financial difficulty. Ship's managers have claimed that they were agents of the owners and successfully avoided settling outstanding items, including the disbursement account. A hint of the shipowner's financial difficulties may come from the charterers, in which case it is in the agent's interest to directly contact the owner.

The second vital action is to provide the owner with a proforma disbursement account including the intended agency fee. The proforma disbursement account will show approximations of expenditure required under the main headings. The object is to receive advance funding from the owner.

Other tasks before the ship's arrival will include liaising with the shippers or consignees to determine where the ship is to berth and to maintain contact with them so that the necessary labour and equipment is ready at the appropriate time. Pilots, tugs and boatmen (for mooring) will all need advance warning.

During this time, contact will be made with the ship itself not only to establish its expected time of arrival and to give berthing details but also to learn in advance of any urgent requirements. The most common request is a supply of cash in local currency.

### On arrival

A good agent meets all ships on arrival unless the captain asks to delay this meeting. At the first meeting, which may include the first officer and the stevedores, all requirements in connection with the cargo, the ship and its personnel will be discussed. Apart from the actual cargo operations, the ship may need some repair work and members of the crew may need medical or dental treatment. The agent must always ensure they bring the captain's cash and the crew's mail to this first meeting.

In some ports, the agent is not allowed to board the ship until port health and/or the customs officials have boarded and cleared the ship. *Free pratique* is the process of confirming that none of the ship's personnel is suffering from an infectious disease. It ensures that the ship has permission from the health authorities to enter port and make contact with people from the shore. Free pratique is normally granted by radio prior to arrival.

The agent will be required to lodge various forms with authorities such as customs, the port authority and the administrators of lights and lighthouses. The agent will also have to pay, or commit themselves to pay, substantial sums of money to cover costs associated with pilotage, towage, customs and port dues. Except for costs associated with stevedoring the largest items on the disbursement account will be committed at this stage. This is why advance funding is necessary.

**Tugs are invariably used by large ocean-going cargo vesselsto manoeuvre in port**

Commercially the agent has to ensure that a written **Notice of Readiness (NOR)** is properly tendered to the shippers or consignees. The NOR is a provision in a voyage charter party which states that the charterer will be advised when the ship has arrived and is ready to load or discharge. The provision will stipulate the particular hours and days when this notice may be tendered and how soon afterwards laytime will commence. The tendering of the NOR 'starts the meter ticking' for the calculation of laytime and, if appropriate, demurrage or despatch. What constitutes a ready ship and issues associated with claims for demurrage or dispatch are amongst the most frequent areas of dispute heard by maritime arbitration.

The times of the actual commencement of loading or discharging are considered separately from the issues of the NOR, the ready ship, demurrage and despatch. Timekeeping is of great importance as costs associated with a ship being in port are high. Daily, or more frequently if circumstances dictate, the agent should advise the owner of the progress concerning the loading or discharging of the ship and prospects for completion.

### Upon departure

Liaison with the ship will continue throughout the ship's stay in port. A careful note of the progress of loading or discharging will be kept in the agent's office. The note will record the times of stoppage and recommencement of loading or discharge along with reasons, which may include bad weather, machinery faults or strikes.

When the loading or discharging is finished, the agent will be in a position to complete a statement of facts. The statement of facts sets out a log of events during the ship's stay in port. If time permits, the agent should ask the ship's captain to check the ship's deck logbook against the statement of facts. If in agreement, the captain will sign the statement. The agent will also seek the signature of the loading or discharging terminal manager. After completion the agent will forward the statement of facts to the owner.

It is upon the statement of facts that claims for demurrage or despatch will be based. It is not for the agent to debate the legal niceties as to whether demurrage is due or despatch earned, but simply to ensure that the facts are 100% accurate.

The agent will organise the linesmen, boatmen, tugs and pilots to coincide with the time of completion and departure of the ship. The owners and the agents at the next port of call will be notified.

### After departure

Following departure of the ship, the agent will gather together the invoices and vouchers associated with the expenditure made on the ship's behalf. When all are to hand, a disbursement account will be produced. An invoice or voucher for every item of expenditure will accompany the account. A balance in favour either of the owner or the agent will be shown. If the balance is in favour of the owner, the balance should be sent back without delay. The agent should lose no time in seeking any balance due.

## 8.5 LINER AGENCY

The work of the liner agent is the same whether carried out by an independent agent or by departments within the liner operator's own company. The following section will consider the tasks as they are found in the office of an independent agent.

Under previous headings which have been considered in this book, the different jobs which fall under the general term of shipbroking have tended to be tasks done by individuals or small teams. Even ship management with its several different departments will tend to comprise of small groups of people. Work associated with liner trades is the only form of shipbroking that can be called labour intensive. In addition to employing a larger number of people, liner work involves a wide variety and different levels of skill. There are some tasks which are purely clerical in nature whilst others require an ability to think on one's feet in considering the legal aspects of the contract of carriage between the liner company and its users. The following part briefly examines the four core areas of work of the liner agent. The four core areas cover dealing with the ship, dealing with the outward cargo, dealing with the inward cargo and dealing with the principal.

The basic activities of liner agency are considered in the context of the traditional liner operation. Additional comment is made on issues associated with container shipping. On the main trade routes, container shipping is dominant.

## Dealing with the ship

Liner agency is not always port-based. The following paragraphs will focus on the agent whose appointment also includes attending the ship in port. Much of what was covered in the first part of this chapter applies to liners' agents as it does to those involved with tramp ships and tankers. The agent will deal with customs, health and port authorities on behalf of the ship and look after the needs of the ship's crew in a similar manner.

The most obvious difference between the work of the liner agent and the agent who deals with a chartered ship is the form of cargo. In the case of the chartered ship, it is likely that the cargo is a single commodity and that the loading or discharging arrangements have been made at the time of the charter.

The liner trade deals with the loading and/or discharging of many different types of consignment, including unitised cargoes. To this end, discussion with the stevedores will start well before the ship arrives at a port. Arranging the stowage to ensure safe trim as well as having the right cargo accessible at each discharging port is the responsibility of the ship's command. The role of the agent is to ensure that all the information about what cargo has been booked is provided to the ship as early as possible. Booking information allows the ship's command the opportunity to establish a cargo plan.

Before the ship arrives, a suitable berth has to be arranged. If the ship is carrying break-bulk cargo, that is, non–containerised cargo, a berth will be required. A liner berth will be equipped with facilities, such as a warehouse where cargo discharged from the ship can be accommodated and cargo to be loaded can be assembled. A liner ship may use its own cargo handling equipment or make use of that provided by the terminal.

## Dealing with outward cargo – marketing

Liners are, by definition, ships which adhere to a pre-planned schedule where arrival and departure dates are known months in advance. Occasionally weather, strikes and other unforeseeable events will impact on the schedule. The many hundreds of different shippers and their forwarding agents need to be aware of the exact schedule and the services offered. The liner company will advertise their schedules in advance making full use of the World Wide Web. In addition, active salesmanship will help inform shippers of the available opportunities. Hard copy advertising tends to be restricted to trade journals. The basic commodity which a liner company has to sell is space on board a ship. The marketing of space is similar to selling an actual physical product. Competition is fierce. The sales force of full time representatives will be fully committed to the task.

While dealing with more than one principal in the same trade is seldom a problem in the tramp/tanker agency world, it is difficult for an agent to act for more than one liner service in the same trade. The question of conflict of interest is a consideration for a principal when choosing an agent. With a number of liner companies operating in the major trades, it can be difficult for principals to find a good quality agent not already committed to certain of the trades.

The outward freight department personnel in a liner shipping company not only take cargo bookings but have to have information available as to when and where the cargo should be delivered to the port. They will also deal with shipper's queries. In addition, freight cost will be calculated and quotes provided to each potential shipper. Liner freight tariffs are notoriously complicated and are based on what the market will bear.

By law it is the shipper's responsibility to declare dangerous goods to the shipowner prior to loading. Dangerous goods are defined in the International Maritime Dangerous Goods (IMDG Code) and cover nine basic categories which include explosives, inflammables and toxic substances. Laws and codes cannot protect a ship from catching fire or the crew from being poisoned. Liner agency personnel need to be able to recognise potentially hazardous cargo and crosscheck any suspect material with the shippers and the IMDG Code.

**Agency personnel need to identify hazardous cargoes before they are loaded**

## Dealing with outward cargo – documentation

Although use is made of electronic processes, a significant number of forms are used in the liner business. A standard shipping note (SSN) will be used if shipping goods overseas. The SSN contains information about the goods and companies involved in sending, shipping and receiving. It is used by customs officials and the shipping company. If shipping dangerous goods by sea, a dangerous goods note (DGN) will need to be completed prior to shipment. It will be forwarded to the carrier, usually the shipping company and receiving authorities, including terminal operators. Cargo received on board the ship will be evidenced by the issue of a mate's receipt, handed to the shipper.

The shipper is required to present a set of bills of lading (B/L) to the liner's agents. A set of bills of lading will comprise three originals and anything up to a dozen copies. The B/L acts as receipt for the goods loaded. The B/L will be signed by the agent, on behalf of the Master having been checked against the mate's receipt. The check will ensure that the description and quantity in the B/L agrees with the cargo that has been loaded. The B/L will then be freighted, meaning that the exact freight due will be calculated and shown on the form.

The liner's agent will retain at least one copy of the B/L. Information from the B/L is used to complete the ship's manifest. The manifest is a comprehensive list of all cargo on board the ship following completion of loading at a particular port. Several copies of the manifest will be required for the file, the owner, the ship, the customs and the port of discharge.

If the freight is to be paid at the loading port, it is customary for a freight account to be produced. Unless there is an arrangement for the shipper to be granted credit, the B/Ls are not passed back to the shipper, with the all-important Freight Paid endorsement, until the money is handed over. If the freight is to be collected at discharging port then the amount due is entered on the B/Ls.

It is not unusual for up to 20 sheets of paper to be involved for a single consignment and there can be many hundreds of consignments carried on an ocean going liner. Widespread use of computer systems ensures that several documents are produced from the same input of information, eliminating the need for much manual checking. Despite computerisation, there is still a significant human involvement in the movement of liner cargoes.

## Dealing with outward cargo – containers

The process described so far relates to cargo loaded directly into the ship referred to either break-bulk cargo or conventional cargo. The terms differentiate the cargo process from the movement of cargo carried in freight containers, sometimes referred to as containerisation.

The introduction of containerisation caused great changes in the liner business, including the movement of manual work away from the quayside and development of additional work for the liner agent.

At the loading port with conventional cargo, the agent will take the booking and advise the shippers of the transit shed where the cargo should be delivered. The stevedores will load it onto the ship. With containerisation, the agent will take the booking and then arrange for the necessary container(s) to be provided to the shipper. All container movements to the shipper and following loading to the container port terminal are monitored. To undertake the task, the agent will establish a container control department. If the shipper elects to use a door-to-door service then it is the agent's responsibility to arrange for the container to move from the depot to the shipper's premises and then to the container port terminal. To provide the facility, the agent will establish a transport department.

The foregoing assumes the shipper has sufficient cargo for a full container load (FCL). If this is not the case and the shipper has insufficient cargo to fill a container it can be forwarded as a less than container load (LCL). The cargo will be presented at a nominated depot as conventional cargo and consolidated by the depot into an FCL. The container company will usually have contracts with depots to consolidate LCL cargoes into containers. The agent will monitor the depot's work and ensure that the LCL container will reach the ship at the right time. A packing list, similar to a miniature manifest, is issued for each for each LCL container.

## Dealing with inward cargo

In advance of a ship's arrival at the discharge port, the manifest of the cargo to be discharged at that port will be received by the agent. The details in the manifest include the name and address of the consignee for each item of cargo or the name and address of the party to notify, referred to as the notify party. When a cargo has been sold under a letter of credit the notify party may be the eventual consignee. But the B/L is issued to 'order' rather than to a named consignee. The purpose of this is to 'open' the B/L, like a cheque drawn to cash, enabling the banks involved in the payment transaction to hold the B/L as security.

Although the notify party is often the consignee, this is not always the case. The consignee named in the manifest may no longer be the consignee when the ship arrives at the discharge port. Not only does the B/L act as a receipt but it is also a document of title and as such the goods which it represents can be traded. A B/L may be endorsed to another party (this can happen an infinite number of times). The party endorsed on the B/L has title to the goods described in the B/L and can claim them on arrival at the port of discharge. A B/L can be held as security for payment.

On receipt of the manifest, the agent will notify the consignees and the B/L holders will present the original bill of lading at the agent's office. Where freight is payable at destination, the consignee will be required to make payment before their goods are released. In most cases, the agent issues a delivery order in exchange for the original B/L. The delivery order is an instruction to the ship, port authority or terminal operator to deliver the consignment to the person named in the order.

There are potentially hundreds of consignments on each vessel. Nearly all of them will require only routine handling. Yet the inward freight department has to be alert to the risk of releasing cargo without receiving an original bill of lading. It may even encounter the occasional forgery. In both cases it is not only the amount of freight at risk but the total value of the cargo.

If the cargo is break-bulk, the agent will have arranged transit shed space before the ship's arrival. Activity associated with containers is the reverse of the loading procedure and involves the return of the empty container to the correct depot, known as resituated.

One further duty of the inward liner agent is dealing with cargo claims. Cargo claims are less prevalent in the container business, but with break-bulk cargo, there can be disputes concerning cargo damage and discrepancy regarding the amount of cargo delivered.

One of the following sets of rules will govern the carriage of goods by sea: The Hague, Hague-Visby or Hamburg Rules. Whichever is used will determine the degree of liability that the ship has to bear.

### Dealing with the principal

When the ship has departed from port, the task of reconciling the financial account is undertaken. Reconciliation of the account can be a complex activity. Apart from the normal disbursements associated with a ship's stay in port, there will be other costs including stevedoring charges, tallying costs, transit shed rental, crane hire and port workers' overtime. If containers are involved there will be road and rail haulage accounts and depot handling charges to be processed.

The shipowner will want any balance of the disbursement account to be returned as quickly as possible. There is an expectation that the disbursement account will be completed and forwarded by the agent to the shipowner as efficiently as possible. As the gross amount of money collected by the liner agent for a port call can be substantial, the prudent principal will take care to investigate the financial stability and reputation of any agents they appoint.

## 8.6 LINER AGENT REMOTE FROM THE PORT

Countries with no coastline of their own still export and import goods and liner companies will want a sales organisation there. Sometimes, lines operating to countries that do have their own ports may find it convenient to have the marketing in the hinterland carried out by a different agent from that handling the ship itself. Even in the UK where it is impossible to live more than 80 miles (130 km) from the sea, it is not unusual for the ship to be looked after by one agent and the cargo to be obtained by a loading broker.

Some container terminals are close to the port while others are far inland

The duties of such agents will vary from case to case; some may simply take the booking and leave all the documentation to the port agent. In other cases, the hinterland agent will complete all the documentation and act as a forwarder responsible for getting the cargo to the port.

## 8.7 AGENCY CONTRACT

In many cases, the contract between the owner and the agent may be no more than one line in the appointment email. Generally though, the duties of a liner agent have to be spelled out in more detail. Furthermore, an agent has to staff-up to handle a liner service and so needs a contract of reasonable duration in order to justify the commitment to several additional employees.

There is no set pattern for a liner agency contract but the Federation of National Associations of Ship Brokers and Agents (FONASBA) has produced a printed draft in the form of their Standard Liner and General Agency Agreement.

A study of the clauses in the FONASBA Standard Liner and General Agency agreement is a useful way of understanding all the different duties a liner agent may be expected to perform, and the way in which they can expect to be remunerated for them.

Chapter 9

# International trade and finance: International terms of sale

*The European Monetary System was established in 1979 by the European Union in order to bring some financial stability to Europe*

## 9.1 INTRODUCTION

Persons involved in the shipping business are concerned with aspects of international trade that are directly related to the transportation of goods. To carry out this service effectively, it is of value to understand the additional activities and relationships that are faced by shippers, merchants and traders.

International seaborne trade represents the many voyages undertaken each year during which cargoes are moved between different countries. A contract for the sale of goods between a buyer in one country and a seller in another country is the core contract in international trade. Other contracts will be established between different parties to facilitate and safeguard the transaction, including contracts for finance, transport, cargo insurance and agency.

The basic elements which apply to all contracts are outlined below.

## 9.2 THE BASIC CONTRACT

**The four elements of a contract are:**

- the offer;
- acceptance which is an agreement to the terms of the offer. Acceptance has to be made in a reasonable manner and time;
- consideration which concerns the price to each party to the bargain. It is what each party will receive in consideration for performing their part of the contract;
- intention to create legal relations recognises that both parties to a contract intend legal consequences to attach to the agreement.

In a contract for the sale of goods there are three considerations:

- the time when ownership of the goods passes from the seller to the buyer;
- the time when payment is due;
- the point when risk in the goods passes from the seller to buyer.

In international sales, one party could make an offer on its standard terms and the other party will accept the offer on its own standard terms. If the terms are different, there is no legal acceptance which can lead to a dispute regarding the validity of the contract. The adoption of an internationally recognised set of standard terms governing international sales prevents the problem arising by ensuring that both parties are in agreement as to the terms contained in the contract. Using internationally recognised standard terms, the buyers and sellers are aware of their rights and obligations.

International commercial terms, referred to as Incoterms, have been produced by the International Chamber of Commerce and have been accepted as providing the international standard terms required.

Under English law, a sale of goods is defined as 'a contract to pass the property in goods for a money consideration, the price'. The word 'property' basically means 'ownership'. A sale of goods means that the ownership of the goods is transferred in exchange for payment.

## 9.3 GOODS

There are two distinct types of goods which are the subject to an international sales contract, namely, specific goods and unascertained goods. Specific goods are those which are readily identifiable at the time the contract is made. For example, '1,000 New Zealand lamb carcasses numbered Y 20,001 to Y 21000'.

Unascertained goods are goods that have yet to be produced by the seller, or are part of a larger bulk and have not been set aside for a specific contract. For example, 'an offer to sell 50 tonnes of wheat from a stock of 200 tonnes stored'. The 50 tonnes of wheat would be unascertained as it is not known which of the 200 tonnes will be the 50 tonnes received by the buyer.

## 9.4 PROPERTY

The next element in the sale of goods is the passing of property. Property means ownership. When property passes, the right of ownership is transferred from the seller to the buyer. Property is not possession. Possession signifies physical control, not ownership. For example, if goods are placed in a warehouse following purchase by a third party, possession of the goods will be with the warehouse owner but the property will be with the third party. When property passes to the buyer, the buyer becomes the owner of the goods.

The passing of the property and payment have the following consequences:

- the buyer must pay the price to the seller; the passing of property and payment of the price are concurrent conditions;
- the risks pass to the buyer;
- certain specific remedies become available to the seller if the buyer breaches the contract by refusing to take the goods.

An important question which needs to be answered is when does property pass? The English Sale of Goods Act provides that 'property passes when the parties intend it to.'

There are more helpful rules which depend on whether the goods are specific or unascertained. Property in specific goods will usually pass at the time the contract is made, depending on what terms and conditions are made in the contract, notwithstanding that the goods may not be delivered immediately.

Property cannot pass at the same stage for unascertained goods. For property to pass, there must be what is known as appropriation. Appropriation means that out of the unascertained goods, a parcel of those goods must be specified for the buyer. The goods then become specific goods and it is at that time the property will pass. For example, if from a warehouse full of grain a certain amount of grain is sold to a buyer, the property will not pass until the grain is irrevocably put aside to be delivered to the buyer.

Essentially property (ownership) passes when the contract is made, or in the case of unascertained goods, when a specific parcel to be delivered is set aside. It is possible for the passing of property to be delayed and this can frequently occur in international sales.

## 9.5 RISK

At the time that property passes, risk will also pass. In the case of goods, risk is associated with the loss or damage to the goods. Whoever bears the risk will bear the burden of loss or damage. For example, when A sells goods to B, the property and risk pass to B. The goods remain in A's warehouse. Fire, for which A is not to blame, destroys the warehouse and its contents. B will bear the loss. In another situation, if A sells the goods to B, who then takes them away, but if B has not yet paid for the goods, the property and risk remain with A. If the goods remain in the possession of B and are damaged it will be A who will bear the loss.

The passing of property and risk is of great importance and it is important to recognise the significance of both concepts and their operation. Whilst risk passes normally at the same time as property in some contracts for international sale, risk may pass before property.

## 9.6 INTERNATIONAL CONTRACTS OF SALE AND INCOTERMS 2010

The basic ideas of a contract have been established. The following section considers the various contracts used for the international sales of goods. It will illustrate how they differ from the basic contractual model.

To ensure a seller and buyer understand the terms of the sales contract to which they agree, the International Chamber of Commerce has published an agreed set of rules which define the responsibilities of seller and buyer for delivery of goods under an international sales contract. They are known as the Incoterms. First published in 1936, the Incoterms are regularly revised. The current edition is *Incoterms 2010*, which became effective from 1 January 2011. The outline of the Incoterms, which are set out below, is only a guide to the buyers' and sellers' responsibilities under the individual contracts. Where possible, reference should be made to the definitive publication, *Incoterms 2010* which is available from the International Chamber of Commerce (ICC).

The *Incoterms 2010* are divided into two categories, namely, (i) terms for any mode or modes of transport and (ii) terms to be used for transport by sea and waterway. The two categories assist Incoterm users to identify the correct term for their particular requirement. Incoterms 2010 have reduced the number of terms used in Incoterms 2000 from 13 to 11.

The ICC publication, *Incoterms 2010*, helps the seller and buyer in international sales in the following ways:

- it provides extensive guidance and illustrative graphics to help users efficiently choose the correct rule for each transaction;
- new classifications are given to help identify the most suitable rule in relation to the mode of transport;
- there is advice for the use of electronic procedures;

- information is provided on security-related clearance for shipments;
- there is advice relating to the use of Incoterms 2010 in domestic intra EU trade.

Parties to a contract intent on being bound by the rules defining their responsibilities must state this explicitly in the contract. Unless they do so there is no certainty that the clarity of the definitions afforded by Incoterms will apply.

Incoterms are designed to cover a wide range of terms of sales. The terms extend from sales made at the point of origin of the goods, for example, the seller's factory, ex-works (EXW) to a sale which is made when the goods are delivered at the buyer's door, delivered duty paid (DDP). The terms are not inventions of the International Chamber of Commerce, but reflect the terms on which international traders prefer to do business. There are many reasons why parties to a sale will decide on different terms to be used, including the type of goods, the forms of transport to be used, payment methods and state of the market at the time of the sale.

International trade is a dynamic business. Customs and practices in international trade change with new forms of transport, improved communication, banking technology, national and international law and changes in demand and supply. As a result, the terms on which traders do business evolve to suit the changing times. The International Chamber of Commerce, regularly consults with trade bodies to regularly review and, if appropriate, revise the Incoterms. Recent amendments reflect the need to facilitate the increased use of electronic data interchange.

*Incoterms 2010* encompass the following terms:

Terms for any mode of transport:

| | |
|---|---|
| EXW | ex-works |
| FCA | free carrier |
| CPT | carriage paid to |
| CIP | carriage and insurance paid to |
| DAT | delivered at terminal |
| DAP | delivered at place |
| DDP | delivered duty paid |

Terms for sea and inland waterways:

| | |
|---|---|
| FAS | free alongside ship |
| FOB | free on board |
| CFR | cost and freight |
| CIF | cost, insurance and freight |

The *Incoterms 2010* revision saw the four terms DAF, delivered at frontier; DES, delivered ex-ship; DEQ, delivered ex-quay; DDU, delivered duty unpaid, in which there was significant overlap, replaced by the two new terms, DAP, delivered at place and DAT, delivered at terminal.

As in previous editions, the Incoterms fall into four alphabetical groups. The 'E' terms, ex-works, is used where the seller makes the goods available at their factory or premises. The 'F' terms indicate that the seller must deliver the goods to a carrier named by the buyer. The 'C' terms apply to situations where the seller arranges for the carriage of the goods, but without bearing the risk for loss or damage after shipment and despatch. The 'D' terms refer to cases where the seller bears all the costs and risks needed to deliver the goods to the country of destination. Each Incoterm defines the duties of buyer and seller in respect of every stage in the transport chain and establishes the division of costs, the stage when payment is made, property passes and risk is transferred from one to the other.

## 9.7 INCOTERMS RELATING TO SEA AND INLAND WATERWAYS

While it is useful to be familiar with the basic implications of each of the 11 terms, it is the four Incoterms relating to sea and inland waterways which are of particular importance to the shipping business. Full details of the terms can be found in Incoterms 2010, but the following explanations illustrate the important points:

### FAS – free alongside ship

Under the term FAS which names the loading port (for example, FAS Rotterdam), the buyer will nominate the port and possibly the berth to which the goods have to be delivered and the date delivery. The seller's obligations cease when the goods are alongside the vessel at the required time. Property and risk pass at this point and the obligation to pay arises.

### FOB – free on board

One of the most popular terms used in the international sales contract is that of FOB. In an FOB contract the seller has responsibility for bringing the goods to the named port and loading them on board the vessel. The goods then become the buyer's property. The buyer is responsible for paying freight and insurance on the goods. For example, FOB sales will always be expressed as FOB Mombasa or FOB Durban.

The buyer has a duty to name the ship and port. The ship will be nominated within a time specified in the contract. If the nomination is ineffective for some reason, the buyer may re-nominate provided that the contract time period has not expired. The buyer usually books the space on, or charters, the nominated ship. The port will be agreed in advance as the seller will need to calculate the cost of delivering the goods to the ship.

It is the seller's duty to arrange delivery of the goods on board the vessel. Risk will pass at the same time as the goods pass over the rail. It is at this time that the price will become payable. Sometimes the passing of property can be delayed, for example, if the transfer of the bill of lading is delayed. The bill of lading will signify transfer of ownership, sometimes known as title.

In an FOB contract the buyer will arrange his/her own insurance, although the seller must give the buyer sufficient information, most of which is in the sale contract, to enable insurance to be effected. If the seller fails to give the information required, risk will remain with the seller.

### Variants on the FOB contract

There are often modifications to the simple FOB format which will be agreed in advance and clearly stated in the contract. Modified FOB contracts are not provided for within the standard Incoterms. Under modified FOB contracts, the passing of property can be delayed.

### FOB stowed

The cost of stowage rests with the seller, so risk and property will pass on stowage and not when the goods pass over the ship's rail.

### FOB stowed and trimmed

The term is only applicable to bulk cargoes. Under the terms FOB stowed and trimmed, the seller will arrange and pay for the cost of trimming. Trimming is the even spreading of cargo across the hold to fill void spaces and reduce the risk of cargo shifting.

### FOB with services

Under the variant FOB with services, the seller may be required to arrange additional needs for the buyer. For example, the seller may agree to arrange the space on a ship.

**Some cargoes are easily trimmed**

### CIF (... named port of destination) cost, insurance and freight

The CIF contract is the most widely used form of international sales contract. As its title suggests, it involves the seller not only supplying the goods but also arranging insurance and carriage. The price of goods sold CIF will be higher than goods sold FOB as freight and insurance elements will be included in the selling price. The contract is based on the discharge port rather than the load port enabling the seller to complete the purchase of the goods when afloat.

The seller has several obligations, the first of which is to ship the goods as described in the contract of sale and in accordance with any further stipulations, such as time and place. The seller also will arrange the contract of carriage based on the usual conditions for the trade, provide assignable insurance for a reasonable value of the goods and prepare an invoice for the goods in accordance with the contract of sale. Finally, the seller must tender the invoice, the bill of lading and the policy of insurance to the buyer and their agent or banker.

The buyer must accept the documents and pay the price. The buyer may, of course, refuse to accept the seller's documents if they are not in accordance with the contract, though they may be re-tendered by the seller in a satisfactory condition within the contract period. Property passes when the documents are transferred. Risk though will have passed at the moment of shipment. If anything has happened to the goods during the voyage, the buyer will be protected, as he will receive the insurance policy when the documents are transferred.

In law, the transfer of the documents represents the transfer of the goods, so even if the goods are lost, the transfer of the documents can still complete the sale. The CIF contract has been judicially described as a 'contract for the sale of goods performed by the sale of documents'.

### CFR – cost and freight

The CFR contract is a variation of the CIF contract. The buyer pays for the goods and the freight. The buyer arranges the insurance. This form of contract is popular in countries that like to ensure that importing buyers place insurance on their own national insurers. As in the CIF contract, property passes and the price becomes payable upon transfer of the documents. The buyer is responsible for risks when the goods are loaded onto the ship.

## 9.8 NON-MARITIME INCOTERMS

In addition to the Incoterms relating to sea and inland waters, it is appropriate to have a basic knowledge of the other seven terms which are used in a contract of sale and cover any mode of transport. A brief outline of the terms is set out below:

### EXW – ex-works

The buyer has all the risk and cost from the seller's factory or premises including loading onto the vehicle at the seller's premises. The buyer will have all the costs of insurance, carriage and arranging for the export of the goods.

### FCA – free carrier named point

In this term of sale, the seller has to arrange delivery to the carrier at a named point. The risk then passes to the buyer at this point who is responsible for the arrangement and payment of insurance and carriage. This term of sale may be used to cover any single mode of transport or multi-modal transport. When using this term, it is important to understand the particular responsibilities of buyer and seller in respect of the different types of transport which may be used.

### CPT (... named place of destination) carriage paid to

In this term, the seller is responsible for paying all the freight or carriage to the destination named by the buyer. The risk, though, passes to the buyer once the goods are delivered to the first carrier regardless of the type of transport used and whether it is multi-modal or not.

### CIP – carriage and insurance paid to

CIP is very similar to CPT except that the seller is responsible for insuring the goods to the final destination, whatever the form of transport.

### DAT – delivered at terminal

The term 'delivered at terminal' is a new term under Incoterms 2010. DAT means that the seller pays for delivery of the goods to a named terminal at the agreed destination. The seller also bears the risks involved in bringing the goods to, and unloading them at, the destination terminal.

The buyer takes responsibility for the goods once they are unloaded at the terminal. The word terminal includes any place, whether covered or not, such as a quay, warehouse, container yard or road, rail or air cargo terminal.

The parties should clearly specify the terminal and, if possible, a specific point within the terminal for the delivery of the goods. The contract of carriage negotiated by the seller with the shipowner should make clear the exact point for delivery. If the parties intend the seller to bear the risks and costs involved in transporting and handling the goods from the terminal to another place, then the contract should be made out under the terms delivered at place (DAP), or delivered duty paid (DDP).

DAT requires the seller to clear the goods for export. The seller has no obligation to clear the goods for import, pay any import duty or carry out any import customs' formalities.

### DAP – delivered at place

The term 'delivered at place' is a new term under Incoterms 2010. The seller pays for and delivers the goods to a specified destination where they are placed at the disposal of the buyer. The buyer pays for the cost of importing the goods. The seller bears all risks in taking the goods to the named place.

The buyer and seller will clearly specify the point within the agreed place of destination to which the goods will be delivered.

Risks to that point are for the account of the seller. The seller will need to agree contracts of carriage to that point. Unless otherwise agreed, the seller is not entitled to recover costs under its contract of carriage relating to unloading at the place of destination. DAP requires the seller to clear the goods for export, but there is no obligation to clear the goods for import, pay any import duty or carry out any import formalities.

If the parties require the seller to clear the goods for import, pay import duty and carry out any import customs formalities, delivered duty paid (DDP) term should be used.

### DDP – delivered duty paid ...named place of destination

Here the seller is responsible for all costs until the goods are delivered to the final destination. This will include the payment of all import duties and taxes that have to be paid on the goods. On occasions, goods will be delivered DDP exclusive of duty and/or taxes when the buyer will be responsible for meeting any import duties or taxes due.

## 9.9 THE USE OF TERMS IN INTERNATIONAL TRADE

Consider the extreme ends of the range of Incoterms EXW and DDP. It seems clear that to expect one party to deal with all aspects of international transport will have drawbacks. For example, a buyer based in Canada wishes to purchase a consignment of washing machines from a manufacturer in Korea under an EXW contract of sale. The buyer would be responsible for arranging and paying for every stage of the transport chain, even the labour and equipment to load the goods at the manufacturer's factory. All the risks involved would be the responsibility of the buyer. In addition, the buyer would have to undertake clearing the export and import customs' formalities.

Given the burden of cost, responsibility and risk, it might be assumed that sellers would prefer to sell on EXW terms and that buyers would refuse to accept any terms other than DDP. In reality, most goods are sold on terms where both parties have some responsibility for aspects of carriage.

In the previous example, it would be easier, and probably cheaper for the Korean seller to arrange and pay for fork-lift trucks to load the washing machines on to vehicles and deliver them to the nearest port, than for a non-Korean-speaking buyer based in a distant continent and time zone to accomplish the same exercise. The Canadian buyer is in a better position to deal with import customs' entry, duty payments and to co-ordinate delivery to their depots than the seller. In addition to practical considerations, there may be advantages to one party or the other in controlling the ocean carriage, cargo-handling and insurance. An international seller of goods may find that buyers regard their arrangements for shipment through to a port in their country as a valuable service, leaving only local arrangements to be made by the buyer. The seller may be able to charge a premium price for their service and increase the profitability on the sale.

The exact terms used depend on the relative bargaining power of the buyer and seller. Under normal, stable market conditions, trading partners may use either FOB or CIF terms. A sudden swing in the market for the goods being traded may alter the terms under which the goods are sold. In a sellers' market, the producer is in a position to dictate the terms upon which they are prepared to sell their goods. It is probable that the terms used will be those which minimise their risk and ensure the most advantageous method of payment. In a buyers' market, sellers will be forced to adapt their terms of sale to the buyers' requirements if they want to enhance their chances of doing business.

Therefore, the terms on which goods are sold in international markets are a compromise, negotiated in the same way as all the other aspects of the business, between the parties who make the deal.

Risk of damage is slight but is always a threat

## 9.10 REMEDIES FOR BREACH OF CONTRACT

No discussion about the international sale of goods is complete without mention of the remedies available for breach of contract. The following is an outline of the most common remedies using English law.

### Remedies of the seller

The buyer will normally be in breach of the contract by refusing to accept the goods or by refusing to pay for them. The remedies depend upon whether the property has passed or not.

If the property has passed, the price will be due and the seller can sue for the price of the goods. Their damages will be the entire contract price. The remedy is also available if it is stipulated that the price is to be paid on a certain day and that day has passed.

If the property has not passed, the seller will have to sue for damages for non-acceptance of the goods. The disadvantage with this is that the seller will still have the goods and will be obliged to mitigate their loss by selling them elsewhere. The recoverable damages will be the difference between the original contract price and the price which was obtained on selling the goods to a third party. Damages for non-acceptance can be small.

### Stoppage in transit

A further valuable remedy for the seller is the right of stoppage in transit, conferred by the English Sale of Goods Act. This gives the seller the right to stop the goods in the course of carriage and to repossess them if the buyer is insolvent. There is an obvious danger that the seller will not be paid.

There are two important conditions, namely, the insolvency of the buyer and the goods which must still be in transit and not have been delivered to the buyer. If the carrier is the buyer's agent, as in an FOB contract, delivery to the carrier will in law be delivery to the buyer and the right of stoppage will not be available. But the courts are fairly lenient and, in the case of FOB contracts where the seller's duty terminates on delivery to the ship, they have tended to regard the carrier as an independent party and not the buyer's agent. The right of stoppage may be exercised. The right is exercised by informing the carrier. The seller will be liable for payment of any freight.

### Lien

If the seller still has the goods in their possession and the buyer becomes insolvent, the seller may retain the goods in defiance of their duty to deliver by exercising their unpaid seller's lien.

## Remedies of the Buyer

If the seller is in breach of a condition of the contract, it may arise because of one of the following circumstances:

- late delivery;
- short delivery, that is, not delivering a sufficient quantity;
- delivery of damaged goods or goods otherwise in breach of the seller's undertakings;
- non-delivery;
- tender of defective documents.

The buyer may reject the goods or, at an earlier stage, the documents. He would then sue for damages or non-delivery of the goods. The acceptance of documents does not necessarily prevent the subsequent rejection of the goods. Damages will be the difference between the contract price and the market price of the goods at the time the goods ought to have been correctly delivered. As with the seller's right to damage for non-acceptance, these may be negligible.

If the buyer decides not to reject the goods, or has lost the right to reject them by having unduly interfered with the goods, they will be kept and the seller sued for damages for defective delivery. Damages will be calculated according to the difference between the value of the goods as and when delivered and the market value of the same goods had they been delivered on time or undamaged.

### Specific performance

The buyer's equivalent of the seller's right to sue for the price is to demand the correct delivery of the goods and performance of the contract. This is known as asking for an order for specific performance and is likely to be granted only if it is impossible to obtain the contract goods at any price elsewhere. It is a very rare order for a court to make.

## 9.11 LAW AND JURISDICTION

The examples above show the position under English law. Whether a particular contract of sale is subject to English law is determined by reference to the contract itself.

The contract may stipulate that it is to be 'governed by English law and that disputes are to be referred to an English court or arbitration proceedings'. In the absence of such a stipulation, reference must be made to the nationalities of the parties and the countries within which performance of the contract is to take place. If the nationality and performance of the contract point to one country, the law of that country will apply.

There may be a difference between the governing law of a contract and the jurisdiction in which claims may be brought. For example, in the absence of a specific provision in the contract, the High Court in England might consider that it has jurisdiction over a particular dispute, while applying the law of some other country to determine the rights and responsibilities of the parties.

The British government, like the governments of other countries, is considering ratification of the UN Convention on Contracts for the International Sale of Goods. If ratified, this will fundamentally alter the existing structure of these contracts.

## 9.12 POSTSCRIPT

The section regarding international contracts of sale is concerned only with the legal relationship between the two parties to the contract for the sale of goods, that is, between the buyer and the seller. It does not consider the relationships between those parties and third parties between which other contracts are made, for example, between the merchant and a carrier.

Chapter 10

# Finance and insurance in international trade

*If the entire population of the world is taken as 100, then half of the total wealth would be held by 6 people*

## 10.1 INTRODUCTION

The distance and time scales inherent in international trade present a number of problems to businesses. The buyer will try to ensure that the agreement made with the seller results in the delivery of the goods at the right place and time and will have minimum impact on cash flow. Likewise, the seller will want to secure payment with the minimum time between producing and/or shipping the goods and receipt of payment. The seller is also concerned with the maintenance of cash flow.

The concerns of the buyer and seller have implications for those involved in the international transportation of goods as the method and timing of payment will depend on the correct preparation and presentation of transport documents, adherence to shipment and delivery dates and any restrictions caused by transshipment.

## 10.2 METHODS OF PAYMENT

Two main aspects concerning the payment and financing of international trade are considered, namely (i) the method and security of payment and (ii) the implications that certain methods of payment or financing will have for those in shipping business.

The method of payment in any sales contract is a matter of negotiation between buyer and seller. It depends upon mutual trust and the financial standing of the buyer. In a competitive buyers' market, the buyer can negotiate more advantageous payment terms than in a sellers' market. Unless cash is used between the buyer and the seller, payment will involve cost.

There is a range of different of payment methods available which provide varying degrees of security and advantages for buyer or seller. Not all payment methods are appropriate for use in international sales.

### Cash with order

Cash with order is the most advantageous form of payment for the seller. Also referred to as advance payment against proforma invoice, cash with order is a form of payment in advance. The method of payment is the most secure for the seller since the full payment for the goods is received before shipment is made. It is of great risk to the buyer because the buyer essentially extends credit to the seller and has little redress against incomplete adherence to the contract.

### Open account

Open account is the most favourable form of payment for a buyer. On receiving the order, the seller will despatch the goods. The invoice will be forwarded to the buyer. The seller will await payment under terms previously agreed. The payment terms will cover an agreed period for payment following receipt of the goods by the buyer. The seller is at risk of the buyer defaulting in payment while already possessing the goods. While the open account method of payment is common for a sale between financially-sound businesses within national boundaries, it is not a common method of payment in international trade except where there are established trading patterns. Open account is increasingly being used in stable areas like the European Union.

## The bill of exchange

The bill of exchange is an alternative to using cash with order or open account. A bill of exchange is defined as: *'an unconditional order in writing addressed by one person to another, signed by the person giving it (usually the seller), requiring the person to whom it is addressed (usually the buyer) to pay on demand or at a fixed or determinable future time, a sum certain in money to, or to the order of, a specified person or to the bearer (usually the seller or their bank)'.*

The bill of exchange is similar in appearance to a cheque and stipulates payment at a future date, for example, 90 days from the date of issue. The future date of payment extends credit to the buyer who may be able to sell a significant proportion of the goods purchased, before being required to pay the sum due on the bill. The buyer's cash flow is therefore under less strain. The buyer may be able to afford to purchase larger quantities than under a less flexible form of payment which in turn can benefit the seller, who is able to do more business with the buyer. The advantage of bills of exchange from the seller's point of view lies in the difference between the bill of exchange and a cheque. Unlike a cheque, a bill of exchange is negotiable. If the seller does not want to wait the full 90 days to collect payment they can discount (sell) the bill to a bank for slightly less than its face value.

In order to spread the cost of the goods to the buyer, different terms could be agreed. For example, '25% of the cost of the goods should be paid on receipt (or on transfer of the documents or whatever terms have been agreed for the sale) with the balance payable on three equal bills of exchange maturing at 30, 60 and 90 days respectively'. The buyer will accept the bills of exchange and hand them to the seller as part payment (in this case) for the goods. If the seller does not discount the bills at an earlier date, he/she will present them on the due date at the buyer's bank (or wherever has been agreed beforehand) for payment. If the seller chooses to discount one or more of the bills, the bank or discount house who buys the debt may sell it on to other institutions or use it as security until the maturity date, when it will be presented for settlement.

## Documentary letter of credit

The documentary letter of credit is the method of payment most frequently used in international trade. It provides a good compromise between the needs of both the buyer or importer and the seller or exporter. It is a flexible and safe form of payment giving security to both parties to the sale. It requires the carrier or the agent to fulfil their role with care. A documentary letter of credit is 'an obligation of the bank that opens the letter of credit to pay the agreed amount to the seller on behalf of the buyer, upon receipt of the documents specified in the letter of credit'.

The bank providing the letter of credit is known as the issuing bank and, acting on the instruction of the buyer, it undertakes to pay an agreed amount to the seller or beneficiary.

The opening of a documentary letter of credit is normally done by the issuing bank through its correspondent bank in the country of residence of the seller or beneficiary. There are exceptions. The buyer or applicant is required to state where the credit is to be paid otherwise it will be paid in the buyer's country. Some countries may restrict where a letter of credit is established and paid because of foreign exchange restrictions. The intermediary through whom the letter of credit is established is known as the advising/confirming or paying bank.

In summary, there are four parties involved in a documentary credit, namely, the buyer (importer) known as applicant, the seller (exporter) known as the beneficiary, the buyer's bank known as the issuing bank and the seller's bank known as the confirming, advising or payment bank.

A bank will not interpret the terms of a documentary letter of credit. The terms must be adhered to exactly as stated.

To ensure uniformity of interpretation by banks in respect of a documentary letter of credit, the International Chamber of Commerce has produced guidelines entitled *'Uniform Customs and Practice for Documentary Credits',* usually abbreviated to 'UCP'. The guidelines are reviewed at irregular intervals. The latest revision was undertaken in 2007 and is identified by the number 600, hence UCP 600.

The documentary letter of credit is normally described as irrevocable, meaning that it cannot be revoked once it has been opened. It will lapse if the documents are not presented within the stipulated time. On the buyer's instruction, the issuing bank irrevocably commits itself to pay the beneficiary on the correct presentation of the requirement documents.

If a seller is uncertain of the financial status of the buyer, they will require the credit to be confirmed. This means that the bank in the buyer's country notifying the letter of credit gives an undertaking to pay without recourse to the seller, unless otherwise stipulated. The seller is certain of receiving payment providing they present the right documents. The correspondent bank may be willing to add their confirmation at the seller's request and expense, if requested and authorised by the issuing bank to do so.

When the buyer instructs his/her bank to open a letter of credit, he/she will state explicitly the type of credit and the conditions under which the bank will pay the seller. The buyer may elect to pay a sight draft providing it is accompanied by certain documents that ensure the delivery of the goods at the correct time and place. Normally transshipment is allowed and documents must be presented for payment within a number of days from the date of shipment. There is usually an expiry date which is the latest date for the presentation of documents by the seller. The seller must forward the right documents to the advising bank within the time limit agreed. The documents must fully comply with the instructions in the letter of credit and be correctly completed in every detail.

## 10.3 DOCUMENTS ASSOCIATED WITH THE LETTER OF CREDIT

To receive payment, the beneficiary (exporter) must present the documents to the advising bank as required by the documentary letter of credit. Typical documents to be presented will depend on the terms in the documentary letter of credit but include financial documents such as a bill of exchange, commercial documents such as the commercial invoice, insurance documents, cargo insurance policy, official documents including certificate of origin, export licence and phytosanitary certificate (for plant life) and transport documents, specifically the bill of lading. Brief comments on the invoice, insurance and the bill of lading are given below:

### Invoice

The invoice must specify the quality and quantity of the goods consigned, together with the unit and total price. In some instances, the buyer will insist upon the invoice being certified by an independent body such as a chamber of commerce. Some countries (because of import restrictions) may require a consular invoice in addition to a commercial invoice.

### Insurance

If the letter of documentary credit covers a sale where the seller (exporter) is responsible for insuring the goods, for example, under a CIF or CIP contract a certificate of insurance will be required.

### Bill of lading (B/L)

The bill of lading is a document of title and is the ultimate security for payment. The letter of documentary credit is most specific about the information contained in the bill of lading. Details in the boxed form of the CONGENBILL 2007 Bill of Lading, shown in the appendices will have to be accurate. Details include the names of the shipper and consignee, the ship's name and names of the ports of loading and discharge, the shipper's description of the goods including gross weight, the date of shipment and a statement about the condition of the goods when received on board, signed by the ship's master. The slightest deviation of detail from the stipulations contained in the letter of documentary credit could result in payment being refused or delayed. In a documentary letter of credit, the use of the word clean is used in describing the bill of lading. The bill of lading is not clean if it contains an endorsement relating to the condition of the cargo. An endorsement would guarantee refusal by the bank to pay. The bill of lading is a receipt for the goods shipped and is evidence of the contract of carriage.

## 10.4 CONFIRMING HOUSES

Direct selling between an exporter and importer is not the only way that international trade can be conducted. Another method is to use a confirming house, sometimes known as an exporting house.

The use of a confirming house as a method of executing international trade evolved in European countries that administered substantial overseas territories during the early 20th century. Today, confirming houses are found in most industrialised countries.

The role of the confirming house is an unusual mix of agent and principal. The purchase negotiations may take place directly between the overseas buyer and the seller. Alternatively, the buyer may choose to have the confirming house act as their agent to locate and order goods. The title 'confirming' is earned because the confirming house 'confirms' responsibility for payment to the seller when the goods are shipped. In some contracts, the confirming house's commitment goes further by accepting full liability as a principal for the seller while retaining a position as agent for the buyer. Regardless of the contract terms relating to the sale, the confirming house will always be a principal in its dealings with the carrier.

## 10.5 RISKS IN INTERNATIONAL TRADING

All business carries an element of risk, but businesses involved in international trade have to deal with additional risks and be able to recognise what mitigating measures they can take.

Risks in international trade can be divided into many types including economic risk, political risk, foreign exchange risk, commercial risk, cultural risk, knowledge inadequacy and transport risk.

For the buyer, risks can be mitigated in many ways, including dealing with a seller who has a sound reputation, agreeing to a secure method of payment, such as the use of a letter of documentary credit, buying and selling in the same currency to reduce foreign exchange risk (or hedging against a foreign exchange risk), ensuring effective insurance cover against transport risks and having a contingency plan against an unfavourable event.

The seller exporter can mitigate against international trade risk in ways which reciprocate those used by the buyer. Risk can be mitigated by dealing with a buyer importer who has a sound reputation, using secured methods of payment such as the letter of documentary credit, taking care that the letter does not contain ambiguous terms, acquiring sufficient expertise to ensure correct preparation of documentation, acknowledging cultural differences and, ideally, selling in the same currency used by the buyer (or hedging against foreign exchange risk by entering into a forward or option foreign exchange contract with a bank). There is also a need to take out adequate insurance cover against transport risks and consider a contingency plan in the case of an unforeseen event occurring.

The following sections are concerned with foreign exchange risk and mitigation and the insurance of the goods in international trade.

## 10.6 FOREIGN EXCHANGE

Foreign exchange is defined as the exchange of one currency for another or the conversion of one currency into another. Foreign exchange may also refer to the global market where currencies are traded. Foreign exchange transactions have increased due to globalisation and are now the largest financial market with daily volumes measured in the trillions of dollars. Foreign exchange is involved in international payment where the parties to a contract of sale are located in countries using different currencies.

### Foreign exchange fluctuations

In any international trade transaction, the buyer or the seller, and sometimes both, will be involved in a foreign exchange transaction, buying or selling currency used in payment for the goods.

Rates of exchange between different currencies constantly fluctuate creating a problem for parties involved in an international sale as the price agreed when the sales contract was made may not be reflected in the money received by the seller or paid by the buyer.

Take a simple example. If the price set for a consignment of goods sent to the USA by a UK exporter was $6,000 calculated at an exchange rate of $1.50 to £1, the exporter would expect to receive £4,000 when the exporter changed the dollars at the bank. If by the time the payment was made the exchange rate had changed to $2.00 to £1, the exporter would only receive £3,000. An anticipated profit on the transaction might be turned into a loss.

Parties to an international transaction have several different options to mitigate the risk of currency fluctuation working against them. After assessing the risks, the parties could decide to do nothing, and take a chance that any unfavourable fluctuation will not be sufficiently serious to put their business in danger. A favourable move of the exchange rate will be to their obvious advantage. If the decision to do nothing is taken, the currency needs will be met by being purchased or sold on the spot market at the time of the transaction. Parties dealing in large amounts of currency or working on small margins may find working on the spot market an unacceptable risk. Banks provide alternatives for hedging against currency losses. Alternatives include the use of forward exchange contracts and foreign currency options. A combination of different methods may be used to spread the risk of currency fluctuation and keep down costs.

Exchange rates have a great impact on international trade

## Spot contract

A spot contract is an agreement to buy or sell one currency in exchange for another at the spot exchange rate prevailing on the day of the agreement.

## Spot exchange rate

The rate at which currencies are exchanged is known as the spot exchange rate, the current value of one currency compared to the other. Currency spot exchange rates are quoted in the financial pages of the press. Two rates are quoted: the bank's selling price and the bank's buying price. Spot exchange rate movements are unpredictable.

## Forward exchange contract

A forward exchange contract allows the purchase or sale of one currency against another for settlement at a fixed time ahead. The forward exchange contract guarantees the value of a future transaction by locking in the spot rate on the day of the deal. It eliminates uncertainty and protects against unfavourable currency fluctuations. For example, a contract made on 16 November that is 'two months forward fixed' becomes due on 16 January. Alternatively, if the exporter wanted some flexibility a 'three-month forward contract with an option over the second and third month' could be chosen.

Further flexibility may be achieved by using an 'option-dated forward contract' which is similar to a regular forward contract except that the owner of the contract can settle it at any time within a pre-set 30-day period

Forward rates are calculated by referring to the spot rate (either bank selling or bank buying) and then using the forward rates to calculate the contract price. The forward rates will be quoted as being at a premium or a discount which reflects the difference in interest rates on the interbank market rather than what the bank regards as the possible exchange rates in the future. For example, currencies with lower interest rates than the pound sterling will be said to stand at a premium while those with higher interest rates will be at a discount.

The example below shows the US$ being quoted as a premium.

| **Spot Rate £1 =** | **$1.5040** | **—** | **$1.5120** |
|---|---|---|---|
| One month | .10c | — | .05c pm |
| Two months | .15c | — | .12c pm |
| Three months | .25c | — | .18c pm |

To calculate a forward rate the bank will deduct the appropriate premium from the spot rate. So, based on the above figures, the forward contract rates would be as follows:

| | **Bank Selling** | **Bank Buying** |
|---|---|---|
| One month | $1.5030 | $1.5115 |
| Two months | $1.5025 | $1.5108 |
| Three months | $1.5015 | $1.5102 |

As the dollar becomes more expensive, fewer dollars will be received for sterling if you are buying from the bank, but more sterling when the bank is buying dollars from you.

Compare this with an example of the dollar being quoted at a discount:

| **Spot Rate £1 =** | **$1.5040** | **—** | **$1.5120** |
|---|---|---|---|
| One month | .03c | — | .08c pm |
| Two months | .10c | — | .15c pm |
| Three months | .17c | — | .23c pm |

To calculate the forward rate in the case of a currency that is becoming cheaper, the appropriate discount will be added giving the following forward rates:

| | **Bank Selling** | **Bank Buying** |
|---|---|---|
| One month | $1.5043 | $1.5128 |
| Two months | $1.5050 | $1.5135 |
| Three months | $1.5057 | $1.5143 |

As the dollar is becoming cheaper, when the bank sells you dollars in the future, you will get more for your pound, but if the bank is buying dollars from you, you will get less in the future than at the spot rate.

If the contract is an option-dated forward option, the bank will have the choice of quoting either the rate at the beginning or the end of the option period. For example, if you had the forward option contract mentioned above, three months forward with the option over the second or third months, the rate could either be the one month rate (the rate at the beginning of the period) or the three months rate (the rate at the end of the period). If the currency is at a premium, then the bank will sell at the rate at the end of the period and buy at the rate at the beginning of the period. If, on the other hand, the currency is at a discount, the bank will sell at the rate at the beginning of the period and buy at the rate at the end of the period.

The bank will always buy or sell at a rate it finds most advantageous. The customer will know exactly what the rate will be when he/she make the contract and so has certainty about what they will receive in the future. The seller may be able to adjust their price to the contract exchange rate.

In summary, the contract rate is set when the contract is made. The option in the contract is there so that the customer may choose exactly when during the option period they will buy or sell the currency concerned. Once the contract is made, it must be completed.

Four considerations need to be recognised when arranging a foreign exchange contract:

- the bank buys high;
- the bank sells low;
- a discount is added to the spot rate;
- a premium is deducted from the spot rate.

A bank is in the business of making a profit and will set the option contract rate that is most advantageous to itself.

## Foreign currency options

The definition of a foreign currency option is that it is a contract that grants the holder the right, but not the obligation, to buy or sell currency at a specified exchange rate during a specified period of time.

Foreign currency options are a flexible way of obtaining protection against currency rate movements. The key difference between foreign currency options and forward exchange contracts is that the holder of a foreign currency option is not obliged to declare the option if it is not advantageous to do so. As defined, the bank confers a right but not an obligation to buy (or sell) currency at an agreed rate. If the currency moves in the holder's favour during the option period, then the option can simply be allowed to lapse. The foreign currency option provides protection against adverse currency rate fluctuations.

Foreign currency options are useful for businesses that may require an amount of a foreign currency at some future date but cannot be sure of this – for example, during the negotiation of prices for an international deal which takes into account a known rate of exchange. If the deal goes ahead, the guaranteed rate could be improved upon, but could never be worse than the option rate. If the deal falls through, the option can be allowed to lapse.

There are two basic types of option available from banks, the European option and the American option. In European options the exercise date (strike date) is fixed and is the only date upon which the option can be exercised. American options can be exercised at any time up to the expiry date, after which it too expires. There is a price (the premium) that is paid upfront to the bank at the time the option is arranged. This is usually quoted as a percentage of the currency amount, and will be a function of the strike rate agreed, the option period and type, as well as the bank's assessment of the volatility of the currencies involved and the interest rate differentials between them.

Assuming that the worst rate an exporter is prepared to accept is $1.65 when exchanging the proceeds of a sale in dollars for pounds sterling, in order to protect themselves against a worse rate, they may decide to buy an American-style currency option to sell one million US dollars at a strike price of $1.65 for expiry in six months' time. If, at any time during the period, the market (spot) rate is worse than $1.65, the option can be exercised and the dollars sold at $1.65 through the bank. Alternatively, if the market rate is better than $1.65 the option can be allowed to lapse and the dollars sold in the market at the spot rate.

Traders who regularly work in particular foreign currencies will operate foreign currency accounts through their banks. They will hold one or more currencies without being forced to buy or sell at a disadvantage when they receive or make payments. In order to protect their own currencies, some countries impose restrictions on the use of foreign currency accounts. Permission may be required from a government department to buy or sell currency.

## 10.7 TRANSACTION COSTS IN INTERNATIONAL TRADE

International trade is a complex business, and buyers and sellers will face many more problems than those who undertake business within national borders. Transaction costs involved in international trade are varied, those involved in arranging international payments having been covered above. Other transaction costs in international trade will include transport, insurance and documentation.

### Transport costs in the bulk shipping sector

In the bulk shipping sector, which is synonymous to a free market, transport costs will fluctuate according to the state of the market and the cost of bunkers, both being factors outside the control of the buyer or seller of goods.

Trading in futures of any type involves forming a view on the movement of prices and what level they are likely to be at some time in the future. There are futures markets in most commodities. In the shipping business, volatile freight rates provide the opportunity to establish a futures freight market.

In the dry bulk trades, if the charterer is the seller of the goods, he may have sold the goods to be shipped at some future date. The charterer will be concerned that freight rates might rise resulting in reduced trading profit. The charterer will protect his position by 'buying' a freight futures contract. If freight rates rise sharply at the time the ship is fixed, the loss they incur on the physical market will be offset, to some extent, by the profit they make on their futures position.

Conversely, shipowners face the opposite risk to charterers. Shipowners will lose money if freight markets fall. Shipowners can protect themselves against falling freight rates by selling futures contracts. If, contrary to expectation, the freight rates rise they will benefit from higher earnings in the physical market, offsetting money lost on futures trading.

Charterers and shipowners can mitigate their risk to freight movements using forward freight agreements (FFA). A forward freight agreement (FFA) is defined as a 'means of hedging exposure to freight market risk through the trading of specified time charter and voyage charter rates for forward position'. Indices, maintained by the Baltic Exchange, are used for the settlement of forward freight agreements. The Baltic Exchange Dry Index (BDI) which succeeded the Baltic Freight Index (BFI) in 1999 is a composite of dry bulk time charter averages of Capesize, Panamax, Supramax and handysize bulk carriers. The BDI is maintained by the Baltic Exchange as a leading indicator of the spot dry bulk cargo market.

In addition to the BDI, the Baltic Exchange has developed a series of indices for the dry bulk and tanker shipping markets. The indices are based on an assessment by global panels of shipbrokers, indicating an underlying understanding of what is happening in the freight markets. Identified by a three or four letter abbreviation, the indices focus on a specific area of the market. For example, BPI refers to the Baltic Exchange Panamax Index; BHSI refers to the Baltic Exchange Handymax Index and BDTI the Baltic Exchange Dirty Tanker Index. The Baltic Dry Index and Tanker Indices are provided by *Lloyd's List*. The Baltic Exchange provides forward assessments on specific dry bulk and tanker routes. With an index-based futures contract, it is not possible to deliver an actual cargo or a ship in settlement of a position, so all the contracts traded in freight futures are settled in cash, based on the actual level of the index on the date that the position matures.

A market for trading dry bulk cargo freight futures was established at the Baltic Exchange, London in 1985. Known as the Baltic International Freight Futures Exchange (BIFFEX) it allowed the trading of ocean freight future contracts, with settlements based on the Baltic Freight Index (BFI). BIFFEX was modestly successful for some years but, by 2001, the volume of dry bulk cargo contracts being traded was insufficient and BIFFEX ceased trading.

Presently, forward freight agreements are arranged through the Forward Freight Agreement Brokers' Association (FFABA), an independent association of FFA broking members of the Baltic Exchange.

The FFA market depends on the willingness of shipowners and charterers to buy and sell contracts. If both parties are involved in the physical market reflected in the appropriate index, they can expect the index to reflect their actual trading conditions. To this extent, their activity in the futures market can be seen as hedging their prospects in the physical market. If they gain in one, they will lose in the other. Their exposure to large fluctuations in freight will be reduced.

Parties who are neither shipowners nor charterers can buy and sell contracts in the freight futures markets. Such trading takes place in most futures markets and lends liquidity to the market. However, as they have no vested interest in the physical market, they are not involved in hedging operations, but are investing on a purely speculative basis, hoping to make a profit by merely trading the futures market.

Trading in forward freight agreements is a specialised form of hedging. It requires considerable expertise and knowledge of the market. It should not be undertaken without careful consideration and expert advice.

## 10.8 INSURANCE

Insurance is a vital aspect in any business as it provides a degree of security to the parties involved. There are many uncertainties and risks in international trade and therefore insurance assumes particular importance. If insurance did not exist, the number of businesses willing to be involved in international trade would diminish. Businesses would have to insure themselves by retaining capital sums against the possibility of loss, hampering management of the business and reducing the opportunity to make profit.

Much marine insurance is booked through Lloyd's of London

## Insurable interest

In general, a person may only take out insurance if they have an interest in the goods or property insured. The assured, the person whom the insurance covers, must be in a position to suffer loss if there is a mishap. If a person does not have an insurable interest, he/she may not look after the property or goods adequately and could benefit if there were a loss. If there is no insurable interest, a claim would be declared void.

The essential features of insurable interest in respect of marine cargo insurance are:

- there must be a physical object exposed to marine peril;
- the insured must have some legal relationship to that object in consequence of which they benefit by its preservation or are prejudiced by its loss or damage.

In the shipping business the insured need not have an insurable interest at the time of placing the insurance, but must have an interest at the time of the loss.

The simplest form of insurable interest is the ownership of the goods insured.

A buyer will have an insurable interest in the goods whether they are FOB or CIF, even though they have the right to reject them and return them to the seller if they are contractually incorrect on being received.

The seller has an insurable interest while they have the risk or property of the goods or both. If the buyer rejects the goods or there is stoppage in transit, then the rights will revert to the seller. If payment is required before ownership passes, then the goods remain the seller's property until payment is made. Having insurance in place that takes effect at the moment of handover, when risk passes from seller to buyer is important, for example, in ship sale and purchase (S&P) transactions.

Carriers have an interest because of their liability to cargo owners, as do shippers, to the extent that they wish to cover freight paid in advance.

A charterer has an insurable interest, as they have a liability to the shipowner. For example, if a ship is fixed to load at 'a good and safe berth, always afloat' and, while loading, the ship grounds due to the water being shallower than expected, the shipowner can hold the charterer responsible for damage to the hull. Or, if the charterer describes the cargo as harmless and it subsequently corrodes the vessel's holds, the charterer will be held responsible for the damage. Time charterers have additional liabilities to the shipowner with regard to their control over the ship on hire. It will be more extensive than for a voyage charterer. Charterers can take out specific insurance cover in respect of the additional liabilities.

The insurer of a subject matter will have an insurable interest in the risk they have written, allowing the risk to be spread through reinsurance.

Commission to agents and brokerage fees may also create an insurable interest. Indeed, some shipbroking companies insure their brokerage as a matter of routine under all their time charter fixtures.

A broker can have an insurable interest. The broker should be able to insure against a significant error made on the fixture of a ship which results in a claim by an owner or a charterer. The form of insurance is known as Professional Indemnity Insurance.

## 10.9 TRADE TERMS IN EXPORT SALES

In any export transaction, the responsibility for arranging insurance will be either with the seller or buyer as agreed in the contract of sale. If the contract includes Incoterms 2010, then the responsibility for the arranging and payment of the insurance will be absolutely clear.

For example, under an FOB sale, the goods are at the risk of the exporter until such time as they have effectively crossed the ship's rail and they will generally arrange their own insurance for that leg of the journey. Once they have crossed the ship's rail, the goods will be at the buyer's risk and it is their responsibility to place the insurance coverage.

If goods are sold CIF then it is the responsibility of the seller to arrange, at his/her cost and in a form that is transferable, a policy of marine insurance.

The transferability of the policy under a CIF sale is vital. While the seller takes out the policy and pays the premium to cover the risk, the most likely time for damage to be discovered is after discharge when the ownership has passed to the buyer.

## 10.10 WARRANTIES

In insurance the word warranty has a very specific meaning. It is an undertaking by the insured to observe certain conditions. The rule is embodied in section 33 of the Marine Insurance Act 1906, which states that 'a warranty…is a condition which must be exactly complied with, whether it is material to the risk or not. If it be not so complied with...the insurer is discharged from liability'.

For example, if there is a warranty that the insured goods have a certain type of packaging and this is not adhered to, then in the event of a loss, the claim may be disallowed on the grounds that the goods were improperly packed. This is regardless of the fact that the loss may not in any way be due to the packaging.

- Express warranties

  An express warranty is an undertaking actually written into the contract to perform a certain act. Failure to carry out the condition may well result in the policy being declared void.

- Implied warranties

  An implied warranty is an undertaking not written in the policy but implied by law to exist in the contract. Two implied warranties in a marine insurance policy cover seaworthiness of the ship and legality to the extent that the insured is in a position to control it.

## 10.11 TYPES OF CARGO POLICIES

Different types of insurance policy are available for cargo:

- Facultative insurance;
- Open insurance contracts (open contracts);
- Floating policy;
- Open cover.

### Facultative insurance

Facultative insurance refers to the placing of a specific or named risk relating to a particular shipment. The effecting of this type of insurance can be a complex process. Exporters regularly involved in international sales would find the placing of facultative insurance for every consignment time-consuming.

### Open insurance contracts

It is to the exporter's advantage if the cost of insurance is standardised. In this way, when making quotations or agreeing particular terms of sale, the exporter will know the approximate cost of insurance cover. The use of open insurance contracts, known more simply as open contracts, has become more popular in recent years. There are three types of open contracts, namely the floating policy, open cover and open policy.

### Floating policy

A floating policy provides insurance, which will cover a certain total value of goods over a certain period of time. For example, a floating policy could cover 'shipments from London to Vancouver over a period of six months for leather goods to a total value of £1 million'. The policy will provide a general description of the risk. The particulars of the goods and the ship to be used will be declared prior to individual shipment. The goods are declared to the insurer until the agreed ceiling is reached and/or the policy is exhausted. Each shipment is declared on a special form and the amount outstanding on the policy is reduced by the amount of that shipment. The assured is bound to declare each shipment and the insurer is bound to accept the shipment providing that it complies with the agreed terms. Since the policy is issued when it is first negotiated, policies will not be issued for each individual shipment, but certificates of insurance will be issued instead. A seller using CIF terms will need to ascertain that the contract of sale allows the presentation of a certificate of insurance rather than a policy of insurance. The disadvantage of a floating policy to the insured is that the insurer expects to be paid a premium deposit related to the total value of the policy. An average premium is estimated and is adjusted when the declarations of actual cargo carried are made.

### Open cover

Under open cover there is automatic cover available for a period of time. The period of time may be for one year or longer. Open cover can be agreed on a permanent basis unless cancelled by either party. Under the open cover agreement, the insurer agrees to cover all consignments and the premium rates are fixed. This form of insurance gives the greatest flexibility and stability of price to the exporter. Open cover insurance can be arranged on varied terms and can be complex. For example, the cover may contain a limit on the value of goods to be carried per consignment on any one ship, or a limitation may be placed on the value of goods to be in one place prior to shipment.

#### Advantages of the use of open cover

The use of open cover and open policies has a number of advantages:

- as there is continuous automatic cover in force, the insured avoids the risk of omitting to effect the necessary insurance cover;
- the cost of obtaining insurance is known in advance, which enables a seller to include a precise figure for the insurance element when calculating the CIF price. For some commodities the insurance element may be very large;
- insurers are prepared to give better terms to an exporter arranging an annual policy than to one arranging cover on an individual basis;
- it may be, from time to time, that claims will arise which are not strictly speaking recoverable. If the insured has had regular dealings with a particular underwriter, they may well be in a better position to negotiate some form of commercial settlement than for insurance arranged on a facultative basis.

## 10.12 EFFECTING INSURANCE

Any person involved in international trade would rather have the safe delivery of a consignment than be involved in an insurance claim but, because of the risks involved in international trade, claims frequently arise. When claims arise, the insurance cover taken out is expected to meet the claims which are made.

Great care needs to be taken when arranging insurance, particularly under an open cover. The failings in any type of cover may only become evident when a claim is being made and then it is too late. Cover should always be as comprehensive as possible and drawn up in such a way that it meets the individual requirements of the company.

In order to understand the considerations, an underwriter will need to consider when deciding whether to accept a risk, it is worth examining the type of information they are likely to require.

## Cargo and packing

The insurer will require a full description of the goods, together with exact details of the way in which they will be packed. If they are containerised, what type of packing will there be within the container? If they are not containerised, will the goods be contained in cartons, drums, crates or bales or other form of packing?

## Method of shipment

The insurer will require full details of the method of shipment of the goods. If the goods are containerised, will the shipment be door-to-door, part of a groupage consignment or a single or multiple drop delivery? If the cargo is not containerised, will it be a conventional shipment, carried in a chartered vessel, or what special arrangements will need to be made regarding transshipment?

## The Voyage

In deciding a premium, the length of the voyage and ultimate destination is of major importance, especially if war and strikes rate charges apply. Where there is a high level of risk, for example, when warlike activities are taking place, additional insurance premium will be charged.
The voyage may involve an element of storage if the goods are being sent to a distribution centre for onward transmission. The insurer will need to know, otherwise the cover will cease at the original distribution centre.

## Basis of valuation

In export transactions, goods are frequently sold and resold and their value may alter as a result. It is useful to agree a value of the goods in advance as it will save a great deal of time and expense in the event of a claim. A policy where the value is agreed in advance is known as a valued policy. The insurer may include expenses and profit in assessing the value. If no fraud is involved, the agreed value will be taken as the basis for a claim of total or partial loss. Whilst there is an agreed value of the goods, the insured can cover the goods at a lower cost

In international trade, the basis of the valuation may be CIF invoice value plus 10%. In a claim against the policy, the claimant would receive the CIF value plus 10%. When making a declaration under an open policy, the same valuation will be used. The insured may include a percentage to cover anticipated profit and/or inflation when agreeing a basis of valuation. The principle in marine insurance is to try and place the insured into a position they would have been in had the venture been successful.

An unvalued policy requires proof of value in the event of a claim.

## 10.13 CONDITIONS OF INSURANCE

The conditions of insurance, which dictate the level of cover, are important and merit special consideration. A marine insurance policy is not like a house comprehensive policy or motor policy where it can be reasonably presumed that all policies offer the same basic protection.

## 10.14 MARINE CARGO INSURANCE POLICIES

Most cargo policies will incorporate one of three sets of clauses known as Institute Cargo Clauses A, B or C. The widest insurance cover is provided under Institute Cargo Clauses A, a more restrictive cover under Institute Cargo Clauses B, and the most restrictive cover under Institute Cargo Clauses C. The Institute Cargo Clauses have been adopted by the international marine insurance sector including the International Underwriting Association of London (IUA).

### Institute Cargo Clauses A

The Institute Cargo Clauses A are the most widely used clauses associated with dry cargoes. The cover afforded is defined by the risks clause, which reads: *'This insurance covers all risks of loss of, or damage to, the subject matter insured ....'* While the clause states all risks, there are exclusions to the cover provided. Excluded risks include losses due to ordinary leakage, ordinary loss in weight or volume and ordinary wear and tear of the subject matter insured. Among risks excluded from A cover are losses due to the inherent nature of the subject matter, losses due to delay, expenses arising from the financial default of the shipowner or charterer, and losses due to deliberate damage to the subject matter by a wrongful act.

### Institute Cargo Clauses B

Institute Cargo Clauses B provide cover against fire, explosion, vessels or craft being stranded, grounded, sunk or capsized, overturning or derailment of land conveyances, collision or contact, discharge of cargo at a port of distress, general average sacrifice and jettison. The B clauses also give protection against losses due to earthquake, volcanic eruption or lightning, washing overboard, entry of sea, lake or river water into a vessel, craft, hold-conveyance, lift van or place of storage, plus total loss of packages lost overboard or dropped overboard during loading or unloading.

The B clauses exclude cover for 'deliberate damage to or deliberate destruction of the subject matter' by the wrongful act of any person or persons, that is, malicious damage. If cover for this is required, it can be included by the addition of the malicious damage clause.

### Institute Cargo Clauses C

The C clauses cover only fire, explosion, vessels or craft being stranded, grounded, sunk or capsized, overturning or derailment of land conveyances, collision or contact, discharge of cargo at a port of distress, general average sacrifice and jettison.

The C clauses exclude cover for 'deliberate damage to or deliberate destruction of the subject matter' by the wrongful act of any person or persons, but, as with the B clauses, cover can be included by the addition of the malicious damage clause in return for paying an additional premium which protects against the major casualties only.

Neither the Institute Cargo Clauses B nor C clauses cover theft.

## Conditions common to Institute Cargo Clauses A, B and C.

The list and descriptions below cover conditions which are common to the Institute Cargo Clauses A, B and C.

- Packing (Clause 4.3)

  The clause excludes claims 'resulting from insufficiency or unsuitability of the packing or preparation of the subject matter...'

- Insolvency (Clause 4.6)

  The clause excludes loss or damage arising from insolvency or financial default of the owners, managers, charterers, or operators of a vessel being used. Again this is something which is not new as it has never been the intention for a marine cargo policy to guarantee the performance of third parties and to meet their liabilities. This clause should encourage the insured to use only creditworthy and reputable sea carriers.

- Atomic Weapons (Clauses 4.7 and 4.8)

  In common with the radioactive contamination exclusion clause, which is used in other branches of insurance, this clause, for clarity, excludes the result of a non-warlike use of an atomic weapon. This obviously relates to misuse or accidental misuse.

<table>
<tr><th>Risk Covered</th><th>ICC "A"</th><th>ICC "B"</th><th>ICC "C"</th></tr>
<tr><td>1. Fire or Explosion</td><td rowspan="14">YES</td><td rowspan="13">YES</td><td rowspan="8">YES</td></tr>
<tr><td>2. Vessel being stranded/ grounded/ sunk/ capsized</td></tr>
<tr><td>3. Overturning/ derailment of land conveyance</td></tr>
<tr><td>4. Collision</td></tr>
<tr><td>5. Discharge of cargo at port of distress</td></tr>
<tr><td>6. General Average sacrifice</td></tr>
<tr><td>7. Jettison</td></tr>
<tr><td>8. General Average Charges, Salvage Charges</td></tr>
<tr><td>9. Liability under contract of affreightment to 'Both to blame collision'</td><td rowspan="6">NO</td></tr>
<tr><td>10. Earthquake, Volcanic Eruption, Lightning</td></tr>
<tr><td>11. Washing overboard</td></tr>
<tr><td>12. Entry of sea/ lake/ river water to vessel/ conveyance container/ liftvan or place of storage</td></tr>
<tr><td>13. Total loss of any package lost overboard or dropped whilst loading/ unloading</td></tr>
<tr><td>14. Malicious Damage</td><td>NO</td></tr>
</table>

- Terrorists (Clause 7.3)

  The clause excludes damage caused by any terrorist or person acting from a political motive. Unfortunately, it is a clause which has particular relevance to some countries and is a point of particular importance in inland transit cases in those countries. To obtain such cover the Institute War Clauses must be incorporated.

Irrespective of the basic conditions of insurance selected, cover against the risk of war and strikes can be a further option. There are a number of popular misconceptions, even amongst people employed in the insurance industry, as to what is and what is not covered under the war and strike clauses. The clauses are discussed below.

### Institute War Clauses

In simple terms, institute war clauses provide for loss or damage to the insured interest caused by hostilities, warlike operations, civil war, revolution, rebellion and insurrection. It is not generally appreciated that cover only attaches as the interest insured is loaded on board the ship and terminates once it has been discharged. In other words, the war risks cover only attaches whilst the goods are at sea. It does not attach whilst the goods are travelling on land. In addition, the cover specifically excludes loss or damage from the use of any atomic/nuclear weaponry.

### Institute strikes, riots and civil commotions clauses

Taking the case of a dock strike while a ship is in port, the following situations will emerge:

- if the cargo is caught up in a strike, the period of transit will be prolonged and normal risks, particularly associated with theft and pilferage, will be enhanced. Under the standard cargo policies, provision is made for cover to continue during this extended period;

- the institute strikes, riots and civil commotions clauses cover physical loss or damage to the property insured, directly caused by strikers, locked-out workmen or persons taking part in labour disturbances, riots, civil commotions and by persons acting maliciously;

- the institute strikes, riots and civil commotions clauses specifically exclude loss or damage caused by the passive action of the strikers in withdrawing their labour.

With some commodities, it will not make any difference whether the voyage takes one week or one month, but with perishable commodities the situation is different. When dealing in perishables, it is possible to negotiate additional cover.

## 10.15 PREMIUMS

Essentially each exporter's insurance rate will depend on the individual claims' record. An underwriter when assessing insurance risk, takes many factors into account including the commodity to be insured, the conditions of insurance requested, the adequacy of packing, the attention given to shipping arrangements and cargo destination. Primarily, when judging the premium to set, the underwriter is guided by the exporter's claims' experience.

There are a number of ways in which an exporter can make a positive contribution towards keeping his or her insurance costs to a minimum.

## 10.16 CLAIMS PROCEDURE

It is important that when claims arise they are handled efficiently so that settlement can be made without delay. For this reason the insured should be familiar with the steps to take when making a claim.

- Any news regarding a claim or even a potential claim should be communicated to insurers at the earliest opportunity.

- If the loss is likely to exceed a minimum amount, underwriters will normally require a survey report. Lloyd's Agents are available in practically every major port throughout the world and are at the service of all underwriters to conduct surveys. When instructed, they carry out inspections and issue recommendations. Where a shipper has sold CIF and has issued the consignee with an insurance certificate, the Lloyd's Agent will appear on that certificate. Once the claim has been quantified and documented, underwriters are normally in a position to transfer the insurance money directly to the consignee.

- A written claim should be made immediately against the carrier or shipowner, as failure to do so can prejudice the insurer's rights of recovery.

In practice, when a claim has been settled between the underwriter and exporter, it is at the discretion of the underwriter to decide whether or not to pursue a claim against the carrier or shipowner concerned. The pursuit of a claim by the insurer is known as subrogation.

- Clean receipts should never be given if there is loss or damage to the cargo. The delivery docket, consignment note should be endorsed accordingly.

- Insurers will require some or all of the following documents:

  - insurance certificate;

  - commercial invoice;

  - bill of lading or consignment note, whichever is applicable;

  - delivery receipt;

  - correspondence with carriers or shipowners;

  - repairs' estimates;

  - surveyor's report.

Marine insurance claims are settled in the currency expressed on the insurance policy/certificate. If the claims are to be paid in the local currency, it is necessary that the insurance certificate is issued and the premium paid in that currency. The surveyor's fees/expenses form an admissible part of the claim once the claim itself is recoverable.

## 10.17 THE PRINCIPLE OF AVERAGE

Average is a technical term relating to partial loss. The concept of partial loss may be sub-divided into particular average or general average.

## Particular average

Particular average is defined in the Marine Insurance Act 1906 as 'a partial loss of the subject matter insured caused by a peril insured against and which is not a general average loss'. It is, in fact, fortuitous partial loss or damage proximately caused by an insured peril.

## General average

A definition of general average is contained in the York-Antwerp Rules 1994, Rule A:

*'There is a general average act when, and only when, any extraordinary sacrifice or expenditure is intentionally made or incurred for the common safety for the purpose of preserving from peril the property involved in a common maritime adventure'.*

Or in the Marine Insurance Act 1906 (Section 66, Sub 2)

'There is a general average act where any extraordinary sacrifice or expenditure is voluntarily and reasonably made or incurred in time of peril for the purpose of preserving the property imperilled in the common adventure.'

Examples of when general average loss may occur include:

- when part of a cargo is sacrificed to save the entire venture;
- part of the ship is sacrificed to save the entire venture;
- a ship and cargo are saved by unloading and reloading the stranded ship;
- water is used to extinguish a fire and damages cargo … damage caused by the fire itself is not general average;
- cargo is lost due to it being used as a fuel because no other is available. General average will only apply if the action undertaken saves the whole venture.

The principle behind general average is that, as all the parties benefited from the sacrifice, they should all contribute to the cost of saving the venture in proportion to the value of their property.

To establish each party's contribution, the list of expenses is passed to specialists known as average adjusters. To ensure that all the parties involved pay their share, their cargo is only released in exchange for an average bond plus in some cases an average guarantee. The cargo owner's insurers provide the latter document and, if it is not forthcoming, the carrying line may demand an actual cash deposit from the consignee.

General average is a highly complex subject and those needing a more extensive knowledge are recommended to study a text on marine insurance.

Chapter 11

# International shipping organisations

*A wide range of maritime organisations provide security and confidence for the shipping industry*

## 11.1 INTRODUCTION

There are a large number of international organisations directly or indirectly connected with the business of shipping. Some of them are intergovernmental but the majority are in the private sector. Some of the more important and influential are included below.

International shipping organisations will be considered in the following categories:

- shipowners' organisations;
- brokers' and agents' organisations;
- United Nations organisations;
- international ship classification;
- international seafarer support organisations;
- maritime insurance;
- other shipping-related international bodies.

All international shipping organisations are dynamic, working in a fast-moving business and an ever-changing world. The internet now provides an ideal medium for keeping track of the latest developments in the work of the organisations. The following thumbnail descriptions contain website addresses which can be consulted for up-to-the-minute information.

## 11.2 SHIPOWNERS' ORGANISATIONS

### International Chamber of Shipping

The International Chamber of Shipping (ICS) was established in 1921 and took its current title in 1948. The ICS is the principal international trade association for the shipping industry. It consists of national shipowners' associations representing all sectors and trades and covers over 80% of the world's merchant fleet. The ICS is concerned with technical, legal, employment and trade policy issues that impact on international ship operations. ICS belongs to the International Chamber of Commerce (ICC) and is involved with many intergovernmental bodies including the International Maritime Organization (IMO), the International Labour Organization (ILO), the World Trade Organization (WTO) and the United National Conference on Trade and Development (UNCTAD). It plays an influential role in the development, implementation and revision of international conventions including the International Convention for the Safety of Life at Sea (SOLAS), and the International Convention on Standards of Training Certification and Watchkeeping for Seafarers (STCW).

The International Shipping Federation (ISF), which was founded in 1909 as an independent broad-based international employers' organisation, was dedicated to maritime manpower issues, providing advice and guidance to members through its range of global contacts. It merged with the ICS in 2011. Its identity is used by the ICS when acting as the international employers' association for ship operations. Labour issues are covered by the Labour Affairs Committee of the ICS.

The International Chamber of Shipping and the International Shipping Federation have a common website http://www.ics-shipping.org/. The website contains a list with hyperlinks to each of the organisations that make up the ICS. Membership includes the Hellenic Chamber of Shipping, the Cyprus Shipping Chamber, the Japanese Shipowners' Association, the China Ocean Shipping Group and the United Kingdom's Chamber of Shipping.

### International Association of Dry Cargo Shipowners (INTERCARGO)

Intercargo is an acronym for the International Association of Dry Cargo Shipowners. It was established in 1980 following recognition for the need of an international organisation to represent the interests of shipowners in the bulk dry cargo sector. It followed the development of Intertanko, which had shown what could be done for independent owners of tanker tonnage.

The first meeting, held in 1980, composed of founding members drawn largely from Greece with a small number from Scandinavia and Hong Kong. Over 35 years, membership has grown to more than 160 companies and groups who operate ships engaged in the transport of dry bulk commodities such as iron ore, coal, grain, timber, steel and other similar cargoes. The importance of the dry bulk industry is that, without the estimated 500 million deadweight tonnes of dry bulk shipping, global trade, industry and ultimately modern lifestyles could not be maintained.

Intercargo is the only international shipowners' group whose objective is the promotion and protection of the interests of private, independent owners in the dry bulk sector. It considers policy issues of a governmental or commercial nature which affect the overall health of the sector. It recognises that many issues involving the operation of bulk carriers are dealt with by other organisations. Under its constitution, Intercargo will not duplicate the work of others.

Services provided by Intercargo to its members include an information service, advice, guidance and representation. An active committee structure covers policy, technical and commercial issues. It participates in the work of the International Maritime Organization (IMO). Intercargo is a member of the Round Table of International Shipping Associations. Intercargo's website can be found at www.intercargo.org.

### International Association of Independent Tanker Owners (INTERTANKO)

INTERTANKO is the acronym for the International Association of Independent Tanker Owners. It was established in 1970. Its three main goals are quoted as 'safe transport, cleaner seas and free competition'.

Independent owners control more than 70% of the world's tanker tonnage, and Intertanko represents over 75% of this sector, acting as a service association gathering intelligence and dispensing advice and information to members. Membership is open to independent owners and managing operators of tankers. It excludes tonnage owned by oil companies and governmental agencies. It numbers some 204 owners and operators from 40 countries who control more than 3,000 tankers of 270 million deadweight tonnes. In addition, there are 236 associate members. Part of the success of Intertanko is that it has shown its worth as a pressure group.

Intertanko gathers information and provides an intelligence centre for members; it is involved in documentary work and has pioneered and published forms for all types of tanker chartering. It takes a keen interest in all aspects of maritime safety, particularly areas affecting tanker operators, their ships, officers and crews.

Intertanko has an informative website at www.intertanko.com where the latest news of its activities can be found alongside useful links to other tanker-related sites.

### Baltic and International Maritime Council (BIMCO)

The Baltic and International Maritime Council (BIMCO) was founded in 1905 by a group of shipowners engaged principally in the Baltic and White Sea trades. At that time it was known as the Baltic and White Sea Conference and concerned itself mainly with regulating and improving the financial rewards of the timber trades. Later, it adopted a wider outlook (albeit still predominantly dry cargo bulk trades) and changed its name to the Baltic and International Maritime Conference. The last word was changed to Council in recent years. It has an international membership of 2,300 organisations representing shipowners and operators, shipbrokers and agents, maritime lawyers and P&I Clubs.

BIMCO's core objective is to facilitate the commercial operations of its members by developing standard contracts and clauses and providing quality information, advice and education. BIMCO pursues all issues affecting its members, seeking co-operation rather than confrontation, and providing input of a practical nature to ensure that the economic impact of new regulations on shipowners is fully appraised.

For over 100 years, the documentary work of BIMCO has been the activity for which it has been best known. Its work has enabled it to contribute to trade facilitation, harmonisation and the raising of contractual standards within the maritime industry. BIMCO issues approved standard documents, including charter parties and bills of lading, sometimes in collaboration with other bodies such as the International Chamber of Shipping and the Federation of National Associations of Ship Brokers and Agents (FONASBA). Innovation in recent years has been the staging of one or two day courses in maritime centres around the world. These have attracted considerable support from local shipping audiences to hear papers delivered by eminent industrial practitioners.

BIMCO was quick to realise the benefits of computer-based communication and information systems for its membership, and began pioneering work in this field as early as the late 1980s. Its members can access its materials and information online. Though much of this is restricted to the membership, a great deal of useful material can be found on www.bimco.org including samples of BIMCO's approved charter parties and bills of lading.

BIMCO has its headquarters in Bagsværd, Copenhagen.

### Oil Companies International Marine Forum (OCIMF)

The Oil Companies International Marine Forum is a voluntary association of 98 oil companies who have an interest in the shipment and terminal activities associated with crude oil, oil products, petrochemicals and gas. The mission of OCIMF is 'to be the foremost authority on the safe and environmentally-responsible operation of oil tankers, terminal and offshore support vessels, promoting continuous improvement in standards of design and operation'. The forum was formed in 1970 in response to growing public concern about marine pollution, particularly following the *Torrey Canyon* incident in 1967. OCIMF has consultative status at the IMO. It is known for the Ship Inspection Report Programme (SIRE) which was set up to address concerns about sub-standard shipping and presently provides a source of technical and operational information to prospective charterers. In addition, OCIMF runs the Maritime Terminal Information System (MTIS), the Offshore Vessel Inspection Database (OVID) and the Tanker Management and Self-Assessment (TMSA) programme.

## 11.3 BROKERS' AND AGENTS' ORGANISATIONS

### The Institute of Chartered Shipbrokers

The Institute of Chartered Shipbrokers was established in 1911. At that time London was, as now, a centre for international shipping activity. The port of London was thriving with busy berths along both banks of the Thames. London was not the only city where the business of shipping played an important role. At many ports, especially those involved with Britain's extensive coal export trade, there were shipping exchanges for the chartering of tramp ships and offices from which ships' agents conducted their business.

Whilst none of the provincial centres handled the volume of business transacted on London's Baltic Exchange, they shared a common desire to form an organisation devoted to the maintenance of the same ethical standards for which the Baltic was renowned. Different local associations of shipbrokers came together in 1911 and formed the Institute of Shipbrokers.

The maintenance of standards needed more than mutual desire and an agreement to act in an ethical manner. A programme of education and training was developed to ensure all members were knowledgeable about their business. Having formed itself into an organisation with the dual aims of 'discipline involved in the maintenance of standards and education for its members' the Institute approached the Privy Council and received its first Royal Charter in 1920. The Privy Council is a uniquely British body. It is the highest-ranking committee in the country presided over by the reigning sovereign. The granting of royal charters is a small but nonetheless important aspect of its work.

Under the bye-laws drawn up under the Royal Charter, the Institute of Chartered Shipbrokers is required to 'devise and impose means for testing the qualifications of candidates for admission to professional membership by examination in theory and practice' and to 'exercise professional supervision over the Members of the Institute and secure for them such definite professional standing as may assist them in the discharge of their duties'.

The professional standing the Institute is able to confer comprises membership (MICS) for those who pass the qualifying examinations and satisfy the Council that they are 'fit and proper persons'. Those who attain positions of influence in the profession may apply for promotion to fellowship (FICS). Fellows may call themselves 'chartered shipbrokers'.

Since 1920, shipping has become more complex to the extent that the name shipbroker, which at one time was thought to apply only to those engaged in chartering dry cargo tramp ships, now embraces separate disciplines in tanker chartering, ship management, sale and purchase, port agency and liner trades. Each discipline is examined separately in the qualifying examinations for membership.

In 1984, the Institute succeeded in obtaining an amendment to its Royal Charter, which permitted several changes in the byelaws, one of which was the formation of an additional class of membership for companies, enabling the Institute to represent the interests of firms and corporations. Another important amendment was the removal of the limitation that restricted membership to UK and the Commonwealth citizens. Today, anyone in the world may be granted admission provided they fulfil the membership qualifications. This has enabled the Institute of Chartered Shipbrokers to become an international organisation. Further information can be found at www.ics.org.uk.

The Baltic Exchange

### The Baltic Exchange

The Baltic Exchange is a limited company owned by its shareholders and comprises member companies, their principals and representatives on the Exchange and individual members.

The Baltic Exchange traces its origins to a club established in 1823 representing the users of the Baltic Coffee House. The club started in a coffee house called the 'Virginia and Maryland' and, after 1744, as the 'Virginia and Baltic'. The Baltic club merged with the London Shipping Exchange in 1900 and moved to the Exchange building, a building which was destroyed by a terrorist bomb in 1992. The event and the development of electronic trading put an end to the daily trading activity on the floor. The present Baltic Exchange building is currently located a short distance from its former site, now occupied by the building known as the London Gherkin.

The Baltic Exchange is the world's only independent source of maritime market information for the trading and settlement of physical and derivative contracts. Its international community of over 600 members encompasses the majority of world shipping interests. The Baltic Exchange generates a number of freight indices which, along with real time market information and a substantial database of shipping information, can be accessed by its members.

The majority of members of the Exchange are brokers acting in the various markets as intermediaries between the principals. All the international trading activities concerned produce foreign exchange. Members of the Baltic are invisible export earners for the UK. They are committed to a code of business conduct which is overseen by the Exchange.

Membership of the Exchange is open to corporations registered in the UK which have to be represented by principals resident in the UK for three years prior to election. It is also open to individuals in their own name or operating in partnerships. Members of the Baltic Exchange who carry on business as 'brokers only' will have signed the Broker's Letter by which they undertake not to trade as principals. Members are required to operate separate bank accounts for clients and must take out appropriate insurance cover against errors and omissions, and breach of warranty of authority.

The Exchange is governed by a board of 15 directors, 12 of whom are elected by shareholders and three by members. It has disciplinary powers of censure, suspension and expulsion over members and is responsible for sustaining proper ethical standards in trading. The secretary of the Exchange acts as chief executive of the organisation, carrying out policy determined by the directors and having responsibility for the administration and organisation of the Exchange and its staff. The Exchange derives its income from membership subscriptions and from rents of the offices which it owns.

The motto of the Exchange, Our Word, Our Bond, symbolises the importance of ethics in trading. Members need to rely on each other and, in turn, on their principals for many contracts which are verbally expressed and only subsequently confirmed in writing. The Baltic Exchange trading community regards the principle of 'treating others as oneself would wish to be treated' as the basis for ethical trading. The Baltic Code of Ethics and Market Practice provides a list of underpinning principles to be observed and also a list of practices unacceptable to the trading community. The Code and other materials about the Baltic Exchange can be found on the Baltic Exchange website www.balticexchange.com.

FONASBA

## The Federation of National Associations of Shipbrokers and Agents (FONASBA)

The Federation of National Associations of Shipbrokers and Agents (FONASBA) was formed in 1969 from national European shipbroker and agent associations to represent the interests of the liner agent, the tramp port agent, and the shipbroker engaged in the chartering of ships. FONASBA membership is made up of 49 countries, represented by 43 national associations of shipbrokers and agents with a further 6 countries represented by associate or candidate members.

FONASBA speaks with authority on all matters concerning the profession of shipbroking and agency. It consults with national and international bodies, authorities and organisations on matters of concern to its members. It encourages fair and equitable professional practice. FONASBA gives support to its members when the basis and general interests of the shipbroker and agent professions are questioned. It also co-ordinates efforts to improve shipping contracts and ensure efficient information exchange of a general and particular interest.

The chartering and documentary committee of FONASBA participates in the revision of charter parties and other shipping documents. It has issued forms of liner and general agency agreements, an International Brokers' Commission Contract, a Time Charter Interpretation Code and a Guide to Standard Port Agency Conditions as well as devising the MULTIFORM charter party as an alternative to the General Voyage Charter party (GENCON).

The Chartering and Documentary Committee of FONASBA has played a leading role in the revision of charter parties such as NORGRAIN 89, NYPE 93 and AMWELSH 93 issued by the Association of Ship Brokers and Agents (USA).The guiding policy in all charter revisions is to remain objective and adopt an even-handed position between charterer and owners irrespective of the current state of the market. The Federation advocates terms that are equitable to both sides, and that are clear, comprehensive and reflect up-to-date conditions.

FONASBA's secretariat is based in London. It has consultative status at the United Nations Committee for Trade and Development, providing the voice of shipbrokers and agents. The European Community Association of Shipbrokers and Agents (ECASBA), founded in 1993 to represent European brokers and agents in their dealings with the European Union, is a sub-committee of FONASBA. Further details of FONASBA's activities can be found on its website at www.fonasba.com.

### The International Federation of Forwarding Agents' Associations (FIATA)

FIATA's initials stem from its French title, as the Fédération Internationale des Associations de Transitaires et Assimilés. The organisation was founded in Vienna in 1926. It is a non-governmental organisation and claims to be the global voice of freight logistics. It represents a sector of industry which is closely allied to shipbroking. FIATA incorporates more than 40,000 freight-forwarding firms in 150 countries worldwide.

The main objectives of FIATA are to unite the freight-forwarding industry worldwide, to represent, promote and protect the interests of the industry by participating as advisors or experts in meetings of international bodies dealing with transportation, and to familiarise trade and industry and the public at large with the services provided by freight forwarders.

FIATA's membership consists of national associations, such as the British International Freight Association (BIFA), freight-forwarding and transport groups and individual members.

FIATA is active in the fields of airfreight, customs and multi-modal transport as well as shipping and working groups and committees which examine developments in sea, rail and air transport. These groups and committees have produced recommended forms of documentation, such as non-negotiable waybills, shippers' dangerous goods' declarations, multi-modal transport bills of lading and warehouse receipts.

Further information about the FIATA list can be found at www.fiata.com.

## 11.4 UNITED NATIONS BODIES

IMO INTERNATIONAL MARITIME ORGANIZATION

### The International Maritime Organization (IMO)

The International Maritime Organization (IMO) is the United Nations (UN) specialised agency with responsibility for the safety and security of shipping and the prevention of marine pollution by ships. Initially established as the International Maritime Consultative Organization (IMCO) in 1948, it achieved full status as an agency of the UN in 1958. Its headquarters are in London.

The governing body of the IMO is the Assembly, which meets once every two years. The Assembly consists of 171 member states and three associate members. A Council of 40 member states elected by the Assembly, acts as IMO's governing body, known as the Council, between the Assembly sessions.

In addition to the Assembly and Council there are five main committees: the Maritime Safety Committee (MSC); the Marine Environment Protection Committee (MEPC); the Legal Committee (LEC); the Technical Co-operation Committee (TCC) and the Facilitation Committee (FAL). A number of subcommittees support the work of the main technical committees.

The committees have contributed to promoting the adoption of some 30 conventions and protocols which fall under three main groups: maritime safety; the prevention of marine pollution; and liability and compensation, especially in relation to damage caused by pollution. Outside the three major groups are a number of other conventions dealing with facilitation, tonnage measurement, unlawful acts against shipping and salvage. IMO has produced more than 600 codes and recommendations on related matters.

The most important conventions are the International Convention for the Safety of Life at Sea (SOLAS), the International Convention for the Prevention of Pollution from Ships (MARPOL) and the International Convention on Standards of Training, Certification and Watchkeeping for Seafarers (STCW).

SOLAS covers many areas including: matters of safety in the ship structure; reduction of fire risk and firefighting equipment; lifesaving equipment; radio communications; navigational safety; the carriage of cargoes, including dangerous goods; the management of ship operation; measures to enhance safety and security including the International Ship and Port Facilities Code and safety measures for ships operating in polar waters.

MARPOL was established to prevent oil pollution from ships. It has developed to cover other areas including the prevention of pollution by the carriage of liquid noxious substances, the prevention of pollution by harmful substances carried in packaged form, the prevention of pollution by sewage and garbage from ships, and the prevention of air pollution.

The STCW convention prescribes minimum standards relating to training, certification and watchkeeping for seafarers, which all countries are obliged to meet or exceed.

The IMO itself has no direct power to enforce its conventions. When they are adopted, they will be incorporated into the laws of the flag state, who are then responsible for ensuring compliance. The work of surveying and the issuing of certificates of compliance is dealt with by classification societies. Inspection and enforcement is undertaken by flag state coastguard agencies and port state control organisations.

IMO measures have proved beneficial in many areas. For example, the number of collisions between ships has been greatly reduced in areas where IMO-approved traffic separation schemes have been introduced. Updated information on the IMO's conventions, codes, rules and publications can be found on the organisation's website: www.imo.org.

UNCTAD

### United Nations Conference for Trade and Development (UNCTAD)

UNCTAD is the UN body responsible for dealing with development issues, particularly international trade – the main driver of development. The work of UNCTAD is wide and can be summed up in three words: think, debate, and deliver.

UNCTAD is based in Geneva and is governed by 194 member states. It has a shipping division staffed by a dedicated team whose efforts have met with a mixed degree of success. Their Non-Mandatory Minimum Standards for Shipping Agents, which were promulgated in March 1988, were endorsed enthusiastically by almost all nations represented. Similarly, their maritime training programmes, tailor-made for developing nations, are held in high regard.

Less successful have been UNCTAD's attempts to regulate liner trading with the Code of Practice for Liner Conferences, remembered for one clause referred to as the '40-40-20 Rule'. The code was overtaken by commercial evolution and attempts to modify it have been unsuccessful.

UNCTAD participated in the preparatory work for the new UN Convention on Contracts for the International Carriage of Goods Wholly or Partly by Sea which was adopted by the UN assembly in 2008 – known as the Rotterdam Rules. The Rotterdam Rules provide mandatory standards of liability for loss or damage arising from the international carriage of goods by sea. On ratification it is intended to be the successor to earlier conventions including the Hague Rules 1924, the Hague-Visby Rules 1968 and the Hamburg Rules 1978. A minimum number of 20 nations are required to ratify the Rotterdam Rules.

Two attempts to standardise the basic clauses in charter parties have so far failed to make progress. This should not be surprising in view of the large volume of chartering which is controlled by groups who are quite happy with existing charter parties.

Despite lack of success indicated in the few well-publicised failures, UNCTAD is a positive forum, and its proceedings and current topics can be perused on their website www.unctad.org

### The International Labour Organization (ILO)

The International Labour Organization (ILO) was founded in 1919, in the wake of a destructive war, to pursue a vision based on the premise that universal, lasting peace can be established only if it is based on social justice. The ILO became the first specialised agency of the UN in 1946. The main aims of the ILO are to promote rights at work, encourage decent employment opportunities and strengthen dialogue on work-related issues.

In 2006 the organisation completed an update and consolidation of all existing international maritime labour law. It produced what has been described as the fourth pillar of maritime law - the Maritime Labour Convention 2006. The Convention entered into force in 2013. It covers five areas which impact on ship operations, namely: the minimum requirements for seafarers to work on a ship; conditions of employment; accommodation, recreational facilities, food and catering; heath protection, medical care welfare and social security provision and compliance and enforcement.

Further information about the work of the ILO can be found on their website www.ilo.org.

## 11.5 INTERNATIONAL SHIP CLASSIFICATION

IACS

INTERNATIONAL ASSOCIATION
OF CLASSIFICATION SOCIETIES

### International Association of Classification Societies (IACS)

There are more than 50 organisations worldwide which define their activities as providing marine classification. They compete with each other for business. The 12 largest societies which cover 90% of the world's cargo-carrying tonnage, make up the membership of IACS. The main purpose of IACS is to help promote consistency, rules and standards of classification, design, construction and through-life compliance by member societies.

IACS has promoted a code of ethics to which it expects its members to adhere. It promotes transparency within the system of classification. In order to obtain membership of IACS, a classification society must satisfy demanding criteria on quality systems and procedures, and individual classification societies have been suspended from membership for failing to uphold the standards required.

The following classification societies are members of IACS:

- American Bureau of Shipping (ABS);
- Bureau Veritas (BV);
- China Classification Society (CCS);

- Croation Register of Shipping (CRS);
- Det Norske Veritas - Germanischer Lloyd (DNV–GL);
- Indian Register of Shipping (IRS);
- Korean Register (KR);
- Lloyd's Register (LR);
- Nippon Kaiji Kyokai (NK);
- Polish Register of Shipping (PRS);
- Registro Italiano Navale (RINA);
- Russian Maritime Register of Shipping (RS).

IACS has had to deal with much criticism of the system of classification following a series of serious maritime accidents where certification issued by one or more of its members has publicly been called into question. It attempts to address the conflict which occurs between the commercial aspects of classification society work and the upholding of standards applied to members' tonnage. The activities of IACS are described on the website www.iacs.org.uk.

Lloyd's Register

### Lloyd's Register

Lloyd's Register of Shipping is a major classification society and a member of IACS. It is a non-profit making concern, obtaining its funds from fees charged for the services of its surveyors and from subscriptions to the Register Book. The society is run by a general committee, composed of underwriters, shipowners, shipbuilders, marine engineers, steel makers and representatives of other shipping organisations.

Confusion often arises over Lloyd's Register of Shipping and the Corporation of Lloyd's. They are two different and independent organisations, though sharing the same origin and name. In the days of Lloyd's coffee house, underwriters collected and catalogued information concerning the characteristics and construction of individual vessels to help them in their insurance activities. The register of ships, known as the underwriters' register or green book, was first published in 1760. In 1797, a dispute over classification methods prompted shipowners to publish their own book, which appeared in 1799 and remained a rival register until 1834 when reconciliation resulted in the formation of Lloyd's Register of Shipping. Since then, Lloyd's Register has remained an independent classification society.

The authority of Lloyd's Register lies in the high standards it maintains, with maritime governments accepting that classification by Lloyd's Register recognises that statutory requirements regarding the structural strength of ships has been met.
The research and technical advisory services of Lloyd's Register are involved in the study of new

developments and projects, providing valuable technical advice to the shipping industry. Lloyd's Register has recently established a Global Technology Centre (GTC) at Southampton University, described as the cornerstone of Lloyd's Register's global marine research and technology network. A sister GTC has been established in Singapore, recognising that an international approach to tackling tomorrow's challenges is appropriate.

An investigation department at Lloyd's Register deals with problems involving technical failures in ships. Records are maintained on damage or failures occurring in ships which are classed by Lloyd's Register. The records may be consulted prior to or during the sale of ships in the secondhand market.

The annual volumes of Lloyd's Register are published jointly with Fairplay, in bound form and on CD-ROM. The Register includes details of all merchant ships over 100 tons, regardless of whether or not they are classed by Lloyd's.

Maintaining a ship in class requires that a special survey is conducted every five years when the hull and machinery are inspected. Various factors including new technology made the five years' survey cycle difficult to operate. Most vessels now undertake the hull and machinery survey on a continuous cycle. The surveys are carried out by a staff of about 1,500 qualified surveyors based worldwide.

The independent status of classification societies, their integrity and the nature of their work have led many of these organisations to widen their sphere of activities. Lloyd's Register, for example, offers many specialist services from its wide range of expertise, from approval of naval architects' plans and computer testing of hull designs to advice on marine engine lubricants and the auditing of ISO 9000 systems. Further information about Lloyd's Register can be found on their website www.lr.org.

## 11.6 INTERNATIONAL SEAFARER SUPPORT ORGANISATIONS

### The International Transport Workers' Federation (ITF)

The International Transport Workers' Federation (ITF) was formed during the closing years of the 19th century as the international secretariat of worldwide transport unions. Its present membership exceeds 400 trade unions from nearly 100 countries. The ITF claims to represent more than four million transport workers.

When the ITF was founded, the use by shipowners of open registries was unknown. The term open registry refers to the registration of a ship in a country of different sovereignty from that of the shipowner. Ships registered under an open registry can reduce operating costs and avoid regulations recognised by the shipowner's country. The use of open registries was seen by the ITF as an attempt to undermine trade unionism in general and the standards of seafarers' working and safety conditions in particular. In 1950, at its Stuttgart Congress, the ITF adopted a plan of action which required all shipowners to adhere to certain defined minimum conditions. Failure to do so would result in a boycott of the ship and encourage the shipowners to the negotiating table.

Much of that resolution remains in place to this day. A somewhat ambitious part of the plan was to force shipowners away from open registries by an international blockade. This did not go beyond a four-day boycott in 1958. A more practical resolution was passed at their 1971 congress in Vienna when a standard agreement was drawn up, for use by all ships whose crews were not covered by an agreement properly negotiated between union and employer.

Such agreements include provision for contributions to an ITF fund which has been set up to sustain the campaign and provide worldwide charitable support for seafarers' welfare facilities.

The strength of the ITF lies in the fact that almost all transport unions are affiliated to it. This means that immobilising a ship by arranging for the withdrawal of services, such as tug crews and lock-keepers, is relatively straightforward. The ideals of the ITF will be supported by affiliated unions. The ITF provides permanent officials in many major ports of the world and takes the lead to help resolve many difficult situations where crews have been in danger or stranded without funds.

The ITF website is www.itfseafarers.org.

ISWAN

## International Seafarers Welfare and Assistance Network (ISWAN)

The International Seafarers Welfare and Assistance Network (ISWAN) is a membership organisation which includes as core members the International Chamber of Shipping, the International Transport Workers' Federation, the International Christian Maritime Association and more than 40 constituent members. The mission of the ISWAN is to promote seafarers' welfare and related issues, and the application of the relevant sections of the Maritime Labour Convention 2006, through raising awareness, supporting front line providers, encouraging and recognising best practice in providing welfare assistance to seafarers, their families and dependants, providing liaison and referral services, undertaking relevant research and building support for the work of the stakeholders. ISWAN provides a 24-hour, 365-day free and confidential support to seafarers through SeafarerHelp.

Further information can be found on www.seafarerswelfare.org.

## 11.7 MARITIME INSURANCE

IUA OF LONDON

### The International Underwriting Association

The International Underwriting Association (IUA) of London represents companies that trade in the London insurance market outside Lloyd's. The IUA was fomed in 1998 through the merger of the Institute of London Underwriters (ILU) and the London International Insurance and Reinsurance Market bringing together representative bodies for the marine and non-marine sectors of the London company insurance market. The ILU's history in marine aviation and transport insurance markets dates back to 1884 which, following many years of informal gatherings in the Jerusalem Coffee House and Jamaica Wine Rooms near the Royal Exchange, was developed to discuss policy wording and other matters of mutual interest.

Of particular interest to the shipping business is the development of the standard clauses associated with cargo and ship insurance.

The website of the IUA is www.iua.co.uk.

LLOYD'S

### The Corporation of Lloyd's ('Lloyd's of London')

Lloyd's is an insurance market of a kind to be found nowhere else in the world. The market began in the late 17th century with its origins involved with the insurance of ships and cargoes. Today it is a diversified market providing the opportunity to place insurance on a wide range of interests from ships to satellites. The scale of risk activity can be illustrated by the fact that £26.1 billion of gross written premiums were placed in the market during 2013.

Lloyd's is not a company. It has no shareholders and accepts no corporate liability for risks insured. Lloyd's is a society of underwriters, all of whom accept insurance risks for their personal profit or loss and are liable to the full extent of their private fortunes to meet their insurance commitments. The 20,000 members of Lloyd's, known as 'names' are grouped into 40 syndicates which vary in size from a few to more than 1000 names. The affairs of each syndicate are managed by an underwriting agent who is responsible for appointing a professional underwriter for each main class of business. Underwriting membership is open to men and women of any nationality provided that they meet the stringent financial requirements of the Council of Lloyd's.

The most recent act of Parliament covering the activities of Lloyd's is the Lloyd's Act 1982 which resulted from an inquiry into the society's constitution and the effectiveness of its powers of self-regulation. The Corporation of Lloyd's provides its members with their premises and a wide variety of centralised supporting services. Details can be found on the Lloyd's of London website www.lloydsoflondon.co.uk.

## Lloyd's agents

Lloyd's of London has always been closely connected with the sea and accordingly has developed a worldwide shipping intelligence system of which a worldwide network of agents send relevant reports associated with shipping, aviation, ports and areas in which they operate to Lloyd's of London. The first Lloyd's agent appointed abroad was in Madeira in 1811 and, by the end of that year, 150 firms had been appointed. Today there are more than 500 agents.

Lloyd's agents are also called upon to appoint surveyors to report on damage or loss. It is the practice for marine policies of Lloyd's underwriters and insurance companies to state that claims' settlement will be assisted if Lloyd's agents are called in to conduct a survey. Arrangements for collecting and processing the large volume of information received from Lloyd's agents throughout the world used to be the responsibility of Lloyd's of London Press until it was taken over by Informa, one of the world's largest knowledge providers. Within Informa, the Lloyd's List Group continues to publish *Lloyd's List*, the world's oldest newspaper but now only available online. The electronic paper provides daily news and analysis of the global shipping market, including maritime casualties. Informa Cargo publishes *Lloyd's Loading List*, a key tool for UK freight forwarders.

## International Group of P&I Clubs

The International Group of P&I (Protection and Indemnity) (IGP&I) Clubs consists of 13 members who provide P&I cover for approximately 90% of the world's ocean-going tonnage. Each member of the group is an independent, non-profit making mutual insurance association. They provide cover for their members against third-party liabilities relating to the use and operation of ships.

The IGP&I provides a forum for its members to develop common policy and promote shipowners' interests in relation to their liability and insurance issues. It also provides an effective conduit for members to speak on important industry issues, for example, on international conventions and legislation affecting shipowners' liabilities and insurance matters. The Group co-ordinates the operation and regulation of the members' clubs' claim-sharing agreement.

For further information see www.igpandi.org.

## 11.8 OTHER SHIPPING-RELATED INTERNATIONAL BODIES

International Chamber of Commerce
*The world business organization*

### The International Chamber of Commerce

Chambers of commerce exist in a wide variety of shapes and sizes. At one end of the spectrum, there are small associations of traders representing the commerce and industry of a town and at the other end are the national chambers of commerce which speak for an entire country.

The membership of chambers of commerce is diverse, with businesses who compete with each other sharing common concerns and interests. Many activities of a chamber of commerce will have no discernable impact upon shipping but others do. An example is that their independence and integrity are sufficient for validation of a certificate of origin to be an acceptable document either in its own right or as a prerequisite before receiving consular approval.

In some countries, businesses must, by law, register with their local or regional chamber of commerce. Other chambers of commerce are given the responsibility for conducting commercial actions and other market activities, making them influential and powerful bodies. They may be involved in commercial arbitrations or provide references for local companies and trade contacts for national or international purposes.

The chambers influence international trade through the International Chamber of Commerce (ICC). In the same way as national shipping associations have benefited from the formation of an international body, the International Chamber of Commerce has more than made its mark by its publication of handbooks including Incoterms 2010, an internationally-agreed glossary of terms used in international trade and the Uniform Customs and Practice for Documentary Credits 600 (UCP 600), a set of rules on the issuance and use of letters of credit.

Of direct importance to the shipping business are two sections of the ICC, namely, the International Maritime Bureau and Commercial Crime Services, both anti-crime organisations which tackle commercial crime including maritime and insurance fraud.

ICC have a publishing arm which can provide copies of ICC Incoterms 2010 and UCP 600. The publications can be ordered from the ICC headquarters in Paris and seen on the ICC website at www.iccwbo.org.

International Maritime Bureau

### The International Maritime Bureau (IMB)

The International Maritime Bureau (IMB) is a specialised division of the ICC. It was established in 1981 to act as a focal point in the fight against all types of maritime crime and malpractice. It uses industry knowledge, experience and access to a large number of well-placed contacts around the world to do this. Amongst its activities, the IMB helps to authenticate suspect bills of lading and other shipping documents. It disseminates information on maritime crime, offers advice and assistance in avoiding the risk of fraud, raises awareness of the dangers of maritime crime and provides help and training with counter-measures.

Maritime fraud by its very nature takes place in several different jurisdictions so that, even when discovered, it is difficult to prosecute the perpetrators. A further problem is the reticence of merchants in admitting to fraud, knowing that restitution is unlikely.

Before 1992, ship masters and ship operators had nowhere to turn to when their ships were attacked, robbed or hijacked either in port or out at sea. In response to problems of increasing violent criminal activity in the Malacca Strait and elsewhere in the Far East which was ignored by the local law enforcement agencies, the IMB set up the Piracy Reporting Centre (PRC) in Kuala Lumpur. Ship masters report any piracy, armed robbery or stowaway incidents to the PRC. The aim of the reporting centre is to raise awareness within the shipping industry of areas of high risk. The PRC has played an invaluable role in helping fight piracy in the Indian Ocean.

A development has been the inauguration of a simple and relatively inexpensive satellite tracking system known as SHIPLOC that allows merchants and shipping companies to monitor the exact location of their ships using a personal computer with internet access.

Information about the activities of the IMB can be found through the ICC website at www. icc-ccs.org/icc/imb.

# APPENDICES

*There are 167 official national currencies in circulation in the world*

# LIST OF APPENDICES


| | | |
|---|---|---|
| 1. | Gencon 94 | 197 |
| 2. | NYPE 93 | 200 |
| 3. | Shellvoy 6 | 214 |
| 4. | Shelltime 4 | 234 |
| 5. | Loadline map | 243 |
| 6. | S & P particulars sheet | 244 |
| 7. | Norwegian Saleform 93 | 245 |
| 8. | Norwegian Saleform 2012 | 251 |
| 9. | Shipman 2009 | 259 |
| 10. | Statement of Facts | 280 |
| 11. | Disbursement account | 282 |
| 12. | Fonasba Agency aggreement | 283 |
| 13. | Certificate of cargo insurance | 288 |
| 14. | Institute Cargo Clauses (A) | 289 |
| 15. | Institute Cargo Clauses (B) | 292 |
| 16. | Institute Cargo Clauses (C) | 295 |
| 17. | Congen Bill of Lading | 298 |
| 18. | Letter of Credit | 300 |
| 19. | UCP600 | 302 |

# APPENDIX I

# GENCON 94

| | |
|---|---|
| 1. Shipbroker | **RECOMMENDED**<br>**THE BALTIC AND INTERNATIONAL MARITIME COUNCIL**<br>**UNIFORM GENERAL CHARTER (AS REVISED 1922,1976 and 1994)**<br>**(To be used for trades for which no specially approved form is in force)**<br>**CODE NAME: "GENCON"** **Part I** |
| | 2. Place and date |
| 3. Owners/Place of business (Cl. 1) | 4. Charterers/Place of business (Cl. 1) |
| 5. Vessel's name (Cl. 1) | 6. GT/NT(Cl. 1) |
| 7. DWT all told on summer load line in metric tons (abt.) (Cl. 1) | 8. Present position (Cl. 1) |
| 9. Expected ready to load (abt.) (Cl. 1) | |
| 10. Loading port or place (Cl. 1) | 11 Discharging port or place (Cl. 1) |
| 12. Cargo (also state quantity and margin in Owners' option, if agreed; if full and complete cargo not agreed state "part cargo" (Cl. 1) | |
| 13. Freight rate (also state whether freight prepaid or payable on delivery) (Cl. 4) | 14. Freight payment (state currency and method of payment; also beneficiary and bank account) (Cl. 4) |
| 15. State if vessel's cargo handling gear shall not be used (Cl. 5) | 16. Laytime (if separate laytime for load. and disch. is agreed, fill in a) and b). If total laytime for load. and disch., fill in c) only) (Cl. 6) |
| 17. Shippers/Place of business (Cl. 6) | a) Laytime for loading |
| 18. Agents (loading) (Cl. 6) | (b) Laytime for discharging |
| 19. Agents (discharging) (Cl. 6) | c) Total laytime for loading and discharging |
| 20. Demurrage rate and manner payable (loading and discharging) (Cl. 7) | 21. Cancelling date (Cl. 9) |
| | 22. General Average to be adjusted at (Cl. 12) |
| 23. Freight Tax (state if for the Owners' account (Cl .13 (c)) | 24. Brokerage commission and to whom payable (Cl. 15) |
| 25. Law and Arbitration (state 19 (a), 19 (b) or 19 (c) of Cl. 19; if 19 (c) agreed also state Place of Arbitration) (if not filled in 19 (a) shall apply) (Cl. 19) | |
| (a) State maximum amount for small claims/shortened arbitration (Cl. 19) | 26. Additional clauses covering special provisions, if agreed |

It is mutually agreed that this Contract shall be performed subject to the conditions contained in this Charter Party which shall include Part I as well as Part II. In the event of a conflict of conditions, the provisions of Part I shall prevail over those of Part II to the extent of such conflict.

| | |
|---|---|
| Signature (Owners) | Signature (Charterers) |

1. It is agreed between the party mentioned in Box 3 as the Owners of the Vessel named in Box 5, of the GT/NT indicated in Box 6 and carrying about the number of metric tons of deadweight capacity all told on summer loadline stated in Box 7, now in position as stated in Box 8 and expected ready to load under this Charter Party about the date indicated in Box 9, and the party mentioned as the Charterers in Box 4 that:

The said Vessel shall, as soon as her prior commitments have been completed, proceed to the loading port(a) or place(s) stated in Box 10 or so near thereto as she may safely get and lie always afloat, and there load a full and complete cargo (if shipment of deck cargo agreed same to be at the Charterers' risk and responsibility) as stated in Box 12, which the Charterers bind themselves to ship, and being so loaded the Vessel shall proceed to the discharging port(s) or place(s) stated in Box 11 as ordered on signing Bills of Lading, or so near thereto as she may safely get and lie always afloat, and there deliver the cargo.

2. **Owners' Responsibility Clause**

The Owners are to be responsible for loss of or damage to the goods or for delay in delivery of the goods only in case the loss, damage or delay has been caused by personal want of due diligence on the part of the Owners or their Manager to make the Vessel in all respects seaworthy and to secure that she is properly manned, equipped and supplied, or by the personal act or default of the Owners or their Manager.

And the Owners are not responsible for loss, damage or delay arising from any other cause whatsoever, even from the neglect or default of the Master or crew or some other person employed by the Owners on board or ashore for whose acts they would, but for this Clause, be responsible, or from unseaworthiness of the Vessel on loading or commencement of the voyage or at any time whatsoever.

3. **Deviation Clause**

The Vessel has liberty to call at any port or ports in any order, for any purpose, to sail without pilots, to tow and/or assist Vessels in all situations, and also to deviate for the purpose of saving life and/or property.

4. **Payment of Freight**

(a) The freight at the rate stated in Box 13 shall be paid in cash calculated on the intaken quantity of cargo.

(b) *Prepaid*. If according to Box 13 freight is to be paid on shipment, it shall be deemed earned and non-returnable, Vessel and/or cargo lost or not lost.

Neither the Owners nor their agents shall be required to sign or endorse bills of lading showing freight prepaid unless the freight due to the Owners has actually been paid.

(c) *On delivery*. If according to Box 13 freight, or part thereof, is payable at destination it shall not be deemed earned until the cargo is thus delivered. Notwithstanding the provisions under (a), if freight or part thereof is payable on delivery of the cargo the Charterers shall have the option of paying the freight on delivered weight/quantity provided such option is declared before breaking bulk and the weight/quantity can be ascertained by official weighing machine, joint draft survey or tally.

Cash for Vessel's ordinary disbursements at the port of loading to be advanced by the Charterers, if required, at highest current rate of exchange, subject to two (2) per cent to cover insurance and other expenses.

5. **Loading/Discharging**

*(a) Costs/Risks*

The cargo shall be brought into the holds, loaded, stowed and/or trimmed, tallied, lashed and/or secured and taken from the holds and discharged by the Charterers, free of any risk, liability and expense whatsoever to the Owners. The Charterers shall provide and lay all dunnage material as required for the proper stowage and protection of the cargo on board, the Owners allowing the use of all dunnage available on board. The Charterers shall be responsible for and pay the cost of removing their dunnage after discharge of the cargo under this Charter Party and time to count until dunnage has been removed.

*(b) Cargo Handling Gear*

Unless the Vessel Is gearless or unless it has been agreed between the parties that the Vessel's gear shall not be used and stated as such in Box 15, the Owners shall throughout the duration of loading/discharging give free use of the Vessel's cargo handling gear and of sufficient motive power to operate all such cargo handling gear. All such equipment to be in good working order. Unless caused by negligence of the stevedores, time lost by breakdown of the Vessel's cargo handling gear or motive power - pro rata the total number of cranes/winches required at that time for the loading/discharging of cargo under this Charter Party - shall not count as laytime or time on demurrage. On request the Owners shall provide free of charge cranemen/winchmen from the crew to operate the Vessel's cargo handling gear, unless local regulations prohibit this, in which latter event shore labourers shall be for the account of the Charterers. Cranemen/winchmen shall be under the Charterers' risk and responsibility and as stevedores to be deemed as their servants but shall always work under the supervision of the Master.

*(c) Stevedore Damage*

The Charterers shall be responsible for damage (beyond ordinary wear and tear) to any part of the Vessel caused by Stevedores. Such damage shall be notified as soon as reasonably possible by the Master to the Charterers or their agents and to their Stevedores, failing which the Charterers shall not be held responsible. The Master shall endeavour to obtain the Stevedores' written acknowledgement of liability.

The Charterers are obliged to repair any stevedore damage prior to completion of the voyage, but must repair stevedore damage affecting the Vessel's seaworthiness or class before the Vessel sails from the port where such damage was caused or found. All additional expenses Incurred shall be for the account of the Charterers and any time lost shall be for the account of and shall be paid to the Owners by the Charterers at the demurrage rate.

6. **Laytime**

** (a) Separate laytime for loading and discharging*

The cargo shall be loaded within the number of running days/hours as indicated in Box 16, weather permitting, Sundays and holidays excepted, unless used, in which event time used shall count.

The cargo shall be discharged within the number of running days/hours as indicated in Box 16, weather permitting, Sundays and holidays excepted, unless used, in which event time used shall count.

** (b) Total laytime for loading and discharging*

The cargo shall be loaded and discharged within the number of total running days/hours as indicated, in Box 16, weather permitting, Sundays and holidays excepted, unless used, in which event time used shall count.

*(c) Commencement of laytime (loading and discharging)*

Laytime for loading and discharging shall commence at 13.00 hours, if notice of readiness is given up to and including 12.00 hours, and at 06.00 hours next working day if notice given during office hours after 12.00 hours. Notice of readiness at loading port to be given to the Shippers named in Box 17 or if not named, to the Charterers or their agents named in Box 18. Notice of readiness at the discharging port to be given to the Receivers or, If not known, to the Charterers or their agents named in Box 19.

If the loading/discharging berth is not available on the Vessel's arrival at or off the port of loading/discharging, the Vessel shall be entitled to give notice of readiness within ordinary office hours on arrival there, whether in free pratique or not, whether customs cleared or not. Laytime or time on demurrage shall then count as if she were In berth and in all respects ready for loading/discharging provided that the Master warrants that she is in fact ready In all respects. Time used in moving from the place of waiting to the loading/discharging berth shall not count as laytime.

If, after inspection, the Vessel Is found not to be ready in all respects to load/discharge time lost after the discovery thereof until the Vessel is again ready to load/discharge shall not count as laytime.

Time used before commencement of laytime shall count.

** Indicate alternative (a) or (b) as agreed, in Box 16.*

7. **Demurrage**

Demurrage at the loading and discharging port is payable by the Charterers at the rate stated in Box 20 in the manner stated in Box 20 per day or pro rata for any part of a day. Demurrage shall fall due day by day and shall be payable upon receipt of the Owners' invoice.

In the event the demurrage is not paid in accordance with the above, the Owners shall give the Charterers 96 running hours written notice to rectify the failure. If the demurrage is not paid at the expiration of this time limit and if the vessel is in or at the loading port, the Owners are entitled at any time to terminate the Charter Party and claim damages for any losses caused thereby.

8. **Lien Clause**

The Owners shall have a lien on the cargo and on all sub-freights payable in respect of the cargo, for freight, deadweight, demurrage, claims for damages and for all other amounts due under this Charter Party including costs of recovering same.

9. **Cancelling Clause**

(a) Should the Vessel not be ready to load (whether in berth or not) on the cancelling date indicated in Box 21, the Charterers shall have the option of cancelling this Charter Party.

(b) Should the Owners anticipate that, despite the exercise of due diligence, the Vessel will not be ready to load by the cancelling date, they shall notify the Charterers thereof without delay stating the expected date of the Vessel's readiness to load and asking whether the Charterers will exercise their option of cancelling the Charter Party, or agree to a new cancelling date.

Such option must be declared by the Charterers within 48 running hours after the receipt of the Owners' notice. If the Charterers do not exercise their option of cancelling, then this Charter Party shall be deemed to be amended such that the seventh day after the new readiness date stated in the Owners' notification to the Charterers shall be the new cancelling date.

The provisions of sub-clause (b) of this Clause shall operate only once, and In case of the Vessel's further delay, the Charterers shall have the option of cancelling the Charter Party as per sub-clause (a) of this Clause.

10. **Bills of Lading**

Bills of Lading shall be presented and signed by the Master as per the "Cangenbill" Bill of Lading form, Edition 1994, without prejudice to this Charter Party, or by the Owners' agents provided written authority has been given by Owners to the agents, a copy of which is to be furnished to the Charterers. The Charterers shall indemnify the Owners against all consequences or liabilities that may arise from the signing of bills of lading as presented to the extent that the terms or contents of such bills of lading impose or result In the imposition of more onerous liabilities upon the Owners than those assumed by the Owners under this Charter Party.

11. **Both-to-Blame Collision Clause**

If the Vessel comes into collision with another vessel as a result of the negligence of the other vessel and any act, neglect or default of the Master, Mariner, Pilot or the servants of the Owners In the navigation or in the management of the Vessel, the owners of the cargo carried hereunder will indemnify the Owners against all loss or liability to the other or non-carrying vessel or her owners in so far as such loss or liability represents loss of, or damage to, or any claim whatsoever of the owners of said cargo, paid or payable by the other or non-carrying vessel or her owners to the owners of said cargo and set-off, recouped or recovered by the other or non-carrying vessel or her owners as part of their claim against the carrying Vessel or the Owners. The foregoing provisions shall also apply where the owners, operators or those in charge of any vessel or vessels or objects other than, or in addition to, the colliding vessels or objects are at fault in respect of a collision or contact.

12. **General Average and New Jason Clause**

General Average shall be adjusted In London unless otherwise agreed in Box 22 according to York-Antwerp Rules 1994 and any subsequent modification thereof. Proprietors of cargo to pay the cargo's share in the general expenses even if same have been necessitated through neglect or default of the Owners' servants (see Clause 2).

If General Average is to be adjusted in accordance with the law and practice of the United States of America, the following Clause shall apply: "In the event of accident, danger, damage or disaster before or after the commencement of the voyage, resulting from any cause whatsoever, whether due to negligence or not, for which, or for the consequence of which, the Owners are not responsible, by statute, contract or otherwise, the cargo shippers, consignees or the owners of the cargo shall contribute with the Owners In General Average to the payment of any sacrifices, losses or expenses of a General Average nature that may be made or incurred and shall pay salvage and special charges incurred in respect of the cargo. If a salving vessel is owned or operated by the Owners, salvage shall be paid for as fully as if the said salving vessel or vessels belonged to strangers. Such deposit as the Owners, or their agents, may deem sufficient to cover the estimated contribution of the goods and any salvage and special charges thereon shall, if required, be made by the cargo, shippers, consignees or owners of the goods to the Owners before delivery".

13. **Taxes and Dues Clause**

(a) *On Vessel* -The Owners shall pay all dues, charges and taxes customarily levied on the Vessel, howsoever the amount thereof may be assessed.

(b) *On cargo* -The Charterers shall pay all dues, charges, duties and taxes customarily levied on the cargo, howsoever the amount thereof may be assessed.

(c) *On freight* -Unless otherwise agreed In Box 23, taxes levied on the freight shall be for the Charterers' account.

# PART II

## "Gencon" Charter (As Revised 1922, 1976 and 1994)

**14. Agency**

In every case the Owners shall appoint their own Agent both at the port of loading and the port of discharge.

**15. Brokerage**

A brokerage commission at the rate stated In Box 24 on the freight, dead-freight and demurrage earned is due to the party mentioned In Box 24.

In case of non-execution 1/3 of the brokerage on the estimated amount of freight to be paid by the party responsible for such non-execution to the Brokers as indemnity for the tatter's expenses and work. In case of more voyages the amount of indemnity to be agreed.

**16. General Strike Clause**

(a) If there is a strike or lock-out affecting or preventing the actual loading of the cargo, or any part of it, when the Vessel is ready to proceed from her last port or at any time during the voyage to the port or ports of loading or after her arrival there, the Master or the Owners may ask the Charterers to declare, that they agree to reckon the laydays as if there were no strike or lock-out. Unless the Charterers have given such declaration in writing (by telegram, if necessary) within 24 hours, the Owners shall have the option of cancelling this Charter Party. If part cargo has already been loaded, the Owners must proceed with same, (freight payable on loaded quantity only) having liberty to complete with other cargo on the way for their own account.

(b) If there is a strike or lock-out affecting or preventing the actual discharging of the cargo on or after the Vessel's arrival at or off port of discharge and same has not been settled within 46 hours, the Charterers shall have the option of keeping the Vessel waiting until such strike or lock-out is at an end against paying half demurrage after expiration of the time provided for discharging until the strike or lock-out terminates and thereafter full demurrage shall be payable until the completion of discharging, or of ordering the Vessel to a safe port where she can safely discharge without risk of being detained by strike or lock-out. Such orders to be given within 48 hours after the Master or the Owners have given notice to the Charterers of the strike or lock-out affecting the discharge. On delivery of the cargo at such port, all conditions of this Charter Party and of the Bill of Lading shall apply and the Vessel shall receive the same freight as if she had discharged at the original port of destination, except that if the distance to the substituted port exceeds 100 nautical miles, the freight on the cargo delivered at the substituted port to be increased in proportion.

(c) Except for the obligations described above, neither the Charterers nor the Owners shall be responsible for the consequences of any strikes or lock-outs preventing or affecting the actual loading or discharging of the cargo.

**17. War Risks ("Voywar 1993")**

(1) For the purpose of this Clause, the words:

(a) The "Owners" shall include the shipowners, bareboat charterers, disponent owners, managers or other operators who are charged with the management of the Vessel, and the Master; and

(b) "War Risks" shall Include any war (whether actual or threatened), act of war, civil war, hostilities, revolution, rebellion, civil commotion, warlike operations, the laying of mines (whether actual or reported), acts of piracy, acts of terrorists, acts of hostility or malicious damage, blockades (whether imposed against all Vessels or imposed selectively against Vessels of certain flags or ownership, or against certain cargoes or crews or otherwise howsoever), by any person, body, terrorist or political group, or the Government of any state whatsoever, which, in the reasonable Judgement of the Master and/or the Owners, may be dangerous or are likely to be or to become dangerous to the Vessel, her cargo, crew or other persons on board the Vessel.

(2) If at any time before the Vessel commences loading, it appears that, in the reasonable judgement of the Master and/or the Owners, performance of the Contract of Carriage, or any part of it, may expose, or is likely to expose, the Vessel, her cargo, crew or other persons on board the Vessel to War Risks, the Owners may give notice to the Charterers cancelling this Contract of Carriage, or may refuse to perform such part of it as may expose, or may be likely to expose, the Vessel, her cargo, crew or other persons on board the Vessel to War Risks; provided always that if this Contract of Carriage provides that loading or discharging is to take place within a range of ports, and at the port or ports nominated by the Charterers the Vessel, her cargo, crew, or other persons onboard the Vessel may be exposed, or may be likely to be exposed, to War Risks, the Owners shall first require the Charterers to nominate any other safe port which lies within the range for loading or discharging, and may only cancel this Contract of Carriage It the Charterers shall not have nominated such safe port or ports within 48 hours of receipt of notice of such requirement.

(3) The Owners shall not be required to continue to load cargo for any voyage, or to sign Bills of Lading for any port or place, or to proceed or continue on any voyage, or on any part thereof, or to proceed through any canal or waterway, or to proceed to or remain at any port or place whatsoever, where it appears, either after the loading of the cargo commences, or at any stage of the voyage thereafter before the discharge of the cargo is completed, that, In the reasonable judgement of the Master and/or the Owners, the Vessel, her cargo (or any part thereof), crew or other persons on board the Vessel (or any one or more of them) may be, or are likely to be, exposed to War Risks, if it should so appear, the Owners may by notice request the Charterers to nominate a safe port for the discharge of the cargo or any part thereof, and if within 48 hours of the receipt of such notice, the Charterers shall not have nominated such a port, the Owners may discharge the cargo at any safe port of their choice (including the port of loading) in complete fulfilment of the Contract of Carriage. The Owners shall be entitled to recover from the Charterers the extra expenses of such discharge and, if the discharge takes place at any port other than the loading port to receive the full freight as though the cargo had been carried to the discharging port and if the extra distance exceeds 100 miles, to additional freight which shall be the same percentage of the freight contracted for as the percentage which the extra distance represents to the distance of the normal and customary route, the Owners having a lien on the cargo for such expenses and freight.

(4) If at any stage of the voyage after the loading of the cargo commences, it appears that, in the reasonable judgement of the Master and/or the Owners, the Vessel, her cargo, crew or other persons on board the Vessel may be, or are likely to be, exposed to War Risks on any part of the route (including any canal or waterway) which is normally and customarily used in a voyage of the nature contracted for, and there is another longer route to the discharging port, the Owners shall give notice to the Charterers that this route will be taken, in this event the Owners shall be entitled, if the total extra distance exceeds 100 miles, to additional freight which shall be the same percentage of the freight contracted for as the percentage which the extra distance represents to the distance of the normal and customary route.

(5) The Vessel shall have liberty:-

(a) to comply with all orders, directions, recommendations or advice as to departure, arrival, routes, sailing in convoy, ports of call, stoppages, destinations, discharge of cargo, delivery or in any way whatsoever which are given by the Government of the Nation under whose flag the Vessel sails, or other Government to whose laws the Owners are subject, or any other Government which so requires, or any body or group acting with the power to compel compliance with their orders or directions;

(b) to comply with the orders, directions or recommendations of any war risks underwriters who have the authority to give the same under the terms of the war risks insurance;

(c) to comply with the terms of any resolution of the Security Council of the United Nations, any directives of the European Community, the effective orders of any other Supranational body which has the right to issue and give the same, and with national laws aimed at enforcing the same to which the Owners are subject, and to obey the orders and directions of those who are charged with their enforcement;

(d) to discharge at any other port any cargo or part thereof which may render the Vessel liable to confiscation as a contraband carrier;

(e) to call at any other port to change the crew or any part thereof or other persons on board the Vessel when there is reason to believe that they may be subject to internment, imprisonment or other sanctions;

(f) where cargo has not been loaded or has been discharged by the Owners under any provisions of this Clause, to load other cargo for the Owners' own benefit and carry it to any other port or ports whatsoever, whether backwards or forwards or in a contrary direction to the ordinary or customary route.

(6) If in compliance with any of the provisions of sub-clauses (2) to (5) of this Clause anything is done or not done, such shall not be deemed to be a deviation, but shall be considered as due fulfilment of the Contract of Carriage.

**18. General Ice Clause**

*Port of loading*

(a) In the event of the loading port being inaccessible by reason of ice when the Vessel is ready to proceed from her last port or at any time during the voyage or on the Vessel's arrival or in case frost sets In after the Vessel's arrival, the Master for fear of being frozen in is at liberty to leave without cargo, and this Charter Party shall be null and void.

(b) If during loading the Master, for fear of the Vessel being frozen In, deems it advisable to leave, he has liberty to do so with what cargo he has on board and to proceed to any other port or ports with option of completing cargo for the Owners' benefit for any port or ports including port of discharge. Any part cargo thus loaded under this Charter Party to be forwarded to destination at the Vessel's expense but against payment of freight, provided that no extra expenses be thereby caused to the Charterers, freight being paid on quantity delivered (in proportion if lumpsum), all other conditions as per this Charter Party.

(c) In case of more than one loading port, and if one or more of the ports are closed by ice, the Master or the Owners to be at liberty either to load the part cargo at the open port and fill up elsewhere for their own account as under section (b) or to declare the Charter Party null and void unless the Charterers agree to load full cargo at the open port.

*Port of discharge*

(a) Should ice prevent the Vessel from reaching port of discharge the Charterers shall have the option of keeping the Vessel waiting until there opening of navigation and paying demurrage or of ordering the Vessel to a safe and immediately accessible port where she can safely discharge without risk of detention by ice. Such orders to be given within 48 hours after the Master or the Owners have given notice to the Charterers of the Impossibility of reaching port of destination.

(b) If during discharging the Master for fear of the Vessel being frozen in deems it advisable to leave, he has liberty to do so with what cargo he has on board and to proceed to the nearest accessible port where she can safely discharge.

(c) On delivery of the cargo at such port, all conditions of the Bill of Lading shall apply and the Vessel shall receive the same freight as if she had discharged at the original port of destination, except that if the distance of the substituted port exceeds 100 nautical miles, the freight on the cargo delivered at the substituted port to be increased in proportion.

**19. Law and Arbitration**

* (a) This Charter Party shall be governed by and construed in accordance with English law and any dispute arising out of this Charter Party shall be referred to arbitration in London in accordance with the Arbitration Acts 1950 and 1979 or any statutory modification or re-enactment thereof for the time being in force. Unless the parties agree upon a sole arbitrator, one arbitrator shall be appointed by each party and the arbitrators so appointed shall appoint a third arbitrator, the decision of the three-man tribunal thus constituted or any two of them, shall be final. On the receipt by one party of the nomination in writing of the other party's arbitrator, that party shall appoint their arbitrator within fourteen days, failing which the decision of the single arbitrator appointed shall be final.

For disputes where the total amount claimed by either party does not exceed the amount stated in Box 25** the arbitration shall be conducted in accordance with the Small Claims Procedure of the London Maritime Arbitrators Association.

* (b) This Charter Party shall be governed by and construed In accordance with Title 9 of the United States Code and the Maritime Law of the United States and should any dispute arise out of this Charter Party, the matter in dispute shall be referred to three persons at New York, one to be appointed by each of the parties hereto, and the third by the two so chosen; their decision or that of any two of them shall be final, and for purpose of enforcing any award, this agreement may be made a rule of the Court. The proceedings shall be conducted in accordance with the rules of the Society of Maritime Arbitrators, Inc..

For disputes where the total amount claimed by either party does not exceed the amount stated in Box 25** the arbitration shall be conducted In accordance with the Shortened Arbitration Procedure of the Society of Maritime Arbitrators, Inc..

* (c) Any dispute arising out of this Charter Party shall be referred to arbitration at the place indicated In Box 25, subject to the procedures applicable there. The laws of the place indicated in Box 25 shall govern this Charter Party.

(d) If Box 25 in Part I is not filled in, sub-clause (a) of this Clause shall apply.

* *(a), (b) and (c) are alternatives; indicate alternative agreed in Box 25.*

** *Where no figure is supplied in Box 25 in Part I, this provision only shall be void but the other provisions of this Clause shall have full force and remain in effect.*

# APPENDIX 2

## NYPE 93

Code Name: 'NYPE 93'
Recommended by: The Baltic and International Maritime Council (BIMCO)
The Federation of National Associations of Ship Brokers and Agents (FONASBA)

TIME CHARTER
New York Produce Exchange Form
Issued by the Association of Ship Brokers and Agents (U.S.A.), Inc.
November 6th. 1913 - Amended October 20th. 1921; August 6th, 1931; October 3rd. 1946;
Revised June 12th, 1981; September 14th 1993,

THIS CHARTER PARTY, made and concluded in ..........................................................
this .......................................... day of ....................................... 1 9...........................
Between ..............................................................................................................................
..............................................................................................................................
Owners of the Vessel described below, and............................................. ...................
..............................................................................................................................
Charterers.

**Description of Vessel**

Name .................................... Flag ................................ Built ........................ (year).
Port and number of Registry .................................................................................
Classed.................................................. in ............................................................
Deadweight.............................long*/metric* tons (cargo and bunkers, including freshwater and stores not exceeding........................long*/metric* tons) on a salt water draft of ..........................
on summer freeboard.
Capacity........................................ cubic feet grain ................................ cubic feet bale space.
Tonnage ........................................ GT/GRT.
Speed about...............knots, fully laden, in good weather conditions up to and including maximum Force ............on the Beaufort wind scale, on a consumption of about ....................long*/metric* tons of ......................................

* Delete as appropriate.
For further description see Appendix "A " (if applicable)

1. **Duration**

The Owners agree to let and the Charterers agree to hire the Vessel from the time of delivery for a period of ..............................................................................................................
..............................................................................................................................
.............................................................. within below mentioned trading limits.

2. **Delivery**

The Vessel shall be placed at the disposal of the Charterers at ...................................................
..............................................................................................................................

............................................................................................…… The Vessel on her delivery shall be ready to receive cargo with clean-swept holds and tight, staunch, strong and in every way fitted for ordinary cargo service, having water ballast and with sufficient power to operate all cargo-handling gear simultaneously.

The Owners shall give the Charterers not less than ............................ days notice of expected date of delivery.

**3. On-Off Hire Survey**

Prior to delivery and redelivery the parties shall, unless otherwise agreed, each appoint surveyors, for their respective accounts, who shall not later than at first loading port/last discharging port respectively, conduct joint on-hire/off-hire surveys, for the purpose of ascertaining quantity of bunkers on board and the condition of the Vessel. A single report shall be prepared on each occasion and signed by each surveyor, without prejudice to his right to file a separate report setting forth items upon which the surveyors cannot agree. If either party fails to have a representative attend the survey and sign the joint survey report, such party shall nevertheless be bound for all purposes by the findings in any report prepared by the other party. On-hire survey shall be on Charterers' time and off-hire survey on Owners' time.

**4. Dangerous Cargo/Cargo Exclusions**

(a) The Vessel shall be employed in carrying lawful merchandise excluding any goods of a dangerous, injurious, flammable or corrosive nature unless carried in accordance with the requirements or recommendations of the competent authorities of the country of the Vessel's registry and of ports of shipment and discharge and of any intermediate countries or ports through whose waters the Vessel must pass. Without prejudice to the generality of the foregoing, in addition the following are specifically excluded: livestock of any description, arms, ammunition, explosives, nuclear and radioactive materials,……………………………………………………………..

…………………………………………………………………………………………………………

…………………………………………………………………………………………………………

…………………………………………………………………………………………………………

(b) If IMO-classified cargo is agreed to be carried, the amount of such cargo shall be limited to… ……………. tons and the Charterers shall provide the Master with any evidence he may reasonably require to show that the cargo is packaged, labelled, loaded and stowed in accordance with IMO regulations, failing which the Master is entitled to refuse such cargo or, if already loaded, to unload it at the Charterers' risk and expense.

**5. Trading Limits**

The Vessel shall be employed in such lawful trades between safe ports and safe places within …....

…………………………………………………………………………………………………………

…………………………………………………………………………………………………………..

.........................................................................................................................………..excluding

…………………………………………………………………………………………………………..

........................................................................................................…... as the Charterers shall direct.

6. **Owners to Provide**

The Owners shall provide and pay for the insurance of the Vessel, except as otherwise provided, and for all provisions, cabin, deck, engine-room and other necessary stores, including boiler water; shall pay for wages, consular shipping and discharging fees of the crew and charges for port services pertaining to the crew; shall maintain the Vessel's class and keep her in a thoroughly efficient state in hull, machinery and equipment for and during the service, and have a full complement of officers and crew.

7. **Charterers to Provide**

The Charterers, while the Vessel is on hire, shall provide and pay for all the bunkers except as otherwise agreed; shall pay for port charges (including compulsory watchmen and cargo watchmen and compulsory garbage disposal), all communication expenses pertaining to the Charterers' business at cost, pilotages, towages, agencies, commissions, consular charges (except those pertaining to individual crew members or flag of the Vessel), and all other usual expenses except those stated in Clause 6, but when the Vessel puts into a port for causes for which the Vessel is responsible (other than by stress of weather), then all such charges incurred shall be paid by the Owners. Fumigations ordered because of illness of the crew shall be for the Owners' account. Fumigations ordered because of cargoes carried or ports visited while theVessel is employed underthis Charter Party shall be for the Charterers' account. All other fumigations shall be for the Charterers'account after the Vessel has been on charter for a continuous period of six months or more.

The Charterers shall provide and pay for necessary dunnage and also any extra fittings requisite for a special trad or unusual cargo, but the Owners shall allow them the use of any dunnage already aboard the Vessel. Prior to redelivery the Charterers shall remove their dunnage and fittings at their cost and in their time.

8. **Performance of Voyage**

(a) The Master shall perform the voyages with due despatch, and shall render all customary assistance with the Vessel's crew. The Master shall be conversant with the English language and (although appointed by the Owners) shall be under the orders and directions of the Charterers as regards employment and agency; and the Charterers shall perform all cargo handling, including but not limited to loading, stowing, trimming, lashing, securing, dunnaging, unlashing, discharging, and tallying, at their risk and expense, under the supervision of the Master.

(b) If the Charterers shall have reasonable cause to be dissatisfied with the conduct of the Master or officers, the Owners shall, on receiving particulars of the complaint, investigate the same, and, if necessary, make a change in the appointments.

9. **Bunkers**

(a) The Charterers on delivery, and the Owners on redelivery, shall take over and pay for all fuel and diesel oil remaining on board the Vessel as hereunder. The Vessel shall be delivered with: ................................ long*/metric* tons of fuel oil at the price of ........................per ton; .................................... tons of diesel oil at the price of .......................... per ton. The vessel shall be redelivered with: ........................................ tons of fuel oil at the price of .................................... per ton; ...................................... tons of diesel oil at the price of ................................. per ton.

** Same tons apply throughout this clause.*

(b) The Charterers shall supply bunkers of a quality suitable for burning in the Vessel's engines and auxiliaries and which conform to the specification(s) as set out in Appendix A.

The Owners reserve their right to make a claim against the Charterers for any damage to the main engines or the auxiliaries caused by the use of unsuitable fuels or fuels not complying with the agreed specification(s). Additionally, if bunker fuels supplied do not conform with the mutually agreed specification(s) or otherwise prove unsuitable for burning in the Vessel's engines or auxiliaries, the Owners shall not be held responsible for any reduction in the Vessel's speed performance and/or increased bunker consumption, nor for any time lost and any other consequences.

**10. Rate of Hire/Redelivery Areas and Notices**

The Charterers shall pay for the use and hire of the said Vessel at the rate of $ .............................. U.S. currency, daily, or $ ................................ U.S. currency per ton on the Vessel's total deadweight carrying capacity, including bunkers and stores, on .................. ..........summer freeboard, per 30 days, commencing on and from the day of her delivery, as afore said, and at and after the same rate for any part of a month; hire shall continue until the hour of the day of her redelivery in like good order and condition, ordinary wear and tear excepted, to the Owners (unless Vessel lost) at ....................................................................................................................

..........................................................................................................................

..................................................................... unless otherwise mutually agreed.

The Charterers shall give the Owners not less than ........................... days notice of the Vessel's expected date and probable port of redelivery.

For the purpose of hire calculations, the times of delivery, redelivery or termination of charter shall be adjusted to GMT.

**11. Hire Payment**

(a) *Payment*

Payment of Hire shall be made so as to be received by the Owners or their designated payee in ........................................................... , viz ...........................................................................

..........................................................................................................................

.......................................................................................................................... in

....................currency, or in United States Currency, in funds available to the Owners on the due date, 15 days in advance, and for the last month or part of same the approximate amount of hire, and should same not cover the actual time, hire shall be paid for the balance day by day as it becomes due, if so required by the Owners. Failing the punctual and regular payment of the hire, or on any fundamental breach whatsoever of this Charter Party, the Owners shall be at liberty to withdraw the Vessel from the service of the Charterers without prejudice to any claims they (the Owners) may otherwise have on the Charterers.

At any time after the expiry of the grace period provided in Sub-clause 11 (b) hereunder and while the hire is outstanding, the Owners shall, without prejudice to the liberty to withdraw, be entitled to withhold the performance of any and all of their obligations hereunder and shall have no responsibility whatsoever for any consequences thereof, in respect of which the Charterers hereby indemnify the Owners, and hire shall continue to accrue and any extra expenses resulting from such withholding shall be for the Charterers' account.

(b) *Grace Period*

Where there is failure to make punctual and regular payment of hire due to oversight, negligence, errors or omissions on the part of the Charterers or their bankers, the Charterers shall be given by the Owners ……………............. clear banking days (as recognized at the agreed place of payment) written notice to rectify the failure, and when so rectified within those ........... days following the Owners' notice, the payment shall stand as regular and punctual.

Failure by the Charterers to pay the hire within ........... days of their receiving the Owners' notice as provided herein, shall entitle the Owners to withdraw as set forth in Sub-clause 11 (a) above.

(c) *Last Hire Payment*

Should the Vessel be on her voyage towards port of redelivery at the time the last and/or the penultimate payment of hire is/are due, said payment(s) is/are to be made for such length of time as the Owners and the Charterers may agree upon as being the estimated time necessary to complete the voyage, and taking into account bunkers actually on board, to be taken over by the Owners and estimated disbursements for the Owners' account before redelivery. Should same not cover the actual time, hire is to be paid for the balance, day by day, as it becomes due. When the Vessel has been redelivered, any difference is to be refunded by the Owners or paid by the Charterers, as the case may be.

(d) *Cash Advances*

Cash for the Vessel's ordinary disbursements at any port may be advanced by the Charterers, as required by the Owners, subject to 2~ percent commission and such advances shall be deducted from the hire.

The Charterers, however, shall in no way be responsible for the application of suc h advances.

**12. Berths**

The Vessel shall be loaded and discharged in any safe dock or at any safe berth or safe place that Charterers or their agents may direct, provided the Vessel can safely enter, lie a nd depart always afloat at any time of tide.

**13. Spaces Available**

(a) The whole reach of the Vessel's holds, decks, and other cargo spaces (not m ore than she can reasonably and safely stow and carry), also accommodations for supercargo, if ca rried, shall be at the Charterers' disposal, reserving only proper and sufficient space for the Vessel's officers, crew, tackle, apparel, furniture, provisions, stores and fuel.

(b) in the event of deck cargo being carried, the Owners are to be and are hereby indemnified by the Charterers for any loss and/or damage and/or liability of whatsoever nature caused to the Vessel as a result of the carriage of deck cargo and which would not have arisen had deck cargo not been loaded.

**14. Supercargo and Meals**

The Charterers are entitled to appoint a supercargo, who shall accompany the Vessel at the Charterers' risk and see that voyages are performed with due despatch. He is to be furnished with free accommodation and same fare as provided for the Master's table, the Charterers paying at the rate of ......................... per day. The Owners shall victual pilots and customs officers, and also, when authorized by the Charterers or their agents, shall victual tally clerks, stevedore's foreman, etc., Charterers paying at the rate of ........................ per meal for all such victualling.

**15. Sailing Orders and Logs**

The Charterers shall furnish the Master from time to time with all requisite instructions and sailing directions, in writing, in the English language, and the Master shall keep full and correct deck and engine logs of the voyage or voyages, which are to be patent to the Charterers or their agents, and furnish the Charterers, their agents or supercargo, when required, with a true copy of such deck and engine logs, showing the course of the Vessel, distance run and the consumption of bunkers. Any log extracts required by the Charterers shall be in the English language.

**16. Delivery/Cancelling**

If required by the Charterers, time shall not commence before .............................. and should the Vessel not be ready for delivery on or before ....................................but not later than.......... hours, the Charterers shall have the option of cancelling this Charter Party.

*Extension of Cancelling*

If the Owners warrant that, despite the exercise of due diligence by them, the Vessel will not be ready for delivery by the cancelling date, and provided the Owners are able to state with reasonable certainty the date on which the Vessel will be ready, they may, at the earliest seven days before the Vessel is expected to sail for the port or place of delivery, require the Charterers to declare whether or not they will cancel the Charter Party. Should the Charterers elect not to cancel, or should they fail to reply within two days or by the cancelling date, which ever shall first occur, then the seventh day after the expected date of readiness for delivery as notified by the Owners shall replace the original cancelling date. Should the Vessel be further delayed, the Owners shall be entitled to require further declarations of the Charterers in accordance with this Clause.

**17. Off Hire**

In the event of loss of time from deficiency and/or default and/or strike of officers or crew, or deficiency of stores, fire, breakdown of, or damages to hull, machinery or equipment, grounding, detention by the arrest of the Vessel, (unless such arrest is caused by events for which the Charterers, their servants, agents or subcontractors are responsible), or detention by average accidents to the Vessel or cargo unless resulting from inherent vice, quality or defect of the cargo, drydocking for the purpose of examination or painting bottom, or by any other similar cause preventing the full working of the Vessel, the payment of hire and overtime, Jf any, shall cease for the time thereby lost. Should the Vessel deviate or put back during a voyage, contrary to the orders or directions of the Charterers, for any reason other than accident to the cargo or where permitted in lines 257 to 258 hereunder, the hire is to be suspended from the time of her deviating or putting back until she is again in the same or equidistant position from the destination and the voyage resumed therefrom. All bunkers used by the Vessel while off hire shall be for the Owners' account. In the event of the Vessel being driven into port or to anchorage through stress of weather, trading to shallow harbors or to rivers or ports with bars, any detention of the Vessel and/or expenses resulting from such detention shall be for the Charterers' account. If upon the voyage the speed be reduced by defect in, or breakdown of, any part of her hull, machinery or equipment, the time so lost, and the cost of any extra bunkers consumed in consequence thereof, and all extra proven expenses may be deducted from the hire.

**1 8. Sublet**

Unless otherwise agreed, the Charterers shall have the liberty to sublet the Vessel for all or any part of the time covered by this Charter Party, but the Charterers remain responsible for the fulfillment of this Charter Party.

**19. Drgdocking**

The Vessel was last drydocked ........................................................................................................

* (a) The Owners shall have the option to place the Vessel in drydock during the currency of this Charter at a convenient time and place, to be mutually agreed upon between the Owners and the Charterers, for bottom cleaning and painting and/or repair as required by class or dictated by circumstances.

*(b) Except in case of emergency no drydocking shall take place during the currency of this Charter Party.

* *Delete as appropriate*

**20. Total Loss**

Should the Vessel be lost, money paid in advance and not earned (reckoning from the date of loss or being last heard of) shall be returned to the Charterers at once.

**21. Exceptions**

The act of God, enemies, fire, restraint of princes, rulers and people, and all dangers and accidents of the seas, rivers, machinery, boilers, and navigation, and errors of navigation throughout this Charter, always mutually excepted.

**22. Liberties**

The Vessel shall have the liberty to sail with or without pilots, to tow and to be towed, to assist vessels in distress, and to deviate for the purpose of saving life and property.

**23. Lien**

The Ow ners shall have a lien upon all cargoes and ail sub-freights and/or sub-hire for any amounts due under this Charter Party, including general average contributions, and the Charterers shall have a li en on the Vessel for all monies paid in advance and not earned, and any overpaid hire or excess deposit to be returned at once.

The Cha rterers will not directly or indirectly suffer, nor permit to be continued, any lien or encumbrance, which might have priority over the title and interest of the Owners in the Vessel. The Charterers undertake that during the period of this Charter Party, they will not procure any supplies or necessaries or services, including any port expenses and bunkers, on the credit of the Owners or in the Owners' time.

**24. Salvage**

All derelicts and salvage shall be for the Owners' and the Charterers' equal benefit after deducting Owners' and Charterers' expenses and crew's proportion.

**25. General Average**

General average shall be adjusted according to York-Antwerp Rules 1974, as amended 1990, or any subsequent modification thereof, in.................................. and settled in ........................ currency.

The Charterers shall procure that all bills of lading issued during the currency of the Charter Party will contain a provision to the effect that general average shall be adjusted according to York-Antwerp Rules 1974, as amended 1990, or any subsequent modification thereof and will include the "New Jason Clause" as per Clause 31.

Time charter hire shall not contribute to general average.

**26, Navigation**

Nothing herein stated is to be construed as a demise of the Vessel to the Time Charterers. The Owners shall remain responsible for the navigation of the Vessel, acts of pilots and tug boats, insurance, crew, and all other matters, same as when trading for their own account.

**27. Cargo Claims**

Cargo claims as between the Owners and the Charterers shall be settled in accordance with the Inter-Club New York Produce Exchange Agreement of February 1970, as amended May, 1984, or any subsequent modification or replacement thereof.

**28. Cargo Gear and Lights**

The Owners shall maintain the cargo handling gear of the Vessel which is as follows: ..........................................................................................................

..........................................................................................................

providing gear (for all derricks or cranes) capable of lifting capacity as described. The Owners shall also provide on the Vessel for night work lights as on board, but all additional lights over those on board shall be at the Charterers' expense. The Charterers shall have the use of any gear on board the Vessel. If required by the Charterers, the Vessel shall work night and day and all cargo handling gear shall be at the Charterers' disposal during loading and discharging. In the event of disabled cargo handling gear, or insufficient power to operate the same, the Vessel is to be considered to be off hire to the extent that time is actually lost to the Charterers and the Owners to pay stevedore stand-by charges occasioned thereby, unless such disablement or insufficiency of power is caused by the Charterers' stevedores. If required by the Charterers, the Owners shall bear the cost of hiring shore gear in lieu thereof, in which case the Vessel shall remain on hire.

**29. Crew Overtime**

In lieu of any overtime payments to officers and crew for work ordered by the Charterers or their agents, the Charterers shall pay the Owners, concurrently with the hire .......................................... per month or pro rata.

**30. Bills of Lading**

(a) The Master shall sign the bills of lading or waybills for cargo as presented in conformity with mates or tally clerk's receipts. However, the Charterers may sign bills of lading or waybills on behalf of the Master, with the Owner's prior written authority, always in conformity with mates or tally clerk's receipts.

(b) All bills of lading or waybills shall be without prejudice to this Charter Party and the

Charterers shall indemnify the Owners against all consequences or liabilities which may arise from any inconsistency between this Charter Party and any bills of lading or waybills signed by the Charterers or by the Master at their request.

(c) Bills of lading covering deck cargo shall be claused: "Shipped on deck at Charterers', Shippers' and Receivers' risk, expense and responsibility, without liability on the part of the Vessel, or her Owners for any loss, damage, expense or delay howsoever caused."

**31. <u>Protective Clauses</u>**

This Charter Party is subject to the following clauses all of which are also to be included in all bills of lading or waybills issued hereunder:

(a) CLAUSE PARAMOUNT

"This bill of lading shall have effect subject to the provisions of the Carriage of Goods by Sea Act of the United States, the Hague Rules, or the Hague-Visby Rules, as applicable, or such other similar national legislation as may mandatorily apply by virtue of origin or destination of the bills of lading, which shall be deemed to be incorporated herein and nothing herein contained shall be deemed a surrender by the carrier of any of its rights or immunities or an increase of any of its responsibilities or liabilities under said applicable Act. If any term of this bill of lading be repugnant to said applicable Act to any extent, such term shall be void to that extent, but no further."

And

(b) BOTH-TO-BLAME COLLISION CLAUSE

'If the ship comes into collision with another ship as a result of the negligence of the oher ship and any act, negl ect or default of the master, mariner, pilot or the servants of the carrier in the navigation or in th e management of the ship, the owners of the goods carried hereuıder will indemnify the car rier against all loss or liability to the other or non-carrying ship or her owners insofar as such loss or liability represents loss of, or damage to, or any claim whatsoever of the owners of said go ods, paid or payable by the other or non-carrying ship or her ownes to the owners of said goo ds and set off, recouped or recovered by the other or non-carrying shp or her owners as part of their claim against the carrying ship or carrier.

The foregoing provisions shall also apply where the owners, operators or those in charge of any ships or objects other than, or in addition to, the colliding ships or objects are at fault in rspect to a collision or conta ct."

and

(c) NEW JASON CLAUSE

'In the event of accident, danger, damage or disaster before or after the commencement of the voyage resulting from any cause whatsoever, whether due to negligence or not, for which, or for the consequences of which, the carrier is not responsible, by statute, contract, or otherwise, the goods, shippers, consignees, or owners of the goods shall contribute with the carrier in general average to the payment of any sacrifices, losses, or expenses of a general average nature that may be made or incurred, and shall pay salvage and special charges incurred in respect of the goods.

If a salving ship is owned or operated by the carrier, salvage shall be paid for as fully as if salving ship or ships belonged to strangers. Such deposit as the carrier or his agents may deem sufficient to cover the estimated contribution of the goods and any salvage and special charges thereon shall, if required, be made by the goods, shippers, consignees or owners of the goods to the carrier before delivery."

and

(d) U.S. TRADE - DRUG CLAUSE

"In pursuance of the provisions of the U.S. Anti Drug Abuse Act 1986 or any re-enactment thereof, the Charterers warrant to exercise the highest degree of care and diligence in preventing unmanifested narcotic drugs and marijuana to be loaded or concealed on board the Vessel.

Non-compliance with the provisions of this clause shall amount to breach of warranty for consequences of which the Charterers shall be liable and shall hold the Owners, the Master and the crew of the Vessel harmless and shall keep them indemnified against all claims whatsoever which may arise and be made against them individually or jointly. Furthermore, all time lost and all expenses incurred, including fines, as a result of the Charterers' breach of the provisions of this clause shall be for the Charterer's account and the Vessel shall remain on hire.

Should the Vessel be arrested as a result of the Charterers' non-compliance with the provisions of this clause, the Charterers shall at their expense take all reasonable steps to secure that within a reasonable time the Vessel is released and at their expense put up the bails to secure release of the Vessel.

The Owners shall remain responsible for all time lost and all expenses incurred, including fines, in the event that unmanifested narcotic drugs and marijuana are found in the possession or effects of the Vessel's personnel."

And

(e) WAR CLAUSES

"(i) No contraband of war shall be shipped. The Vessel shall not be required, without the consent of the Owners, which shall not be unreasonably withheld, to enter any port or zone which is involved in a state of war, warlike operations, or hostilities, civil strife, insurrection or piracy whether there be a declaration of war or not, where the Vessel, cargo or crew might reasonably be expected to be subject to capture, seizure or arrest, or to a hostile act by a belligerent power (the term "power" meaning any de jure or de facto authority or any purported governmental organization maintaining naval, military or air forces).

(ii) If such consent is given by the Owners, the Charterers will pay the provable additional cost of insuring the Vessel against hull war risks in an amount equal to the value under her ordinary hull policy but not exceeding a valuation of .............................................. In addition, the Owners may purchase and the Charterers will pay for war risk insurance on ancillary risks such as loss of hire, freight disbursements, total loss, blocking and trapping, etc. If such insurance is not obtainable commercially or through a government program, the Vessel shall not be required to enter or remain at any such port or zone.

(iii) In the event of the existence of the conditions described in (i) subsequent to the date of this

Charter, or while the Vessel is on hire under this Charter, the Charterers shall, in respect of voyages to any such port or zone assume the provable additional cost of wages and insurance properly incurred in connection with master, officers and crew as a consequence of such war, warlike operations or hostilities.
(iv) Any war bonus to officers and crew due to the Vessel's trading or cargo carried shall be for the Charterers' account."

**32. War Cancellation**

In the event of the outbreak of war (whether there be a declaration of war or not) between any two or more of the following countries: ..................................................................................................
either the Owners or the Charterers may cancel this Charter Party. Whereupon, the Charterers shall redeliver the Vessel to the Owners in accordance with Clause 10; if she has cargo on board, after discharge thereof at destination, or, if debarred under this Clause from reaching or entering it, at a near open and safe port as directed by the Owners; or, if she has no cargo on board, at the port at which she then is; or, if at sea, at a near open and safe port as directed by the Owners. In all cases hire shall continue to be paid in accordance with Clause 11 and except as aforesaid all other provisions of this Charter Party shall apply until redelivery.

**33. Ice**

The Vessel shall not be required to enter or remain in any icebound port or area, nor any port or area where lights or lightships have been or are about to be withdrawn by reason of ice, nor where there is risk that in the ordinary course of things the Vessel will not be able on account of ice to safely enter and remain in the port or area or to get out after having completed loading or discharging. Subject to the Owners' prior approval the Vessel is to follow ice-breakers when reasonably required with regard to her size, construction and ice class.

**34. Requisition**

Should the Vessel be requisitioned by the government of the Vessel's flag during the period of this Charter Party, the Vessel shall be deemed to be off hire during the period of such requisition, and any hire paid by the said government in respect of such requisition period shall be retained by the Owners. The period during which the Vessel is on requisition to the said government shall count as part of the period provided for in this Charter Party.
If the period of requisition exceeds .................................. months, either party shall have the option of cancelling this Charter Party and no consequential claim may be made by either party.

**35. Stevedore Damage**

Notwithstanding anything contained herein to the contrary, the Charterers shall pay for any and all damage to the Vessel caused by stevedores provided the Master has notified the Charterers and/or their agents in writing as soon as practical but not later than 48 hours after any damage is discovered. Such notice to specify the damage in detail and to invite Charterers to appoint a surveyor to assess the extent of such damage.
(a) In case of any and all damage(s) affecting the Vessel's seaworthiness and/or the safety of the crew and/or affecting the trading capabilities of the Vessel, the Charterers shall immediately arrange for repairs of such damage(s) at their expense and the Vessel is to remain on hire until

such repairs are completed and if required passed by the Vessel's classification society.
(b) Any and all damage(s) not described under point (a) above shall be repaired at the Charterers' option, before or after redelivery concurrently with the Owners' work. In such case no hire and/or expenses will be paid to the Owners except and insofar as the time and/or the expenses required for the repairs for which the Charterers are responsible, exceed the time and/or expenses necessary to carry out the Owners' work.

**36. Cleaning of Holds**

The Charterers shall provide and pay extra for sweeping and/or washing and/or cleaning of holds between voyages and/or between cargoes provided such work can be undertaken by the crew and is permitted by local regulations, at the rate of ....... .................... per hold.
In connection with any such operation, the Owners shall not be responsible if the Vessel's holds are not accepted or passed by the port or any other authority. The Charterers shall have the option to re-deliver the Vessel with unclean/unswept holds against a lumpsum payment of ...................... in lieu of cleaning.

**37. Taxes**

Charterers to pay all local, State, National taxes and/or dues assessed on the Vessel or the Owners resulting from the Charterers' orders herein, whether assessed during or after the currency of this Charter Party including any taxes and/or dues on cargo and/or freights and/or sub-freights and/or hire (excludig taxes levied by the country of the flag of the Vessel or the Owners).

**38. Charterers' Colors**

The Charterers shall have the privilege of flying their own house flag and painting the Vessel with their own markings. The Vessel shall be repainted in the Owners' colors before termination of the Charter Party.Cost and time of painting, maintaining and repainting those changes e ffected by the Charterers shall be for the Charterers' account.

**39. Laid Up Return**

The Charterers shall have the benefit of any return insurance premium receivable b y the Owners from their underwriters as and when received from underwriters by reason of the Vessel being in port for a minimum period of 30 days if on full hire for this period or pro rata for the time actually on hire.

**40. Documentation**

The Owners shall provide any documentation relating to the Vessel that may be required to permit the Vessel to trade within the agreed trade limits, including, but not limited to certificates of financial responsibility for oil pollution, provided such oil pollution certificates are obtainable from the Owners' P & I club, valid international tonnage certificate, Suez and Panama tonnage certificates, valid certificate of registry and certificates relating to the strength and/or serviceability of the Vessel's gear.

**41. Stowaways**

(a) (i) The Charterers warrant to exercise due care and diligence in preventing stowaways in gaining access to the Vessel by means of secreting away in the goods and/or containers shipped by the Charterers.

(ii) If, despite the exercise of due care and diligence by the Charterers, stowaways have gained access to the Vessel by means of secreting away in the goods and/or containers shipped by the Charterers, this shall amount to breach of charter for the consequences of which the Charterers shall be liable and shall hold the Owners harmless and shall keep them indemnified against all claims whatsoever which may arise and be made against them. Furthermore, all time lost and all expenses whatsoever and howsoever incurred, including fines, shall be for the Charterers' account and the Vessel shall remain on hire.

(iii) Should the Vessel be arrested as a result of the Charterers' breach of charter according to sub-clause (a)(ii) above, the Charterers shall take all reasonable steps to secure that, within a reasonable time, the Vessel is released and at their expense put up bail to secure release of the Vessel.

(b) (i) If, despite the exercise of due care and diligence by the Owners, stowaways have gained access to the Vessel by means other than secreting away in the goods and/or containers shipped by the Charterers, all time lost and all expenses whatsoever and howsoever incurred, including fines, shall be for the Owners' account and the Vessel shall be off hire.

(ii) Should the Vessel be arrested as a result of stowaways having gained access to the Vessel by means other than secreting away in the goods and/or containers shipped by the Charterers, the Owners shall take all reasonable steps to secure that, within a reasonable time, the Vessel is released and at their expense put up bail to secure release of the Vessel.

**42. Smuggling**

In the event of smuggling by the Master, Officers and/or crew, the Owners shall bear the cost of any fines, taxes, or imposts levied and the Vessel shall be off hire for any time lost as a result thereof.

**43. Commissions**

A commission of ....................percent is payable by the Vessel and the Owners to .. ...................... on hire earned and paid under this Charter, and also upon any continuation or extension of this Charter.

**44. Address Commission**

An address commission of......................... percent is payable to ...................................................... ........................................................ on hire earned and paid under this Charter.

**45. Arbitration**

(a) NEW YORK

All disputes arising out of this contract shall be arbitrated at New York in the following manner, and subject to U.S. Law:

One Arbitrator is to be appointed by each of the parties hereto and a third by the two so chosen. Their decision or that of any two of them shall be final, and for the purpose of enforcing any

award, this agreement may be made a rule of the court. The Arbitrators shall be commercial men, conversant with shipping matters. Such Arbitration is to be conducted in accordance with the rules of the Society of Maritime Arbitrators Inc.
For disputes where the total amount claimed by either party does not exceed US $ ................ ** the arbitration shall be conducted in accordance with the Shortened Arbitration Procedure of the Society of Maritime Arbitrators Inc.

(b) LONDON
All disputes arising out of this contract shall be arbitrated at London and, unless the parties agree forthwith on a single Arbitrator, be referred to the final arbitrament of two Arbitrators carrying on business in London who shall be members of the Baltic Mercantile & Shipping Exchange and engaged in Shipping, one to be appointed by each of the parties, with power to such Arbitrators to appoint an Umpire. No award shall be questioned or invalidated on the ground that any of the Arbitrators is not qualified as above, unless objection to his action be taken before the award is made. Any dispute arising hereunder shall be governed by English Law.
For disputes where the total amount claimed by either party does not exceed US $ ................ ** the arbitration shall be conducted in accordance with the Small Claims Procedure of the London Maritime Arbitrators Association.

** Delete para (a) or (b) as appropriate*
*** Where no figure is supplied in the blank space this provision only shall be void but the other provisions of this clause shall have full force and remain in effect.*

If mutually agreed, clauses ............... to ................ both inclusive, as attached hereto are fully incorporated in this Charter Party.

# APPENDIX 3

# SHELLVOY 6

*Issued March 2005*

Code word for this Charter Party
**"SHELLVOY 6"**

**VOYAGE CHARTER PARTY**
LONDON,

**PREAMBLE**

IT IS THIS DAY AGREED between

of (hereinafter referred to as "Owners"), being owners /disponent owners of the____

motor/steam tank vessel called with an IMO number of

(hereinafter referred to as "the vessel")

and

(hereinafter referred to as "Charterers"):

that the service for which provision is herein made shall be subject to the terms and conditions of this Charter which includes Part I, Part II and Part III. In the event of any conflict between the provisions of Part I, Part II and Part III hereof, the provisions of Part I shall prevail.

**PART I**

(A) Description of vessel

(I) Owners warrant that at the date hereof, and from the time when the obligation to proceed to the loadport(s) attaches, the Vessel

(i) Is classed

(ii) (a) Has a deadweight of ………… (1000 kg) on a salt-water draft on assigned summer freeboard of ………m. and if applicable,

(b) Has on board documentation showing the following additional drafts and deadweights

(iii) Has capacity for cargo of ……………. $m^3$,

(iv) Is fully fitted with heating systems for all cargo tanks capable of maintaining cargo at a temperature of up to degrees Celsius and can accept a cargo temperature on loading of up to a maximum of degrees Celsius.

(v) Has tanks coated as follows:

(vi) Is equipped with cranes/derricks capable of lifting to and supporting at the vessel's port and starboard manifolds submarine hoses of up to tonnes (1000 kg) in weight.

(vii) Can discharge a full cargo (whether homogenous or multi grade) either within 24 hours, or can maintain a back pressure of 100 PSI at the vessel's manifold and Owners warrant such minimum performance provided receiving facilities permit and subject always to the obligation of utmost despatch set out in Part II, clause 3 (1) .
The discharge warranty shall only be applicable provided the kinematic viscosity does not exceed 600 centistokes at the discharge temperature required by Charterers. If the kinematic viscosity only exceeds 600 centistokes on part of the cargo or particular grade(s) then the discharge warranty shall continue to apply to all other cargo/grades.

(viii) Has or will have carried, for the named Charterers, the following three cargoes (all grades to be identified) immediately prior to loading under this Charter:-
Last Cargo/Charterer
2nd Last Cargo/Charterer
3rd Last Cargo/Charterer

(ix) Has a crude oil washing system complying with the requirements of the International Convention for the Prevention of Pollution from Ships 1973 as modified by the Protocol of 1978 ("MARPOL 73/78").

(x) Has an operational inert gas system and is equipped for and able to carry out closed sampling/ullaging/loading and discharging operations in full compliance with the International Safety Guide for Oil Tankers and Terminals ("ISGOTT") guidelines current at the date of this Charter.

(xi) Has on board all papers and certificates required by any applicable law, in force as at the date of this Charter, to enable the vessel to perform the charter service without any delay.

(xii) Is entered in the P&I Club, being a member of the International Group of P&I Clubs.

(xiii) Has in full force and effect Hull and Machinery insurance placed through reputable Brokers on Institute Time Clauses-Hull dated for the value of

(xiv) Complies with the latest edition of the Oil Companies International Marine Forum ("OCIMF") standards for oil tankers' manifolds and associated equipment applicable to its size for cargo manifolds and vapour recovery systems.

(xv) Is equipped to comply with, and is operated in accordance with, and has on board, the latest edition of the International Chamber of Shipping ("ICS") and/or OCIMF guidelines / publications covering:

(a) Ship to Ship Operations
(b) ISGOTT
(c) Clean Seas Guide for Oil Tankers
(d) Bridge Procedure Guide

(II) Throughout the charter service, Owners shall ensure that the vessel shall be maintained, or that they take all steps necessary to promptly restore vessel to be, within the description in Part I clause (A)(I) and any questionnaires requested by Charterers or within information provided by Owners.

(III) Owners warrant that any information provided on any Questionnaire(s) requested by Charterers or any other vessel information/details provided by Owners to Charterers is always complete and correct as at the date hereof, and from the time when the obligation to proceed to the loadport attaches and throughout the charter service. This information is an integral part of this Charter but if there is any conflict between the contents of the Questionnaire(s), or information provided by Owners, and any other provisions of this Charter then such other provisions shall govern.

(B) Position/ Readiness — Now Expected ready to load

In addition to the above details on the position of the vessel Owners will advise Charterers of the known programme, including any contractual options available to the Charterers in Part I clause (A)(I) (viii) above between current position up to expected ready to load date at Charterers nominated or indicated first load port/area. Owners will not, unless with Charterers' prior consent, negotiate or enter into any business or give current Charterers any further options that may affect or alter the programme of the vessel as given in this clause.



(C) Laydays — Commencing Noon Local Time on (Commencement Date)

Terminating Noon Local Time on (Termination Date)

(D) Loading port(s)/ Range

(E) Discharging port(s)/ Range

(F) Cargo description — Charterers' option

Owners warrant that where different grades of cargo are carried pursuant to this Part I clause (F), they will be kept in complete segregation from each other during loading, transit, and discharge, to include the use of different pumps/lines for each grade. If, however, Charterers so require it, the vessel may be required to:

(a) co-mingle different grades of cargo providing such grades fall within the cargo description set out in this Part I clause (F);
(b) otherwise breach the vessel's natural segregation;
(c) add dye to the cargo after loading, and/or
(d) carry out such other cargo operations as Charterers may reasonably require as long as the vessel is capable of such operations

provided that the Charterers will indemnify Owners for any loss damage delay or expense caused by following Charterers' instructions, except to the extent that such loss damage delay or expense could have been avoided by the exercise of due diligence by Owners.

(G) Freight rate — At % of the rate for the voyage as provided for in the New Worldwide Tanker Nominal Freight Scale current at the date of commencement of loading (hereinafter referred to as "Worldscale") per ton (2240 lbs)/tonne (1000 Kg) or, if agreed, the following lumpsum amount(s)/or freight per tonne for named load and discharge area(s)/port(s) combinations

*Issued March 2005* **"SHELLVOY 6"**

| | |
|---|---|
| (H) Freight payable to | |
| (I) Laytime | running hours |
| (J) Demurrage per day (or pro rata) | |
| (K) ETAs | All radio/telex/e-mail messages sent by the master to Charterers shall be addressed to<br><br>All telexes must begin with the vessel name at the start of the subject line (no inverted commas, or use of MT / SS preceding the vessel name) |
| (L) Speed | The vessel shall perform the ballast passage with utmost despatch and the laden passage at knots weather and safe navigation permitting at a consumption of tonnes of Fuel oil (state grade ) per day.<br>Charterers shall have the option to instruct the vessel to increase speed with Charterers reimbursing Owners for the additional bunkers consumed, at replacement cost.<br>Charterers shall also have the option to instruct the vessel to reduce speed on laden passage. Additional voyage time caused by such instructions shall count against laytime or demurrage, if on demurrage, and the value of any bunkers saved shall be deducted from any demurrage claim Owners may have under this Charter with the value being calculated at original purchase price.<br>Owners shall provide documentation to fully support the claims and calculations under this clause. |
| (M) Worldscale | Worldscale Terms and Conditions apply / do not apply to this Charter. [delete as applicable] |
| (N) Casualty/ Accident contacts | In the event of an accident / marine casualty involving the vessel, Owners' technical managers can be contacted on a 24 hour basis as follows:<br>Company Full Name:<br>Contact Person:<br>Full Address:<br>Telephone Number:<br>Fax Number:<br>Telex Number:<br>Email Address:<br>24 Hour Emergency Telephone number: |
| (O) Special provisions | |
| Signatures | IN WITNESS WHEREOF, the parties have caused this Charter consisting of the Preamble, Parts I, II and III to be executed as of the day and year first above written.<br><br>By<br><br>By |

*Issued March 2005* **"SHELLVOY 6"**

PART II

**Condition of vessel**

1. Owners shall exercise due diligence to ensure that from the time when the obligation to proceed to the loading port(s) attaches and throughout the charter service -

(a) the vessel and her hull, machinery, boilers, tanks, equipment and facilities are in good order and condition and in every way equipped and fit for the service required; and

(b) the vessel has a full and efficient complement of master, officers and crew and the senior officers shall be fully conversant in spoken and written English language

and to ensure that before and at the commencement of any laden voyage the vessel is in all respects fit to carry the cargo specified in Part I clause (F). For the avoidance of doubt, references to equipment in this Charter shall include but not be limited to computers and computer systems, and such equipment shall (inter alia) be required to continue to function, and not suffer a loss of functionality and accuracy (whether logical or mathematical) as a result of the run date or dates being processed.

**Cleanliness of tanks**

2. Whilst loading, carrying and discharging the cargo the master shall at all times keep the tanks, lines and pumps of the vessel always clean for the cargo. Unless otherwise agreed between Owners and Charterers the vessel shall present for loading with cargo tanks ready and, subject to the following paragraphs, if vessel is fitted with Inert Gas System ("IGS"), fully inerted.

Charterers shall have the right to inspect vessel's tanks prior to loading and the vessel shall abide by Charterers' instructions with regard to tank or tanks which the vessel is required to present ready for entry and inspection. If Charterer's inspector is not satisfied with the cleanliness of the vessel's tanks, Owners shall clean them in their time and at their expense to the satisfaction of Charterers' inspector, provided that nothing herein shall affect the responsibilities and obligations of the master and Owners in respect of the loading, carriage and care of cargo under this Charter nor prejudice the rights of Charterers, should any contamination or damage subsequently be found, to contend that the same was caused by inadequate cleaning and/or some breach of this or any other clause of this Charter.

Notwithstanding that the vessel, if equipped with IGS, shall present for loading with all cargo tanks fully inerted, any time used for de-inerting (provided that such de-inerting takes place after laytime or demurrage time has commenced or would, but for this clause, have commenced) and/or re-inerting those tanks that at Charterers' specific request were gas freed for inspection, shall count as laytime or if on demurrage as demurrage, provided the tank or tanks inspected are found to be suitable. In such case Charterers will reimburse Owners for bunkers consumed for de-inerting/re-inerting, at replacement cost.

If the vessel's tanks are inspected and rejected, time used for de-inerting shall not count towards laytime or demurrage, and laytime or demurrage time shall not commence or recommence, as the case may be, until the tanks have been re-inspected, approved by Charterers' inspector, and re-inerted.

**Voyage**

3. (1) Subject to the provisions of this Charter the vessel shall perform her service with utmost despatch and shall proceed to such berths as Charterers may specify, in any port or ports within Part I clause (D) nominated by Charterers, or so near thereunto as she may safely get and there, always safely afloat, load thecargo specified in Part I clause (F) of this Charter, but not in excess of the maximum quantity consistent with the International Load Line Convention for the time being in force and, being so loaded, proceed as ordered on signing bills of lading to such berths as Charterers may specify, in any port or ports within Part I clause (E) nominated by Charterers, or so near thereunto as she may safely get and there, always safely afloat, discharge the cargo.

Charterers shall nominate loading and discharging ports, and shall specify loading and discharging berths and, where loading or discharging is interrupted, shall provide fresh orders in relation thereto.
In addition Charterers shall have the option at any time of ordering the vessel to safe areas at sea for wireless orders. Any delay or deviation arising as a result of the exercise of such option shall be compensated by Charterers in accordance with the terms of Part II clause 26 (1).

(2) Owners shall be responsible for and indemnify Charterers for any ***direct*** time, costs, delays or loss including but not limited to use of laytime, demurrage, deviation expenses, replacement tonnage, lightening costs and associated fees and expenses due to any failure whatsoever to comply fully with Charterers' voyage instructions and clauses in this Charter which specify requirements concerning Voyage Instructions and/ or Owners'/masters' duties including, without limitation to the generality of the foregoing, loading more cargo than permitted under the International Load Line Convention, for the time being in force, or for not leaving sufficient space for expansion of cargo or loading more or less cargo than Charterers specified or for not loading/discharging in accordance with Charterers' instructions regarding the cargo quantity or draft requirements.
This clause 3(2) shall have effect notwithstanding the provision of Part II clause 32 (a) of this Charter or Owners' defences under the Hague-Visby Rules

(3) Owners shall always employ pilots for berthing and unberthing of vessels at all ports and/or berths under this Charter unless prior exemption is given by correct and authorised personnel. Owners to confirm in writing if they have been exempt from using a pilot and provide Charterers with the details, including but not limited to, the authorising organisation with person's name.

(4) Without prejudice to the provisions of sub-clause (2) of this clause, and unless a specific prior agreement exists, if a conflict arises between terminal orders and Charterers' voyage instructions, the master shall stop cargo operations, and/or other operations under dispute, and contact Charterers immediately. Terminal orders shall never

*Issued March 2005* **"SHELLVOY 6"**

PART II

supersede Charterers' voyage instructions and any conflict shall be resolved prior to resumption of cargo, or other, operations in dispute. Where such a conflict arises the vessel shall not sail from the port or resume cargo operations, and/or other operations under dispute, until Charterers have directed the vessel to do so.
Time spent resolving the vessel/terminal conflict will count as laytime or demurrage except that failure of Owners/master to comply with the procedure set forth above shall result in the deduction from laytime or demurrage time of the time used in resolving the vessel/terminal instruction conflict

(5) In this Charter, "berth" means any berth, wharf, dock, anchorage, submarine line, a position alongside any vessel or lighter or any other loading or discharging point whatsoever to which Charterers are entitled to order the vessel hereunder, and "port" means any port or location at sea to which the vessel may proceed in accordance with the terms of this Charter.

Safe berth

4. Charterers shall exercise due diligence to order the vessel only to ports and berths which are safe for the vessel and to ensure that transhipment operations conform to standards not less than those set out in the latest edition of ICS/OCIMF Ship-to-Ship Transfer Guide (Petroleum). Notwithstanding anything contained in this Charter, Charterers do not warrant the safety of any port, berth or transhipment operation and Charterers shall not be liable for loss or damage arising from any unsafety if they can prove that due diligence was exercised in the giving of the order or if such loss or damage was caused by an act of war or civil commotion within the trading areas defined in Part I clauses (D/E).

Freight

5. (1) Freight shall be earned concurrently with delivery of cargo at the nominated discharging port or ports and shall be paid by Charterers to Owners without any deductions, except as may be required in the Singapore Income Tax Act and/or under Part II clause 48 and/or under clause 55 and/or under Part III clause 4(a), in United States Dollars at the rate(s) specified in Part I clause (G) on the gross bill of lading quantity as furnished by the shipper (subject to Part II clauses 8 and 40), upon receipt by Charterers of notice of completion of final discharge of cargo, provided that no freight shall be payable on any quantity in excess of the maximum quantity consistent with the International Load Line Convention for the time being in force.

If the vessel is ordered to proceed on a voyage for which a fixed differential is provided in Worldscale, such fixed differential shall be payable without applying the percentage referred to in Part I clause (G).

If cargo is carried between ports and/or by an agreed route for which no freight rate is expressly quoted in Worldscale, then the parties shall, in the absence of agreement as to the appropriate freight rate, apply to Worldscale Association (London) Ltd., or Worldscale Association (NYC) Inc., for the determination of an appropriate Worldscale freight rate. If Owners or master unilaterally elect to proceed by a route that is different to that specified in Worldscale, or different to a route agreed between Owners and Charterers, freight shall always be paid in accordance with the Worldscale rate as published or in accordance with any special rate applicable for the agreed route.

Save in respect of the time when freight is earned, the location of any transhipment at sea pursuant to Part II clause 26(2) shall not be an additional nominated port, unless otherwise agreed, for the purposes of this Charter (including this clause 5) and the freight rate for the voyage shall be the same as if such transhipment had not taken place.

(2) If the freight in Part I clause (G) is a lumpsum amount and such lumpsum freight is connected with a specific number of load and discharge ports given in Part I clause (L) and Owners agree that Charterers may order the vessel to additional load and/or discharge ports not covered by the agreed lumpsum freight, the following shall apply:

(a) the first load port and the final discharge port shall be deemed to be the port(s) that form the voyage and on which the lumpsum freight included in Part I clause (G) refers to;

(b) freight for such additional ports shall be calculated on basis of deviation. Deviation shall be calculated on the difference in distance between the specified voyage (for which freight is agreed) and the voyage actually performed.

BP Shipping Marine Distance Tables (2004), produced by AtoBriac shall be used in both cases.
Deviation time/bunker consumption shall be calculated using the charter speed and bunker consumption as per the speed and consumptions given in Part I clause (L) of this Charter.
Deviation time and time spent in port shall be charged at the demurrage rate in Part I clause (J) of this Charter except that time used in port which would otherwise qualify for half rate laytime and/or demurrage under Part II clause (15) (2) of this Charter will be charged at half rate.
Additional bunkers consumed shall be paid at replacement cost, and actual port costs shall be paid as incurred.
Such deviation costs shall be paid against Owners' fully documented claim.

Claims, dues and other charges

6. (1) Dues and other charges upon the vessel, including those assessed by reference to the quantity of cargo loaded or discharged, and any taxes on freight whatsoever shall be paid by Owners, and dues and other charges upon the cargo shall be paid by Charterers. However, notwithstanding the foregoing, where under a provision of Worldscale a due or charge is expressly for the account of Owners or Charterers then such due or charge shall be payable in accordance with such provision.

(2) Any costs including those itemised under applicable "Worldscale" as being for Charterers' account shall,

*Issued March 2005*

**"SHELLVOY 6"**

PART II

unless otherwise instructed by Charterers, be paid by Owners and reimbursed by Charterers against Owners' fully documented claim.

(3) Charterers shall be discharged and released from all liability in respect of any charges/claims (other than demurrage and Worldscale charges/dues and indemnity claims) including but not limited to additional bunkers, detention, deviation, shifting, heating, deadfreight, speed up, slow down, drifting, port costs, additional freight, insurance, Owner may send to Charterers under this Charter unless any such charges/claims have been received by Charterer in writing, fully and correctly documented, within ninety (90) days from completion of discharge of the cargo concerned under this Charter. Part II clause 15 (3) of this Charter covers the notification and fully documented claim procedure for demurrage.

(4) If, after disconnection of hoses, the vessel remains at berth for vessel's purposes, Owners shall be responsible for all direct and indirect costs whether advised to Owners in advance or not, and including charges by Terminal/Suppliers/Receivers.

Loading and discharging cargo

7. The cargo shall be loaded into the vessel at the expense of Charterers and, up to the vessel's permanent hose connections, at Charterers' risk. The cargo shall be discharged from the vessel at the expense of Owners and, up to the vessel's permanent hose connections, at Owners' risk. Owners shall, unless otherwise notified by Charterers or their agents, supply at Owners' expense all hands, equipment and facilities required on board for mooring and unmooring and connecting and disconnecting hoses for loading and discharging.

Deadfreight

8. Charterers need not supply a full cargo, but if they do not freight shall nevertheless be paid as if the vessel had been loaded with a full cargo.

The term "full cargo" as used throughout this Charter means a cargo which, together with any collected washings (as defined in Part II clause 40) retained on board pursuant to the requirements of MARPOL 73/78, fills the vessel to either her applicable deadweight or her capacity stated in Part I clause (A) (I) (iii), whichever is less, while leaving sufficient space in the tanks for the expansion of cargo. If under Part I clause (F) vessel is chartered for a minimum quantity and the vessel is unable to load such quantity due to having reached her capacity as stated in Part I clause (A) (I) (iii), always leaving sufficient space for expansion of cargo, then without prejudice to any claims which Charterers may have against Owners, no deadfreight between the quantity loaded and the quantity shown in Part I clause (F) shall be due.

Shifting

9. Charterers shall have the right to require the vessel to shift at ports of loading and/or discharging from a loading or discharging berth within port limits and/or to a waiting place inside or outside port limits and back to the same or to another such berth/place once or more often on payment of all additional expenses incurred. For the purposes of and shifting the places grouped in Port and Terminal Combinations in Worldscale are to be considered as berths within a single port. If at any time before cargo operations are completed it becomes dangerous for the vessel to remain at the specified berth as a result of wind or water conditions, Charterers shall pay all additional expenses of shifting from any such berth and back to that or any other specified berth within port limits (except to the extent that any fault of the vessel contributed to such danger).

Subject to Part II clause 14(a) and (c) time spent shifting shall count against laytime or if the vessel is on demurrage for demurrage.

Charterers' failure to give orders

10. If the vessel is delayed due to Charterers' breach of Part II clause 3 Charterers shall, subject to the terms hereof, compensate Owners in accordance with Part II clause 15(1) and (2) as if such delay were time exceeding the laytime. Such compensation shall be Owners' sole remedy in respect of such delay.

The period of such delay shall be calculated:

(i) from 6 hours after Owners notify Charterers that the vessel is delayed awaiting nomination of loading or discharging port until such nomination has been received by Owners, or

(ii) from 6 hours after the vessel gives notice of readiness at the loading or discharging port until commencement of loading or discharging,

as the case may be, subject always to the same exceptions as those set out in Part II clause 14. Any period of delay in respect of which Charterers pay compensation pursuant to this clause 10 shall be excluded from any calculation of time for laytime or demurrage made under any other clause of this Charter.

Periods of delay hereunder shall be cumulative for each port, and Owners may demand compensation after the vessel has been delayed for a total of 20 running days, and thereafter after each succeeding 5 running days of delay and at the end of any delay. Each such demand shall show the period in respect of which compensation is claimed and the amount due. Charterers shall pay the full amount due within 14 days after receipt of Owners' demand. Should Charterers fail to make any such payments Owners shall have the right to terminate this Charter by giving written notice to Charterers or their agents, without prejudice to any claims which Charterers or Owners may have against each other under this Charter or otherwise.

Laydays/ Termination

11. Should the vessel not be ready to load by noon local time on the termination date set out in Part I clause (C) Charterers shall have the option of terminating this Charter unless the vessel has been delayed due to Charterers' change of orders pursuant to Part II clause 26, in which case the laydays shall be extended by the period of such delay.

PART II

As soon as Owners become aware that the vessel will not be ready to load by noon on the termination date, Owners will give notice to Charterers declaring a new readiness date and ask Charterers to elect whether or not to terminate this Charter.

Within 4 days after such notice, Charterers shall either:

(i) declare this Charter terminated or

(ii) confirm a revised set of laydays which shall be amended such that the new readiness date stated shall be the commencement date and the second day thereafter shall be the termination date or,

(iii) agree a new set of laydays or an extension to the laydays mutually acceptable to Owners and Charterers

The provisions of this clause and the exercise or non-exercise by Charterers of their option to terminate shall not prejudice any claims which Charterers or Owners may have against each other.

Laytime

12. (1) The laytime for loading, discharging and all other Charterers' purposes whatsoever shall be the number of running hours specified in Part I clause (I). Charterers shall have the right to load and discharge at all times, including night, provided that they shall pay for all extra expenses incurred ashore.

(2) If vessel is able to, and Charterers so instruct, the vessel shall load earlier than the commencement of of laydays and Charterers shall have the benefit of such time saved by way of offset from any demurrage incurred. Such benefit shall be the time between commencement of loading until the commencement of the original laydays.

Notice of readiness/ Running time

13. (1) Subject to the provisions of Part II clauses 13(3) and 14,

(a) Time at each loading or discharging port shall commence to run 6 hours after the vessel is in all respects ready to load or discharge and written notice thereof has been tendered by the master or Owners' agents to Charterers or their agents and the vessel is securely moored at the specified loading or discharging berth. However, if the vessel does not proceed immediately to such berth time shall commence to run 6 hours after (i) the vessel is lying in the area where she was ordered to wait or, in the absence of any such specific order, in a usual waiting area and (ii) written notice of readiness has been tendered and (iii) the specified berth is accessible. A loading or discharging berth shall be deemed inaccessible only for so long as the vessel is or would be prevented from proceeding to it by bad weather, tidal conditions, ice, awaiting daylight, pilot or tugs, or port traffic control requirements (except those requirements resulting from the unavailability of such berth or of the cargo). If Charterers fail to specify a berth at any port, the first berth at which the vessel loads or discharges the cargo or any part thereof shall be deemed to be the specified berth at such port for the purposes of this clause.

Notice shall not be tendered before commencement of laydays and notice tendered by radio shall qualify as written notice provided it is confirmed in writing as soon as reasonably possible.

Time shall never commence before six hours after commencement of laydays unless loading commences prior to this time as provided in clause 13 (3).

If Owners fail;

(i) to obtain Customs clearance; and/or

(ii) to obtain free pratique unless this is not customary prior to berthing; and/or

(iii) to have on board all papers/certificates required to perform this Charter, either within the 6 hours after notice of readiness originally tendered or when time would otherwise normally commence under this Charter, then the original notice of readiness shall not be valid. A new notice of readiness may only be tendered when Customs clearance and/or free pratique has been granted and/or all papers/certificates required are in order in accordance with relevant authorities' requirements. Laytime or demurrage, if on demurrage, would then commence in accordance with the terms of this Charter. All time, costs and expenses as a result of delays due to any of the foregoing shall be for Owners' account.

(b) Time shall:

(i) continue to run until the cargo hoses have been disconnected.

(ii) recommence two hours after disconnection of hoses if the vessel is delayed for Charterers' purposes and shall continue until the termination of such delay provided that if the vessel waits at any place other than the berth, any time or part of the time on passage to such other place that occurs after two hours from disconnection of hoses shall not count.

(2) If the vessel loads or discharges cargo by transhipment at sea time shall commence in accordance with Part II clause 13 (I) (a), and run until transhipment has been completed and the vessels have separated, always subject to Part II clause 14.

(3) Notwithstanding anything else in this clause 13, if Charterers start loading or discharging the vessel before time would otherwise start to run under this Charter, time shall run from commencement of such loading or discharging.

(4) For the purposes of this clause 13 and of Part II clause 14 and Part II clause 15 "time" shall mean laytime

or time counting for demurrage, as the case may be.

**Suspension of time**

14. Time shall not count when:

(a) spent on inward passage from the vessel's waiting area to the loading or discharging berth specified by Charterers, even if lightening occurred at such waiting area; or

(b) spent in carrying out vessel operations, including but not limited to bunkering, discharging slops and tank washings, and handling ballast, except to the extent that cargo operations are carried on concurrently and are not delayed thereby; or

(c) lost as a result of:

(i) breach of this Charter by Owners; or

(ii) any cause attributable to the vessel, (including but not limited to the warranties in Part I (A) of this Charter) including breakdown or inefficiency of the vessel; or

(iii) strike, lock-out, stoppage or restraint of labour of master, officers or crew of the vessel or tug boats or pilot.

**Demurrage**

15. (1) Charterers shall pay demurrage at the rate specified in Part I clause (J).

If the demurrage rate specified in Part I clause (J) is expressed as a percentage of Worldscale such percentage shall be applied to the demurrage rate applicable to vessels of a similar size to the vessel as provided in Worldscale or, for the purpose of clause 10 and/or if this Charter is terminated prior to the commencement of loading, in Worldscale current at the termination date specified in Part I clause (C).

Demurrage shall be paid per running day or pro rata for part thereof for all time which, under the provisions of this Charter, counts against laytime or for demurrage and which exceeds the laytime specified in Part I clause (I). Charterers' liability for exceeding the laytime shall be absolute and shall not in any case be subject to the provisions of Part II clause 32.

(2) If, however, all or part of such demurrage arises out of or results from fire or explosion or strike or failure/breakdown of plant and/or machinery at ports of loading and/or discharging in or about the plant of Charterers, shippers or consignees of the cargo (not being a fire or explosion caused by the negligence or wilful act or omission of Charterers, shippers or consignees of the cargo or their respective servants or agents), act of God, act of war, riot, civil commotion, or arrest or restraint of princes, rulers or peoples, the laytime used and/or the rate of demurrage shall be reduced by half for such laytime used and/or for such demurrage or such parts thereof.

(3) Owners shall notify Charterers within 60 days after completion of discharge if demurrage has been incurred and any demurrage claim shall be fully and correctly documented, and received by Charterers, within 90 days after completion of discharge . If Owners fail to give notice of or to submit any such claim with documentation, as required herein, within the limits aforesaid, Charterers' liability for such demurrage shall be extinguished.

(4) If any part cargo for other Charterers, shippers or consignees (as the case may be) is loaded or discharged at the same berth, then any time used by the vessel waiting at or for such berth and in loading or discharging which would otherwise count as laytime or if the vessel is on demurrage for demurrage, shall be pro-rated in the proportion that Charterers' cargo bears to the total cargo to be loaded or discharged at such berth. If however, the running of laytime or demurrage, if on demurrage, is solely attributable to other parties' cargo operations then such time shall not count in calculating laytime or demurrage, if on demurrage, against Charterers under this Charter.

**Vessel inspection**

16. Charterers shall have the right, but no duty, to have a representative attend on board the vessel at any loading and/or discharging ports and the master and Owners shall co-operate to facilitate his inspection of the vessel and observation of cargo operations. However, such right, and the exercise or non-exercise thereof, shall in no way reduce the master's or Owners' authority over, or responsibility to Charterers and third parties for, the vessel and every aspect of her operation, nor increase Charterers' responsibilities to Owners or third parties for the same.

**Cargo inspection**

17. This clause 17 is without prejudice to Part II clause 2 hereof. Charterers shall have the right to require inspection of the vessel's tanks at loading and/or discharging ports to ascertain the quantity and quality of the cargo, water and residues on board. Depressurisation of the tanks to permit inspection and/or ullaging shall be carried out in accordance with the recommendations in the latest edition of the ISGOTT guidelines. Charterers shall also have the right to inspect and take samples from the bunker tanks and other non-cargo spaces. Any delay to the vessel caused by such inspection and measurement or associated depressurising/repressurising of tanks shall count against laytime, or if the vessel is on demurrage, for demurrage.

**Cargo measurement**

18. The master shall ascertain the contents of all tanks before and after loading and before and after discharging, and shall prepare tank-by-tank ullage reports of the cargo, water and residues on board which shall be promptly made available to Charterers or their representative if requested. Each such ullage report shall show actual ullage/dips, and densities at observed and standard temperature (15° Celsius). All quantities shall be expressed in cubic metres at both observed and standard temperature.

**Inert gas**

19. The vessel's inert gas system (if any) shall comply with Regulation 62, Chapter II-2 of the 1974 Safety of

Life at Sea Convention as modified by the Protocol of 1978, and any subsequent amendments, and Owners warrant that such system shall be operated (subject to the provisions of Part II clause 2), during loading, throughout the voyage and during discharge, and in accordance with the guidance given in the IMO publication "Inert Gas System (1983)". Should the inert gas system fail, Section 8 (Emergency Procedures) of the said IMO publication shall be strictly adhered to and time lost as a consequence of such failure shall not count against laytime or, if the vessel is on demurrage, for demurrage.

Crude oil washing

20. If the vessel is equipped for crude oil washing Charterers shall have the right to require the vessel to crude oil wash, concurrently with discharge, those tanks in which Charterers' cargo is carried. If crude oil washing is required by Charterers any additional discharge time thereby incurred, always subject to the next succeeding sentences, shall count against laytime or, if the vessel is on demurrage, for demurrage. The number of hours specified in Part I clause (A) (I) (vii) shall be increased by 0.6 hours per cargo tank washed, always subject to a maximum increase of 8 hours. If vessel fails to maintain 100 PSI throughout the discharge then any time over 24 hours, plus the additional discharge performance allowance under this clause, shall not count as laytime or demurrage, if on demurrage. This clause 20 does not reduce Owners' liability for the vessel to perform her service with utmost despatch as setout in Part II, Clause 3(1). The master shall provide Charterers with a crude oil washing log identifying each tank washed, and stating whether such tank has been washed to the MARPOL minimum standard or has been the subject of additional crude oil washing and whether requested by Charterers or otherwise.

Overage insurance

21. Any additional insurance on the cargo required because of the age of the vessel shall be for Owners' account.

Ice

22. The vessel shall not be required to force ice or to follow icebreakers. If the master finds that a nominated port is inaccessible due to ice, the master shall immediately notify Charterers requesting revised orders and shall remain outside the ice-bound area; and if after arrival at a nominated port there is danger of the vessel being frozen in, the vessel shall proceed to the nearest safe and ice free position and at the same time request Charterers to give revised orders.

In either case if the affected port is:

(i) the first or only loading port and no cargo has been loaded, Charterers shall either nominate another port,or give notice cancelling this Charter in which case they shall pay at the demurrage rate in Part I clause (J)for the time from the master's notification aforesaid or from notice of readiness on arrival, as the case may be,until the time such cancellation notice is given;

(ii) a loading port and part of the cargo has been loaded, Charterers shall either nominate another port, or order the vessel to proceed on the voyage without completing loading in which case Charterers shall pay for any deadfreight arising therefrom;

(iii) a discharging port, Charterers shall either nominate another port or order the vessel to proceed to or return to and discharge at the nominated port. If the vessel is ordered to proceed to or return to a nominated port, Charterers shall bear the risk of the vessel being damaged whilst proceeding to or returning to or at such port, and the whole period from the time when the master's request for revised orders is received by Charterers until the vessel can safely depart after completion of discharge shall count against laytime or, if the vessel is on demurrage, for demurrage.

If, as a consequence of Charterers revising orders pursuant to this clause, the nominated port(s) or the number or rotation of ports is changed, freight shall nevertheless be paid for the voyage which the vessel would otherwise have performed had the orders not been so revised, such freight to be increased or reduced by the amount by which, as a result of such revision of orders,

(a) the time used including any time awaiting revised orders (which shall be valued at the demurrage rate in Part I clause (J)), and

(b) the bunkers consumed, at replacement cost and

(c) the port charges

for the voyage actually performed are greater or less than those that would have been incurred on the voyage which, but for the revised orders under this clause, the vessel would have performed.

Quarantine

23. Time lost due to quarantine shall not count against laytime or for demurrage unless such quarantine was in force at the time when the affected port was nominated by Charterers.

Agency

24. The vessel's agents shall be nominated by Charterers at nominated ports of loading and discharging. Such agents, although nominated by Charterers, shall be employed and paid by Owners.

Charterers' obligation at shallow draft port/ Lightening in port

25.(1) If the vessel, with the quantity of cargo then on board, is unable due to inadequate depth of water in the port safely to reach any specified discharging berth and discharge the cargo there always safely afloat, Charterers shall specify a location within port limits where the vessel can discharge sufficient cargo into vessels or lighters to enable the vessel safely to reach and discharge cargo at such discharging berth, and the vessel shall lighten at such location.

(2) If the vessel is lightened pursuant to clause 25(1) then, for the purposes of the calculation

of laytime and demurrage, the lightening place shall be treated as the first discharging berth within the port where such lightening occurs.

**Charterers' orders/ Change of orders/ Part cargo transhipment**

26. (1) If, after loading and/or discharging ports have been nominated, Charterers wish to vary such nominations or their rotation, Charterers may give revised orders subject to Part I clause (D) and/or (E), as the case may be. Charterers shall reimburse Owners at the demurrage rate provided in Part I clause (J) for any deviation or delay which may result therefrom and shall pay at replacement cost for any extra bunkers consumed. Charterers shall not be liable for any other loss or expense which is caused by such variation.

(2) Subject to Part II clause 33(6), Charterers may order the vessel to load and/or discharge any part of the cargo by transhipment at sea in the vicinity of any nominated port or en route between two nominated ports, in which case unless Charterers elect, (which they may do at any time) to treat the place of such transhipment as a load or discharge port (subject to the number of ports and ranges in Part I clauses (D) and (E) of this Charter), Charterers shall reimburse Owners at the demurrage rate specified in Part I clause (J) for any additional steaming time and/or delay which may be incurred as a consequence of proceeding to and from the location at sea of such transhipment and, in addition, Charterers shall pay at replacement cost for any extra bunkers consumed.

(3) Owners warrant that the vessel, master, officers and crew are, and shall remain during this Charter, capable of safely carrying out all the procedures in the current edition of the ICS/ OCIMF Ship to Ship Transfer Guide (Petroleum). Owners further warrant that when instructed to perform a ship to ship transfer the master Officers and crew shall, at all times, comply with such procedures. Charterers shall provide, and pay for, the necessary equipment and, if necessary, mooring master, for such ship to ship operation.

**Heating of cargo**

27. If Charterers require cargo heating the vessel shall, on passage to and whilst at discharging port(s), Maintain the cargo at the loaded temperature or at the temperature stated in Part I clause (A) (I) (iv), whichever is the lower. Charterers may request that the temperature of the cargo be raised above or lowered below that at which it was loaded, in which event Owners shall use their best endeavours to comply with such request and Charterers shall pay at replacement cost for any additional bunkers consumed and any consequential delay to the vessel shall count against laytime or, if the vessel is on demurrage, for demurrage.

**ETA**

28. (1) Owners shall give Charterers a time and date of expected arrival at the first load port or if the loading range is in the Arabian Gulf, the time of her expected arrival off Quoin Island (hereinafter called "load port" in this clause) at the date of this Charter. Owners shall further advise Charterers at any time between the Charter date and arrival at load port of any variation of 6 hours or more in vessel's expected arrival time/date at the load port.

(2) Owners undertake that, unless Charterers require otherwise, the master shall:

(a) advise Charterers immediately on leaving the final port of call on the previous voyage of the time and date of the vessel's expected arrival at the first loading port and shall further advise Charterers 72, 48, 36, and 24 hours before the expected arrival time/date.

(b) advise Charterers immediately after departure from the final loading port, of the vessel's expected time of arrival at the first discharging port or the area at sea to which the vessel has been instructed to proceed for wireless orders, and confirm or amend such advice not later than 72, 48, 36 and 24 hours before the vessel is due at such port or area;

(c) advise Charterers immediately of any variation of more than six hours from expected times of arrival at loading or discharging ports, Quoin Island or such area at sea to Charterers;

(d) address all messages as specified in Part I clause (K).

Owners shall be responsible for any consequences or additional expenses arising as a result of non-compliance with this clause.

(3) If at any time prior to the tender of notice of readiness at the first load port, the vessel ceases to comply with the description set out in Part I clause (A) and in any questionnaire(s), the Owners shall immediately notify Charterers of the same, providing full particulars, and explaining what steps Owners are taking to ensure that the vessel will so comply. Any silence or failure on the part of Charterers to respond to or any inaction taken in respect of any such notice shall not amount to a waiver of any rights or remedies which Charterers may have in respect of the matters notified by Owners.

**Packed cargo**

29. Charterers have the option of shipping products and/or general cargo in available dry cargo space, the Quantity being subject to the master's discretion. Freight shall be payable at the bulk rate in accordance with Part II clause 5 and Charterers shall pay in addition all expenses incurred solely as a result of the packed cargo being carried. Delay occasioned to the vessel by the exercise of such option shall count against laytime or, if the vessel is on demurrage, for demurrage.

**Subletting/ Assignment**

30. Charterers shall have the option of sub-chartering the vessel and/or of assigning this Charter to any person or persons, but Charterers shall always remain responsible for the due fulfilment of all the terms and conditions of this Charter. Additionally Charterers may Novato this charter to any company of the Royal Dutch/ Shell Group of Companies.

*Issued March 2005* **"SHELLVOY 6"**

PART II

**Liberty**

31. The vessel shall be at liberty to tow or be towed, to assist vessels in all positions of distress and to deviate for the purpose of saving life or property. On the laden voyage the vessel shall not take on bunkers or deviate or stop, except as allowed in this clause 31, without prior permission of Charterers , Cargo Insurers, and Owners' P&I Club.

**Exceptions**

32. (1) The vessel, her master and Owners shall not, unless otherwise in this Charter expressly provided, be liable for any loss or damage or delay or failure arising or resulting from any act, neglect or default of the master, pilots, mariners or other servants of Owners in the navigation or management of the vessel; fire, unless caused by the actual fault or privity of Owners; collision or stranding; dangers and accidents of the sea; explosion, Bursting of boilers, breakage of shafts or any latent defect in hull, equipment or machinery; provided, however, that Part I clause (A) and Part II clauses 1 and 2 hereof shall be unaffected by the foregoing. Further, neither the vessel, her master or Owners, nor Charterers shall, unless otherwise in this Charter expressly provided, be liable for any loss or damage or delay or failure in performance hereunder arising or resulting from act of God, act of war, act of public enemies, seizure under legal process, quarantine restrictions, strikes, lock-outs, restraints of labour, riots, civil commotions or arrest or restraint of princes, rulers or people.

(2) Nothing in this Charter shall be construed as in any way restricting, excluding or waiving the right of Owners or of any other relevant persons to limit their liability under any available legislation or law.

(3) Clause 32(1) shall not apply to or affect any liability of Owners or the vessel or any other relevant person in respect of

(a) loss or damage caused to any berth, jetty, dock, dolphin, buoy, mooring line, pipe or crane or other works or equipment whatsoever at or near any port to which the vessels may proceed under this Charter, whether or not such works or equipment belong to Charterers, or

(b) any claim (whether brought by Charterers or any other person) arising out of any loss of or damage to or in connection with the cargo. Any such claim shall be subject to the Hague-Visby Rules or the Hague Rules, or the Hamburg Rules as the case may be, which ought pursuant to Part II clause 37 hereof to have been incorporated in the relevant bill of lading (whether or not such Rules were so incorporated) or, if no such bill of lading is issued, to the Hague-Visby rules unless the Hamburg Rules compulsory apply in which case to the Hamburg Rules.

**Bills of lading**

33. (1) Subject to the provisions of this clause Charterers may require the master to sign lawful bills of lading for any cargo in such form as Charterers direct.

(2) The signing of bills of lading shall be without prejudice to this Charter and Charterers hereby indemnify Owners against all liabilities that may arise from signing bills of lading to the extent that the same impose liabilities upon Owners in excess of or beyond those imposed by this Charter.

(3) All bills of lading presented to the master for signature, in addition to complying with the Requirements of Part II clauses 35, 36 and 37, shall include or effectively incorporate clauses substantially similar to the terms of Part II clauses 22, 33(7) and 34.

(4) All bills of lading presented for signature hereunder shall show a named port of discharge. If when bills of lading are presented for signature discharging port(s) have been nominated hereunder, the discharging port(s) shown on such bills of lading shall be in conformity with the nominated port(s). If at the time of such presentation no such nomination has been made hereunder, the discharging port(s) shown on such bills of lading must be within Part I clause (E) and shall be deemed to have been nominated hereunder by virtue of such presentation.

(5) Article III Rules 3 and 5 of the Hague-Visby Rules shall apply to the particulars included in the bills of lading as if Charterers were the shippers, and the guarantee and indemnity therein contained shall apply to the description of the cargo furnished by or on behalf of Charterers.

(6) Notwithstanding any other provisions of this Charter, Owners shall be obliged to comply with any orders from Charterers to discharge all or part of the cargo provided that they have received from Charterers written confirmation of such orders.

If Charterers by telex, facsimile or other form of written communication that specifically refers to this clause request Owners to discharge a quantity of cargo either:

(a) without bills of lading and/or

(b) at a discharge place other than that named in a bill of lading and/or

(c) that is different from the bill of lading quantity

then Owners shall discharge such cargo in accordance with Charterers' instructions in consideration of receiving the Following indemnity which shall be deemed to be given by Charterers on each and every such occasion and which is limited in value to 200 per cent of the C.I.F. value of the cargo on board:

(i) Charterers shall indemnify Owners, and Owners' servants and agents in respect of any liability loss or damage of whatsoever nature (including legal costs as between attorney or solicitor and client and associated expenses) which Owners may sustain by reason of delivering such cargo in accordance with Charterers' request.

(ii) If any proceeding is commenced against Owners or any of Owners' servants or agents in connection with the vessel having delivered cargo in accordance with such request, Charterers shall provide Owners or any of Owners' servants or agents from time to time on demand with sufficient funds to defend the said proceedings.

(iii) If the vessel or any other vessel or property belonging to Owners should be arrested or detained, or if the arrest or detention thereof should be threatened, by reason of discharge in accordance with Charterers' instruction as aforesaid, Charterers shall provide on demand such bail or other security as may be required to prevent such arrest or detention or to secure the release of such vessel or property and Charterers shall indemnify Owners in respect of any loss, damage or expenses caused by such arrest or detention whether or not the same may be justified.

(iv) Charterers shall, if called upon to do so at any time while such cargo is in Charterers' possession, custody or control, redeliver the same to Owners.

(v) As soon as all original bills of lading for the above cargo which name as discharge port the place where delivery actually occurred shall have arrived and/or come into Charterers' possession, Charterers shall produce and deliver the same to Owners, whereupon Charterers' liability hereunder shall cease. Provided however, if Charterers have not received all such original bills of lading by 24.00 hours on the day 36 calendar months after the date of discharge, then this indemnity shall terminate at that time unless before that time Charterers have received from Owners written notice that:

(a) some person is making a claim in connection with Owners delivering cargo pursuant to Charterers' request or

(b) legal proceedings have been commenced against Owners and/or carriers and/Charterers and/or any of their respective servants or agents and/or the vessel for the same reason.

When Charterers have received such a notice, then this indemnity shall continue in force until such claim or legal proceedings are settled. Termination of this indemnity shall not prejudice any legal rights a party may have outside this indemnity.

(vi) Owners shall promptly notify Charterers if any person (other than a person to whom Charterers ordered cargo to be delivered) claims to be entitled to such cargo and/or if the vessel or any other property belonging to Owners is arrested by reason of any such discharge of cargo.

(vii) This indemnity shall be governed and construed in accordance with the English law and each and any dispute arising out of or in connection with this indemnity shall be subject to the jurisdiction of the High Court of Justice of England.

(7) The master shall not be required or bound to sign bills of lading for any blockaded port or for any port which the master or Owners in his or their discretion consider dangerous or impossible to enter or reach.

(8) Charterers hereby warrant that on each and every occasion that they issue orders under Part II clauses 22, 26, 34 or 38 they will have the authority of the holders of the bills of lading to give such orders, and that such bills of lading will not be transferred to any person who does not concur therein.

(9) Owners hereby agree that original bill(s) of lading, if available, will be allowed to be placed on board. If original bill(s) of lading are placed on board, Owners agree that vessel will discharge cargo against such bill(s) of lading carried on board, on receipt of receivers' proof of identity.

War risks

34.(1) If

(a) any loading or discharging port to which the vessel may properly be ordered under the provisions of this Charter or bills of lading issued pursuant to this Charter be blockaded, or

(b) owing to any war, hostilities, warlike operation, civil commotions, revolutions, or the operation of international law (i) entry to any such loading or discharging port or the loading or discharging of cargo at any such port be considered by the master or Owners in his or their discretion dangerous or prohibited or (ii) it be considered by the master or Owners in his or their discretion dangerous or impossible or prohibited for the vessel to reach any such loading or discharging port,

Charterers shall have the right to order the cargo or such part of it as may be affected to be loaded or discharged at any other loading or discharging port within the ranges specified in Part I clause (D) or (E) respectively (provided such other port is not blockaded and that entry thereto or loading or discharging of cargo thereat or reaching the same is not in the master's or Owners' opinion dangerous or impossible or prohibited).

(2) If no orders be received from Charterers within 48 hours after they or their agents have received from Owners a request for the nomination of a substitute port, then

(a) if the affected port is the first or only loading port and no cargo has been loaded, this Charter shall terminate forthwith;

(b) if the affected port is a loading port and part of the cargo has already been loaded, the vessel may proceed on passage and Charterers shall pay for any deadfreight so incurred;

(c) if the affected port is a discharging port, Owners shall be at liberty to discharge the cargo at any port which they or the master may in their or his discretion decide on (whether within the range specified in Part I clause (E) or not) and such discharging shall be deemed to be due fulfilment of the Contract or Contracts of Affreightment so far as cargo so discharged is concerned.

(3) If in accordance with clause 34(1) or (2) cargo is loaded or discharged at any such other port, freight shall be paid as for the voyage originally nominated, such freight to be increased or reduced by the amount by which, as a result of loading or discharging at such other port,

(a) the time on voyage including any time awaiting revised orders (which shall be valued at the demurrage rate in Part I clause (J)), and

*Issued March 2005* **"SHELLVOY 6"**

PART II

(b) the bunkers consumed, at replacement cost, and

(c) the port charges

for the voyage actually performed are greater or less than those which would have been incurred on the voyage originally nominated save as aforesaid, the voyage actually performed shall be treated for the purpose of this Charter as if it were the voyage originally nominated.

(4) The vessel shall have liberty to comply with any directions or recommendations as to departure, arrival, routes, ports of call, stoppages, destinations, zones, waters, delivery or in any otherwise whatsoever given by the government of the nation under whose flag the vessel sails or any other government or local authority including any de facto government or local authority or by any person or body acting or purporting to act as or with the authority of any such government or authority or by any committee or person having under the terms of the war risks insurance on the vessel the right to give any such directions or recommendations. If by reason of or in compliance with any such directions or recommendations anything is done or is not done, such shall not be deemed a deviation.

If, by reason of or in compliance with any such directions or recommendations as are mentioned in clause 34 (4), the vessel does not proceed to the discharging port or ports originally nominated or to which she may have been properly ordered under the provisions of this Charter or bills of lading issued pursuant to this Charter, the vessel may proceed to any discharging port on which the master or Owners in his or their discretion may decide and there discharge the cargo. Such discharging shall be deemed to be due fulfilment of the contract or contracts of Affreightment and Owners shall be entitled to freight as if discharging had been effected at the port or ports originally nominated or to which the vessel may have been properly ordered under the provisions of this Charter or bills of lading issued pursuant to this Charter. All extra expenses involved in reaching and discharging the cargo at any such other discharging port shall be paid by Charterers and Owners shall have a lien on the cargo for all such extra expenses.

(5) Owners shall pay for all additional war risk insurance premiums, both for annual periods and also for the specific performance of this Charter, on the Hull and Machinery value, as per Part I clause (A) (I) (xiii) applicable at the date of this Charter, or the date the vessel was fixed "on subjects" (whichever is the earlier), and all reasonable crew war bonus. The period of voyage additional war risks premium shall commence when the vessel enters a war risk zone as designated by the London insurance market and cease when the vessel leaves such zone. If the vessel is already in such a zone the period shall commence on tendering notice of readiness under this Charter.

Any increase or decrease in voyage additional war risk premium and any period in excess of the first fourteen days shall be for Charterers' account and payable against proven documentation. Any discount or rebate refunded to Owners for whatever reason shall be passed on to Charterers. Any premiums, and increase thereto, attributable to closure insurance (i.e. blocking and trapping) shall be for Owners' account.

Both to blame clause

35. If the liability for any collision in which the vessel is involved while performing this Charter falls to be determined in accordance with the laws of the United States of America, the following clause, which shall be included in all bills of lading issued pursuant to this Charter shall apply:

"If the vessel comes into collision with another vessel as a result of the negligence of the other vessel and any act, neglect or default of the master, mariner, pilot or the servants of the Carrier in the navigation or in the management of the vessel, the owners of the cargo carried hereunder will indemnify the Carrier against all loss or liability to the other or non-carrying vessel or her owners in so far as such loss or liability represents loss of, or damage to, or any claim whatsoever of the owners of the said cargo, paid or payable by the other or non-carrying vessel or her owners to the owners of the said cargo and set off, recouped or recovered by the other or non-carrying vessel or her owners as part of their claim against the carrying vessel or the Carrier.

The foregoing provisions shall also apply where the owners, operators or those in charge of any vessel or vessels or objects other than, or in addition to, the colliding vessels or objects are at fault in respect of a collision or contact."

General average/ New Jason clause

36. General average shall be payable according to the York/Antwerp Rules 1994, as amended from time to time, and shall be adjusted in London. All disputes relating to General Average shall be resolved in London in accordance with English Law. Without prejudice to the foregoing, should the adjustment be made in accordance with the Law and practice of the United States of America, the following clause, which shall be included in all bills of lading issued pursuant to this Charter, shall apply:

"In the event of accident, danger, damage or disaster before or after the commencement of the voyage, resulting from any cause whatsoever, whether due to negligence or not, for which, or for the consequence of which, the Carrier is not responsible, by statute, contract or otherwise, the cargo, shippers, consignees or owners of the cargo shall contribute with the Carrier in general average to the payment of any sacrifices, losses or expenses of a general average nature that may be made or incurred and shall pay salvage and special charges incurred in respect of the cargo.

If a salving vessel is owned or operated by the Carrier, salvage shall be paid for as fully as if the said salving vessel or vessels belonged to strangers. Such deposit as the Carrier or its agents may deem sufficient to cover the estimated contribution of the cargo and any salvage and special charges thereon shall, if required, be made by the cargo, shippers, consignees or owners of the cargo to the Carrier before delivery."

Clause Paramount

37. The following clause shall be included in all bills of lading issued pursuant to this Charter:

(1) Subject to sub-clauses (2) or (3) hereof, this bill of lading shall be governed by, and have effect subject to the rules contained in the International Convention for the Unification of Certain Rules relating to bills of lading signed at Brussels on 25th August 1924 (hereafter the "Hague Rules") as amended by the Protocol signed at Brussels on 23rd February 1968 (hereafter the "Hague-Visby Rules"). Nothing contained herein shall be deemed to be either a surrender by the carrier of any of his rights or

immunities or any increase of any of his responsibilities or liabilities under the Hague-Visby Rules.

(2) If there is governing legislation which applies the Hague Rules compulsorily to this bill of lading, to the exclusion of the Hague-Visby Rules, then this bill of lading shall have effect subject to the Hague Rules. Nothing herein contained shall be deemed to be either a surrender by the carrier of any of his rights or immunities or an increase of any of his responsibilities or liabilities under the Hague Rules.

(3) If there is governing legislation which applies the United Nations Convention on the Carriage of Goods By Sea 1978 (hereafter the "Hamburg Rules") compulsorily to this bill of lading to the exclusion of the Hague-Visby Rules, then this bill of lading shall have effect subject to the Hamburg Rules. Nothing herein contained shall be deemed to be either a surrender by the carrier of any of his rights or immunities or an increase of any of his responsibilities or liabilities under the Hamburg Rules.

(4) If any term of this bill of lading is repugnant to the Hague-Visby Rules, or Hague Rules or Hamburg Rules, if applicable, such term shall be void to that extent but no further.

(5) Nothing in this bill of lading shall be construed as in any way restricting, excluding or waiving the right of any relevant party or person to limit his liability under any available legislation and/or law.

**Back loading**

38. Charterers may order the vessel to discharge and/or backload a part or full cargo at any nominated port within the loading / discharging ranges specified within Part I clauses (D/E) and within the rotation of the ports previously nominated, provided that any cargo loaded is of the description specified in Part I clause (F) and that the master in his reasonable discretion determines that the cargo can be loaded, segregated and discharged without risk of contamination by, or of any other cargo.

Charterers shall pay in respect of loading, carrying and discharging such cargo as follows:

(a) a lumpsum freight calculated at the demurrage rate specified in Part I clause (J) on any additional port time used by the vessel; and

(b) any additional expenses, including bunkers consumed (at replacement cost) over above those required to load and discharge one full cargo and port costs which included additional agency costs: and

(c) if the vessel is fixed on a Worldscale rate in Part I clause (G) then freight shall always be paid for the whole voyage at the rate(s) specified in Part I clause (G) on the largest cargo quantity carried on any ocean leg.

**Bunkers**

39. Owners shall give Charterers or any other company in the Royal Dutch/Shell Group of Companies first option to quote for the supply of bunker requirements for the performance of this Charter.

**Oil pollution prevention/ Ballast management**

40.(1) Owners shall ensure that the master shall:

(a) comply with MARPOL 73/78 including any amendments thereof;

(b) collect the drainings and any tank washings into a suitable tank or tanks and, after maximum separation of free water, discharge the bulk of such water overboard, consistent with the above regulations; and

(c) thereafter notify Charterers promptly of the amounts of oil and free water so retained on board and details of any other washings retained on board from earlier voyages (together called the "collected washings").

(d) not to load on top of such 'collected washings' without specific instructions from Charterers.

(e) provide Charterers with a slops certificate to be made up and signed by the master and an independent surveyor/terminal representative. The certificate shall indicate:
Origin and composition of slops, Volume, Free water and API measured in barrels at 60 deg F.

(2) On being so notified, Charterers, in accordance with their rights under this clause (which shall include without limitation the right to determine the disposal of the collected washings), shall before the vessel's arrival at the loading berth (or if already arrived as soon as possible thereafter) give instructions as to how the collected washings shall be dealt with. Owners shall ensure that the master on the vessel's arrival at the loading berth (or if already arrived as soon as possible thereafter) shall arrange in conjunction with the cargo suppliers for the measurement of the quantity of the collected washings and shall record the same in the vessel's ullage record.

(3) Charterers may require the collected washings to be discharged ashore at the loading port, in which case no freight shall be payable on them.

(4) Alternatively Charterers may require either that the cargo be loaded on top of the collected washings and the collected washings be discharged with the cargo, or that they be kept separate from the cargo in which case Charterers shall pay for any deadfreight incurred thereby in accordance with Part II clause 8 and shall, if practicable, accept discharge of the collected washings at the discharging port or ports.

In either case, provided that the master has reduced the free water in the collected washings to a minimum consistent with the retention on board of the oil residues in them and consistent with sub-clause (1)(a) above, freight in accordance with Part II clause 5shall be payable on the quantity of the collected washings as if such quantity were included in a bill of lading and the figure therefore furnished by the shipper provided, however, that

(i) if there is a provision in this Charter for a lower freight rate to apply to cargo in excess of an agreed quantity, freight on the collected washings shall be paid at such lower rate (provided such agreed quantity of cargo has been loaded) and

(ii) if there is provision in this Charter for a minimum cargo quantity which is less than a full cargo, then whether or not such minimum cargo quantity is furnished, freight on the collected washings shall be paid as if such minimum cargo quantity had been furnished, provided that no freight shall be payable in respect of any collected washings which are kept separate from the cargo and not discharged at the discharge port.

(5) Whenever Charterers require the collected washings to be discharged ashore pursuant to this clause, Charterers shall

PART II

provide and pay for the reception facilities, and the cost of any shifting there for shall be for Charterers' account. Any time lost discharging the collected washings and/or shifting therefore shall count against laytime or, if the vessel is on demurrage, for demurrage.

(6) Owners warrant that the vessel will arrive at the load port with segregated/ clean ballast as defined by Annex I of MARPOL 73/78 including any amendments thereof.

Oil response pollution and insurance

41. (1) Owners warrant that throughout the duration of this Charter the vessel will be:

(i) owned or demise chartered by a member of the 'International Tanker Owners Pollution Federation Limited, and

(ii) entered in the Protection and Indemnity (P&I) Club stated in Part I clause (A) I (xii) .

(2) It is a condition of this Charter that Owners have in place insurance cover for oil pollution for the maximum on offer through the International Group of P&I Clubs but always a minimum of United States Dollars1,000,000,000 (one thousand million). If requested by Charterers, Owners shall immediately furnish to Charterers full and proper evidence of the coverage.

(3) Owners warrant that the vessel carries on board a certificate of insurance as required by the Civil Liability Convention for Oil Pollution damage. Owners further warrant that said certificate will be maintained effective throughout the duration of performance under this Charter. All time, costs and expense as a result of Owners' failure to comply with the foregoing shall be for Owners' account.

(4) Owners warrant that where the vessel is a "Relevant Ship", they are a "Participating Owner", both as defined in the Small Tanker Oil Pollution Indemnification Agreement ("STOPIA") and that the vessel is entered in STOPIA, and shall so remain during the currency of this Charter, provided always that STOPIA is not terminated in accordance with Clause VIII of its provisions.

Lien

42. Owners shall have an absolute lien upon the cargo and all subfreights for all amounts due under this charter and the cost of recovery thereof including any expenses whatsoever arising from the exercise of such lien.

Drugs and alcohol

43. Owners are aware of the problem of drug and alcohol abuse and warrant that they have a written policy in force, covering the vessel, which meets or exceeds the standards set out in the "Guidelines for the Control of Drugs and Alcohol on board Ship" as published by OCIMF dated June 1995.
Owners further warrant that this policy shall remain in force during the period of this Charter and such policy shall be adhered to throughout this Charter.

ITWF

44. Owners warrant that the terms of employment of the vessel's staff and crew will always remain acceptable to the International Transport Workers Federation on a worldwide basis. All time, costs and expenses incurred as a result of Owners' failure to comply with foregoing shall be for Owners' account.

Letters of protest/ Deficiencies

45. It is a condition of this Charter that from the time the vessel sails to the first load port there will be no Letter(s) of Protest ("LOP"'s) or deficiencies outstanding against the vessel. This refers to LOP's or deficiencies issued by Terminal Inspectorate or similar Port or Terminal or Governmental Authorities.

Document-ation

46. Owners shall ensure that the master and agents produce documentation and provide Charterers with copies of all such documentation relevant to each port and berth call and all transhipments at sea, including but not limited to:
Notice of Readiness / Statement of Facts / Shell Form 19x (if Charterers nominate agents under Part II clause 24) / Time sheet(s) / LOPs/ Hourly pumping logs /COW performance logs by facsimile (to the number advised in the voyage instructions). These documents to be faxed within 48 hours from sailing from each load or discharge port or transhipment area. If the vessel does not have a facsimile machine on board the master shall advise Charterers, within 48 hours from sailing from each port under this Charter, of the documents he has available and ensure copies of such documents are faxed by agents to Charterers from the relevant port of call or at latest from the next port of call. Complying with this clause does not affect the terms of Part II clause 15(3) with regard to notification and submission of a fully documented claim for demurrage or a claim described in Part II clause 6(3) of this Charter. Any documents to be faxed under this clause may be, alternatively, scanned and e-mailed to Charterers.
If any actions or facilities of Suppliers / Receivers / Terminal/ Transhipment vessels or Charterers, as applicable, impinge on the vessel's ability to perform the warranties and / or guarantees of performance under this Charter the master must issue a LOP to such effect. If the master fails to issue such LOP then Owners shall be deemed to have waived any rights to claim. Master and agents shall ensure that all documents concerning port/berth and cargo activities at all ports/berths and transhipment at sea places are signed by both an officer of the vessel and a representative of either Suppliers / Receivers / Terminal / Transhipment vessels or Charterers, as applicable.
If such a signature from Suppliers / Receivers / Terminal/ Transhipment vessels or Charterers, as applicable, is not obtainable the master or his agents should issue a LOP to such effect.
All LOP's issued by master or his agents or received by master or his agents must be forwarded to Charterers as per the terms of this clause.

Administra-tion

47. The agreed terms and conditions of this Charter shall be recorded and evidenced by the production of a fixture note sent to both Charterers and Owners within 24 hours of the fixture being concluded. This fixture note shall state the name and date of the standard pre-printed Charter Party Form, on which the Charter is based, along with all amendments / additions/ deletions to such charter party form. All further additional clauses agreed shall be reproduced in the fixture note with full wording. This fixture note shall be approved and acknowledged as correct by both Owners and Charterers to either the Ship Broker through whom they negotiated or, if no Ship Broker was involved, to each other within two working days after fixture concluded.
No formal written and signed Charter Party will be produced unless specifically requested by Charterers or Owners or is required

by additional clauses of this Charter.

Cargo retention

48. If on completion of discharge any liquid cargo of a pumpable nature remains on board (the presence and quantity of such cargo having been established, by application of the wedge formula in respect of any tank the contents of which do not reach the forward bulkhead, by an independent surveyor, appointed by Charterers and paid jointly by Owners and Charterers), Charterers shall have the right to deduct from freight an amount equal to the FOB loading port value of such cargo, cargo insurance plus freight thereon; provided, however, that any action or lack of action hereunder shall be without prejudice to any other rights or obligations of Charterers, under this Charter or otherwise, and provided further that if Owners are liable to any third party in respect of failure to discharge such pumpable cargo, or any part thereof, Charterers shall indemnify Owners against such liability up to the total amount deducted under this clause.

Hydrogen sulphide

49. Owners shall comply with the requirements in ISGOTT (as amended from time to time) concerning Hydrogen Sulphide and shall ensure that prior to arrival at the load port the Hydrogen Sulphide (ppm by volume in vapour) level in all bunker, ballast and empty cargo spaces is below the Threshold Limit Value ("TLV") - Time Weighted Average ("TWA")
If on arrival at the loading terminal, the loading authorities, inspectors or other authorised and qualified personnel declare that the Hydrogen Sulphide levels in the vessels' tanks exceed the TLV- TWA and request the vessel to reduce the said level to within the TLV-TWA then the original notice of readiness shall not be valid. A valid notice of readiness can only be tendered and laytime, or demurrage time, if on demurrage, to the relevant authorities can only start to run in accordance with Part II clause 13 when the TLV-TWA is acceptable.
If the vessel is unable to reduce the levels of Hydrogen Sulphide within a reasonable time Charterers shall have the option of cancelling this Charter without penalty and without prejudice to any claims which Charterers may have against Owners under this Charter.

Port regulations

50. Owners warrant that the vessel will fully comply with all port and terminal regulations at any named port in this Charter, and any ports to which Charterers may order the vessel to under this Charter in accordance with Part I clauses (D/E) provided that Owners have a reasonable opportunity to acquaint themselves with the regulations at such ports.

Single Point/ Buoy and jetty mooring

51. (1) Owners warrant that:

(a) the vessel complies with the OCIMF recommendations, current at the date of this Charter, for equipment employed in the mooring of ships at single point moorings in particular for tongue type or hinged bar type chain stoppers and that the messenger from the Chain Stopper(s) is secured on a winch drum (not a drum end) and that the operation is totally hands free.

(b) the vessel complies and operates in accordance with the recommendations, current at the date of this Charter, contained in the latest edition of OCIMF's "Mooring Equipment Procedures"

(2) If requested by Charterers, or in the event of an emergency situation arising whilst the vessel is at a Single Buoy Mooring ("SBM"), the vessel shall pump sea water, either directly from the sea or from vessel's clean ballast tanks, to flush SBMs floating hoses prior to, during or /after loading and/or discharge of the cargo; this operation to be carried out at Charterers' expense and with time counting against laytime, or demurrage, if on demurrage. Subject to Owners exercising due diligence in carrying out such an operation Charterers hereby indemnify Owners for any cargo loss or contamination directly resulting from this request.
If master or Owners are approached by Suppliers/Receivers or Terminal Operators to undertake such an operation Owners shall obtain Charterers' agreement before proceeding.

ISPS/MTSA

52. (1) (a) From the date of coming into force of the International Code for the Security of Ships and of Port Facilities and the relevant amendments to Chapter XI of SOLAS ("ISPS Code") and the US Maritime Transportation Security Act 2002 ("MTSA") in relation to the vessel, and thereafter during the currency of this Charter, Owners shall procure that both the vessel and "the Company" (as defined by the ISPS Code) and the "owner" (as defined by the MTSA) shall comply with the requirements of the ISPS Code relating to the vessel and "the Company" and the requirements of MTSA relating to the vessel and the "owner". Upon request Owners shall provide a copy of the relevant International Ship Security Certificate to Charterers. Owners shall provide documentary evidence of compliance with this clause 52 (1) (a).
(b) Except as otherwise provided in this Charter, loss, damage, expense or delay caused by failure on the part of Owners or "the Company"/"owner" to comply with the requirements of the ISPS Code/MTSA or this clause shall be for Owners' account.

(2) (a) Charterers shall provide the Owners with their full style contact details and other relevant information reasonably required by Owners to comply with the requirements of the ISPS Code/MTSA. Additionally, Charterers shall ensure that the contact details of any sub-Charterers are likewise provided to Owners. Furthermore, Charterers shall ensure that all sub-charter parties they enter into shall contain the following provision:
"The Charterers shall provide the Owners with their full style contact details and, where sub-letting is permitted under the terms of the charter party, shall ensure that contact details of all sub-Charterers are likewise provided to the Owners".
(b) Except as otherwise provided in this Charter, loss, damage, expense or delay caused by failure on the part of Charterers to comply with this sub clause (2) shall be for Charterers' account.

*Issued March 2005* **"SHELLVOY 6"**

PART II

(3) (a) Without prejudice to the foregoing, Owners right to tender notice of readiness and Charterers' liability for demurrage in respect of any time delays caused by breaches of this clause 52 shall be dealt with in accordance with Part II clauses 13, (Notice of readiness/Running time), 14, (Suspension of Time), and 15,(Demurrage), of the charter.

(b) Except where the delay is caused by Owners and/or Charterers failure to comply, respectively, with clauses (1) and (2) of this clause 52, then any delay arising or resulting from measures imposed by a port facility or by any relevant authority, under the ISPS Code/MTSA, shall count as half rate laytime, or, if the vessel is on demurrage, half rate demurrage.

(4) Except where the same are imposed as a cause of Owners and/or Charterers failure to comply, respectively, with clauses (1) and (2) of this clause 52 , then any costs or expenses related to security regulations or measures required by the port facility or any relevant authority in accordance with the ISPS Code/MTSA including, but not limited to, security guards, launch services, tug escorts, port security fees or taxes and inspections, shall be shared equally between Owners and Charterers. All measures required by the Owners to comply with the Ship Security Plan shall be for Owners' account.

(5) If either party makes any payment which is for the other party's account according to this clause, the other party shall indemnify the paying party.

Business principles

53. Owners will co-operate with Charterers to ensure that the "Business Principles", as amended from time to time, of the Royal Dutch/Shell Group of Companies, which are posted on the Shell Worldwide Web (www.Shell.com), are complied with.

Law and litigation

54. (a) This Charter shall be construed and the relations between the parties determined in accordance with the laws of England.

Arbitration

(b) All disputes arising out of this Charter shall be referred to Arbitration in London in accordance with the Arbitration Act 1996 (or any re-enactment or modification thereof for the time being in force) subject to the following appointment procedure:

(i) The parties shall jointly appoint a sole arbitrator not later than 28 days after service of a request in writing by either party to do so.

(ii) If the parties are unable or unwilling to agree the appointment of a sole arbitrator in accordance with (i) then each party shall appoint one arbitrator, in any event not later than 14 days after receipt of a further request in writing by either party to do so. The two arbitrators so appointed shall appoint a third arbitrator before any substantive hearing or forthwith if they cannot agree on a matter relating to the arbitration.

(iii) If a party fails to appoint an arbitrator within the time specified in (ii) (the "Party in Default"), the party who has duly appointed his arbitrator shall give notice in writing to the Party in Default that he proposes to appoint his arbitrator to act as sole arbitrator.

(iv) If the Party in Default does not within 7 days of the notice given pursuant to (iii) make the required appointment and notify the other party that he has done so the other party may appoint his arbitrator as sole arbitrator whose award shall be binding on both parties as if he had been so appointed by agreement.

(v) Any award of the arbitrator(s) shall be final and binding and not subject to appeal.

(vi) For the purposes of this clause 54 any requests or notices in writing shall be sent by fax, e-mail or telex and shall be deemed received on the day of transmission.

(c) It shall be a condition precedent to the right of any party to a stay of any legal proceedings in which maritime property has been, or may be, arrested in connection with a dispute under this Charter, that that party furnishes to the other party security to which that other party would have been entitled in such legal proceedings in the absence of a stay.

Small claims

(d) In cases where neither the claim nor any counterclaim exceeds the sum of United States Dollars 50,000 (or such other sum as Owners/Charterers may agree) the arbitration shall be conducted in accordance with the London Maritime Arbitrators' Association Small Claims Procedure current at the time when the arbitration proceedings are commenced.

Address commission

55. Charterers shall deduct address commission of 1.25% from all payments under this Charter.

Construction

56. The side headings have been included in this Charter for convenience of reference and shall in no way affect the construction hereof.

*Issued March 2005* **"SHELLVOY 6"**

PART III

**Australia**

(1)(a) The vessel shall not transit the Great Barrier Reef Inner Passage, whether in ballast en route to a loadport or laden, between the Torres Strait and Cairns, Australia. If the vessel transits the Torres Strait, the vessel shall use the outer reef passage as approved by the Australian Hydrographer. Owners shall always employ a pilot, when transiting the Torres Strait and for entry and departure through the Reef for ports North of Brisbane.

(b) The vessel shall discharge all ballast water on board the vessel and take on fresh ballast water, always in accordance with safe operational procedures, prior to entering Australian waters.

(c) On entering, whilst within and whilst departing from the port of Sydney Owners and master shall ensure that the water line to highest fixed point distance does not exceed 51.8 (fifty one point eight) metres.

(d) If Charterers or Terminal Operators instruct the vessel to slow the cargo operations down or stop entirely the cargo operations in Sydney during the hours of darkness due to excessive noise caused by the vessel then all additional time shall be for Owners' account.

**Goods Services Tax**

(e)(i) Goods Services Tax ("GST") imposed in Australia has application to any supply made under this Charter, the parties agree that the Charterer shall account for GST in accordance with Division 83 of the GST Act even if the Owner becomes registered. The Owner acknowledges that it will not recover from the Charterer an additional amount on account of GST.

(ii) The Owner acknowledges that it is a non-resident and that it does not make supplies through an enterprise carried on in Australia as defined in section 995-1 of the Income Tax Assessment Act 1997.

(iii) The Charterer acknowledges that it is registered. Where appropriate, terms in this clause have the meaning set out in section 195-1 of the GST Act.

**Brazil**

(2) (a) Owners acknowledge the vessel will have, if Charterers so require, to enter a port or place of clearance within mainland Brazil, to obtain necessary clearance from the Brazilian authorities and/or to pick-up personnel required to be on board during the loading of the cargo at Fluminense FPSO. The vessel then proceeds to the Fluminense FPSO where she can tender her notice of readiness. Time at the port of clearance, taken from arrival at pilot station to dropping outward pilot to be for Charterers' account and payable at the agreed demurrage rate together with freight. However this time not to count as laytime or demurrage if on demurrage.

(b) Freight payment under Part II clause 5 of this Charter shall be made within 5 banking days of receipt by Charterers of notice of completion of final discharge

**Canada**

(3) Owners warrant that the vessel complies with all the Canadian Oil Spill response regulations currently in force and that the Owner is a member of a certified oil spill response organisation and that the Owners/vessel shall continue to be members of such organisation and comply with the regulations and requirements of such organisation throughout the period of this Charter.

**Egypt**

(4)(a) Any costs incurred by Charterers for vessel garbage or in vessel deballasting at Sidi Kerir shall be for Owners' account and Charterers shall deduct such costs from freight

(b) Charterers shall have the option for the discharge range Euromed and/or United Kingdom/ Continent (Gibraltar Hamburg range) to instruct the vessel to transit via Suez Canal. In the event that Charterers exercise this option the following shall apply:
Charterers option to part discharge Ain Sukhna and reload Sidi Kerir.
Charterers will pay the following with freight against Owners' fully documented claim:

(c) time incurred at the demurrage rate on the passage from the point at which the vessel deviates from the direct sailing route between last loadport and Port Suez, till the tendering of notice of readiness at Ain Sukhna, less any time lost by reason of delay beyond Charterers' reasonable control;

(d) time incurred at the demurrage rate on the passage from disconnection of hoses at Sidi Kerir to the point at which the vessel rejoins the direct sailing route between Port Said and the first discharge port UK Continent or Mediterranean, less any time lost by reason of delay beyond Charterers' reasonable control;

(e) time incurred at the demurrage rate between tendering of notice of readiness at Ain Sukhna and disconnection of hoses there;

(f) time incurred at the demurrage rate between tendering of notice of readiness at Sidi Kerir and disconnection of hoses there:

(g) all bunkers consumed during the periods (c) to (f) above at replacement cost;

(h) all port charges incurred at Ain Sukhna and Sidi Kerir.

Freight rate via Suez shall be based on the Suez/Suez flat rate without the fixed Suez rate differential, other than as described below (the Worldscale rates in Part I clause (G) of this Charter to apply). All canal dues related to Suez laden transit, including Suez Canal port costs, agency fees and expenses, including but not limited to escort tugs and other expenses for canal laden transit, to be for Charterers' account and to be settled directly by them. Charterers' to pay Owners the 'ballast transit only' fixed rate differential as per Worldscale together with freight.

**India**

(5) (a) In assessing the pumping efficiency under this Charter at ports in India, Owners agree to accept the record of pressure maintained as stated in receiver's statement of facts signed by the ship's representative.

PART III

(b) Owners shall be aware of and comply with the mooring requirements of Indian ports. All time, costs and expenses as a result of Owners' failure to comply with the foregoing shall be for Owners' account.

(c) Charterers shall not be liable for demurrage unless the following conditions are satisfied:

(i) the requirements of Part II clause 15 (3) are met in full; and

(ii) a copy of this Charter signed by Owners is received by Charterers at least 2 (two) working days prior to the vessel's arrival in an Indian port.

Charterers undertake to pay agreed demurrage liabilities promptly if the above conditions have been satisfied.

Japan

(6) (a) Owners shall supply Charterers with copies of:-

(i) General Arrangement/Capacity plan; and

(ii) Piping/Fire Fighting Diagrams

as soon as possible, but always within 4 working days after subjects lifted on this Charter.

(b) If requested by Charterers, Owners shall ensure a Superintendent, fully authorised by Owners to act on Owners' and/or master's behalf, is available at all ports within Japan to attend safety meetings prior to vessel's arrival at the port(s) and be in attendance throughout the time in each port and during each cargo operation.

(c) Vessel to record and print out the position with date/time by Global Positioning System when vessel enters Japanese Territorial Waters ("JTW") in order to perform vessel's declaration of entering JTW for crude oil stock piling purpose.

(d) If under Part I clause (E) of this Charter Japan, or in particular ports or berths in Tokyo Bay and/or the SBM at UBE Refinery, are discharge options and if the vessel is over 220,000 metric tons deadweight and has not previously discharged in Tokyo Bay or the SBM at UBE Refinery then:

(i) Owners shall submit an application of Safety Pledge Letter confirming that all safety measures will be complied with; and

(ii) Present relevant ship data to the Japanese Maritime Safety Agency.

Owners shall comply with the above requirements as soon as possible but always within 4 working days after subjects lifted on this Charter.

(e) If Charterers instruct the vessel to make adjustment to vessel's arrival date/time at discharge port(s) in Japan, any adjustments shall be compensated in accordance with Part I clause (L) of this Charter. If vessel is ordered to drift off Japan, at a location in Owners'/master's option, then the following shall apply:-

(i) Time from vessel's arrival at drifting location to the time vessel departs, on receipt of Charterers' instructions, from such location shall be for Charterers' account at the demurrage rate stipulated in Part I clause (J) of this Charter.

(ii) Bunkers consumed whilst drifting as defined in sub clause (e)(i) above shall be for Charterers' account at replacement cost.

Owners shall provide full documentation to support any claim under this clause.

New Zealand

(7) (a) Owners of vessels carrying Persistent Oil - as defined by the International Group of P&I Clubs - which shall always incorporate Crude and Fuel Oil, Non Persistent Oil as defined by the International Group of P&I Clubs - which shall always incorporate Petroleum Products; and Chemicals, warrant that the vessel shall comply at all times with the Maritime Safety Authority of New Zealand's Voluntary Routeing Code for Shipping whilst transiting the New Zealand coast and / or en route to or from ports in New Zealand and whether laden or in ballast.

(b) the following voyage routing will apply:

(i) vessel is to keep a minimum of 5 miles off the New Zealand coast (and outlying islands) until approaching the port's pilot station, with the following exceptions:

a) to pass a minimum of 4 miles off the coast when transiting Cook Strait;

b) to pass a minimum of 5 miles to the east of Poor Knights Islands and High Peaks Rocks;

c) to pass a minimum of 3 miles from land when transiting the Colville or Jellicoe Channels.

If due to safe navigation and or other weather related reasons the vessel proceeds on a different route to those set out above, the Owners and master shall immediately advise Charterers and Owner's agents in New Zealand of the route being followed and the reasons for such deviation from the above warranted route.

Thailand

(8) If Part I clause (E) of this Charter includes option to discharge at a port/berth in Thailand then the following, which is consistent with industry practice for ships discharging in Thailand, shall apply over and above any other terms contained within this Charter:-

(a) Laytime shall be 96 running hours

(b) Freight payment under Part II clause 5 of this Charter shall be made within 15 days of receipt by Charterers of notice of completion of final discharge of cargo.

(c) Cargo quantity and quality measurements shall be carried out at load and discharge ports by mutually appointed independent surveyors, with costs to be shared equally between Owners and Charterers.

PART III

This is additional to any independent surveyors used for the Cargo Retention clause 48 in Part II of this Charter.

**United Kingdom**

(9) (a) It is a condition of this Charter that Owners ensure that the vessel fully complies with the latest Sullom Voe regulations, including but not limited to:-

i) current minimum bulk loading rates; and

ii) pilot boarding ladder arrangements.

Owners shall also comply with Charterers' instructions regarding the disposal of ballast from the vessel. Charterers shall accept any deadfreight claim that may arise by complying with such instructions.

(b) It is also a condition of this Charter that Owners ensure that the vessel fully complies with the latest Tranmere and Shellhaven regulations, including but not limited to:-

i) being able to ballast concurrently with discharge ; or

ii) maintaining double valve segregation at all times between cargo and ballast if the vessel has to part discharge, stop to ballast, then resume discharge.

(c) In the event of loading or discharge at Tranmere, Shell U.K. Ltd. shall appoint tugs, pilots and boatmen on behalf of Owners. The coordinator of these services shall be OBC., who will submit all bills to Owners direct, irrespective of whether OBC are appointed agents or not. Owners warrant they will put OBC in funds accordingly.

**United States of America**

(10) (a) It is a condition of this Charter that in accordance with U.S. Customs Regulations, 19 CFR 4.7a and 178.2 as amended, Owners have obtained a Standard Carrier Alpha Code (SCAC) and shall include same in the Unique Identifier which they shall enter, in the form set out in the above Customs Regulations, on all the bills of lading, Cargo manifest, Cargo declarations and other cargo documents issued under this Charter allowing carriage of goods to ports in the U.S.

Owners shall be liable for all time, costs and expenses and shall indemnify Charterers against all consequences whatsoever arising directly or indirectly from Owners' failure to comply with the above provisions of this clause.

Owners warrant that they are aware of the requirements of the U.S Bureau of Customs and Border Protection ruling issued on December 5th 2003 under Federal Register Part II Department of Homeland Security 19 CFR Parts 4, 103, et al. and will comply fully with these requirements for entering U.S ports.

**Coastguard compliance**

(b) Owners warrant that during the term of this Charter the vessel will comply with all applicable U.S. Coast Guard (USCG) Regulations in effect as of the date the vessel is tendered for first loading hereunder. If waivers are held to any USCG regulation Owners to advise Charterers of such waivers, including period of validation and reason(s) for waiver. All time costs and expense as a result of Owners' failure to comply with the foregoing shall be for Owners' account.

(c) Owners warrant that they will

(i) comply with the U.S. Federal Water Pollution Control Act as amended, and any amendments or successors to said Act

**Laws and regulation**

(ii) comply with all U.S. State Laws and regulations applicable during this Charter, as they apply to the U.S. States that Charterers may order vessel to under Part I clauses (D/E) of this Charter.

(iii) have secured, carry aboard the vessel, and keep current any certificates or other evidence of financial responsibility required under applicable U.S. Federal or State Laws and regulations and documentation recording compliance with the requirements of OPA 90, any amendments or succeeding legislation, and any regulations promulgated thereunder. Owners shall confirm that these documents will be valid throughout this Charter.

**W-8BEN**

(d) If the recipient of the freight due under this Charter does not file taxes within the US, then such recipient shall complete an IRS Form W-8BEN and forward the original by mail to Charterers, attention "Freight Payments". Should this not be received in a timely manner, then Charterers shall not be liable for interest on late payment of freight, or be in default of this Charter for such late payment.

**Vapour Recovery System**

Owners warrant that the vessel's vapour recovery system complies with the requirements of the United States Coastguard.

**Vietnam**

(11) If required by Charterers, when loading Bach Ho crude oil, Owners will instruct the master to start the cargo heating system(s) prior to loading commencing.

# APPENDIX 4

# SHELLTIME 4

**Code word for this Charter Party**
**"SHELLTIME 4"**

*Issued December 1984*

## Time Charter Party

LONDON. 19

IT IS THIS DAY AGREED between

of (hereinafter referred to as "Owners"), being owners of the

good vessel called

(hereinafter referred to as "the vessel") described as per Clause 1 hereof and

of (hereinafter referred to as "Charterers"):

**Description and Condition of Vessel**

1. At the date of delivery of the vessel under this charter
(a) she shall be classed:
(b) she shall be in every way fit to carry crude petroleum and/or its products;

(c) she shall be tight, staunch, strong, in good order and condition, and in every way fit for the service, with her machinery, boilers, hull and other equipment (including but not limited to hull stress calculator and radar) in a good and efficient state:
(d) her tanks, valves and pipelines shall be oil-tight;
(e) she shall be in every way fitted for burning

at sea - fueloil with a maximum viscosity of Centistokes at 50 degrees Centigrade/any commercial grade of fueloil ("ACGFO") for main propulsion, marine diesel oil/ACGFO for auxiliaries
in port - marine diesel oil/ACGFO for auxiliaries;

(f) she shall comply with the regulations in force so as to enable her to pass through the Suez and Panama Canals by day and night without delay;
(g) she shall have on board all certificates, documents and equipment required from time to time by any applicable law to enable her to perform the charter service without delay;
(h) she shall comply with the description in Form B appended hereto, provided however that if there is any conflict between the provisions of Form B and any other provision, including this Clause 1, of this charter such other provision shall govern.

**Shipboard Personnel and their Duties**

2. (a) At the date of delivery of the vessel under this charter
(i) she shall have a full and efficient complement of master, officers and crew for a vessel of her tonnage, who shall in any event be not less than the number required by the laws of the flag state and who shall be trained to operate the vessel and her equipment competently and safely;
(ii) all shipboard personnel shall hold valid certificates of competence in accordance with the requirements of the law of the flag state;
(iii) all shipboard personnel shall be trained in accordance with the relevant provisions of the International Convention on Standards of Training, Certification and Watchkeeping for Seafarers, 1978;
(iv) there shall be on board sufficient personnel with a good working knowledge of the English language to enable cargo operations at loading and discharging places to be carried out efficiently and safely and to enable communications between the vessel and those loading the vessel or accepting discharge therefrom to be carried out quickly and efficiently.
(b) Owners guarantee that throughout the charter service the master shall with the vessel's officers and crew, unless otherwise ordered by Charterers,
(i) prosecute all voyages with the utmost despatch;
(ii) render all customary assistance; and
(iii) load and discharge cargo as rapidly as possible when required by Charterers or their agents to do so, by night or by day, but always in accordance with the laws of the place of loading or discharging (as the case may be) and in each case in accordance with any applicable laws of the flag state.

**Duty to Maintain**

3. (i) Throughout the charter service Owners shall, whenever the passage of time, wear and tear or any event (whether or not coming within Clause 27 hereof) requires steps to be taken to maintain or restore the conditions stipulated in Clauses 1 and 2(a), exercise due diligence so to maintain or restore the vessel.
(ii) If at any time whilst the vessel is on hire under this charter the vessel fails to comply with the requirements of Clauses 1.2(a) or 10 then hire shall be reduced to the extent necessary to indemnify Charterers for such failure. If and to the extent that such failure affects the time taken by the vessel to perform any services under this charter, hire shall be reduced by an amount equal to the value, calculated at the rate of hire, of the time so lost.

Any reduction of hire under this sub-Clause (ii) shall be without prejudice to any other remedy available to Charterers, but where such reduction of hire is in respect of time lost, such time shall be excluded from any calculation under Clause 24.
(iii) If Owners are in breach of their obligation under Clause 3(i) Charterers may so notify Owners in writing: and if, after the expiry of 30 days following the receipt by Owners of any such notice, Owners have failed

to demonstrate to Charterers' reasonable satisfaction the exercise of due diligence as required in Clause 3(i), the vessel shall be off-hire, and no further hire payments shall be due, until Owners have so demonstrated that they are exercising such due diligence.

Furthermore, at any time while the vessel is off-hire under this Clause 3 Charterers have the option to terminate this charter by giving notice in writing with effect from the date on which such notice of termination is received by Owners or from any later date stated in such notice. This sub-Clause (iii) is without prejudice to any rights of Charterers or obligations of Owners under this charter or otherwise (including without limitation Charterers rights under Clause 21 hereof).

**Period Trading Limits**

4. Owners agree to let and Charterers agree to hire the vessel for a period of
commencing from the time and date of delivery of the vessel, for the purpose of carrying all lawful merchandise (subject always to Clause 28) including in particular

in any part of the world, as Charterers shall direct, subject to the limits of the current British Institute Warranties and any subsequent amendments thereof. Notwithstanding the foregoing, but subject to Clause 35, Charterers may order the vessel to ice-bound waters or to any part of the world outside such limits provided that Owners consent thereto (such consent not to be unreasonably withheld) and that Charterers pay for any insurance premium required by the vessel's underwriters as a consequence of such order.

Charterers shall use due diligence to ensure that the vessel is only employed between and at safe places (which expression when used in this charter shall include ports, berths, wharves, docks, anchorages, submarine lines, alongside vessels or lighters, and other locations including locations at sea) where she can safely lie always afloat. Notwithstanding anything contained in this or any other clause of this charter, Charterers do not warrant the safety of any place to which they order the vessel and shall be under no liability in respect thereof except for loss or damage caused by their failure to exercise due diligence as aforesaid. Subject as above, the vessel shall be loaded and discharged at any places as Charterers may direct, provided that Charterers shall exercise due diligence to ensure that any ship-to-ship transfer operations shall conform to standards not less than those set out in the latest published edition of the ICS/OCIMF Ship-to-Ship Transfer Guide.

The vessel shall be delivered by Owners at a port in

at Owners' option and redelivered to Owners at a port in

at Charterers' option.

**Laydays/ Cancelling**

5. The vessel shall not be delivered to Charterers before and Charterers shall have the option of cancelling this charter if the vessel is not ready and at their disposal on or before

**Owners to Provide**

6. Owners undertake to provide and to pay for all provisions, wages, and shipping and discharging fees and all other expenses of the master, officers and crew; also, except as provided in Clauses 4 and 34 hereof, for all insurance on the vessel, for all deck, cabin and engine-room stores, and for water; for all drydocking, overhaul, maintenance and repairs to the vessel; and for all fumigation expenses and de-rat certificates. Owners' obligations under this Clause 6 extend to all liabilities for customs or import duties arising at any time during the performance of this charter in relation to the personal effects of the master, officers and crew, and in relation to the stores, provisions and other matters aforesaid which Owners are to provide and pay for and Owners shall refund to Charterers any sums Charterers or their agents may have paid or been compelled to pay in respect of any such liability. Any amounts allowable in general average for wages and provisions and stores shall be credited to Charterers insofar as such amounts are in respect of a period when the vessel is on-hire.

**Charterers to Provide**

7. Charterers shall provide and pay for all fuel (except fuel used for domestic services), towage and pilotage and shall pay agency fees, port charges, commissions, expenses of loading and unloading cargoes. canal dues and all charges other than those payable by Owners in accordance with Clause 6 hereof, provided that all charges for the said items shall be for Owners' account when such items are consumed, employed or incurred for Owners' purposes or while the vessel is off-hire (unless such items reasonably relate to any service given or distance made good and taken into account under Clause 21 or 22); and provided further that any fuel used in connection with a general average sacrifice or expenditure shall be paid for by Owners.

**Rate of Hire**

8. Subject as herein provided, Charterers shall pay for the use and hire of the vessel at the rate of
per day, and pro rata for any part of a day, from the time and date of her delivery (local time) until the time and date of her redelivery (local time) to Owners.

**Payment of Hire**

9. Subject to Clause 3(iii), payment of hire shall be made in immediately available funds to:

Account

in per calendar month in advance, less:

(i) any hire paid which Charterers reasonably estimate to relate to off-hire periods, and

(ii) any amounts disbursed on Owners' behalf, any advances and commission thereon, and charges which are for Owners' account pursuant to any provision hereof, and

(iii) any amounts due or reasonably estimated to become due to Charterers under Clause 3(ii) or 24 hereof,

any such adjustments to be made at the due date for the next monthly payment after the facts have been ascertained. Charterers shall not be responsible for any delay or error by Owners' bank in crediting Owners' account provided that Charterers have made proper and timely payment.

In default of such proper and timely payment,

(a) Owners shall notify Charterers of such default and Charterers shall within seven days of receipt of such notice pay to Owners the amount due including interest, failing which Owners may withdraw the vessel from the service of Charterers without prejudice to any other rights Owners may have under this charter or otherwise; and

(b) Interest on any amount due but not paid on the due date shall accrue from the day after that date up to and including the day when payment is made, at a rate per annum which shall be 1% above the U.S. Prime

Interest Rate as published by the Chase Manhattan Bank in New York at 12.00 New York time on the due date, or, if no such interest rate is published on that day, the interest rate published on the next preceding day on which such a rate was so published, computed on the basis of a 360 day year of twelve 30-day months, compounded semi-annually.

**Space Available to Charterers**

10. The whole reach, burthen and decks of the vessel and any passenger accommodation (including Owners' suite) shall be at Charterers' disposal, reserving only proper and sufficient space for the vessel's master, officers, crew, tackle, apparel, furniture, provisions and stores, provided that the weight of stores on board shall not, unless specially agreed, exceed tonnes at any time during the charter period.

**Overtime**

11. Overtime pay of the master, officers and crew in accordance with ship's articles shall be for Charterers' account when incurred, as a result of complying with the request of Charterers or their agents, for loading, discharging, heating of cargo, bunkering or tank cleaning.

**Instructions and Logs**

12. Charterers shall from time to time give the master all requisite instructions and sailing directions, and he shall keep a full and correct log of the voyage or voyages, which Charterers or their agents may inspect as required. The master shall when required furnish Charterers or their agents with a true copy of such log and with properly completed loading and discharging port sheets and voyage reports for each voyage and other returns as Charterers may require. Charterers shall be entitled to take copies at Owners' expense of any such documents which are not provided by the master.

**Bills of Lading**

13. (a) The master (although appointed by Owners) shall be under the orders and direction of Charterers as regards employment of the vessel, agency and other arrangements, and shall sign bills of lading as Charterers or their agents may direct (subject always to Clauses 35(a) and 40) without prejudice to this charter. Charterers hereby indemnify Owners against all consequences or liabilities that may arise

(i) from signing bills of lading in accordance with the directions of Charterers, or their agents, to the extent that the terms of such bills of lading fail to conform to the requirements of this charter, or (except as provided in Clause 13(b)) from the master otherwise complying with Charterers or their agents orders:

(ii) from any irregularities in papers supplied by Charterers or their agents.

(b) Notwithstanding the foregoing, Owners shall not be obliged to comply with any orders from Charterers to discharge all or part of the cargo

(i) at any place other than that shown on the bill of lading and/or

(ii) without presentation of an original bill of lading

unless they have received from Charterers both written confirmation of such orders and an indemnity in a form acceptable to Owners.

**Conduct of Vessel's Personnel**

14. If Charterers complain of the conduct of the master or any of the officers or crew, Owners shall immediately investigate the complaint. If the complaint proves to be well founded, Owners shall, without delay, make a change in the appointments and Owners shall in any event communicate the result of their investigations to Charterers as soon as possible.

**Bunkers at Delivery and Redelivery**

15. Charterers shall accept and pay for all bunkers on board at the time of delivery, and Owners shall on redelivery (whether it occurs at the end of the charter period or on the earlier termination of this charter) accept and pay for all bunkers remaining on board, at the then-current market prices at the port of delivery or redelivery, as the case may be, or if such prices are not available payment shall be at the then-current market prices at the nearest port at which such prices are available; provided that if delivery or redelivery does not take place in a port payment shall be at the price paid at the vessel's last port of bunkering before delivery or redelivery, as the case may be. Owners shall give Charterers the use and benefit of any fuel contracts they may have in force from time to time, if so required by Charterers, provided suppliers agree.

**Stevedores, Pilots, Tugs**

16. Stevedores when required shall be employed and paid by Charterers, but this shall not relieve Owners from responsibility at all times for proper stowage, which must be controlled by the master who shall keep a strict account of all cargo loaded and discharged. Owners hereby indemnify Charterers, their servants and agents against all losses, claims, responsibilities and liabilities arising in any way whatsoever from the employment of pilots, tugboats or stevedores, who although employed by Charterers shall be deemed to be the servants of and in the service of Owners and under their instructions (even if such pilots, tugboat personnel or stevedores are in fact the servants of Charterers their agents or any affiliated company); provided, however, that

(i) the foregoing indemnity shall not exceed the amount to which Owners would have been entitled to limit their liability if they had themselves employed such pilots, tugboats or stevedores, and

(ii) Charterers shall be liable for any damage to the vessel caused by or arising out of the use of stevedores, fair wear and tear excepted, to the extent that Owners are unable by the exercise of due diligence to obtain redress therefor from stevedores.

**Supernumeraries**

17. Charterers may send representatives in the vessel's available accommodation upon any voyage made under this charter, Owners finding provisions and all requisites as supplied to officers, except liquors. Charterers paying at the rate of per day for each representative while on board the vessel.

**Sub-letting**

18. Charterers may sub-let the vessel, but shall always remain responsible to Owners for due fulfilment of this charter.

**Final Voyage**

19. If when a payment of hire is due hereunder Charterers reasonably expect to redeliver the vessel before the next payment of hire would fall due, the hire to be paid shall be assessed on Charterers' reasonable estimate of the time necessary to complete Charterers' programme up to redelivery, and from which estimate Charterers may deduct amounts due or reasonably expected to become due for

(i) disbursements on Owners' behalf or charges for Owners' account pursuant to any provision hereof, and

(ii) bunkers on board at redelivery pursuant to Clause 15.

Promptly after redelivery any overpayment shall be refunded by Owners or any underpayment made good by Charterers.

If at the time this charter would otherwise terminate in accordance with Clause 4 the vessel is on a ballast voyage to a port of redelivery or is upon a laden voyage, Charterers shall continue to have the use of the vessel at the same rate and conditions as stand herein for as long as necessary to complete such ballast voyage, or to complete such laden voyage and return to a port of redelivery as provided by this charter, as the case may be.

**Loss of Vessel**

20. Should the vessel be lost, this charter shall terminate and hire shall cease at noon on the day of her loss; should the vessel be a constructive total loss, this charter shall terminate and hire shall cease at noon on the day on which the vessel's underwriters agree that the vessel is a constructive total loss; should the vessel be missing, this charter shall terminate and hire shall cease at noon on the day on which she was last heard of. Any hire paid in advance and not earned shall be returned to Charterers and Owners shall reimburse Charterers for the value of the estimated quantity of bunkers on board at the time of termination, at the price paid by Charterers at the last bunkering port.

**Off-hire**

21. (a) On each and every occasion that there is loss of time (whether by way of interruption in the vessel's service or, from reduction in the vessel's performance, or in any other manner)

(i) due to deficiency of personnel or stores; repairs; gas-freeing for repairs; time in and waiting to enter dry dock for repairs; breakdown (whether partial or total) of machinery, boilers or other parts of the vessel or her equipment (including without limitation tank coatings); overhaul, maintenance or survey; collision, stranding, accident or damage to the vessel; or any other similar cause preventing the efficient working of the vessel; and such loss continues for more than three consecutive hours (if resulting from interruption in the vessel's service) or cumulates to more than three hours (if resulting from partial loss of service); or

(ii) due to industrial action, refusal to sail, breach of orders or neglect of duty on the part of the master, officers or crew; or

(iii) for the purpose of obtaining medical advice or treatment for or landing any sick or injured person (other than a Charterers' representative carried under Clause 17 hereof) or for the purpose of landing the body of any person (other than a Charterers' representative), and such loss continues for more than three consecutive hours; or

(iv) due to any delay in quarantine arising from the master, officers or crew having had communication with the shore at any infected area without the written consent or instructions of Charterers or their agents, or to any detention by customs or other authorities caused by smuggling or other infraction of local law on the part of the master, officers, or crew; or

(v) due to detention of the vessel by authorities at home or abroad attributable to legal action against or breach of regulations by the vessel, the vessel's owners, or Owners (unless brought about by the act or neglect of Charterers); then

without prejudice to Charterers' rights under Clause 3 or to any other rights of Charterers hereunder or otherwise the vessel shall be off-hire from the commencement of such loss of time until she is again ready and in an efficient state to resume her service from a position not less favourable to Charterers than that at which such loss of time commenced; provided, however, that any service given or distance made good by the vessel whilst off-hire shall be taken into account in assessing the amount to be deducted from hire.

(b) If the vessel fails to proceed at any guaranteed speed pursuant to Clause 24, and such failure arises wholly or partly from any of the causes set out in Clause 21(a) above, then the period for which the vessel shall be off-hire under this Clause 21 shall be the difference between

(i) the time the vessel would have required to perform the relevant service at such guaranteed speed, and

(ii) the time actually taken to perform such service (including any loss of time arising from interruption in the performance of such service).

For the avoidance of doubt, all time included under (ii) above shall be excluded from any computation under Clause 24.

(c) Further and without prejudice to the foregoing, in the event of the vessel deviating (which expression includes without limitation putting back, or putting into any port other than that to which she is bound under the instructions of Charterers) for any cause or purpose mentioned in Clause 21(a), the vessel shall be off-hire from the commencement of such deviation until the time when she is again ready and in an efficient state to resume her service from a position not less favourable to Charterers than that at which the deviation commenced, provided, however, that any service given or distance made good by the vessel whilst so off-hire shall be taken into account in assessing the amount to be deducted from hire. If the vessel, for any cause or purpose mentioned in Clause 21 (a), puts into any port other than the port to which she is bound on the instructions of Charterers, the port charges, pilotage and other expenses at such port shall be borne by Owners. Should the vessel be driven into any port or anchorage by stress of weather hire shall continue to be due and payable during any time lost thereby.

(d) If the vessel's flag state becomes engaged in hostilities, and Charterers in consequence of such hostilities find it commercially impracticable to employ the vessel and have given Owners written notice thereof then from the date of receipt by Owners of such notice until the termination of such commercial impracticability the vessel shall be off-hire and Owners shall have the right to employ the vessel on their own account.

(e) Time during which the vessel is off-hire under this charter shall count as part of the charter period.

**Periodical Drydocking**

22. (a) Owners have the right and obligation to drydock the vessel at regular intervals of

On each occasion Owners shall propose to Charterers a date on which they wish to drydock the vessel, not less than before such date, and Charterers shall offer a port for such periodical drydocking and shall take all reasonable steps to make the vessel available as near to such date as practicable.

Owners shall put the vessel in drydock at their expense as soon as practicable after Charterers place the vessel at Owners' disposal clear of cargo other than tank washings and residues. Owners shall be responsible for and pay for the disposal into reception facilities of such tank washings and residues and shall have the right to retain any monies received therefor, without prejudice to any claim for loss of cargo under any bill of lading or this charter.

(b) If a periodical drydocking is carried out in the port offered by Charterers (which must have suitable accommodation for the purpose and reception facilities for tank washings and residues), the vessel shall be off-hire from the time she arrives at such port until drydocking is completed and she is in every way ready to resume Charterers' service and is at the position at which she went off-hire or a position no less favourable to Charterers, whichever she first attains. However,

(i) provided that Owners exercise due diligence in gas-freeing, any time lost in gas-freeing to the standard required for entry into drydock for cleaning and painting the hull shall not count as off-hire, whether lost on passage to the drydocking port or after arrival there (notwithstanding Clause 21), and

(ii) any additional time lost in further gas-freeing to meet the standard required for hot work or entry to cargo tanks shall count as off-hire, whether lost on passage to the drydocking port or after arrival there.

Any time which, but for sub-Clause (i) above, would be off-hire, shall not be included in any calculation under Clause 24.

The expenses of gas-freeing, including without limitation the cost of bunkers, shall be for Owners account.

(c) If Owners require the vessel, instead of proceeding to the offered port, to carry out periodical drydocking at a special port selected by them, the vessel shall be off-hire from the time when she is released to proceed to the special port until she next presents for loading in accordance with Charterers' instructions, provided, however, that Charterers shall credit Owners with the time which would have been taken on passage at the service speed had the vessel not proceeded to drydock. All fuel consumed shall be paid for by Owners but Charterers shall credit Owners with the value of the fuel which would have been used on such notional passage calculated at the guaranteed daily consumption for the service speed, and shall further credit Owners with any benefit they may gain in purchasing bunkers at the special port.

(d) Charterers shall, insofar as cleaning for periodical drydocking may have reduced the amount of tank-cleaning necessary to meet Charterers' requirements, credit Owners with the value of any bunkers which Charterers calculate to have been saved thereby, whether the vessel drydocks at an offered or a special port.

Ship Inspection

23. Charterers shall have the right at any time during the charter period to make such inspection of the vessel as they may consider necessary. This right may be exercised as often and at such intervals as Charterers in their absolute discretion may determine and whether the vessel is in port or on passage. Owners affording all necessary co-operation and accommodation on board provided, however,

(i) that neither the exercise nor the non-exercise, nor anything done or not done in the exercise or non-exercise, by Charterers of such right shall in any way reduce the master's or Owners' authority over, or responsibility to Charterers or third parties for, the vessel and every aspect of her operation, nor increase Charterers' responsibilities to Owners or third parties for the same; and

(ii) that Charterers shall not be liable for any act, neglect or default by themselves, their servants or agents in the exercise or non-exercise of the aforesaid right.

Detailed Description and Performance

24. (a) Owners guarantee that the speed and consumption of the vessel shall be as follows:-

| Average speed in knots | Maximum average bunker consumption main propulsion fuel oil/diesel oil | - auxiliaries fuel oil/diesel oil |
|---|---|---|
| Laden | tonnes | tonnes |
| | | |
| Ballast | | |

The foregoing bunker consumptions are for all purposes except cargo heating and tank cleaning and shall be pro-rated between the speeds shown.

The service speed of the vessel is knots laden and knots in ballast and in the absence of Charterers' orders to the contrary the vessel shall proceed at the service speed. However if more than one laden and one ballast speed are shown in the table above Charterers shall have the right to order the vessel to steam at any speed within the range set out in the table (the "ordered speed").

If the vessel is ordered to proceed at any speed other than the highest speed shown in the table, and the average speed actually attained by the vessel during the currency of such order exceeds such ordered speed plus 0.5 knots (the "maximum recognised speed"), then for the purpose of calculating any increase or decrease of hire under this Clause 24 the maximum recognised speed shall be used in place of the average speed actually attained.

For the purposes of this charter the "guaranteed speed" at any time shall be the then-current ordered speed or the service speed, as the case may be

The average speeds and bunker consumptions shall for the purposes of this Clause 24 be calculated by reference to the observed distance from pilot station to pilot station on all sea passages during each period stipulated in Clause 24 (c), but excluding any time during which the vessel is (or but for Clause 22(b) (i) would be) off-hire and also excluding "Adverse Weather Periods", being (i) any periods during which reduction of speed is necessary for safety in congested waters or in poor visibility (ii) any days, noon to noon, when winds exceed force 8 on the Beaufort Scale for more than 12 hours.

(b) If during any year from the date on which the vessel enters service (anniversary to anniversary) the vessel falls below or exceeds the performance guaranteed in Clause 24(a) then if such shortfall or excess results

(i) from a reduction or an increase in the average speed of the vessel, compared to the speed guaranteed in Clause 24(a), then an amount equal to the value at the hire rate of the time so lost or gained, as the case may be, shall be deducted from or added to the hire paid:

(ii) from an increase or a decrease in the total bunkers consumed, compared to the total bunkers which would have been consumed had the vessel performed as guaranteed in Clause 24(a), an amount equivalent to the value of the additional bunkers consumed or the bunkers saved, as the case may be, based on the average price paid by Charterers for the vessel's bunkers in such period, shall be deducted from or added to the hire paid.

The addition to or deduction from hire so calculated for laden and ballast mileage respectively shall be adjusted to take into account the mileage steamed in each such condition during Adverse Weather Periods, by dividing such addition or deduction by the number of miles over which the performance has been calculated and multiplying by the same number of miles plus the miles steamed during the Adverse Weather Periods, in order to establish the total addition to or deduction from hire to be made for such period.

Reduction of hire under the foregoing sub-Clause (b) shall be without prejudice to any other remedy available to Charterers.

(c) Calculations under this Clause 24 shall be made for the yearly periods terminating on each successive anniversary of the date on which the vessel enters service, and for the period between the last such anniversary and the date of termination of this charter if less than a year. Claims in respect of reduction of hire arising under this Clause during the final year or part year of the charter period shall in the first instance be settled in accordance with Charterers' estimate made two months before the end of the charter period. Any necessary adjustment after this charter terminates shall be made by payment by Owners to Charterers or by Charterers to Owners as the case may require.

Payments in respect of increase of hire arising under this Clause shall be made promptly after receipt by Charterers of all the information necessary to calculate such increase.

**Salvage**

25. Subject to the provisions of Clause 21 hereof, all loss of time and all expenses ( excluding any damage to or loss of the vessel or tortious liabilities to third parties) incurred in saving or attempting to save life or in successful or unsuccessful attempts at salvage shall be borne equally by Owners and Charterers provided that Charterers shall not be liable to contribute towards any salvage payable by Owners arising in any way out of services rendered under this Clause 25.

All salvage and all proceeds from derelicts shall be divided equally between Owners and Charterers after deducting the master's, officers' and crew's share.

**Lien**

26. Owners shall have a lien upon all cargoes and all freights, sub-freights and demurrage for any amounts due under this charter; and Charterers shall have a lien on the vessel for all monies paid in advance and not earned, and for all claims for damages arising from any breach by Owners of this charter.

**Exceptions**

27. (a) The vessel, her master and Owners shall not, unless otherwise in this charter expressly provided, be liable for any loss or damage or delay or failure arising or resulting from any act, neglect or default of the master, pilots, mariners or other servants of Owners in the navigation or management of the vessel: fire, unless caused by the actual fault or privity of Owners; collision or stranding; dangers and accidents of the sea; explosion, bursting of boilers, breakage of shafts or any latent defect in hull, equipment or machinery: provided, however, that Clauses 1, 2, 3 and 24 hereof shall be unaffected by the foregoing. Further, neither the vessel, her master or Owners, nor Charterers shall, unless otherwise in this charter expressly provided, be liable for any loss or damage or delay or failure in performance hereunder arising or resulting from act of God, act of war, seizure under legal process, quarantine restrictions, strikes, lock-outs, riots, restraints of labour, civil commotions or arrest or restraint of princes, rulers or people.

(b) The vessel shall have liberty to sail with or without pilots, to tow or go to the assistance of vessels in distress and to deviate for the purpose of saving life or property.

(c) Clause 27(a) shall not apply to or affect any liability of Owners or the vessel or any other relevant person in respect of

(i) loss or damage caused to any berth, jetty, dock, dolphin, buoy, mooring line, pipe or crane or other works or equipment whatsoever at or near any place to which the vessel may proceed under this charter, whether or not such works or equipment belong to Charterers, or

(ii) any claim (whether brought by Charterers or any other person) arising out of any loss of or damage to or in connection with cargo. All such claims shall be subject to the Hague-Visby Rules or the Hague Rules, as the case may be, which ought pursuant to Clause 38 hereof to have been incorporated in the relevant bill of lading (whether or not such Rules were so incorporated) or, if no such bill of lading is issued, to the Hague-Visby Rules.

(d) In particular and without limitation, the foregoing subsections (a) and (b) of this Clause shall not apply to or in any way affect any provision in this charter relating to off-hire or to reduction of hire.

**Injurious Cargoes**

28. No acids, explosives or cargoes injurious to the vessel shall be shipped and without prejudice to the foregoing any damage to the vessel caused by the shipment of any such cargo, and the time taken to repair such damage, shall be for Charterers' account. No voyage shall be undertaken, nor any goods or cargoes loaded, that would expose the vessel to capture or seizure by rulers or governments.

**Grade of Bunkers**

29. Charterers shall supply marine diesel oil/fuel oil with a maximum viscosity of Centistokes at 50 degrees Centigrade/ACGFO for main propulsion and diesel oil/ACGFO for the auxiliaries. If Owners require the vessel to be supplied with more expensive bunkers they shall be liable for the extra cost thereof.

Charterers warrant that all bunkers provided by them in accordance herewith shall be of a quality complying with the International Marine Bunker Supply Terms and Conditions of Shell International Trading Company and with its specification for marine fuels as amended from time to time.

**Disbursements**

30. Should the master require advances for ordinary disbursements at any port, Charterers or their agents shall make such advances to him, in consideration of which Owners shall pay a commission of two and a half per cent, and all such advances and commission shall be deducted from hire.

**Laying-up**

31. Charterers shall have the option, after consultation with Owners, of requiring Owners to lay up the vessel at a safe place nominated by Charterers, in which case the hire provided for under this charter shall be adjusted to reflect any net increases in expenditure reasonably incurred or any net saving which should reasonably be made by Owners as a result of such lay-up. Charterers may exercise the said option any number of times during the charter period.

**Requisition**

32. Should the vessel be requisitioned by any government, de facto or de jure, during the period of this charter, the vessel shall be off-hire during the period of such requisition. and any hire paid by such government in respect of such requisition period shall be for Owners' account. Any such requisition period shall count as part of the charter period.

**Outbreak of War**

33. If war or hostilities break out between any two or more of the following countries: U.S.A., U.S.S.R., P.R.C., U.K., Netherlands-both Owners and Charterers shall have the right to cancel this charter.

**Additional War Expenses**

34. If the vessel is ordered to trade in areas where there is war (de facto or de jure) or threat of war, Charterers shall reimburse Owners for any additional insurance premia, crew bonuses and other expenses which are reasonably incurred by Owners as a consequence of such orders, provided that Charterers are given notice of such expenses as soon as practicable and in any event before such expenses are incurred, and provided further that Owners obtain from their insurers a waiver of any subrogated rights against Charterers in respect of any claims by Owners under their war risk insurance arising out of compliance with such orders.

**War Risks**

35. (a) The master shall not be required or bound to sign bills of lading for any place which in his or Owners' reasonable opinion is dangerous or impossible for the vessel to enter or reach owing to any blockade, war, hostilities, warlike operations, civil war, civil commotions or revolutions.

(b) If in the reasonable opinion of the master or Owners it becomes, for any of the reasons set out in Clause 35(a) or by the operation of international law, dangerous, impossible or prohibited for the vessel to reach or enter, or to load or discharge cargo at, any place to which the vessel has been ordered pursuant to this charter (a "place of peril"), then Charterers or their agents shall be immediately notified by telex or radio messages, and Charterers shall thereupon have the right to order the cargo, or such part of it as may be affected, to be loaded or discharged, as the case may be, at any other place within the trading limits of this charter (provided such other place is not itself a place of peril). If any place of discharge is or becomes a place of peril, and no orders have been received from Charterers or their agents within 48 hours after dispatch of such messages, then Owners shall be at liberty to discharge the cargo or such part of it as may be affected at any place which they or the master may in their or his discretion select within the trading limits of this charter and such discharge shall be deemed to be due fulfilment of Owners' obligations under this charter so far as cargo so discharged is concerned.

(c) The vessel shall have liberty to comply with any directions or recommendations as to departure, arrival, routes, ports of call, stoppages, destinations, zones, waters, delivery or in any other wise whatsoever given by the government of the state under whose flag the vessel sails or any other government or local authority or by any person or body acting or purporting to act as or with the authority of any such government or local authority including any de facto government or local authority or by any person or body acting or purporting to act as or with the authority of any such government or local authority or by any committee or person having under the terms of the war risks insurance on the vessel the right to give any such directions or recommendations. If by reason of or in compliance with any such directions or recommendations anything is done or is not done, such shall not be deemed a deviation.

If by reason of or in compliance with any such direction or recommendation the vessel does not proceed to any place of discharge to which she has been ordered pursuant to this charter, the vessel may proceed to any place which the master or Owners in his or their discretion select and there discharge the cargo or such part of it as may be affected. Such discharge shall be deemed to be due fulfilment of Owners obligations under this charter so far as cargo so discharged is concerned.

Charterers shall procure that all bills of lading issued under this charter shall contain the Chamber of Shipping War Risks Clause 1952.

**Both to Blame Collision Clause**

36. If the liability for any collision in which the vessel is involved while performing this charter falls to be determined in accordance with the laws of the United States of America, the following provision shall apply:

"If the ship comes into collision with another ship as a result of the negligence of the other ship and any act, neglect or default of the master, mariner, pilot or the servants of the carrier in the navigation or in the management of the ship, the owners of the cargo carried hereunder will indemnify the carrier against all loss, or liability to the other or non-carrying ship or her owners in so far as such loss or liability represents loss of, or damage to, or any claim whatsoever of the owners of the said cargo, paid or payable by the other or non-carrying ship or her owners to the owners of the said cargo and set off, recouped or recovered by the other or non-carrying ship or her owners as part of their claim against the carrying ship or carrier."

"The foregoing provisions shall also apply where the owners, operators or those in charge of any ship or ships or objects other than, or in addition to, the colliding ships or objects are at fault in respect of a collision or contact."

Charterers shall procure that all bills of lading issued under this charter shall contain a provision in the foregoing terms to be applicable where the liability for any collision in which the vessel is involved falls to be determined in accordance with the laws of the United States of America.

**New Jason Clause**

37. General average contributions shall be payable according to the York/Antwerp Rules, 1974, and shall be adjusted in London in accordance with English law and practice but should adjustment be made in accordance with the law and practice of the United States of America, the following provision shall apply:

"In the event of accident, danger, damage or disaster before or after the commencement of the voyage, resulting from any cause whatsoever, whether due to negligence or not, for which, or for the consequence of which, the carrier is not responsible by statute, contract or otherwise, the cargo, shippers, consignees or owners of the cargo shall contribute with the carrier in general average to the payment of any sacrifices, losses or expenses of a general average nature that may be made or incurred and shall pay salvage and special charges incurred in respect of the cargo."

"If a salving ship is owned or operated by the carrier, salvage shall be paid for as fully as if the said salving ship or ships belonged to strangers. Such deposit as the carrier or his agents may deem sufficient to cover the estimated contribution of the cargo and any salvage and special charges thereon shall, if required, be made by the cargo, shippers, consignees or owners of the cargo to the carrier before delivery."

Charterers shall procure that all bills of lading issued under this charter shall contain a provision in the foregoing terms, to be applicable where adjustment of general average is made in accordance with the laws and practice of the United States of America.

**Clause Paramount**

38. Charterers shall procure that all bills of lading issued pursuant to this charter shall contain the following clause:

"(1) Subject to sub-clause (2) hereof, this bill of lading shall be governed by, and have effect subject to, the rules contained in the International Convention for the Unification of Certain Rules relating to Bills of Lading signed at Brussels on 25th August 1924 (hereafter the "Hague Rules") as amended by the Protocol signed at Brussels on 23rd February 1968 (hereafter the "Hague-Visby Rules"). Nothing contained herein shall be deemed to be either a surrender by the carrier of any of his rights or immunities or any increase of any of his responsibilities or liabilities under the "Hague-Visby Rules."

"(2) If there is governing legislation which applies the Hague Rules compulsorily to this bill of lading, to the exclusion of the Hague-Visby Rules, then this bill of lading shall have effect subject to the Hague Rules. Nothing herein contained shall be deemed to be either a surrender by the carrier of any of his rights or immunities or an increase of any of his responsibilities or liabilities under the Hague Rules."

"(3) If any term of this bill of lading is repugnant to the Hague-Visby Rules, or Hague Rules if applicable, such term shall be void to that extent but no further."

"(4) Nothing in this bill of lading shall be construed as in any way restricting, excluding or waiving the right of any relevant party or person to limit his liability under any available legislation and/or law."

TOVALOP

39. Owners warrant that the vessel is:

(i) a tanker in TOVALOP and

(ii) properly entered in P & I Club

and will so remain during the currency of this charter.

When an escape or discharge of Oil occurs from the vessel and causes or threatens to cause Pollution Damage, or when there is the threat of an escape or discharge of Oil (i.e. a grave and imminent danger of the escape or discharge of Oil which, if it occurred, would create a serious danger of Pollution Damage, whether or not an escape or discharge in fact subsequently occurs), then Charterers may, at their option, upon notice to Owners or master, undertake such measures as are reasonably necessary to prevent or minimise such Pollution Damage or to remove the Threat, unless Owners promptly undertake the same. Charterers shall keep Owners advised of the nature and result of any such measures taken by them and, if time permits, the nature of the measures intended to be taken by them. Any of the aforementioned measures taken by Charterers shall be deemed taken on Owners' authority as Owners' agent, and shall be at Owners' expense except to the extent that:

(1) any such escape or discharge or Threat was caused or contributed to by Charterers, or

(2) by reason of the exceptions set out in Article III, paragraph 2, of the 1969 International Convention on Civil Liability for Oil Pollution Damage, Owners are or, had the said Convention applied to such escape or discharge or to the Threat, would have been exempt from liability for the same, or

(3) the cost of such measures together with all other liabilities, costs and expenses of Owners arising out of or in connection with such escape or discharge or Threat exceeds one hundred and sixty United States Dollars (US $160) per ton of the vessel's Tonnage or sixteen million eight hundred thousand United States Dollars (US $16,800,000), whichever is the lesser, save and insofar as Owners shall be entitled to recover such excess under either the 1971 International Convention on the Establishment of an International Fund for Compensation for Oil Pollution Damage or under CRISTAL;

PROVIDED ALWAYS that if Owners in their absolute discretion consider said measures should be discontinued, Owners shall so notify Charterers and thereafter Charterers shall have no right to continue said measures under the provisions of this Clause 39 and all further liability to Charterers under this Clause 39 shall thereupon cease.

The above provisions are not in derogation of such other rights as Charterers or Owners may have under this charter or may otherwise have or acquire by law or any International Convention or TOVALOP.

The term "TOVALOP" means the Tanker Owners' Voluntary Agreement Concerning Liability for Oil Pollution dated 7th January 1969, as amended from time to time, and the term "CRISTAL" means the Contract Regarding an Interim Supplement to Tanker Liability for Oil Pollution dated 14th January 1971, as amended from time to time. The terms "Oil", "Pollution Damage", and "Tonnage" shall for the purposes of this Clause 39 have the meanings ascribed to them in TOVALOP.

Export Restrictions

40. The master shall not be required or bound to sign bills of lading for the carriage of cargo to any place to which export of such cargo is prohibited under the laws, rules or regulations of the country in which the cargo was produced and/or shipped.

Charterers shall procure that all bills of lading issued under this charter shall contain the following clause:

"If any laws rules or regulations applied by the government of the country in which the cargo was produced and/or shipped, or any relevant agency thereof, impose a prohibition on export of the cargo to the place of discharge designated in or ordered under this bill of lading, carriers shall be entitled to require cargo owners forthwith to nominate an alternative discharge place for the discharge of the cargo, or such part of it as may be affected, which alternative place shall not be subject to the prohibition, and carriers shall be entitled to accept orders from cargo owners to proceed to and discharge at such alternative place. If cargo owners fail to nominate an alternative place within 72 hours after they or their agents have received from carriers notice of such prohibition, carriers shall be at liberty to discharge the cargo or such part of it as may be affected by the prohibition at any safe place on which they or the master may in their or his absolute discretion decide and which is not subject to the prohibition, and such discharge shall constitute due performance of the contract contained in this bill of lading so far as the cargo so discharged is concerned".

The foregoing provision shall apply mutatis mutandis to this charter, the references to a bill of lading being deemed to be references to this charter.

Law and Litigation

41. (a) This charter shall be construed and the relations between the parties determined in accordance with the laws of England.

(b) Any dispute arising under this charter shall be decided by the English Courts to whose jurisdiction the parties hereby agree.

(c) Notwithstanding the foregoing, but without prejudice to any party's right to arrest or maintain the arrest of any maritime property, either party may, by giving written notice of election to the other party, elect to have any such dispute referred to the arbitration of a single arbitrator in London in accordance with the provisions of the Arbitration Act 1950, or any statutory modification or re-enactment thereof for the time being in force.

(i) A party shall lose its right to make such an election only if:

(a) it receives from the other party a written notice of dispute which -

(1) states expressly that a dispute has arisen out of this charter:

(2) specifies the nature of the dispute: and

(3) refers expressly to this clause 41(c)

and

(b) it fails to give notice of election to have the dispute referred to arbitration not later than 30 days from the date of receipt of such notice of dispute.

(ii) The parties hereby agree that either party may -

(a) appeal to the High Court on any question of law arising out of an award:

(b) apply to the High Court for an order that the arbitrator state the reasons for his award:

(c) give notice to the arbitrator that a reasoned award is required: and

(d) apply to the High Court to determine any question of law arising in the course of the reference.

(d) It shall be a condition precedent to the right of any party to a stay of any legal proceedings in which maritime property has been, or may be, arrested in connection with a dispute under this charter, that that party furnishes to the other party security to which that other party would have been entitled in such legal proceedings in the absence of a stay.

Construction

42. The side headings have been included in this charter for convenience of reference and shall in no way affect the construction hereof.

# APPENDIX 5

## LOADLINE MAP

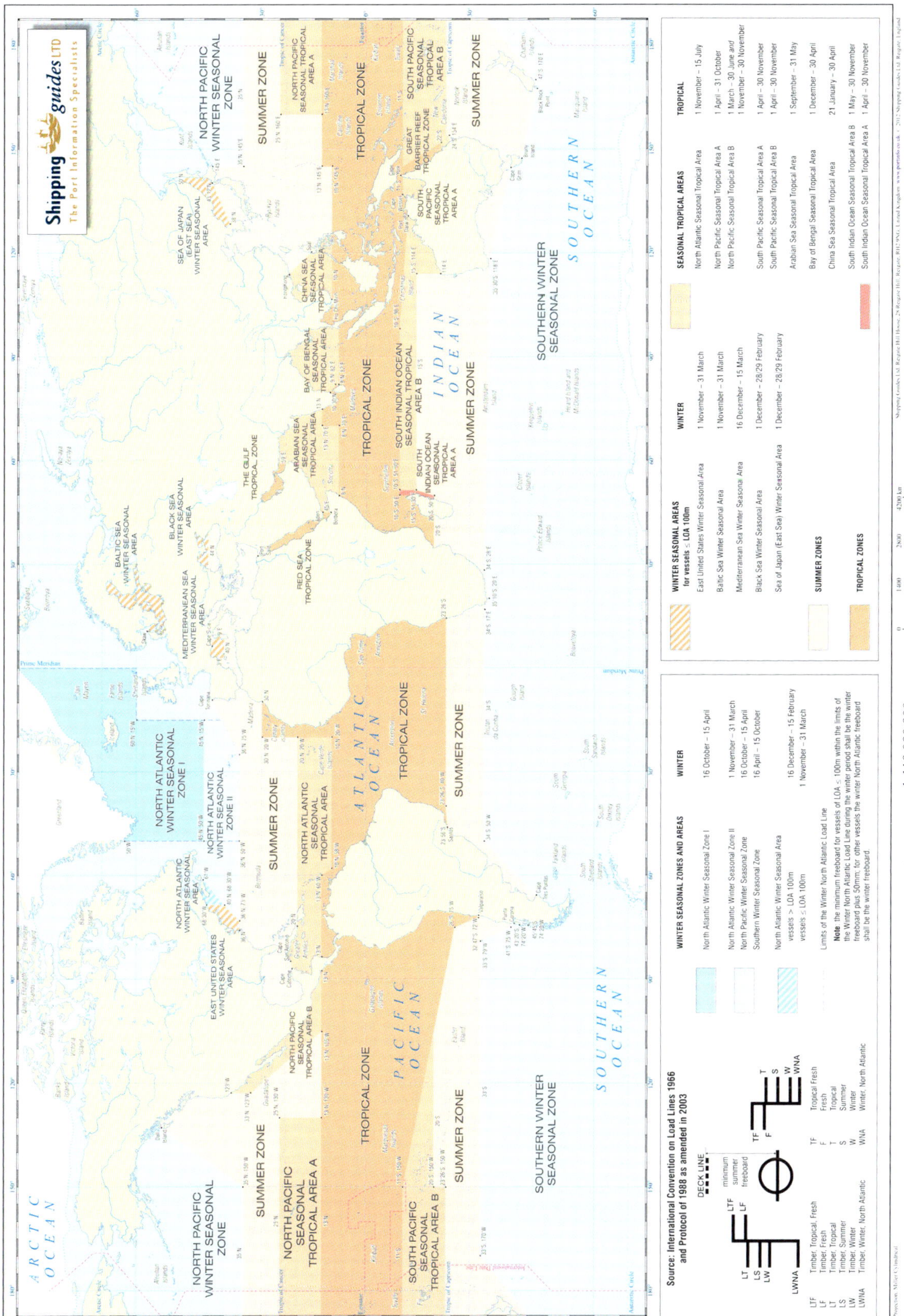

# APPENDIX 6

# S & P PARTICULARS SHEET

**S & P Particulars Sheet**

*Particulars of*

Flag

Year Built and Builders

Tons gross/nett

Cubic Capacity (about)

DEADWEIGHT
including Bunkers of about Draught Loaded

Dimensions

Bunkers

Water Ballast

ENGINES

BOILERS

Donkey Boiler

Winches Derricks DECK PLAN 'Tween Decks

AVERAGE SPEED (about) CONSUMPTION (about)

Passengers

No. of Bulkheads

" of Holds

" of Hatchways and dimensions

CLASS AND SURVEY

Remarks

(These particulars are given without any guarantee for their accuracy

# APPENDIX 7

# NORWEGIAN SALEFORM 93

Norwegian Shipbrokers' Association's Memorandum of Agreement for sale and purchase of ships. Adopted by The Baltic and International Maritime Council (BIMCO) in 1956.
Code-name
**SALEFORM 1993**
Revised 1966, 1983 and 1986/87.

## MEMORANDUM OF AGREEMENT

Dated:

hereinafter called the Sellers, have agreed to sell, and

hereinafter called the Buyers, have agreed to buy

Name:

Classification Society/Class:

Built: By:

Flag: Place of Registration:

Call Sign: Grt/Nrt:

Register Number:

hereinafter called the Vessel, on the following terms and conditions:

**Definitions**

"Banking days" are days on which banks are open both in the country of the currency stipulated for the Purchase Price in Clause 1 and in the place of closing stipulated in Clause 8.

"In writing" or "written" means a letter handed over from the Sellers to the Buyers or vice versa, a registered letter, telex, telefax or other modern form of written communication.

"Classification Society" or "Class" means the Society referred to in line 4.

**1. Purchase Price**

**2. Deposit**

As security for the correct fulfilment of this Agreement the Buyers shall pay a deposit of 10 % (ten per cent) of the Purchase Price within banking days from the date of this Agreement. This deposit shall be placed with

and held by them in a joint account for the Sellers and the Buyers, to be released in accordance with joint written instructions of the Sellers and the Buyers. Interest, if any, to be credited to the Buyers. Any fee charged for holding the said deposit shall be borne equally by the Sellers and the Buyers.

**3. Payment**

The said Purchase Price shall be paid in full free of bank charges to

on delivery of the Vessel, but not later than 3 banking days after the Vessel is in every respect physically ready for delivery in accordance with the terms and conditions of this Agreement and Notice of Readiness has been given in accordance with Clause 5.

**4. Inspections**

a)* The Buyers have inspected and accepted the Vessel's classification records. The Buyers have also inspected the Vessel at/in on and have accepted the Vessel following this inspection and the sale is outright and definite, subject only to the terms and conditions of this Agreement.

b)* The Buyers shall have the right to inspect the Vessel's classification records and declare whether same are accepted or not within

The Sellers shall provide for inspection of the Vessel at/in

The Buyers shall undertake the inspection without undue delay to the Vessel. Should the Buyers cause undue delay they shall compensate the Sellers for the losses thereby incurred.

The Buyers shall inspect the Vessel without opening up and without cost to the Sellers.
During the inspection, the Vessel's deck and engine log books shall be made available for examination by the Buyers. If the Vessel is accepted after such inspection, the sale shall become outright and definite, subject only to the terms and conditions of this Agreement, provided the Sellers receive written notice of acceptance from the Buyers within 72 hours after completion of such inspection.
Should notice of acceptance of the Vessel's classification records and of the Vessel not be received by the Sellers as aforesaid, the deposit together with interest earned shall be released immediately to the Buyers, whereafter this Agreement shall be null and void.

* *4a) and 4b) are alternatives; delete whichever is not applicable. In the absence of deletions, alternative 4a) to apply.*

**5. Notices, time and place of delivery**

a) The Sellers shall keep the Buyers well informed of the Vessel's itinerary and shall provide the Buyers with , , and days notice of the estimated time of arrival at the intended place of drydocking/underwater inspection/delivery. When the Vessel is at the place of delivery and in every respect physically ready for delivery in accordance with this Agreement, the Sellers shall give the Buyers a written Notice of Readiness for delivery.

b) The Vessel shall be delivered and taken over safely afloat at a safe and accessible berth or anchorage at/in

in the Sellers' option.

Expected time of delivery:

Date of cancelling (see Clauses 5 c), 6 b) (iii) and 14):

c) If the Sellers anticipate that, notwithstanding the exercise of due diligence by them, the Vessel will not be ready for delivery by the cancelling date they may notify the Buyers in writing stating the date when they anticipate that the Vessel will be ready for delivery and propose a new cancelling date. Upon receipt of such notification the Buyers shall have the option of either cancelling this Agreement in accordance with Clause 14 within 7 running days of receipt of the notice or of accepting the new date as the new cancelling date. If the Buyers have not declared their option within 7 running days of receipt of the Sellers' notification or if the Buyers accept the new date, the date proposed in the Sellers' notification shall be deemed to be the new cancelling date and shall be substituted for the cancelling date stipulated in line 61.

If this Agreement is maintained with the new cancelling date all other terms and conditions hereof including those contained in Clauses 5 a) and 5 c) shall remain unaltered and in full force and effect. Cancellation or failure to cancel shall be entirely without prejudice to any claim for damages the Buyers may have under Clause 14 for the Vessel not being ready by the original cancelling date.

d) Should the Vessel become an actual, constructive or compromised total loss before delivery the deposit together with interest earned shall be released immediately to the Buyers whereafter this Agreement shall be null and void.

**6. Drydocking/Divers Inspection**

a)** The Sellers shall place the Vessel in drydock at the port of delivery for inspection by the Classification Society of the Vessel's underwater parts below the deepest load line, the extent of the inspection being in accordance with the Classification Society's rules. If the rudder, propeller, bottom or other underwater parts below the deepest load line are found broken, damaged or defective so as to affect the Vessel's class, such defects shall be made good at the Sellers' expense to the satisfaction of the Classification Society without condition/recommendation*.

b)** (i) The Vessel is to be delivered without drydocking. However, the Buyers shall have the right at their expense to arrange for an underwater inspection by a diver approved by the Classification Society prior to the delivery of the Vessel. The Sellers shall at their cost make the Vessel available for such inspection. The extent of the inspection and the conditions under which it is performed shall be to the satisfaction of the Classification

Society. If the conditions at the port of delivery are unsuitable for such inspection, the Sellers shall make the Vessel available at a suitable alternative place near to the delivery port.

(ii) If the rudder, propeller, bottom or other underwater parts below the deepest load line are found broken, damaged or defective so as to affect the Vessel's class, then unless repairs can be carried out afloat to the satisfaction of the Classification Society, the Sellers shall arrange for the Vessel to be drydocked at their expense for inspection by the Classification Society of the Vessel's underwater parts below the deepest load line, the extent of the inspection being in accordance with the Classification Society's rules. If the rudder, propeller, bottom or other underwater parts below the deepest load line are found broken, damaged or defective so as to affect the Vessel's class, such defects shall be made good by the Sellers at their expense to the satisfaction of the Classification Society without condition/recommendation*. In such event the Sellers are to pay also for the cost of the underwater inspection and the Classification Society's attendance.

(iii) If the Vessel is to be drydocked pursuant to Clause 6 b) (ii) and no suitable dry-docking facilities are available at the port of delivery, the Sellers shall take the Vessel to a port where suitable drydocking facilities are available, whether within or outside the delivery range as per Clause 5 b). Once drydocking has taken place the Sellers shall deliver the Vessel at a port within the delivery range as per Clause 5 b) which shall, for the purpose of this Clause, become the new port of delivery. In such event the cancelling date provided for in Clause 5 b) shall be extended by the additional time required for the drydocking and extra steaming, but limited to a maximum of 14 running days.

c) If the Vessel is drydocked pursuant to Clause 6 a) or 6 b) above

(i) the Classification Society may require survey of the tailshaft system, the extent of the survey being to the satisfaction of the Classification surveyor. If such survey is not required by the Classification Society, the Buyers shall have the right to require the tailshaft to be drawn and surveyed by the Classification Society, the extent of the survey being in accordance with the Classification Society's rules for tailshaft survey and consistent with the current stage of the Vessel's survey cycle. The Buyers shall declare whether they require the tailshaft to be drawn and surveyed not later than by the completion of the inspection by the Classification Society. The drawing and refitting of the tailshaft shall be arranged by the Sellers. Should any parts of the tailshaft system be condemned or found defective so as to affect the Vessel's class, those parts shall be renewed or made good at the Sellers' expense to the satisfaction of the Classification Society without condition/recommendation*.

(ii) the expenses relating to the survey of the tailshaft system shall be borne by the Buyers unless the Classification Society requires such survey to be carried out, in which case the Sellers shall pay these expenses. The Sellers shall also pay the expenses if the Buyers require the survey and parts of the system are condemned or found defective or broken so as to affect the Vessel's class*.

(iii) the expenses in connection with putting the Vessel in and taking her out of drydock, including the drydock dues and the Classification Society's fees shall be paid by the Sellers if the Classification Society issues any condition/recommendation* as a result of the survey or if it requires survey of the tailshaft system. In all other cases the Buyers shall pay the aforesaid expenses, dues and fees.

(iv) the Buyers' representative shall have the right to be present in the drydock, but without interfering with the work or decisions of the Classification surveyor.

(v) the Buyers shall have the right to have the underwater parts of the Vessel cleaned and painted at their risk and expense without interfering with the Sellers' or the Classification surveyor's work, if any, and without affecting the Vessel's timely delivery. If, however, the Buyers' work in drydock is still in progress when the Sellers have completed the work which the Sellers are required to do, the additional docking time needed to complete the Buyers' work shall be for the Buyers' risk and expense. In the event that the Buyers' work requires such additional time, the Sellers may upon completion of the Sellers' work tender Notice of Readiness for delivery whilst the Vessel is still in drydock and the Buyers shall be obliged to take delivery in accordance with Clause 3, whether the Vessel is in drydock or not and irrespective of Clause 5 b).

* Notes, if any, in the surveyor's report which are accepted by the Classification Society without condition/recommendation are not to be taken into account.

** *6 a) and 6 b) are alternatives; delete whichever is not applicable. In the absence of deletions, alternative 6 a) to apply.*

**7. Spares/bunkers, etc.**

The Sellers shall deliver the Vessel to the Buyers with everything belonging to her on board and on shore. All spare parts and spare equipment including spare tail-end shaft(s) and/or spare propeller(s)/propeller blade(s), if any, belonging to the Vessel at the time of inspection used or unused, whether on board or not shall become the Buyers' property, but spares on order are to be excluded. Forwarding charges, if any, shall be for the Buyers' account. The Sellers are not required to replace spare parts including spare tail-end shaft(s) and spare propeller(s)/propeller blade(s) which are taken out of spare and used as replacement prior to delivery, but the replaced items shall be the property of the Buyers. The radio installation and navigational equipment shall be included in the sale without extra payment if they are the property of the Sellers. Unused stores and provisions shall be included in the sale and be taken over by the Buyers without extra payment.

The Sellers have the right to take ashore crockery, plates, cutlery, linen and other articles bearing the Sellers' flag or name, provided they replace same with similar unmarked items. Library, forms, etc., exclusively for use in the Sellers' vessel(s), shall be excluded without compensation. Captain's, Officers' and Crew's personal belongings including the slop chest are to be excluded from the sale, as well as the following additional items (including items on hire):

The Buyers shall take over the remaining bunkers and unused lubricating oils in storage tanks and sealed drums and pay the current net market price (excluding barging expenses) at the port and date of delivery of the Vessel.
Payment under this Clause shall be made at the same time and place and in the same currency as the Purchase Price.

**8. Documentation**

The place of closing:

In exchange for payment of the Purchase Price the Sellers shall furnish the Buyers with delivery documents, namely:

a) Legal Bill of Sale in a form recordable in (the country in which the Buyers are to register the Vessel), warranting that the Vessel is free from all encumbrances, mortgages and maritime liens or any other debts or claims whatsoever, duly notarially attested and legalized by the consul of such country or other competent authority.

b) Current Certificate of Ownership issued by the competent authorities of the flag state of the Vessel.

c) Confirmation of Class issued within 72 hours prior to delivery.

d) Current Certificate issued by the competent authorities stating that the Vessel is free from registered encumbrances.

e) Certificate of Deletion of the Vessel from the Vessel's registry or other official evidence of deletion appropriate to the Vessel's registry at the time of delivery, or, in the event that the registry does not as a matter of practice issue such documentation immediately, a written undertaking by the Sellers to effect deletion from the Vessel's registry forthwith and furnish a Certificate or other official evidence of deletion to the Buyers promptly and latest within 4 (four) weeks after the Purchase Price has been paid and the Vessel has been delivered.

f) Any such additional documents as may reasonably be required by the competent authorities for the purpose of registering the Vessel, provided the Buyers notify the Sellers of any such documents as soon as possible after the date of this Agreement.

At the time of delivery the Buyers and Sellers shall sign and deliver to each other a Protocol of Delivery and Acceptance confirming the date and time of delivery of the Vessel from the Sellers to the Buyers.

At the time of delivery the Sellers shall hand to the Buyers the classification certificate(s) as well as all plans etc., which are on board the Vessel. Other certificates which are on board the Vessel shall also be handed over to the Buyers unless the Sellers are required to retain same, in which case the Buyers to have the right to take copies. Other technical documentation which may be in the Sellers' possession shall be promptly forwarded to the Buyers at their expense, if they so request. The Sellers may keep the Vessel's log books but the Buyers to have the right to take copies of same.

**9. Encumbrances**

The Sellers warrant that the Vessel, at the time of delivery, is free from all charters, encumbrances, mortgages and maritime liens or any other debts whatsoever. The Sellers hereby undertake to indemnify the Buyers against all consequences of claims made against the Vessel which have been incurred prior to the time of delivery.

**10. Taxes, etc.**

Any taxes, fees and expenses in connection with the purchase and registration under the Buyers' flag shall be for the Buyers' account, whereas similar charges in connection with the closing of the Sellers' register shall be for the Sellers' account.

**11. Condition on delivery**

The Vessel with everything belonging to her shall be at the Sellers' risk and expense until she is delivered to the Buyers, but subject to the terms and conditions of this Agreement she shall be delivered and taken over as she was at the time of inspection, fair wear and tear excepted.
However, the Vessel shall be delivered with her class maintained without condition/recommendation*, free of average damage affecting the Vessel's class, and with her classification certificates and national certificates, as well as all other certificates the Vessel had at the time of inspection, valid and unextended without condition/recommendation* by Class or the relevant authorities at the time of delivery.
"Inspection" in this Clause 11, shall mean the Buyers' inspection according to Clause 4 a) or 4 b), if applicable, or the Buyers' inspection prior to the signing of this Agreement. If the Vessel is taken over without inspection, the date of this Agreement shall be the relevant date.

* Notes, if any, in the surveyor's report which are accepted by the Classification Society without condition/recommendation are not to be taken into account.

**12. Name/markings**

Upon delivery the Buyers undertake to change the name of the Vessel and alter funnel markings.

**13. Buyers' default**

Should the deposit not be paid in accordance with Clause 2, the Sellers have the right to cancel this Agreement, and they shall be entitled to claim compensation for their losses and for all expenses incurred together with interest.
Should the Purchase Price not be paid in accordance with Clause 3, the Sellers have the right to cancel the Agreement, in which case the deposit together with interest earned shall be released to the Sellers. If the deposit does not cover their loss, the Sellers shall be entitled to claim further compensation for their losses and for all expenses incurred together with interest.

**14. Sellers' default**

Should the Sellers fail to give Notice of Readiness in accordance with Clause 5 a) or fail to be ready to validly complete a legal transfer by the date stipulated in line 61 the Buyers shall have the option of cancelling this Agreement provided always that the Sellers shall be granted a maximum of 3 banking days after Notice of Readiness has been given to make arrangements for the documentation set out in Clause 8. If after Notice of Readiness has been given but before the Buyers have taken delivery, the Vessel ceases to be physically ready for delivery and is not made physically ready again in every respect by the date stipulated in line 61 and new Notice of

Readiness given, the Buyers shall retain their option to cancel. In the event that the Buyers elect to cancel this Agreement the deposit together with interest earned shall be released to them immediately.
Should the Sellers fail to give Notice of Readiness by the date stipulated in line 61 or fail to be ready to validly complete a legal transfer as aforesaid they shall make due compensation to the Buyers for their loss and for all expenses together with interest if their failure is due to proven negligence and whether or not the Buyers cancel this Agreement.

**15. Buyers' representatives**

After this Agreement has been signed by both parties and the deposit has been lodged, the Buyers have the right to place two representatives on board the Vessel at their sole risk and expense upon arrival at on or about
These representatives are on board for the purpose of familiarisation and in the capacity of observers only, and they shall not interfere in any respect with the operation of the Vessel. The Buyers' representatives shall sign the Sellers' letter of indemnity prior to their embarkation.

**16. Arbitration**

a)* This Agreement shall be governed by and construed in accordance with English law and any dispute arising out of this Agreement shall be referred to arbitration in London in accordance with the Arbitration Acts 1950 and 1979 or any statutory modification or re-enactment thereof for the time being in force, one arbitrator being appointed by each party. On the receipt by one party of the nomination in writing of the other party's arbitrator, that party shall appoint their arbitrator within fourteen days, failing which the decision of the single arbitrator appointed shall apply. If two arbitrators properly appointed shall not agree they shall appoint an umpire whose decision shall be final.

b)* This Agreement shall be governed by and construed in accordance with Title 9 of the United States Code and the Law of the State of New York and should any dispute arise out of this Agreement, the matter in dispute shall be referred to three persons at New York, one to be appointed by each of the parties hereto, and the third by the two so chosen; their decision or that of any two of them shall be final, and for purpose of enforcing any award, this Agreement may be made a rule of the Court.
The proceedings shall be conducted in accordance with the rules of the Society of Maritime Arbitrators, Inc. New York.

c)* Any dispute arising out of this Agreement shall be referred to arbitration at , subject to the procedures applicable there.

The laws of shall govern this Agreement.

* *16 a), 16 b) and 16 c) are alternatives; delete whichever is not applicable. In the absence of deletions, alternative 16 a) to apply.*

# APPENDIX 8

# NORWEGIAN SALEFORM 2012

## MEMORANDUM OF AGREEMENT

Norwegian Shipbrokers' Association's Memorandum of Agreement for sale and purchase of ships. Adopted by BIMCO in 1956.
Code-name
**SALEFORM 2012**
Revised 1966, 1983 and 1986/87, 1993 and 2012

Dated:

(*Name of sellers*), hereinafter called the "Sellers", have agreed to sell, and

(*Name of buyers*), hereinafter called the "Buyers", have agreed to buy:

Name of vessel:

IMO Number:

Classification Society:

Class Notation:

Year of Build: Builder/Yard:

Flag: Place of Registration: GT/NT: /

hereinafter called the "Vessel", on the following terms and conditions:

**Definitions**

"Banking Days" are days on which banks are open both in the country of the currency stipulated for the Purchase Price in Clause 1 (Purchase Price) and in the place of closing stipulated in Clause 8 (Documentation) and (*add additional jurisdictions as appropriate).*

"Buyers' Nominated Flag State" means (*state flag state).*

"Class" means the class notation referred to above.

"Classification Society" means the Society referred to above.

"Deposit" shall have the meaning given in Clause 2 (Deposit)

"Deposit Holder" means (*state name and location of Deposit Holder)* or, if left blank, the Sellers' Bank, which shall hold and release the Deposit in accordance with this Agreement.

"In writing" or "written" means a letter handed over from the Sellers to the Buyers or vice versa, a registered letter, e-mail or telefax.

"Parties" means the Sellers and the Buyers.

"Purchase Price" means the price for the Vessel as stated in Clause 1 (Purchase Price).

"Sellers' Account" means (*state details of bank account*) at the Sellers' Bank.

"Sellers' Bank" means (*state name of bank, branch and details*) or, if left blank, the bank notified by the Sellers to the Buyers for receipt of the balance of the Purchase Price.

1. **Purchase Price**
The Purchase Price is (*state currency and amount both in words and figures*).

2. **Deposit**
As security for the correct fulfilment of this Agreement the Buyers shall lodge a deposit of % ( per cent) or, if left blank, 10% (ten per cent), of the Purchase Price (the "Deposit") in an interest bearing account for the Parties with the Deposit Holder within three (3) Banking Days after the date that:

   **(i)** this Agreement has been signed by the Parties and exchanged in original or by e-mail or telefax; and

   **(ii)** the Deposit Holder has confirmed in writing to the Parties that the account has been opened.

The Deposit shall be released in accordance with joint written instructions of the Parties. Interest, if any, shall be credited to the Buyers. Any fee charged for holding and releasing the Deposit shall be borne equally by the Parties. The Parties shall provide to the Deposit Holder all necessary documentation to open and maintain the account without delay.

3. **Payment**
On delivery of the Vessel, but not later than three (3) Banking Days after the date that Notice of Readiness has been given in accordance with Clause 5 (Time and place of delivery and notices):

**(i)** the Deposit shall be released to the Sellers; and

**(ii)** the balance of the Purchase Price and all other sums payable on delivery by the Buyers to the Sellers under this Agreement shall be paid in full free of bank charges to the Sellers' Account.

4. **Inspection**
**(a)*** The Buyers have inspected and accepted the Vessel's classification records. The Buyers have also inspected the Vessel at/in (*state place*) on (*state date*) and have accepted the Vessel following this inspection and the sale is outright and definite, subject only to the terms and conditions of this Agreement.

**(b)*** The Buyers shall have the right to inspect the Vessel's classification records and declare whether same are accepted or not within (*state date/period*).

The Sellers shall make the Vessel available for inspection at/in (*state place/range*) within (*state date/period*).

The Buyers shall undertake the inspection without undue delay to the Vessel. Should the Buyers cause undue delay they shall compensate the Sellers for the losses thereby incurred.

The Buyers shall inspect the Vessel without opening up and without cost to the Sellers.

During the inspection, the Vessel's deck and engine log books shall be made available for examination by the Buyers.

The sale shall become outright and definite, subject only to the terms and conditions of this Agreement, provided that the Sellers receive written notice of acceptance of the Vessel from the Buyers within seventy-two (72) hours after completion of such inspection or after the date/last day of the period stated in Line 59, whichever is earlier.

Should the Buyers fail to undertake the inspection as scheduled and/or notice of acceptance of the Vessel's classification records and/or of the Vessel not be received by the Sellers as aforesaid, the Deposit together with interest earned, if any, shall be released immediately to the Buyers, whereafter this Agreement shall be null and void.

**4(a) and 4(b) are alternatives; delete whichever is not applicable. In the absence of deletions, alternative 4(a) shall apply.*

5. **Time and place of delivery and notices**
**(a)** The Vessel shall be delivered and taken over safely afloat at a safe and accessible berth or anchorage at/in (*state place/range*) in the Sellers' option.

Notice of Readiness shall not be tendered before: (*date*)

Cancelling Date (see Clauses 5(c), 6 (a)(i), 6 (a) (iii) and 14):

**(b)** The Sellers shall keep the Buyers well informed of the Vessel's itinerary and shall provide the Buyers with twenty (20), ten (10), five (5) and three (3) days' notice of the date the Sellers intend to tender Notice of Readiness and of the intended place of delivery.

When the Vessel is at the place of delivery and physically ready for delivery in accordance with this Agreement, the Sellers shall give the Buyers a written Notice of Readiness for delivery.

**(c)** If the Sellers anticipate that, notwithstanding the exercise of due diligence by them, the Vessel will not be ready for delivery by the Cancelling Date they may notify the Buyers in writing stating the date when they anticipate that the Vessel will be ready for delivery and proposing a new Cancelling Date. Upon receipt of such notification the Buyers shall have the option of either cancelling this Agreement in accordance with Clause 14 (Sellers' Default) within three (3) Banking Days of receipt of the notice or of accepting the new date as the new Cancelling Date. If the Buyers have not declared their option within three (3) Banking Days of receipt of the Sellers' notification or if the Buyers accept the new date, the date proposed in the Sellers' notification shall be deemed to be the new Cancelling Date and shall be substituted for the

Cancelling Date stipulated in line 79.

If this Agreement is maintained with the new Cancelling Date all other terms and conditions hereof including those contained in Clauses 5(b) and 5(d) shall remain unaltered and in full force and effect.

**(d)** Cancellation, failure to cancel or acceptance of the new Cancelling Date shall be entirely without prejudice to any claim for damages the Buyers may have under Clause 14 (Sellers' Default) for the Vessel not being ready by the original Cancelling Date.

**(e)** Should the Vessel become an actual, constructive or compromised total loss before delivery the Deposit together with interest earned, if any, shall be released immediately to the Buyers whereafter this Agreement shall be null and void.

**6. Divers Inspection / Drydocking**

(a)*

(i) The Buyers shall have the option at their cost and expense to arrange for an underwater inspection by a diver approved by the Classification Society prior to the delivery of the Vessel. Such option shall be declared latest nine (9) days prior to the Vessel's intended date of readiness for delivery as notified by the Sellers pursuant to Clause 5(b) of this Agreement. The Sellers shall at their cost and expense make the Vessel available for such inspection. This inspection shall be carried out without undue delay and in the presence of a Classification Society surveyor arranged for by the Sellers and paid for by the Buyers. The Buyers' representative(s) shall have the right to be present at the diver's inspection as observer(s) only without interfering with the work or decisions of the Classification Society surveyor. The extent of the inspection and the conditions under which it is performed shall be to the satisfaction of the Classification Society. If the conditions at the place of delivery are unsuitable for such inspection, the Sellers shall at their cost and expense make the Vessel available at a suitable alternative place near to the delivery port, in which event the Cancelling Date shall be extended by the additional time required for such positioning and the subsequent re-positioning. The Sellers may not tender Notice of Readiness prior to completion of the underwater inspection.

(ii) If the rudder, propeller, bottom or other underwater parts below the deepest load line are found broken, damaged or defective so as to affect the Vessel's class, then (1) unless repairs can be carried out afloat to the satisfaction of the Classification Society, the Sellers shall arrange for the Vessel to be drydocked at their expense for inspection by the Classification Society of the Vessel's underwater parts below the deepest load line, the extent of the inspection being in accordance with the Classification Society's rules (2) such defects shall be made good by the Sellers at their cost and expense to the satisfaction of the Classification Society without condition/recommendation** and (3) the Sellers shall pay for the underwater inspection and the Classification Society's attendance.

Notwithstanding anything to the contrary in this Agreement, if the Classification Society do not require the aforementioned defects to be rectified before the next class drydocking survey, the Sellers shall be entitled to deliver the Vessel with these defects against a deduction from the Purchase Price of the estimated direct cost (of labour and materials) of carrying out the repairs to the satisfaction of the Classification Society, whereafter the Buyers shall have no further rights whatsoever in respect of the defects and/or repairs. The estimated direct cost of the repairs shall be the average of quotes for the repair work obtained from two reputable independent shipyards at or in the vicinity of the port of delivery, one to be obtained by each of the Parties within two (2) Banking Days from the date of the imposition of the condition/recommendation, unless the Parties agree otherwise. Should either of the Parties fail to obtain such a quote within the stipulated time then the quote duly obtained by the other Party shall be the sole basis for the estimate of the direct repair costs. The Sellers may not tender Notice of Readiness prior to such estimate having been established.

(iii) If the Vessel is to be drydocked pursuant to Clause 6(a)(ii) and no suitable dry-docking facilities are available at the port of delivery, the Sellers shall take the Vessel to a port where suitable drydocking facilities are available, whether within or outside the delivery range as per Clause 5(a). Once drydocking has taken place the Sellers shall deliver the Vessel at a port within the delivery range as per Clause 5(a) which shall, for the purpose of this Clause, become the new port of delivery. In such event the Cancelling Date shall be extended by the additional time required for the drydocking and extra steaming, but limited to a maximum of fourteen (14) days.

**(b)*** The Sellers shall place the Vessel in drydock at the port of delivery for inspection by the Classification Society of the Vessel's underwater parts below the deepest load line, the extent of the inspection being in accordance with the Classification Society's rules. If the rudder, propeller, bottom or other underwater parts below the deepest load line are found broken, damaged or defective so as to affect the Vessel's class, such defects shall be made good at the Sellers' cost and expense to the satisfaction of the Classification Society without condition/recommendation**. In such event the Sellers are also to pay for the costs and expenses in connection with putting the Vessel in and taking her out of drydock, including the drydock dues and the Classification Society's fees. The Sellers shall also pay for these costs and expenses if parts of the tailshaft system are condemned or found defective or broken so as to affect the Vessel's class. In all other cases, the Buyers shall pay the aforesaid costs and expenses, dues and fees.

**(c)** If the Vessel is drydocked pursuant to Clause 6 (a)(ii) or 6 (b) above:

**(i)** The Classification Society may require survey of the tailshaft system, the extent of the survey being to the satisfaction of the Classification surveyor. If such survey is not required by the Classification Society, the Buyers shall have the option to require the tailshaft to be drawn and surveyed by the Classification Society, the extent of the survey being in accordance with the Classification Society's rules for tailshaft survey and consistent with the current stage of the Vessel's survey cycle. The Buyers shall declare whether they require the tailshaft to be drawn and surveyed not later than by the completion of the inspection by the Classification Society. The drawing and refitting of the tailshaft shall be arranged by the Sellers. Should any parts of the tailshaft system be condemned or found defective so as to affect the Vessel's class, those parts shall be renewed or made good at the Sellers' cost and expense to the satisfaction of Classification Society without condition/recommendation**.

**(ii)** The costs and expenses relating to the survey of the tailshaft system shall be borne by the Buyers unless the Classification Society requires such survey to be carried out or if parts of the system are condemned or found defective or broken so as to affect the Vessel's class, in which case the Sellers shall pay these costs and expenses.

**(iii)** The Buyers' representative(s) shall have the right to be present in the drydock, as observer(s) only without interfering with the work or decisions of the Classification Society surveyor.

**(iv)** The Buyers shall have the right to have the underwater parts of the Vessel cleaned and painted at their risk, cost and expense without interfering with the Sellers' or the Classification Society surveyor's work, if any, and without affecting the Vessel's timely delivery. If, however, the Buyers' work in drydock is still in progress when the Sellers have completed the work which the Sellers are required to do, the additional docking time needed to complete the Buyers' work shall be for the Buyers' risk, cost and expense. In the event that the Buyers' work requires such additional time, the Sellers may upon completion of the Sellers' work tender Notice of Readiness for delivery whilst the Vessel is still in drydock and, notwithstanding Clause 5(a), the Buyers shall be obliged to take delivery in accordance with Clause 3 (Payment), whether the Vessel is in drydock or not.

**6 (a) and 6 (b) are alternatives; delete whichever is not applicable. In the absence of deletions, alternative 6 (a) shall apply.*

***Notes or memoranda, if any, in the surveyor's report which are accepted by the Classification Society without condition/recommendation are not to be taken into account.*

**Spares, bunkers and other items**
The Sellers shall deliver the Vessel to the Buyers with everything belonging to her on board and on shore. All spare parts and spare equipment including spare tail-end shaft(s) and/or spare propeller(s)/propeller blade(s), if any, belonging to the Vessel at the time of inspection used or unused, whether on board or not shall become the Buyers' property, but spares on order are excluded. Forwarding charges, if any, shall be for the Buyers' account. The Sellers are not required to replace spare parts including spare tail-end shaft(s) and spare propeller(s)/propeller blade(s) which are taken out of spare and used as replacement prior to delivery, but the replaced items shall be the property of the Buyers. Unused stores and provisions shall be included in the sale and be taken over by the Buyers without extra payment.

Library and forms exclusively for use in the Sellers' vessel(s) and captain's, officers' and crew's personal belongings including the slop chest are excluded from the sale without compensation, as well as the following additional items: *(include list)*

Items on board which are on hire or owned by third parties, listed as follows, are excluded from the sale without compensation: *(include list)*

Items on board at the time of inspection which are on hire or owned by third parties, not listed above, shall be replaced or procured by the Sellers prior to delivery at their cost and expense.

The Buyers shall take over remaining bunkers and unused lubricating and hydraulic oils and greases in storage tanks and unopened drums and pay either:

**(a)** *the actual net price (excluding barging expenses) as evidenced by invoices or vouchers; or

**(b)** *the current net market price (excluding barging expenses) at the port and date of delivery of the Vessel or, if unavailable, at the nearest bunkering port,

for the quantities taken over.

Payment under this Clause shall be made at the same time and place and in the same currency as the Purchase Price.

"inspection" in this Clause 7, shall mean the Buyers' inspection according to Clause 4(a) or 4(b) (Inspection), if applicable. If the Vessel is taken over without inspection, the date of this Agreement shall be the relevant date.

**(a) and (b) are alternatives, delete whichever is not applicable. In the absence of deletions alternative (a) shall apply.*

**Documentation**
The place of closing:

**(a)** In exchange for payment of the Purchase Price the Sellers shall provide the Buyers with the following delivery documents:

**(i)** Legal Bill(s) of Sale in a form recordable in the Buyers' Nominated Flag State, transferring title of the Vessel and stating that the Vessel is free from all mortgages, encumbrances and maritime liens or any other debts whatsoever, duly notarially attested and legalised or apostilled, as required by the Buyers' Nominated Flag State;

**(ii)** Evidence that all necessary corporate, shareholder and other action has been taken by the Sellers to authorise the execution, delivery and performance of this Agreement;

**(iii)** Power of Attorney of the Sellers appointing one or more representatives to act on behalf of the Sellers in the performance of this Agreement, duly notarially attested and legalised or apostilled (as appropriate);

**(iv)** Certificate or Transcript of Registry issued by the competent authorities of the flag state on the date of delivery evidencing the Sellers' ownership of the Vessel and that the Vessel is free from registered encumbrances and mortgages, to be faxed or e-mailed by such authority to the closing meeting with the original to be sent to the Buyers as soon as possible after delivery of the Vessel;

**(v)** Declaration of Class or (depending on the Classification Society) a Class Maintenance Certificate issued within three (3) Banking Days prior to delivery confirming that the Vessel is in Class free of condition/recommendation;

**(vi)** Certificate of Deletion of the Vessel from the Vessel's registry or other official evidence of deletion appropriate to the Vessel's registry at the time of delivery, or, in the event that the registry does not as a matter of practice issue such documentation immediately, a written undertaking by the Sellers to effect deletion from the Vessel's registry forthwith and provide a certificate or other official evidence of deletion to the Buyers promptly and latest within four (4) weeks after the Purchase Price has been paid and the Vessel has been delivered;

**(vii)** A copy of the Vessel's Continuous Synopsis Record certifying the date on which the Vessel ceased to be registered with the Vessel's registry, or, in the event that the registry does not as a matter of practice issue such certificate immediately, a written undertaking from the Sellers to provide the copy of this certificate promptly upon it being issued together with evidence of submission by the Sellers of a duly executed Form 2 stating the date on which the Vessel shall cease to be registered with the Vessel's registry;

(viii) Commercial Invoice for the Vessel;

(ix) Commercial Invoice(s) for bunkers, lubricating and hydraulic oils and greases;

(x) A copy of the Sellers' letter to their satellite communication provider cancelling the Vessel's communications contract which is to be sent immediately after delivery of the Vessel;

(xi) Any additional documents as may reasonably be required by the competent authorities of the Buyers' Nominated Flag State for the purpose of registering the Vessel, provided the Buyers notify the Sellers of any such documents as soon as possible after the date of this Agreement; and

(xii) The Sellers' letter of confirmation that to the best of their knowledge, the Vessel is not black listed by any nation or international organisation.

**(b)** At the time of delivery the Buyers shall provide the Sellers with:

(i) Evidence that all necessary corporate, shareholder and other action has been taken by the Buyers to authorise the execution, delivery and performance of this Agreement; and

(ii) Power of Attorney of the Buyers appointing one or more representatives to act on behalf of the Buyers in the performance of this Agreement, duly notarially attested and legalised or apostilled (as appropriate).

**(c)** If any of the documents listed in Sub-clauses (a) and (b) above are not in the English language they shall be accompanied by an English translation by an authorised translator or certified by a lawyer qualified to practice in the country of the translated language.

**(d)** The Parties shall to the extent possible exchange copies, drafts or samples of the documents listed in Sub-clause (a) and Sub-clause (b) above for review and comment by the other party not later than *(state number of days)*, or if left blank, nine (9) days prior to the Vessel's intended date of readiness for delivery as notified by the Sellers pursuant to Clause 5(b) of this Agreement.

**(e)** Concurrent with the exchange of documents in Sub-clause (a) and Sub-clause (b) above, the Sellers shall also hand to the Buyers the classification certificate(s) as well as all plans, drawings and manuals, (excluding ISM/ISPS manuals), which are on board the Vessel. Other certificates which are on board the Vessel shall also be handed over to the Buyers unless the Sellers are required to retain same, in which case the Buyers have the right to take copies.

**(f)** Other technical documentation which may be in the Sellers' possession shall promptly after delivery be forwarded to the Buyers at their expense, if they so request. The Sellers may keep the Vessel's log books but the Buyers have the right to take copies of same.

**(g)** The Parties shall sign and deliver to each other a Protocol of Delivery and Acceptance confirming the date and time of delivery of the Vessel from the Sellers to the Buyers.

**9. Encumbrances**

The Sellers warrant that the Vessel, at the time of delivery, is free from all charters, encumbrances, mortgages and maritime liens or any other debts whatsoever, and is not subject to Port State or other administrative detentions. The Sellers hereby undertake to indemnify the Buyers against all consequences of claims made against the Vessel which have been incurred prior to the time of delivery.

**10. Taxes, fees and expenses**

Any taxes, fees and expenses in connection with the purchase and registration in the Buyers' Nominated Flag State shall be for the Buyers' account, whereas similar charges in connection with the closing of the Sellers' register shall be for the Sellers' account.

**11. Condition on delivery**

The Vessel with everything belonging to her shall be at the Sellers' risk and expense until she is delivered to the Buyers, but subject to the terms and conditions of this Agreement she shall be delivered and taken over as she was at the time of inspection, fair wear and tear excepted.

However, the Vessel shall be delivered free of cargo and free of stowaways with her Class maintained without condition/recommendation*, free of average damage affecting the Vessel's class, and with her classification certificates and national certificates, as well as all other certificates the Vessel had at the time of inspection, valid and unextended without condition/recommendation* by the Classification Society or the relevant authorities at the time of delivery.

"inspection" in this Clause 11, shall mean the Buyers' inspection according to Clause 4(a) or 4(b) (Inspections), if applicable. If the Vessel is taken over without inspection, the date of this Agreement shall be the relevant date.

**Notes and memoranda, if any, in the surveyor's report which are accepted by the Classification Society without condition/recommendation are not to be taken into account.*

**12. Name/markings**
Upon delivery the Buyers undertake to change the name of the Vessel and alter funnel markings.

**13. Buyers' default**
Should the Deposit not be lodged in accordance with Clause 2 (Deposit), the Sellers have the right to cancel this Agreement, and they shall be entitled to claim compensation for their losses and for all expenses incurred together with interest.

Should the Purchase Price not be paid in accordance with Clause 3 (Payment), the Sellers have the right to cancel this Agreement, in which case the Deposit together with interest earned, if any, shall be released to the Sellers. If the Deposit does not cover their loss, the Sellers shall be entitled to claim further compensation for their losses and for all expenses incurred together with interest.

**14. Sellers' default**
Should the Sellers fail to give Notice of Readiness in accordance with Clause 5(b) or fail to be ready to validly complete a legal transfer by the Cancelling Date the Buyers shall have the option of cancelling this Agreement. If after Notice of Readiness has been given but before the Buyers have taken delivery, the Vessel ceases to be physically ready for delivery and is not made physically ready again by the Cancelling Date and new Notice of Readiness given, the Buyers shall retain their option to cancel. In the event that the Buyers elect to cancel this Agreement, the Deposit together with interest earned, if any, shall be released to them immediately.

Should the Sellers fail to give Notice of Readiness by the Cancelling Date or fail to be ready to validly complete a legal transfer as aforesaid they shall make due compensation to the Buyers for their loss and for all expenses together with interest if their failure is due to proven negligence and whether or not the Buyers cancel this Agreement.

**15. Buyers' representatives**
After this Agreement has been signed by the Parties and the Deposit has been lodged, the Buyers have the right to place two (2) representatives on board the Vessel at their sole risk and expense.

These representatives are on board for the purpose of familiarisation and in the capacity of observers only, and they shall not interfere in any respect with the operation of the Vessel. The Buyers and the Buyers' representatives shall sign the Sellers' P&I Club's standard letter of indemnity prior to their embarkation.

**16. Law and Arbitration**
**(a)** *This Agreement shall be governed by and construed in accordance with English law and any dispute arising out of or in connection with this Agreement shall be referred to arbitration in London in accordance with the Arbitration Act 1996 or any statutory modification or re-enactment thereof save to the extent necessary to give effect to the provisions of this Clause.

The arbitration shall be conducted in accordance with the London Maritime Arbitrators Association (LMAA) Terms current at the time when the arbitration proceedings are commenced.

The reference shall be to three arbitrators. A party wishing to refer a dispute to arbitration shall appoint its arbitrator and send notice of such appointment in writing to the other party requiring the other party to appoint its own arbitrator within fourteen (14) calendar days of that notice and stating that it will appoint its arbitrator as sole arbitrator unless the other party appoints its own arbitrator and gives notice that it has done so within the fourteen (14) days specified. If the other party does not appoint its own arbitrator and give notice that it has done so within the fourteen (14) days specified, the party referring a dispute to arbitration may, without the requirement of any further prior notice to the other party, appoint its arbitrator as sole arbitrator and shall advise the other party accordingly. The award of a sole arbitrator shall be binding on both Parties as if the sole arbitrator had been appointed by agreement.

In cases where neither the claim nor any counterclaim exceeds the sum of US$100,000 the arbitration shall be conducted in accordance with the LMAA Small Claims Procedure current at the time when the arbitration proceedings are commenced.

**(b)** *This Agreement shall be governed by and construed in accordance with Title 9 of the United States Code and the substantive law (not including the choice of law rules) of the State of New York and any dispute arising out of or in connection with this Agreement shall be referred to three (3) persons at New York, one to be appointed by each of the parties hereto, and the third by the two so chosen; their decision or that of any two of them shall be final, and for the purposes of enforcing any award, judgment may be entered on an award by any court of competent jurisdiction. The proceedings shall be conducted in accordance with the rules of the Society of Maritime Arbitrators, Inc.

In cases where neither the claim nor any counterclaim exceeds the sum of US$ 100,000 the arbitration shall be conducted in accordance with the Shortened Arbitration Procedure of the Society of Maritime Arbitrators, Inc.

**(c)** This Agreement shall be governed by and construed in accordance with the laws of *(state place)* and any dispute arising out of or in connection with this Agreement shall be referred to arbitration at *(state place)*, subject to the procedures applicable there.

**16(a), 16(b) and 16(c) are alternatives; delete whichever is not applicable. In the absence of deletions, alternative 16(a) shall apply.*

**17. Notices**
All notices to be provided under this Agreement shall be in writing.

Contact details for recipients of notices are as follows:

For the Buyers:

For the Sellers:

**18. Entire Agreement**
The written terms of this Agreement comprise the entire agreement between the Buyers and the Sellers in relation to the sale and purchase of the Vessel and supersede all previous agreements whether oral or written between the Parties in relation thereto.

Each of the Parties acknowledges that in entering into this Agreement it has not relied on and shall have no right or remedy in respect of any statement, representation, assurance or warranty (whether or not made negligently) other than as is expressly set out in this Agreement.

Any terms implied into this Agreement by any applicable statue or law are hereby excluded to the extent that such exclusion can legally be made. Nothing in this Clause shall limit or exclude any liability for fraud.

| For and on behalf of the Sellers | For and on behalf of the Buyers |
|---|---|
| ______________________ | ______________________ |
| Name: | Name: |
| Title: | Title: |

# APPENDIX 9

# SHIPMAN 2009

Explanatory Notes for SHIPMAN 2009 are available from BIMCO at www.bimco.org



BIMCO

## SHIPMAN 2009

STANDARD SHIP MANAGEMENT AGREEMENT

PART I

| | |
|---|---|
| 1. Place and date of Agreement | 2. Date of commencement of Agreement (Cls. 2, 12, 21 and 25) |
| 3. Owners (name, place of registered office and law of registry) (Cl. 1)<br>(i) Name:<br>(ii) Place of registered office:<br>(iii) Law of registry: | 4. Managers (name, place of registered office and law of registry) (Cl. 1)<br>(i) Name:<br>(ii) Place of registered office:<br>(iii) Law of registry: |
| 5. The Company (with reference to the ISM/ISPS Codes) (state name and IMO Unique Company Identification number. If the Company is a third party then also state registered office and principal place of business) (Cls. 1 and 9(c)(i))<br>(i) Name:<br>(ii) IMO Unique Company Identification number:<br>(iii) Place of registered office:<br>(iv) Principal place of business: | 6. Technical Management (state "yes" or "no" as agreed) (Cl. 4)<br>7. Crew Management (state "yes" or "no" as agreed) (Cl. 5(a))<br>8. Commercial Management (state "yes" or "no" as agreed) (Cl. 6) |
| 9. Chartering Services period (only to be filled in if "yes" stated in Box 8) (Cl 6(a)) | 10. Crew Insurance arrangements (state "yes" or "no" as agreed)<br>(i) Crew Insurances* (Cl. 5(b)):<br>(ii) Insurance for persons proceeding to sea onboard (Cl. 5(b)(i)):<br>*only to apply if Crew Management (Cl. 5(a)) agreed (see Box 7)* |
| 11. Insurance arrangements (state "yes" or "no" as agreed) (Cl. 7) | 12. Optional insurances (state optional insurance(s) as agreed, such as piracy, kidnap and ransom, loss of hire and FD & D) (Cl. 10(a)(iv)) |
| 13. Interest (state rate of interest to apply after due date to outstanding sums) (Cl. 9(a)) | 14. Annual management fee (state annual amount) (Cl. 12(a)) |
| 15. Manager's nominated account (Cl.12(a)) | 16. Daily rate (state rate for days in excess of those agreed in budget) (Cl. 12(c))<br>17. Lay-up period / number of months (Cl.12(d)) |
| 18. Minimum contract period (state number of months) (Cl. 21(a)) | 19. Management fee on termination (state number of months to apply) (Cl. 22(g)) |
| 20. Severance Costs (state maximum amount) (Cl. 22(h)(ii)) | 21. Dispute Resolution (state alternative Cl. 23(a), 23(b) or 23(c); if Cl. 23(c) place of arbitration must be stated) (Cl. 23) |

**SHIPMAN 2009**
**Standard ship management agreement** **PART I**

(continued)

| | |
|---|---|
| 22. Notices (state full style contact details for serving notice and communication to the Owners) (Cl. 24) | 23. Notices (state full style contact details for serving notice and communication to the Managers) (Cl. 24) |

It is mutually agreed between the party stated in Box 3 and the party stated in Box 4 that this Agreement consisting of PART I and PART II as well as Annexes "A" (Details of Vessel or Vessels), "B" (Details of Crew), "C" (Budget), "D" (Associated Vessels) and "E" (Fee Schedule) attached hereto, shall be performed subject to the conditions contained herein. In the event of a conflict of conditions, the provisions of PART I and Annexes "A", "B", "C", "D" and "E" shall prevail over those of PART II to the extent of such conflict but no further.

| | |
|---|---|
| Signature(s) (Owners) | Signature(s) (Managers) |

## PART II
## SHIPMAN 2009
### Standard ship management agreement

**SECTION 1 – Basis of the Agreement**

1. **Definitions**
In this Agreement save where the context otherwise requires, the following words and expressions shall have the meanings hereby assigned to them:

"Company" (with reference to the ISM Code and the ISPS Code) means the organization identified in **Box 5** or any replacement organization appointed by the Owners from time to time (see Sub-clauses 9(b)(i) or 9(c)(ii), whichever is applicable).

"Crew" means the personnel of the numbers, rank and nationality specified in Annex "B" hereto.

"Crew Insurances" means insurance of liabilities in respect of crew risks which shall include but not be limited to death, permanent disability, sickness, injury, repatriation, shipwreck unemployment indemnity and loss of personal effects (see Sub-clause 5(b) (Crew Insurances) and Clause 7 (Insurance Arrangements) and Clause 10 (Insurance Policies) and **Boxes 10** and **11**).

"Crew Support Costs" means all expenses of a general nature which are not particularly referable to any individual vessel for the time being managed by the Managers and which are incurred by the Managers for the purpose of providing an efficient and economic management service and, without prejudice to the generality of the foregoing, shall include the cost of crew standby pay, training schemes for officers and ratings, cadet training schemes, sick pay, study pay, recruitment and interviews.

"Flag State" means the State whose flag the Vessel is flying.

"ISM Code" means the International Management Code for the Safe Operation of Ships and for Pollution Prevention and any amendment thereto or substitution therefor.

"ISPS Code" means the International Code for the Security of Ships and Port Facilities and the relevant amendments to Chapter XI of SOLAS and any amendment thereto or substitution therefor.

"Managers" means the party identified in **Box 4**.

"Management Services" means the services specified in SECTION 2 - Services (Clauses 4 through 7) as indicated affirmatively in **Boxes 6** through **8, 10 and 11,** and all other functions performed by the Managers under the terms of this Agreement.

"Owners" means the party identified in **Box 3**.

"Severance Costs" means the costs which are legally required to be paid to the Crew as a result of the early termination of any contracts for service on the Vessel.

"SMS" means the Safety Management System (as defined by the ISM Code).

"STCW 95" means the International Convention on Standards of Training, Certification and Watchkeeping for Seafarers, 1978, as amended in 1995 and any amendment thereto or substitution therefor.

"Vessel" means the vessel or vessels details of which are set out in Annex "A" attached hereto.

2. **Commencement and Appointment**
With effect from the date stated in **Box 2** for the commencement of the Management Services and continuing unless and until terminated as provided herein, the Owners hereby appoint the Managers and the Managers hereby agree to act as the Managers of the Vessel in respect of the Management Services.

3. **Authority of the Managers**
Subject to the terms and conditions herein provided, during the period of this Agreement the Managers shall carry out the Management Services in respect of the Vessel as agents for and on behalf of the Owners. The Managers shall have authority to take such actions as they may from time to time in their absolute discretion consider to be necessary to enable them to perform the Management Services in accordance with sound ship management practice, including but not limited to compliance with all relevant rules and regulations.

**PART II**
**SHIPMAN 2009**
**Standard ship management agreement**

**SECTION 2 – Services**

4. **Technical Management**
*(only applicable if agreed according to* ***Box 6****).*
The Managers shall provide technical management which includes, but is not limited to, the following services:

**(a)** ensuring that the Vessel complies with the requirements of the law of the Flag State;

**(b)** ensuring compliance with the ISM Code;

**(c)** ensuring compliance with the ISPS Code;

**(d)** providing competent personnel to supervise the maintenance and general efficiency of the Vessel;

**(e)** arranging and supervising dry dockings, repairs, alterations and the maintenance of the Vessel to the standards agreed with the Owners provided that the Managers shall be entitled to incur the necessary expenditure to ensure that the Vessel will comply with all requirements and recommendations of the classification society, and with the law of the Flag State and of the places where the Vessel is required to trade;

**(f)** arranging the supply of necessary stores, spares and lubricating oil;

**(g)** appointing surveyors and technical consultants as the Managers may consider from time to time to be necessary;

**(h)** in accordance with the Owners' instructions, supervising the sale and physical delivery of the Vessel under the sale agreement. However services under this Sub-clause 4(h) shall not include negotiation of the sale agreement or transfer of ownership of the Vessel;

**(i)** arranging for the supply of provisions unless provided by the Owners; and

**(j)** arranging for the sampling and testing of bunkers.

5. **Crew Management and Crew Insurances**
**(a)** *Crew Management*
*(only applicable if agreed according to* ***Box 7****)*
The Managers shall provide suitably qualified Crew who shall comply with the requirements of STCW 95. The provision of such crew management services includes, but is not limited to, the following services:

(i) selecting, engaging and providing for the administration of the Crew, including, as applicable, payroll arrangements, pension arrangements, tax, social security contributions and other mandatory dues related to their employment payable in each Crew member's country of domicile;

(ii) ensuring that the applicable requirements of the law of the Flag State in respect of rank, qualification and certification of the Crew and employment regulations, such as Crew's tax and social insurance, are satisfied;

(iii) ensuring that all Crew have passed a medical examination with a qualified doctor certifying that they are fit for the duties for which they are engaged and are in possession of valid medical certificates issued in accordance with appropriate Flag State requirements or such higher standard of medical examination as may be agreed with the Owners. In the absence of applicable Flag State requirements the medical certificate shall be valid at the time when the respective Crew member arrives on board the Vessel and shall be maintained for the duration of the service on board the Vessel;

(iv) ensuring that the Crew shall have a common working language and a command of the English language of a sufficient standard to enable them to perform their duties safely;

(v) arranging transportation of the Crew, including repatriation;

(vi) training of the Crew;

PART II
SHIPMAN 2009
**Standard ship management agreement**

(vii) conducting union negotiations; and

(viii) if the Managers are the Company, ensuring that the Crew, on joining the Vessel, are given proper familiarisation with their duties in relation to the Vessel's SMS and that instructions which are essential to the SMS are identified, documented and given to the Crew prior to sailing.

(ix) if the Managers are **not** the Company:

(1) ensuring that the Crew, before joining the Vessel, are given proper familiarisation with their duties in relation to the ISM Code; and

(2) instructing the Crew to obey all reasonable orders of the Company in connection with the operation of the SMS.

(x) Where Managers are **not** providing technical management services in accordance with Clause 4 (Technical Management):

(1) ensuring that no person connected to the provision and the performance of the crew management services shall proceed to sea on board the Vessel without the prior consent of the Owners (such consent not to be unreasonably withheld); and

(2) ensuring that in the event that the Owners' drug and alcohol policy requires measures to be taken prior to the Crew joining the Vessel, implementing such measures;

**(b)** Crew Insurances
*(only applicable if Sub-clause 5(a) applies* ***and*** *if agreed according to* ***Box 10****)*
The Managers shall throughout the period of this Agreement provide the following services:

(i) arranging Crew Insurances in accordance with the best practice of prudent managers of vessels of a similar type to the Vessel, with sound and reputable insurance companies, underwriters or associations. Insurances for any other persons proceeding to sea onboard the Vessel may be separately agreed by the Owners and the Managers (see **Box 10**);

(ii) ensuring that the Owners are aware of the terms, conditions, exceptions and limits of liability of the insurances in Sub-clause 5(b)(i);

(iii) ensuring that all premiums or calls in respect of the insurances in Sub-clause 5(b)(i) are paid by their due date;

(iv) if obtainable at no additional cost, ensuring that insurances in Sub-clause 5(b)(i) name the Owners as a joint assured with full cover and, unless otherwise agreed, on terms such that Owners shall be under no liability in respect of premiums or calls arising in connection with such insurances.

(v) providing written evidence, to the reasonable satisfaction of the Owners, of the Managers' compliance with their obligations under Sub-clauses 5(b)(ii), and 5(b)(iii) within a reasonable time of the commencement of this Agreement, and of each renewal date and, if specifically requested, of each payment date of the insurances in Sub-clause 5(b)(i).

**6. Commercial Management**
*(only applicable if agreed according to* ***Box 8****)*.
The Managers shall provide the following services for the Vessel in accordance with the Owners' instructions, which shall include but not be limited to:

**(a)** seeking and negotiating employment for the Vessel and the conclusion (including the execution thereof) of charter parties or other contracts relating to the employment of the Vessel. If such a contract exceeds the period stated in **Box 9**, consent thereto in writing shall first be obtained from the Owners;

**(b)** arranging for the provision of bunker fuels of the quality specified by the Owners as required for the Vessel's trade;

**PART II**
**SHIPMAN 2009**
**Standard ship management agreement**

**(c)** voyage estimating and accounting and calculation of hire, freights, demurrage and/or despatch monies due from or due to the charterers of the Vessel; assisting in the collection of any sums due to the Owners related to the commercial operation of the Vessel in accordance with Clause 11 (Income Collected and Expenses Paid on Behalf of Owners);

*If any of the services under Sub-clauses 6(a), 6(b) and 6(c) are to be excluded from the Management Fee, remuneration for these services must be stated in Annex E (Fee Schedule). See Sub-clause 12(e).*

**(d)** issuing voyage instructions;

**(e)** appointing agents;

**(f)** appointing stevedores; and

**(g)** arranging surveys associated with the commercial operation of the Vessel.

**7. Insurance Arrangements**
*(only applicable if agreed according to **Box 11**).*
The Managers shall arrange insurances in accordance with Clause 10 (Insurance Policies), on such terms as the Owners shall have instructed or agreed, in particular regarding conditions, insured values, deductibles, franchises and limits of liability.

## PART II
## SHIPMAN 2009
### Standard ship management agreement

**SECTION 3 – Obligations**

8. **Managers' Obligations**
**(a)** The Managers undertake to use their best endeavours to provide the Management Services as agents for and on behalf of the Owners in accordance with sound ship management practice and to protect and promote the interests of the Owners in all matters relating to the provision of services hereunder.

Provided however, that in the performance of their management responsibilities under this Agreement, the Managers shall be entitled to have regard to their overall responsibility in relation to all vessels as may from time to time be entrusted to their management and in particular, but without prejudice to the generality of the foregoing, the Managers shall be entitled to allocate available supplies, manpower and services in such manner as in the prevailing circumstances the Managers in their absolute discretion consider to be fair and reasonable.

**(b)** Where the Managers are providing technical management services in accordance with Clause 4 (Technical Management), they shall procure that the requirements of the Flag State are satisfied and they shall agree to be appointed as the Company, assuming the responsibility for the operation of the Vessel and taking over the duties and responsibilities imposed by the ISM Code and the ISPS Code, if applicable.

9. **Owners' Obligations**
**(a)** The Owners shall pay all sums due to the Managers punctually in accordance with the terms of this Agreement. In the event of payment after the due date of any outstanding sums the Manager shall be entitled to charge interest at the rate stated in **Box 13**.

**(b)** Where the Managers are providing technical management services in accordance with Clause 4 (Technical Management), the Owners shall:

(i) report (or where the Owners are not the registered owners of the Vessel procure that the registered owners report) to the Flag State administration the details of the Managers as the Company as required to comply with the ISM and ISPS Codes;

(ii) procure that any officers and ratings supplied by them or on their behalf comply with the requirements of STCW 95; and

(iii) instruct such officers and ratings to obey all reasonable orders of the Managers (in their capacity as the Company) in connection with the operation of the Managers' safety management system.

**(c)** Where the Managers are **not** providing technical management services in accordance with Clause 4 (Technical Management), the Owners shall:

(i) procure that the requirements of the Flag State are satisfied and notify the Managers upon execution of this Agreement of the name and contact details of the organization that will be the Company by completing **Box 5**;

(ii) if the Company changes at any time during this Agreement, notify the Managers in a timely manner of the name and contact details of the new organization;

(iii) procure that the details of the Company, including any change thereof, are reported to the Flag State administration as required to comply with the ISM and ISPS Codes. The Owners shall advise the Managers in a timely manner when the Flag State administration has approved the Company; and

(iv) unless otherwise agreed, arrange for the supply of provisions at their own expense.

**(d)** Where the Managers are providing crew management services in accordance with Sub-clause 5(a) the Owners shall:

(i) inform the Managers prior to ordering the Vessel to any excluded or additional premium area under any of the Owners' Insurances by reason of war risks and/or piracy or like perils and pay whatever additional costs may properly be incurred by the Managers as a consequence of such orders including, if necessary, the costs of replacing any member of the Crew. Any delays resulting from negotiation with or replacement of any member of the Crew as a result of the Vessel being ordered to such an area

PART II
SHIPMAN 2009
**Standard ship management agreement**

shall be for the Owners' account. Should the Vessel be within an area which becomes an excluded or additional premium area the above provisions relating to cost and delay shall apply;

(ii) agree with the Managers prior to any change of flag of the Vessel and pay whatever additional costs may properly be incurred by the Managers as a consequence of such change. If agreement cannot be reached then either party may terminate this Agreement in accordance with Sub-clause 22(e); and

(iii) provide, at no cost to the Managers, in accordance with the requirements of the law of the Flag State, or higher standard, as mutually agreed, adequate Crew accommodation and living standards.

**(e)** Where the Managers are **not** the Company, the Owners shall ensure that Crew are properly familiarised with their duties in accordance with the Vessel's SMS and that instructions which are essential to the SMS are identified, documented and given to the Crew prior to sailing.

PART II
SHIPMAN 2009
Standard ship management agreement

**SECTION 4 – Insurance, Budgets, Income, Expenses and Fees**

**10. Insurance Policies**

The Owners shall procure, whether by instructing the Managers under Clause 7 (Insurance Arrangements) or otherwise, that throughout the period of this Agreement:

**(a)** at the Owners' expense, the Vessel is insured for not less than its sound market value or entered for its full gross tonnage, as the case may be for:

(i) hull and machinery marine risks (including but not limited to crew negligence) and excess liabilities;

(ii) protection and indemnity risks (including but not limited to pollution risks, diversion expenses and, except to the extent insured separately by the Managers in accordance with Sub-clause 5(b)(i), Crew Insurances;

*NOTE: If the Managers are not providing crew management services under Sub-clause 5(a) (Crew Management) or have agreed not to provide Crew Insurances separately in accordance with Sub-clause 5(b)(i), then such insurances must be included in the protection and indemnity risks cover for the Vessel (see Sub-clause 10(a)(ii) above).*

(iii) war risks (including but not limited to blocking and trapping, protection and indemnity, terrorism and crew risks); and

(iv) such optional insurances as may be agreed (such as piracy, kidnap and ransom, loss of hire and FD & D) (see **Box 12**)

Sub-clauses 10(a)(i) through 10(a)(iv) all in accordance with the best practice of prudent owners of vessels of a similar type to the Vessel, with sound and reputable insurance companies, underwriters or associations ("the Owners' Insurances");

**(b)** all premiums and calls on the Owners' Insurances are paid by their due date;

**(c)** the Owners' Insurances name the Managers and, subject to underwriters' agreement, any third party designated by the Managers as a joint assured, with full cover. It is understood that in some cases, such as protection and indemnity, the normal terms for such cover may impose on the Managers and any such third party a liability in respect of premiums or calls arising in connection with the Owners' Insurances.

If obtainable at no additional cost, however, the Owners shall procure such insurances on terms such that neither the Managers nor any such third party shall be under any liability in respect of premiums or calls arising in connection with the Owners' Insurances. In any event, on termination of this Agreement in accordance with Clause 21 (Duration of the Agreement) and Clause 22 (Termination), the Owners shall procure that the Managers and any third party designated by the Managers as joint assured shall cease to be joint assured and, if reasonably achievable, that they shall be released from any and all liability for premiums and calls that may arise in relation to the period of this Agreement; and

**(d)** written evidence is provided, to the reasonable satisfaction of the Managers, of the Owners' compliance with their obligations under this Clause 10 within a reasonable time of the commencement of the Agreement, and of each renewal date and, if specifically requested, of each payment date of the Owners' Insurances.

**11. Income Collected and Expenses Paid on Behalf of Owners**

**(a)** Except as provided in Sub-clause 11(c) all monies collected by the Managers under the terms of this Agreement (other than monies payable by the Owners to the Managers) and any interest thereon shall be held to the credit of the Owners in a separate bank account.

**(b)** All expenses incurred by the Managers under the terms of this Agreement on behalf of the Owners (including expenses as provided in Clause 12(c)) may be debited against the Owners in the account referred to under Sub-clause 11(a) but shall in any event remain payable by the Owners to the Managers on demand.

**(c)** All monies collected by the Managers under Clause 6 (Commercial Management) shall be paid into a bank account in the name of the Owners or as may be otherwise advised by the Owners in writing.

## PART II
## SHIPMAN 2009
### Standard ship management agreement

**12. Management Fee and Expenses**

(a) The Owners shall pay to the Managers an annual management fee as stated in **Box 14** for their services as Managers under this Agreement, which shall be payable in equal monthly instalments in advance, the first instalment (pro rata if appropriate) being payable on the commencement of this Agreement (see Clause 2 (Commencement and Appointment) and **Box 2**) and subsequent instalments being payable at the beginning of every calendar month. The management fee shall be payable to the Managers' nominated account stated in **Box 15**.

**(b)** The management fee shall be subject to an annual review and the proposed fee shall be presented in the annual budget in accordance with Sub-clause 13(a).

**(c)** The Managers shall, at no extra cost to the Owners, provide their own office accommodation, office staff, facilities and stationery. Without limiting the generality of this Clause 12 (Management Fee and Expenses) the Owners shall reimburse the Managers for postage and communication expenses, travelling expenses, and other out of pocket expenses properly incurred by the Managers in pursuance of the Management Services. Any days used by the Managers' personnel travelling to or from or attending on the Vessel or otherwise used in connection with the Management Services in excess of those agreed in the budget shall be charged at the daily rate stated in **Box 16**.

**(d)** If the Owners decide to layup the Vessel and such layup lasts for more than the number of months stated in **Box 17**, an appropriate reduction of the Management Fee for the period exceeding such period until one month before the Vessel is again put into service shall be mutually agreed between the parties. If the Managers are providing crew management services in accordance with Sub-clause 5(a), consequential costs of reduction and reinstatement of the Crew shall be for the Owners' account. If agreement cannot be reached then either party may terminate this Agreement in accordance with Sub-clause 22(e).

**(e)** Save as otherwise provided in this Agreement, all discounts and commissions obtained by the Managers in the course of the performance of the Management Services shall be credited to the Owners.

**13. Budgets and Management of Funds**

**(a)** The Managers' initial budget is set out in Annex "C" hereto. Subsequent budgets shall be for twelve month periods and shall be prepared by the Managers and presented to the Owners not less than three months before the end of the budget year.

**(b)** The Owners shall state to the Managers in a timely manner, but in any event within one month of presentation, whether or not they agree to each proposed annual budget. The parties shall negotiate in good faith and if they fail to agree on the annual budget, including the management fee, either party may terminate this Agreement in accordance with Sub-clause 22(e).

**(c)** Following the agreement of the budget, the Managers shall prepare and present to the Owners their estimate of the working capital requirement for the Vessel and shall each month request the Owners in writing to pay the funds required to run the Vessel for the ensuing month, including the payment of any occasional or extraordinary item of expenditure, such as emergency repair costs, additional insurance premiums, bunkers or provisions. Such funds shall be received by the Managers within ten running days after the receipt by the Owners of the Managers' written request and shall be held to the credit of the Owners in a separate bank account.

**(d)** The Managers shall at all times maintain and keep true and correct accounts in respect of the Management Services in accordance with the relevant International Financial Reporting Standards or such other standard as the parties may agree, including records of all costs and expenditure incurred, and produce a comparison between budgeted and actual income and expenditure of the Vessel in such form and at such intervals as shall be mutually agreed.

The Managers shall make such accounts available for inspection and auditing by the Owners and/or their representatives in the Managers' offices or by electronic means, provided reasonable notice is given by the Owners.

**(e)** Notwithstanding anything contained herein, the Managers shall in no circumstances be required to use or commit their own funds to finance the provision of the Management Services.

## PART II
## SHIPMAN 2009
### Standard ship management agreement

**SECTION 5 – Legal, General and Duration of Agreement**

**14. Trading Restrictions**
If the Managers are providing crew management services in accordance with Sub-clause 5(a) (Crew Management), the Owners and the Managers will, prior to the commencement of this Agreement, agree on any trading restrictions to the Vessel that may result from the terms and conditions of the Crew's employment.

**15. Replacement**
If the Managers are providing crew management services in accordance with Sub-clause 5(a) (Crew Management), the Owners may require the replacement, at their own expense, at the next reasonable opportunity, of any member of the Crew found on reasonable grounds to be unsuitable for service. If the Managers have failed to fulfil their obligations in providing suitable qualified Crew within the meaning of Sub-clause 5(a) (Crew Management), then such replacement shall be at the Managers' expense.

**16. Managers' Right to Sub-Contract**
The Managers shall not subcontract any of their obligations hereunder without the prior written consent of the Owners which shall not be unreasonably withheld. In the event of such a sub-contract the Managers shall remain fully liable for the due performance of their obligations under this Agreement.

**17. Responsibilities**
**(a)** *Force Majeure* - Neither party shall be liable for any loss, damage or delay due to any of the following force majeure events and/or conditions to the extent that the party invoking force majeure is prevented or hindered from performing any or all of their obligations under this Agreement, provided they have made all reasonable efforts to avoid, minimise or prevent the effect of such events and/or conditions:

(i) acts of God;

(ii) any Government requisition, control, intervention, requirement or interference;

(iii) any circumstances arising out of war, threatened act of war or warlike operations, acts of terrorism, sabotage or piracy, or the consequences thereof;

(iv) riots, civil commotion, blockades or embargoes;

(v) epidemics;

(vi) earthquakes, landslides, floods or other extraordinary weather conditions;

(vii) strikes, lockouts or other industrial action, unless limited to the employees (which shall not include the Crew) of the party seeking to invoke force majeure;

(viii) fire, accident, explosion except where caused by negligence of the party seeking to invoke force majeure; and

(ix) any other similar cause beyond the reasonable control of either party.

**(b)** *Liability to Owners*
(i) Without prejudice to Sub-clause 17(a), the Managers shall be under no liability whatsoever to the Owners for any loss, damage, delay or expense of whatsoever nature, whether direct or indirect, (including but not limited to loss of profit arising out of or in connection with detention of or delay to the Vessel) and howsoever arising in the course of performance of the Management Services **UNLESS** same is proved to have resulted solely from the negligence, gross negligence or wilful default of the Managers or their employees or agents, or sub-contractors employed by them in connection with the Vessel, in which case (save where loss, damage, delay or expense has resulted from the Managers' personal act or omission committed with the intent to cause same or recklessly and with knowledge that such loss, damage, delay or expense would probably result) the Managers' liability for each incident or series of incidents giving rise to a claim or claims shall never exceed a total of ten (10) times the annual management fee payable hereunder.

(ii) *Acts or omissions of the Crew* - Notwithstanding anything that may appear to the contrary in this Agreement, the Managers shall not be liable for any acts or omissions of the Crew, even if such acts

**PART II**
**SHIPMAN 2009**
**Standard ship management agreement**

or omissions are negligent, grossly negligent or wilful, except only to the extent that they are shown to have resulted from a failure by the Managers to discharge their obligations under Clause 5(a) (Crew Management), in which case their liability shall be limited in accordance with the terms of this Clause 17 (Responsibilities).

**(c)** *Indemnity* - Except to the extent and solely for the amount therein set out that the Managers would be liable under Sub-clause 17(b), the Owners hereby undertake to keep the Managers and their employees, agents and sub-contractors indemnified and to hold them harmless against all actions, proceedings, claims, demands or liabilities whatsoever or howsoever arising which may be brought against them or incurred or suffered by them arising out of or in connection with the performance of this Agreement, and against and in respect of all costs, loss, damages and expenses (including legal costs and expenses on a full indemnity basis) which the Managers may suffer or incur (either directly or indirectly) in the course of the performance of this Agreement.

**(d)** *"Himalaya"* - It is hereby expressly agreed that no employee or agent of the Managers (including every sub-contractor from time to time employed by the Managers) shall in any circumstances whatsoever be under any liability whatsoever to the Owners for any loss, damage or delay of whatsoever kind arising or resulting directly or indirectly from any act, neglect or default on his part while acting in the course of or in connection with his employment and, without prejudice to the generality of the foregoing provisions in this Clause 17 (Responsibilities), every exemption, limitation, condition and liberty herein contained and every right, exemption from liability, defence and immunity of whatsoever nature applicable to the Managers or to which the Managers are entitled hereunder shall also be available and shall extend to protect every such employee or agent of the Managers acting as aforesaid and for the purpose of all the foregoing provisions of this Clause 17 (Responsibilities) the Managers are or shall be deemed to be acting as agent or trustee on behalf of and for the benefit of all persons who are or might be their servants or agents from time to time (including sub-contractors as aforesaid) and all such persons shall to this extent be or be deemed to be parties to this Agreement.

**18. General Administration**

**(a)** The Managers shall keep the Owners and, if appropriate, the Company informed in a timely manner of any incident of which the Managers become aware which gives or may give rise to delay to the Vessel or claims or disputes involving third parties.

**(b)** The Managers shall handle and settle all claims and disputes arising out of the Management Services hereunder, unless the Owners instruct the Managers otherwise. The Managers shall keep the Owners appropriately informed in a timely manner throughout the handling of such claims and disputes.

**(c)** The Owners may request the Managers to bring or defend other actions, suits or proceedings related to the Management Services, on terms to be agreed.

**(d)** The Managers shall have power to obtain appropriate legal or technical or other outside expert advice in relation to the handling and settlement of claims in relation to Sub-clauses 18(a) and 18(b) and disputes and any other matters affecting the interests of the Owners in respect of the Vessel, unless the Owners instruct the Managers otherwise.

**(e)** On giving reasonable notice, the Owners may request, and the Managers shall in a timely manner make available, all documentation, information and records in respect of the matters covered by this Agreement either related to mandatory rules or regulations or other obligations applying to the Owners in respect of the Vessel (including but not limited to STCW 95, the ISM Code and ISPS Code) to the extent permitted by relevant legislation.

On giving reasonable notice, the Managers may request, and the Owners shall in a timely manner make available, all documentation, information and records reasonably required by the Managers to enable them to perform the Management Services.

**(f)** The Owners shall arrange for the provision of any necessary guarantee bond or other security.

**(g)** Any costs incurred by the Managers in carrying out their obligations according to this Clause 18 (General Administration) shall be reimbursed by the Owners.

PART II
SHIPMAN 2009
Standard ship management agreement

**19. Inspection of Vessel**
The Owners may at any time after giving reasonable notice to the Managers inspect the Vessel for any reason they consider necessary.

**20. Compliance with Laws and Regulations**
The parties will not do or permit to be done anything which might cause any breach or infringement of the laws and regulations of the Flag State, or of the places where the Vessel trades.

**21. Duration of the Agreement**
**(a)** This Agreement shall come into effect at the date stated in **Box 2** and shall continue until terminated by either party by giving notice to the other; in which event this Agreement shall terminate upon the expiration of the later of the number of months stated in **Box 18** or a period of two (2) months from the date on which such notice is received, unless terminated earlier in accordance with Clause 22 (Termination).

**(b)** Where the Vessel is not at a mutually convenient port or place on the expiry of such period, this Agreement shall terminate on the subsequent arrival of the Vessel at the next mutually convenient port or place.

**22. Termination**
**(a)** *Owners' or Managers' default.*
If either party fails to meet their obligations under this Agreement, the other party may give notice to the party in default requiring them to remedy it. In the event that the party in default fails to remedy it within a reasonable time to the reasonable satisfaction of the other party, that party shall be entitled to terminate this Agreement with immediate effect by giving notice to the party in default.

**(b)** Notwithstanding Sub-clause 22(a):

(i) The Managers shall be entitled to terminate the Agreement with immediate effect by giving notice to the Owners if any monies payable by the Owners and/or the owners of any associated vessel, details of which are listed in Annex "D", shall not have been received in the Managers' nominated account within ten days of receipt by the Owners of the Managers' written request, or if the Vessel is repossessed by the Mortgagee(s).

(ii) If the Owners proceed with the employment of or continue to employ the Vessel in the carriage of contraband, blockade running, or in an unlawful trade, or on a voyage which in the reasonable opinion of the Managers is unduly hazardous or improper, the Managers may give notice of the default to the Owners, requiring them to remedy it as soon as practically possible. In the event that the Owners fail to remedy it within a reasonable time to the satisfaction of the Managers, the Managers shall be entitled to terminate the Agreement with immediate effect by notice.

(iii) If either party fails to meet their respective obligations under Sub-clause 5(b) (Crew Insurances) and Clause 10 (Insurance Policies), the other party may give notice to the party in default requiring them to remedy it within ten (10) days, failing which the other party may terminate this Agreement with immediate effect by giving notice to the party in default.

**(c)** *Extraordinary Termination*
This Agreement shall be deemed to be terminated in the case of the sale of the Vessel or, if the Vessel becomes a total loss or is declared as a constructive or compromised or arranged total loss or is requisitioned or has been declared missing or, if bareboat chartered, unless otherwise agreed, when the bareboat charter comes to an end.

**(d)** For the purpose of Sub-clause 22(c) hereof:

(i) the date upon which the Vessel is to be treated as having been sold or otherwise disposed of shall be the date on which the Vessel's owners cease to be the registered owners of the Vessel;

(ii) the Vessel shall be deemed to be lost either when it has become an actual total loss or agreement has been reached with the Vessel's underwriters in respect of its constructive total loss or if such agreement with the Vessel's underwriters is not reached it is adjudged by a competent tribunal that a constructive loss of the Vessel has occurred; and

(iii) the date upon which the Vessel is to be treated as declared missing shall be ten (10) days after the Vessel was last reported or when the Vessel is recorded as missing by the Vessel's underwriters, whichever occurs first. A missing vessel shall be deemed lost in accordance with the provisions of Sub-clause 22(d)(ii).

**(e)** In the event the parties fail to agree the annual budget in accordance with Sub-clause 13(b), or to agree a change of flag in accordance with Sub-clause 9(d)(ii), or to agree to a reduction in the Management Fee in accordance with Sub-clause 12(d), either party may terminate this Agreement by giving the other party not less than one month's notice, the result of which will be the expiry of the Agreement at the end of the current budget period or on expiry of the notice period, whichever is the later.

**(f)** This Agreement shall terminate forthwith in the event of an order being made or resolution passed for the winding up, dissolution, liquidation or bankruptcy of either party (otherwise than for the purpose of reconstruction or amalgamation) or if a receiver or administrator is appointed, or if it suspends payment, ceases to carry on business or makes any special arrangement or composition with its creditors.

**(g)** In the event of the termination of this Agreement for any reason other than default by the Managers the management fee payable to the Managers according to the provisions of Clause 12 (Management Fee and Expenses), shall continue to be payable for a further period of the number of months stated in **Box 19** as from the effective date of termination. If **Box 19** is left blank then ninety (90) days shall apply.

**(h)** In addition, where the Managers provide Crew for the Vessel in accordance with Clause 5(a) (Crew Management):

(i) the Owners shall continue to pay Crew Support Costs during the said further period of the number of months stated in **Box 19**; and

(ii) the Owners shall pay an equitable proportion of any Severance Costs which may be incurred, not exceeding the amount stated in **Box 20**. The Managers shall use their reasonable endeavours to minimise such Severance Costs.

**(i)** On the termination, for whatever reason, of this Agreement, the Managers shall release to the Owners, if so requested, the originals where possible, or otherwise certified copies, of all accounts and all documents specifically relating to the Vessel and its operation.

**(j)** The termination of this Agreement shall be without prejudice to all rights accrued due between the parties prior to the date of termination.

**23. BIMCO Dispute Resolution Clause**

**(a)** This Agreement shall be governed by and construed in accordance with English law and any dispute arising out of or in connection with this Agreement shall be referred to arbitration in London in accordance with the Arbitration Act 1996 or any statutory modification or re-enactment thereof save to the extent necessary to give effect to the provisions of this Clause.

The arbitration shall be conducted in accordance with the London Maritime Arbitrators Association (LMAA) Terms current at the time when the arbitration proceedings are commenced.

The reference shall be to three arbitrators. A party wishing to refer a dispute to arbitration shall appoint its arbitrator and send notice of such appointment in writing to the other party requiring the other party to appoint its own arbitrator within 14 calendar days of that notice and stating that it will appoint its arbitrator as sole arbitrator unless the other party appoints its own arbitrator and gives notice that it has done so within the 14 days specified. If the other party does not appoint its own arbitrator and give notice that it has done so within the 14 days specified, the party referring a dispute to arbitration may, without the requirement of any further prior notice to the other party, appoint its arbitrator as sole arbitrator and shall advise the other party accordingly. The award of a sole arbitrator shall be binding on both parties as if he had been appointed by agreement.

Nothing herein shall prevent the parties agreeing in writing to vary these provisions to provide for the appointment of a sole arbitrator.

In cases where neither the claim nor any counterclaim exceeds the sum of USD50,000 (or such other sum as the parties may agree) the arbitration shall be conducted in accordance with the LMAA Small Claims Procedure current at the time when the arbitration proceedings are commenced.

PART II
SHIPMAN 2009
Standard ship management agreement

**(b)** This Agreement shall be governed by and construed in accordance with Title 9 of the United States Code and the Maritime Law of the United States and any dispute arising out of or in connection with this Agreement shall be referred to three persons at New York, one to be appointed by each of the parties hereto, and the third by the two so chosen; their decision or that of any two of them shall be final, and for the purposes of enforcing any award, judgment may be entered on an award by any court of competent jurisdiction. The proceedings shall be conducted in accordance with the rules of the Society of Maritime Arbitrators, Inc.

In cases where neither the claim nor any counterclaim exceeds the sum of USD50,000 (or such other sum as the parties may agree) the arbitration shall be conducted in accordance with the Shortened Arbitration Procedure of the Society of Maritime Arbitrators, Inc. current at the time when the arbitration proceedings are commenced.

**(c)** This Agreement shall be governed by and construed in accordance with the laws of the place mutually agreed by the parties and any dispute arising out of or in connection with this Agreement shall be referred to arbitration at a mutually agreed place, subject to the procedures applicable there.

**(d)** Notwithstanding Sub-clauses 23(a), 23(b) or 23(c) above, the parties may agree at any time to refer to mediation any difference and/or dispute arising out of or in connection with this Agreement.

(i) In the case of a dispute in respect of which arbitration has been commenced under Sub-clauses 23(a), 23(b) or 23(c) above, the following shall apply:

(ii) Either party may at any time and from time to time elect to refer the dispute or part of the dispute to mediation by service on the other party of a written notice (the "Mediation Notice") calling on the other party to agree to mediation.

(iii) The other party shall thereupon within 14 calendar days of receipt of the Mediation Notice confirm that they agree to mediation, in which case the parties shall thereafter agree a mediator within a further 14 calendar days, failing which on the application of either party a mediator will be appointed promptly by the Arbitration Tribunal ("the Tribunal") or such person as the Tribunal may designate for that purpose. The mediation shall be conducted in such place and in accordance with such procedure and on such terms as the parties may agree or, in the event of disagreement, as may be set by the mediator.

(iv) If the other party does not agree to mediate, that fact may be brought to the attention of the Tribunal and may be taken into account by the Tribunal when allocating the costs of the arbitration as between the parties.

(v) The mediation shall not affect the right of either party to seek such relief or take such steps as it considers necessary to protect its interest.

(vi) Either party may advise the Tribunal that they have agreed to mediation. The arbitration procedure shall continue during the conduct of the mediation but the Tribunal may take the mediation timetable into account when setting the timetable for steps in the arbitration.

(vii) Unless otherwise agreed or specified in the mediation terms, each party shall bear its own costs incurred in the mediation and the parties shall share equally the mediator's costs and expenses.

(viii) The mediation process shall be without prejudice and confidential and no information or documents disclosed during it shall be revealed to the Tribunal except to the extent that they are disclosable under the law and procedure governing the arbitration.

*(Note: The parties should be aware that the mediation process may not necessarily interrupt time limits.)*

**(e)** If **Box 21** in Part I is not appropriately filled in, Sub-clause 23(a) of this Clause shall apply.

*Note: Sub-clauses 23(a), 23(b) and 23(c) are alternatives; indicate alternative agreed in **Box 21**. Sub-clause 23(d) shall apply in all cases.*

**24. Notices**

**(a)** All notices given by either party or their agents to the other party or their agents in accordance with the provisions of this Agreement shall be in writing and shall, unless specifically provided in this Agreement to

**PART II**
**SHIPMAN 2009**
**Standard ship management agreement**

the contrary, be sent to the address for that other party as set out in **Boxes 22** and **23** or as appropriate or to such other address as the other party may designate in writing.

A notice may be sent by registered or recorded mail, facsimile, electronically or delivered by hand in accordance with this Sub-clause 24(a).

**(b)** Any notice given under this Agreement shall take effect on receipt by the other party and shall be deemed to have been received:

(i) if posted, on the seventh (7th) day after posting;

(ii) if sent by facsimile or electronically, on the day of transmission; and

(iii) if delivered by hand, on the day of delivery.

And in each case proof of posting, handing in or transmission shall be proof that notice has been given, unless proven to the contrary.

**25. Entire Agreement**
This Agreement constitutes the entire agreement between the parties and no promise, undertaking, representation, warranty or statement by either party prior to the date stated in **Box 2** shall affect this Agreement. Any modification of this Agreement shall not be of any effect unless in writing signed by or on behalf of the parties.

**26. Third Party Rights**
Except to the extent provided in Sub-clauses 17(c) (Indemnity) and 17(d) (Himalaya), no third parties may enforce any term of this Agreement.

**27. Partial Validity**
If any provision of this Agreement is or becomes or is held by any arbitrator or other competent body to be illegal, invalid or unenforceable in any respect under any law or jurisdiction, the provision shall be deemed to be amended to the extent necessary to avoid such illegality, invalidity or unenforceability, or, if such amendment is not possible, the provision shall be deemed to be deleted from this Agreement to the extent of such illegality, invalidity or unenforceability, and the remaining provisions shall continue in full force and effect and shall not in any way be affected or impaired thereby.

**28. Interpretation**
In this Agreement:

**(a)** *Singular/Plural*
The singular includes the plural and vice versa as the context admits or requires.

**(b)** *Headings*
The index and headings to the clauses and appendices to this Agreement are for convenience only and shall not affect its construction or interpretation.

**(c)** Day
"Day" means a calendar day unless expressly stated to the contrary.

ANNEX "A" (DETAILS OF VESSEL OR VESSELS)
TO THE BIMCO STANDARD SHIP MANAGEMENT AGREEMENT
CODE NAME: SHIPMAN 2009

Date of Agreement:

Name of Vessel(s):

Particulars of Vessel(s):

**ANNEX "B" (DETAILS OF CREW)**
**TO THE BIMCO STANDARD SHIP MANAGEMENT AGREEMENT**
**CODE NAME: SHIPMAN 2009**

Date of Agreement:

Details of Crew:

| Numbers | Rank | Nationality |
|---|---|---|

**ANNEX "C" (BUDGET)**
**TO THE BIMCO STANDARD SHIP MANAGEMENT AGREEMENT**
**CODE NAME: SHIPMAN 2009**

Date of Agreement:

Managers´ initial budget with effect from the commencement date of this Agreement (see **Box 2**):

ANNEX "D" (ASSOCIATED VESSELS)
TO THE BIMCO STANDARD SHIP MANAGEMENT AGREEMENT
CODE NAME: SHIPMAN 2009

NOTE: PARTIES SHOULD BE AWARE THAT BY COMPLETING THIS ANNEX "D" THEY WILL BE SUBJECT TO THE PROVISIONS OF SUB-CLAUSE 22(b)(i) OF THIS AGREEMENT.

Date of Agreement:

Details of Associated Vessels:

ANNEX "E" (FEE SCHEDULE)
TO THE BIMCO STANDARD SHIP MANAGEMENT AGREEMENT
CODE NAME: SHIPMAN 2009

# APPENDIX 10

# STATEMENT OF FACTS

**STANDARD STATEMENT OF FACTS (SHORT FORM)**
RECOMMENDED BY
THE BALTIC AND INTERNATIONAL MARITIME CONFERENCE (BIMCO)
AND THE FEDERATION OF NATIONAL ASSOCIATIONS
OF SHIP BROKERS AND AGENTS (FONASBA)

| | | | |
|---|---|---|---|
| 1. Agents | | | |
| 2. Vessel's name | | 3. Port | |
| 4. Owners/Disponent Owners | | 5. Vessel berthed | |
| | | 6. Loading commenced | 7. Loading completed |
| 8. Cargo | | 9. Discharging commenced | 10. Discharging completed |
| | | 11. Cargo documents on board | 12. Vessel sailed |
| 13. Charter Party* | | 14. Working hours/meal hours of the port* | |
| 15. Bill of Lading weight/quantity | 16. Outturn weight/quantity | | |
| 17. Vessel arrived on roads | | 18. | |
| 19. Notice of readiness tendered | | 20. | |
| 21. Next tide available | | 22. | |

DETAILS OF DAILY WORKING*

| Date | Day | Hours worked | | Hours stopped | | No. of gangs | Quantity load./disch. | Remarks* |
|---|---|---|---|---|---|---|---|---|
| | | From | to | From | to | | | |
| | | | | | | | | |

| | |
|---|---|
| General remarks* | |
| Place and date | Name and signature (Master)* |
| Name and signature (Agents)* | Name and signature (for the Charterers/Shippers/Receivers)* |

* See Explanatory Notes overleaf for filling in the boxes

Printed and sold by Fr. G. Knudtzons Bogtrykkeri A/S, 61 Vallensbækvej, DK-2625 Vallensbæk, Telefax +45 4366 0304, by authority of BIMCO

Published by The Baltic and International Maritime Conference (BIMCO), Copenhagen

# INSTRUCTIONS FOR FILLING IN THE BOXES

## General

It is recommended to fill in the boxes with a short text. When it is a matter of figures to be inserted as is the case in most of the boxes, this should be done as follows:

| 6. Loading commenced |
|---|
| 1975-03-15-0800 |

the figures being mentioned in the following order: year–month–date–time.

## Boxes Calling for Special Attention

### Charter Party*:

Insert name and date of charter, for instance, "Gencon" dated 1975-03-01.

### Working hours/meal hours of the port*:

Indicate normal working hours/meal hours of the port and not the actual hours worked on board the vessel which may be longer or shorter than the hours normally worked in the port. Such day-by-day figures should be indicated in the box provided for under "Details of Daily Working".

Some empty boxes are made available in which other relevant information applying to the particular port or vessel could be inserted, such as, time of granting free pratique, if applicable, etc.

### Details of Daily Working*:

Insert day-by-day figures and indicate in the vertical column marked "Remarks *" all relevant details as to reasons for stoppages such as bad weather, strikes, breakdown of winches/cranes, shortage of cargo, etc.

### General Remarks*:

This box should be used for insertion of such general observations which are not covered in any of the boxes provided for in the first main group of boxes, for instance, reasons for berthing delay or other general observations.

### Signatures*:

It is of importance that the boxes provided for signatures are duly signed by the parties concerned.

# APPENDIX 11

# DISBURSEMENT ACCOUNT

**Disbursement Account**

* See Explanatory Notes overleaf for filling in the boxes

## SHIPPING LTD

**DISBURSEMENT ACCOUNT**

| | | | | | |
|---|---|---|---|---|---|
| Vessel: | | | | | |
| Voy No: 031/03 | | Disch: | Containers | Invoice No: | 02005/03 |
| Port: Tilbury | | Sailed: | 17.03.2004 | Date: | 31.03.2004 |
| Arrived: 15.03.2003 | | To: | Rotterdam | Ref: | T1460 |
| From: Hamburg | | Loaded: | Containers | | |

| Detail | Voucher No | Item | Total |
|---|---|---|---|
| *Port Charges* | | £ | £ |
| Conservancy Dues | 1 | 6,588.00 | |
| Pilotage – River | 2 & 3 | 4,224.50 | |
| Pilotage – Dock | 4 & 5 | 2,149.00 | |
| Towage | 6 & 7 | 3,985.00 | |
| Light Dues | 8 | 3,208.00 | 20,154.50 |
| *Cargo Handling Charges* | | | |
| Stevedoring | 9 to 17 | 35,216.30 | |
| Landing & Terminal Charges | 18 to 22 | 5,204.00 | |
| Sundry | 23 | 274.00 | 40,694.30 |
| *Ship's Expenses* | | | |
| Cash to Master | 24 | 4,500.00 | |
| Cash returned by Master | 25 | –650.00 | |
| Crew Expenses – Hotels | 26 & 27 | 654.32 | |
| Crew Expenses – Travel | 28 to 36 | 1,059.46 | |
| Supply of Fresh Water | 37 | 78.92 | |
| Deck Stores – Chandlery | 38 & 39 | 1,026.15 | |
| Agency Fee | | 600.00 | 7,256.85 |
| Total Disbursements | | | 68,117.65 |
| Less: Received on Account | | | 60,000.00 |
| Balance due to us | | | £8,117.65 |
| VAT: Zero Rate | | | |

# APPENDIX 12

# FONASBA AGENCY AGREEMENT

FONASBA The Federation of National Associations of Ship Brokers and Agents FONASBA

## STANDARD LINER AND GENERAL AGENCY AGREEMENT

Revised and adopted 2001

Approved by BIMCO 2001

It is hereby agreed between:

..........................................................of...................................................(hereinafter referred to as the Principal)

and

..........................................................of...................................................(hereinafter referred to as the Agent)

on the ...............................................................day of ......................................................................20.........

that:

1.00 The Principal hereby appoints the Agent as its Liner Agent for all its owned and/or chartered vessels including any space or slot charter agreement serving the trade between ............................................................................ and ..................................................................

1.01 This Agreement shall come into effect on .........................and shall continue until.....................

Thereafter it shall continue until terminated by either party giving to the other notice in writing, in which event the Agreement shall terminate upon the expiration of a period of .....months from the date upon which such notice was given.

1.02 The territory in which the Agent shall perform its duties under the Agreement shall be.............. hereinafter referred to as the "Territory".

1.03 This Agreement covers the activities described in section 3..............................

1.04 The Agent undertakes not to accept the representation of other shipping companies nor to engage in NVOCC or such freight forwarding activities in the Territory, which are in direct competition to any of the Principal's transportation activities, without prior written consent, which shall not unreasonably be withheld.

1.05 The Principal undertakes not to appoint any other party in the Agent's Territory for the services defined in this Agreement.

1.06 The established custom of the trade and/or port shall apply and form part of this Agreement.

1.07 In countries where the position of the agent is in any way legally protected or regulated, the Agent shall have the benefit of such protection or regulation.

1.08 All aspects of the Principal's business are to be treated confidentially and all files and records pertaining to this business are the property of the Principal.

**2.0 Duties of the Agent**

2.01 To represent the Principal in the Territory, using his best endeavours to comply at all times with any reasonable specific instructions which the Principal may give, including the use of Principal's documentation, terms and conditions.

2.02 In consultation with the Principal to recommend and/or appoint on the Principal's behalf and account, Sub-Agents.

2.03 In consultation with the Principal to recommend and/or to appoint on the Principal's behalf and account, Stevedores, Watchmen, Tallymen, Terminal Operators, Hauliers and all kinds of suppliers.

2.04 The Agent will not be responsible for the negligent acts or defaults of the Sub-Agent or Sub-Contractor unless the Agent fails to exercise due care in the appointment and supervision of such Sub-Agent or Sub- Contractor. Notwithstanding the foregoing the Agent shall be responsible for the acts of his subsidiary companies appointed within the context of this Clause.

2.05 The Agent will always strictly observe the shipping laws and regulations of the country and will indemnify the Principal for fines, penalties, expenses or restrictions that may arise due to the failure of the Agent to comply herewith.

3.0 **Activities of Agent** (Delete those which do not apply)

3.1 **Marketing and Sales**

3.11 To provide marketing and sales activities in the Territory, in accordance with general guidelines laid down by the Principal, to canvass and book cargo, to publicise the services and to maintain contact with Shippers, Consignees, Forwarding Agents, Port and other Authorities and Trade Organisations.

3.12 To provide statistics and information and to report on cargo bookings and use of space allotments. To announce sailing and/or arrivals, and to quote freight rates and announce freight tariffs and amendments.

3.13 To arrange for public relations work (including advertising, press releases, sailing schedules and general promotional material) in accordance with the budget agreed with the Principal and for his account.

3.14 To attend to conference, consortia and /or alliance matters on behalf of the Principal and for the Principal's account.

3.15 To issue on behalf of the Principal Bills of Landing and Manifests, delivery orders, certificates and such other documents.

3.2 **Port Agency**

3.21 To arrange for berthing of vessels, loading and discharging of the cargo, in accordance with the local custom and conditions.

3.22 To arrange and co-ordinate all activities of the Terminal Operators, Stevedores, Tallymen and all other Contractors, in the interest of obtaining the best possible operation and despatch of the Principal's vessel.

3.23 To arrange for calling forward, reception and loading of outward cargo and discharge and release of inward cargo and to attend to the transhipment of through cargo.

3.24 To arrange for bunkering, repairs, husbandry, crew changes, passengers, ship's stores, spare parts, technical and nautical assistance and medical assistance.

3.25 To carry out the Principal's requirements concerning claims handling, P & I matters, General Average and/or insurance, and the appointment of Surveyors.

3.26 To attend to all necessary documentation and to attend to consular requirements.

3.27 To arrange for and attend to the clearance of the vessel and to arrange for all other services appertaining to the vessel's movements through the port.

3.28 To report to the Principal the vessel's position and to prepare a statement of facts of the call and/or a port log.

3.29 To keep the Principal regularly and timely informed on Port and working conditions likely to affect the despatch of the Principal's vessels.

3.3 **Container and Ro/Ro Traffic**

Where "equipment" is referred to in the following section it shall comprise container, flat racks, trailers or similar cargo carrying devices, owned, leased or otherwise controlled by the Principal.

3.31 To arrange for the booking of equipment on the vessel.

3.32 To arrange for the stuffing and unstuffing of LCL cargo at the port and to arrange for the provision of inland LCL terminals.

3.33 To provide and administer a proper system, or to comply with the principal's system for the control and registration of equipment. To organise equipment stock within the Territory and make provision for storage, positioning and repositioning of the equipment.

3.34 To comply with Customs requirements and arrange for equipment interchange documents in respect of the movements for which the Agent is responsible and to control the supply and use of locks, seals and labels.

3.35 To make equipment available and to arrange inland haulage.

3.36 To undertake the leasing of equipment into and re-delivery out of the system.

3.37 To operate an adequate equipment damage control system in compliance with the Principal's instructions. To arrange for equipment repairs and maintenance, when and where necessary and to report on the condition of equipment under the Agent's control.

**General Agency**

3.41 To supervise, activities and co-ordinate all marketing and sales activities of Port, Inland Agents and/or Sub-agents in the Territory, in accordance with general guidelines laid down by the Principal and to use every effort to obtain business from prospective clients and to consolidate the flow of statistics and information.

3.42 To supervise and co-ordinate all activities of Port, Inland Agents and/or Sub-agents as set forth in the agreement, in order to ensure the proper performance of all customary requirements for the best possible operation of the Principal's vessel in the G.A.'s Territory.

3.43 In consultation with the Principal to recommend and/or appoint on the Principal's behalf and account Port, Inland Agents, and/or Sub-Agents if required.

3.44 To provide Port, Inland Agents and/or Sub-agents with space allocations in accordance with the Principal's requirements.

3.45 To arrange for an efficient rotation of vessels within the Territory, in compliance with the Principal's instructions and to arrange for the most economical despatch in the ports of its area within the scope of the sailing schedule.

3.46 To liaise with Port Agents and/or Sub-agents if and where required, in the Territory in arranging for such matters as bunkering, repairs, crew changes, ship's stores, spare parts, technical, nautical, medical assistance and consular requirements

3.47 To instruct and supervise Port, Inland Agents and/or Sub-Agents regarding the Principal's requirements concerning claims handling. P & I matters and/or insurance, and the appointment of Surveyors. All expenses involved with claims handling other than routine claims are for Principal's account.

**3.5 Accounting and Finance**

3.51 To provide for appropriate records of the Principal's financial position to be maintained in the Agent's books, which shall be available for inspection and to prepare periodic financial statements.

3.52 To check all vouchers received for services rendered and to prepare a proper disbursement account in respect of each voyage or accounting period.

3.53 To advise the Principal of all amendments to port tariffs and other charges as they become known.

3.54 To calculate freight and other charges according to Tariffs supplied by the Principal and exercise every care and diligence in applying all terms and conditions of such Tariffs or other freight agreements. If the Principal organises or employs an organisation for checking freight calculations and documentation the costs for such checking to be entirely for the Principal's account.

3.55 To collect freight and related accounts and remit to the Principal all freights and other monies belonging to the Principal at such periodic intervals as the Principal may require. All bank charges to be for the Principal's account. The Agent shall advise the Principal of the customary credit terms and arrangements. If the Agent is required to grant credit to customers due to commercial reasons, the risk in respect of outstanding collections is for the Principal's account unless the Agent has granted credit without the knowledge and prior consent of the Principal.

3.56 The Agent shall have authority to retain money from the freight collected to cover all past and current disbursements, subject to providing regular cash position statements to the Principal.

3.57 The Agent in carrying out his duties under this Agreement shall not be responsible to the Principal for loss or damage caused by any Banker, Broker or other person, instructed by the Agent in good faith unless the same happens by or through the wilful neglect or default of the Agent. The burden of proving the wilful neglect of the Agent shall be on the Principal.

**4.0 Principal's Duties**

4.01 To provide all documentation, necessary to fulfil the Agent's task together with any stationery specifically required by the Principal.

4.02 To give full and timely information regarding the vessel's schedules, ports of call and line policy insofar as it affects the port and sales agency activities.

4.03 To provide the Agents immediately upon request with all necessary funds to cover advance disbursements unless the Agent shall have sufficient funds from the freights collected.

4.04 The Principal shall at all times indemnify the Agent against all claims, charges, losses, damages and expenses which the Agent may incur in connection with the fulfilment of his duties under this Agreement. Such indemnity shall extend to all acts, matters and things done, suffered or incurred by the Agent during the duration of this Agreement, notwithstanding any termination thereof, provided always, that this indemnity shall not extend to matters arising by reason of the wilful misconduct or negligence of the Agent.

4.05 Where the Agent provides bonds, guarantees and any other forms of security to Customs or other statutory authorities then the Principal shall indemnify and reimburse the Agent immediately such claims are made, provided they do not arise by reason of the wilful misconduct or the negligence of the Agent.

4.06 If mutually agreed the Principal shall take over the conduct of any dispute which may arise between the Agent and any third party as a result of the performance of the Agent's duties.

**5.0 Remuneration**

5.01 The Principal agrees to pay the agent and the Agent accepts, as consideration for the services rendered, the commissions and fees set forth on the schedule attached to this Agreement. Any fees specified in monetary units in the attached schedule shall be reviewed every 12 months and if necessary adjusted in accordance with such recognised cost of living index as is published in the country of the Agent.

5.02 Should the Principal require the Agent to undertake full processing and settlement of claims, then the Agent is entitled to a separate remuneration as agreed with the Principal and commensurate with the work involved.

5.03 The remuneration specified in the schedule attached is in respect of the ordinary and anticipated duties of the Agent within the scope of this Agreement. Should the Agent be required to perform duties beyond the scope of this Agreement then the terms on which the Agent may agree to perform such duties will be subject to express agreement between the parties. Without prejudice to the generality of the foregoing such duties may include e.g. participating in conference activities on behalf of the Principal, booking fare-paying passengers, sending out general average notices and making collections under average bonds insofar as these duties are not performed by the average adjuster.

5.04 If the Tariff currency varies in value against the local currency by more than 10% after consideration of any currency adjustment factor existing in the trade the basis for calculation of remuneration shall be adjusted accordingly.

5.05 Any extra expenses occasioned by specific additional requirements of the Principal in the use of computer equipment and systems for the performance of the Agent's duties to the Principal shall be borne by the Principal.

5.06 The Principal is responsible for all additional expenses incurred by the Agent in connecting its computers to any national or local port community system.

**6.0 Duration**

6.01 This agreement shall remain in force as specified in clause 1.01 of this Agreement. Any notice of termination shall be sent by registered or recorded mail.

6.02 If the Agreement for any reason other than negligence or wilful misconduct of the Agent should by cancelled at an earlier date than on the expiry of the notice given under clause 1.01 hereof, the Principal shall compensate the Agent. The compensation payable by the Principal to the agent shall be determined in accordance with clause 6.04 below.

6.03 If for any reason the Principal withdraws or suspends the service, the Agent may withdraw from this agreement forthwith, without prejudice to its claim for compensation.

6.04 The basis of compensation shall be the monthly average of the commission and fees earned during the previous 12 months or if less than 12 months have passed then a reasonable estimate of the same, multiplied by the number of months from the date of cancellation until the contract would have been terminated in accordance with clause 1.01 above. Furthermore the gross redundancy payments, which the Agent and/or Sub-Agent(s) is compelled to make to employees made redundant by reason of the withdrawal or suspension of the Principal's service, or termination of this Agreement, shall also be taken into account.

6.05 The Agent shall have a general lien on amounts payable to the Principal in respect of any undisputed sums due and owing to the Agent including but not limited to commissions, disbursements and duties.

**7.0 Jurisdiction**

7.01 a) This Agreement shall be governed by and construed in accordance with the laws of the country in which the Agent has its principle place of business and any dispute arising out of or in connection with this Agreement shall be referred to arbitration in that country subject to the procedures applicable there.

b) This Agreement shall be governed by and construed in accordance with the laws of .............................................. and any dispute arising out of or in connection with this Agreement shall be referred to arbitration at ...................., subject to the procedures applicable there.

c) Any dispute arising out of this Agreement shall be referred to arbitration at.....................subject to the law and procedures applicable there.

*( subclauses [a] [b] & [c] are options. If [b] or [c] are not filled in then [a] shall apply.)*

**REMUNERATION SCHEDULE BELONGING TO STANDARD LINER AND GENERAL AGENCY AGREEMENT**

Between..................................................................and........................................................date.............................
(As Principal) (As Agent)

---

The Agent is entitled to the following remuneration based <u>on all total freight</u> earnings (including any surcharges,(eg BAF, CAF) handling charges (eg THC) and freight additionals including inland transport which may be agreed) of the Principal's liner service to and from the Territory to be paid in Agent's local currency. The total remuneration per call shall not in any case be lower than the local fee applicable

I A. Where the Agent provides all the services enumerated in this Agreement the Commission shall be:

Services outward.......................% [ Min ......... per cont or tonne/cbm ] } MIN

inward.........................% [ Min ......... per cont or tonne/cbm ] } LUMP SUM

2. ........................% for cargo when only booking is involved. [ Min ........ per cont ] } PER

3. .........................% for cargo when only handling is involved. [ Min......... per cont ] } CALL .....................

("only handling" in the remuneration schedule is so defined that the duties of an Agent are to call forward and otherwise arrange for the cargo to be loaded on board, where the specific booking has been made elsewhere and acknowledged as such by the shipper as nominated for the Principal's service.

4. In respect of movements of cargo outside the Agent's Territory.....................% of the gross total freight is payable in cases where only collection of freight is involved.

5. An additional fee for containers and/or units entering or leaving the inventory control system of the Agent a fee of....................... per unit.

II A. ...................................% for cargo loaded on board in bulk. [ Min .......... per tonne / cbm ]

2. ....................................% for cargo discharged in bulk. [ Min ........... per tonne / cbm ]

III Where the Agent provides only the services as non-port agent the remuneration shall be:

When actually booked/originating from this area:

1. Services outward ........................% [ Min ............ per cont or tonne / cbm ]

inward .........................% [ Min ............ per cont or tonne / cbm ]

2. An additional fee for containers and/or units entering or leaving the inventory control system of the Agent a fee of ....................... per unit.

IV Where the Agent provides only the services as non-port agent the remuneration shall be:

1. ............................% for cargo loaded on board in bulk. [ Min ........... per tonne / cbm ]

2. .............................% for cargo discharged in bulk. [ Min ........... per tonne / cbm ]

5. Clearance and ship's husbandry fee shall be as agreed.

6. A Commission of ..................... % shall be paid on all ancillary charges collected by the Agent on behalf of the Principal such as Depot Charges, Container Demurrage, Container Damage etc.

7. Communications: The Principal will either pay actual communication expenses on a cost plus basis or pay a lumpsum monthly on an average cost plus basis, to be review able.

8. Travelling expenses: When the Agent is requested by the Principal to undertake journeys of any significant distance and/or duration, all travel expenses including accommodation and other expenses will be for the Principal's account.

9. Documentary and Administrative Charges: Such charges to be levied as appropriate by the Agent to cargo interests and to remain with the Agent even if related to the trade of the principal.

10. In case of Transhipment Cargo, a transhipment fee of .......................... per cont / tonne / cbm is charged by the Agent.

................................................................................ ............................................................................
**PRINCIPAL** **AGENT**

# APPENDIX 13

# CERTIFICATE OF CARGO INSURANCE

ACIS
CARGO UNDERWRITING AGENCY LTD

**Original**

Surveyor Reference

2nd Floor, 72 High Street,
Sevenoaks, Kent TN13 1JR
Tel: +44 (0) 1732 452020
Fax: +44 (0) 1732 464950
www.aciscargoinsurance.com

## CERTIFICATE OF MARINE INSURANCE No. 15002

This is to Certify that the Underwriters have insured the goods specified below

under Policy No.

subject to the Policy Terms, Conditions and other details shown hereon

In favour of

| | | |
|---|---|---|
| Conveyance | From (Commencement of transit) | |
| Via/to | To (final destination) | Insured Value and Currency |
| Marks and Numbers | Interest | |

**SURVEYS**

In the event of loss or damage for which the Underwriters may be liable, immediate application must be made by the INSURED or his agents or the consignee to the UNDERWRITERS or the following agents to arrange for a Surveyor to be appointed:-

**CLAIMS** payable at

by

Please refer to instructions printed overleaf

Failure to comply with these instructions may prejudice any claim.

If the insured shall make any claim knowing the same to be false or fraudulent, as regards amount or otherwise, this insurance shall become void and all claims hereunder shall be forfeited.

SHIPPED UNDER DECK BUT CONTAINER SHIPMENTS ON OR UNDER DECK

**CONDITIONS OF INSURANCE:**
Subject to the conditions printed overleaf, as applicable to the type of interest shown above.

Signed for the Underwriters by

Underwriter
ACIS Cargo Underwriting Agency Limited

(The Institute Clauses referred to are those current at time of commencement of transit or risk)

**THIS CERTIFICATE REQUIRES ENDORSEMENT BY THE INSURED.**

This certificate is not valid unless countersigned by an authorised person

| |
|---|
| Place and Date of Issue |
| Authorised Signatory |

AUTHORISED AND REGULATED BY THE FINANCIAL SERVICES AUTHORITY (FSA) AND ENTERED IN THE FSA REGISTER UNDER FIRM REFERENCE No. [illegible]

# APPENDIX 14

# INSTITUTE CARGO CLAUSES (A)

**RISKS COVERED**

Risks

1. This insurance covers all risks of loss of or damage to the subject-matter insured except as excluded by the provisions of Clauses 4, 5, 6 and 7 below.

General Average

2. This insurance covers general average and salvage charges, adjusted or determined according to the contract of carriage and/or the governing law and practice, incurred to avoid or in connection with the avoidance of loss from any cause except those excluded in Clauses 4, 5, 6 and 7 below.

"Both to Blame Collision Clause"

3. This insurance indemnifies the Assured, in respect of any risk insured herein, against liability incurred under any Both to Blame Collision Clause in the contract of carriage. In the event of any claim by carriers under the said Clause, the Assured agree to notify the Insurers who shall have the right, at their own cost and expense, to defend the Assured against such claim.

**EXCLUSIONS**

4. In no case shall this insurance cover
   - 4.1 loss damage or expense attributable to wilful misconduct of the Assured
   - 4.2 ordinary leakage, ordinary loss in weight or volume, or ordinary wear and tear of the subject-matter insured
   - 4.3 loss damage or expense caused by insufficiency or unsuitability of packing or preparation of the subject-matter insured to withstand the ordinary incidents of the insured transit where such packing or preparation is carried out by the Assured or their employees or prior to the attachment of this insurance (for the purpose of these Clauses "packing" shall be deemed to include stowage in a container and "employees" shall not include independent contractors)
   - 4.4 loss damage or expense caused by inherent vice or nature of the subject-matter insured
   - 4.5 loss damage or expense caused by delay, even though the delay be caused by a risk insured against (except expenses payable under Clause 2 above)
   - 4.6 loss damage or expense caused by insolvency or financial default of the owners managers charterers or operators of the vessel where, at the time of loading of the subject-matter insured on board the vessel, the Assured are aware, or in the ordinary course of business should be aware, that such insolvency or financial default could prevent the normal prosecution of the voyage
     This exclusion shall not apply where the contract of insurance has been assigned to the party claiming hereunder who has bought or agreed to buy the subject-matter insured in good faith under a binding contract
   - 4.7 loss damage or expense directly or indirectly caused by or arising from the use of any weapon or device employing atomic or nuclear fission and/or fusion or other like reaction or radioactive force or matter.

5. 5.1 In no case shall this insurance cover loss damage or expense arising from
   - 5.1.1 unseaworthiness of vessel or craft or unfitness of vessel or craft for the safe carriage of the subject-matter insured, where the Assured are privy to such unseaworthiness or unfitness, at the time the subject-matter insured is loaded therein
   - 5.1.2 unfitness of container or conveyance for the safe carriage of the subject-matter insured, where loading therein or thereon is carried out
     prior to attachment of this insurance or
     by the Assured or their employees and they are privy to such unfitness at the time of loading.
   - 5.2 Exclusion 5.1.1 above shall not apply where the contract of insurance has been assigned to the party claiming hereunder who has bought or agreed to buy the subject-matter insured in good faith under a binding contract.
   - 5.3 The Insurers waive any breach of the implied warranties of seaworthiness of the ship and fitness of the ship to carry the subject-matter insured to destination.

6. In no case shall this insurance cover loss damage or expense caused by
   - 6.1 war civil war revolution rebellion insurrection, or civil strife arising therefrom, or any hostile act by or against a belligerent power
   - 6.2 capture seizure arrest restraint or detainment (piracy excepted), and the consequences thereof or any attempt thereat
   - 6.3 derelict mines torpedoes bombs or other derelict weapons of war.

7. In no case shall this insurance cover loss damage or expense
   - 7.1 caused by strikers, locked-out workmen, or persons taking part in labour disturbances, riots or civil commotions
   - 7.2 resulting from strikes, lock-outs, labour disturbances, riots or civil commotions
   - 7.3 caused by any act of terrorism being an act of any person acting on behalf of, or in connection with, any organisation which carries out activities directed towards the overthrowing or influencing, by force or violence, of any government whether or not legally constituted

7.4 caused by any person acting from a political, ideological or religious motive.

**DURATION**

Transit Clause

**8.** 8.1 Subject to Clause 11 below, this insurance attaches from the time the subject-matter insured is first moved in the warehouse or at the place of storage (at the place named in the contract of insurance) for the purpose of the immediate loading into or onto the carrying vehicle or other conveyance for the commencement of transit,

continues during the ordinary course of transit

and terminates either

8.1.1 on completion of unloading from the carrying vehicle or other conveyance in or at the final warehouse or place of storage at the destination named in the contract of insurance,

8.1.2 on completion of unloading from the carrying vehicle or other conveyance in or at any other warehouse or place of storage, whether prior to or at the destination named in the contract of insurance, which the Assured or their employees elect to use either for storage other than in the ordinary course of transit or for allocation or distribution, or

8.1.3 when the Assured or their employees elect to use any carrying vehicle or other conveyance or any container for storage other than in the ordinary course of transit or

8.1.4 on the expiry of 60 days after completion of discharge overside of the subject-matter insured from the oversea vessel at the final port of discharge,

whichever shall first occur.

8.2 If, after discharge overside from the oversea vessel at the final port of discharge, but prior to termination of this insurance, the subject-matter insured is to be forwarded to a destination other than that to which it is insured, this insurance, whilst remaining subject to termination as provided in Clauses 8.1.1 to 8.1.4, shall not extend beyond the time the subject-matter insured is first moved for the purpose of the commencement of transit to such other destination.

8.3 This insurance shall remain in force (subject to termination as provided for in Clauses 8.1.1 to 8.1.4 above and to the provisions of Clause 9 below) during delay beyond the control of the Assured, any deviation, forced discharge, reshipment or transhipment and during any variation of the adventure arising from the exercise of a liberty granted to carriers under the contract of carriage.

Termination of Contract of Carriage

**9.** If owing to circumstances beyond the control of the Assured either the contract of carriage is terminated at a port or place other than the destination named therein or the transit is otherwise terminated before unloading of the subject-matter insured as provided for in Clause 8 above, then this insurance shall also terminate *unless prompt notice is given to the Insurers and continuation of cover is requested when this insurance shall remain in force, subject to an additional premium if required by the Insurers*, either

9.1 until the subject-matter insured is sold and delivered at such port or place, or, unless otherwise specially agreed, until the expiry of 60 days after arrival of the subject-matter insured at such port or place, whichever shall first occur,

or

9.2 if the subject-matter insured is forwarded within the said period of 60 days (or any agreed extension thereof) to the destination named in the contract of insurance or to any other destination, until terminated in accordance with the provisions of Clause 8 above.

Change of Voyage

**10.** 10.1 Where, after attachment of this insurance, the destination is changed by the Assured, *this must be notified promptly to Insurers for rates and terms to be agreed. Should a loss occur prior to such agreement being obtained cover may be provided but only if cover would have been available at a reasonable commercial market rate on reasonable market terms.*

10.2 Where the subject-matter insured commences the transit contemplated by this insurance (in accordance with Clause 8.1), but, without the knowledge of the Assured or their employees the ship sails for another destination, this insurance will nevertheless be deemed to have attached at commencement of such transit.

**CLAIMS**

Insurable Interest

**11.** 11.1 In order to recover under this insurance the Assured must have an insurable interest in the subject-matter insured at the time of the loss.

11.2 Subject to Clause 11.1 above, the Assured shall be entitled to recover for insured loss occurring during the period covered by this insurance, notwithstanding that the loss occurred before the contract of insurance was concluded, unless the Assured were aware of the loss and the Insurers were not.

Forwarding Charges

**12.** Where, as a result of the operation of a risk covered by this insurance, the insured transit is terminated at a port or place other than that to which the subject-matter insured is covered under this insurance, the

Insurers will reimburse the Assured for any extra charges properly and reasonably incurred in unloading storing and forwarding the subject-matter insured to the destination to which it is insured.

This Clause 12, which does not apply to general average or salvage charges, shall be subject to the exclusions contained in Clauses 4, 5, 6 and 7 above, and shall not include charges arising from the fault negligence insolvency or financial default of the Assured or their employees.

Constructive Total Loss

**13.** No claim for Constructive Total Loss shall be recoverable hereunder unless the subject-matter insured is reasonably abandoned either on account of its actual total loss appearing to be unavoidable or because the cost of recovering, reconditioning and forwarding the subject-matter insured to the destination to which it is insured would exceed its value on arrival.

Increased Value

**14.** 14.1 If any Increased Value insurance is effected by the Assured on the subject-matter insured under this insurance the agreed value of the subject-matter insured shall be deemed to be increased to the total amount insured under this insurance and all Increased Value insurances covering the loss, and liability under this insurance shall be in such proportion as the sum insured under this insurance bears to such total amount insured.

In the event of claim the Assured shall provide the Insurers with evidence of the amounts insured under all other insurances.

14.2 **Where this insurance is on Increased Value the following clause shall apply:**
The agreed value of the subject-matter insured shall be deemed to be equal to the total amount insured under the primary insurance and all Increased Value insurances covering the loss and effected on the subject-matter insured by the Assured, and liability under this insurance shall be in such proportion as the sum insured under this insurance bears to such total amount insured.

In the event of claim the Assured shall provide the Insurers with evidence of the amounts insured under all other insurances.

**BENEFIT OF INSURANCE**

**15.** This insurance

15.1 covers the Assured which includes the person claiming indemnity either as the person by or on whose behalf the contract of insurance was effected or as an assignee,

15.2 shall not extend to or otherwise benefit the carrier or other bailee.

**MINIMISING LOSSES**

Duty of Assured

**16.** It is the duty of the Assured and their employees and agents in respect of loss recoverable hereunder

16.1 to take such measures as may be reasonable for the purpose of averting or minimising such loss, and

16.2 to ensure that all rights against carriers, bailees or other third parties are properly preserved and exercised

and the Insurers will, in addition to any loss recoverable hereunder, reimburse the Assured for any charges properly and reasonably incurred in pursuance of these duties.

Waiver

**17.** Measures taken by the Assured or the Insurers with the object of saving, protecting or recovering the subject-matter insured shall not be considered as a waiver or acceptance of abandonment or otherwise prejudice the rights of either party.

**AVOIDANCE OF DELAY**

**18.** It is a condition of this insurance that the Assured shall act with reasonable despatch in all circumstances within their control.

**LAW AND PRACTICE**

**19.** This insurance is subject to English law and practice.

*NOTE:- Where a continuation of cover is requested under Clause 9, or a change of destination is notified under Clause 10, there is an obligation to give prompt notice to the Insurers and the right to such cover is dependent upon compliance with this obligation.*



**CL382**
**01/01/2009**

# APPENDIX 15

# INSTITUTE CARGO CLAUSES (B)

**RISKS COVERED**

Risks

**1.** This insurance covers, except as excluded by the provisions of Clauses 4, 5, 6 and 7 below,

1.1 loss of or damage to the subject-matter insured reasonably attributable to

1.1.1 fire or explosion

1.1.2 vessel or craft being stranded grounded sunk or capsized

1.1.3 overturning or derailment of land conveyance

1.1.4 collision or contact of vessel craft or conveyance with any external object other than water

1.1.5 discharge of cargo at a port of distress

1.1.6 earthquake volcanic eruption or lightning,

1.2 loss of or damage to the subject-matter insured caused by

1.2.1 general average sacrifice

1.2.2 jettison or washing overboard

1.2.3 entry of sea lake or river water into vessel craft hold conveyance container or place of storage,

1.3 total loss of any package lost overboard or dropped whilst loading on to, or unloading from, vessel or craft.

General Average

**2.** This insurance covers general average and salvage charges, adjusted or determined according to the contract of carriage and/or the governing law and practice, incurred to avoid or in connection with the avoidance of loss from any cause except those excluded in Clauses 4, 5, 6 and 7 below.

"Both to Blame Collision Clause"

**3.** This insurance indemnifies the Assured, in respect of any risk insured herein, against liability incurred under any Both to Blame Collision Clause in the contract of carriage. In the event of any claim by carriers under the said Clause, the Assured agree to notify the Insurers who shall have the right, at their own cost and expense, to defend the Assured against such claim.

**EXCLUSIONS**

**4.** In no case shall this insurance cover

4.1 loss damage or expense attributable to wilful misconduct of the Assured

4.2 ordinary leakage, ordinary loss in weight or volume, or ordinary wear and tear of the subject-matter insured

4.3 loss damage or expense caused by insufficiency or unsuitability of packing or preparation of the subject-matter insured to withstand the ordinary incidents of the insured transit where such packing or preparation is carried out by the Assured or their employees or prior to the attachment of this insurance (for the purpose of these Clauses "packing" shall be deemed to include stowage in a container and "employees" shall not include independent contractors)

4.4 loss damage or expense caused by inherent vice or nature of the subject-matter insured

4.5 loss damage or expense caused by delay, even though the delay be caused by a risk insured against (except expenses payable under Clause 2 above)

4.6 loss damage or expense caused by insolvency or financial default of the owners managers charterers or operators of the vessel where, at the time of loading of the subject-matter insured on board the vessel, the Assured are aware, or in the ordinary course of business should be aware, that such insolvency or financial default could prevent the normal prosecution of the voyage
This exclusion shall not apply where the contract of insurance has been assigned to the party claiming hereunder who has bought or agreed to buy the subject-matter insured in good faith under a binding contract

4.7 deliberate damage to or deliberate destruction of the subject-matter insured or any part thereof by the wrongful act of any person or persons

4.8 loss damage or expense directly or indirectly caused by or arising from the use of any weapon or device employing atomic or nuclear fission and/or fusion or other like reaction or radioactive force or matter.

**5.** 5.1 In no case shall this insurance cover loss damage or expense arising from

5.1.1 unseaworthiness of vessel or craft or unfitness of vessel or craft for the safe carriage of the subject-matter insured, where the Assured are privy to such unseaworthiness or unfitness, at the time the subject-matter insured is loaded therein

5.1.2 unfitness of container or conveyance for the safe carriage of the subject-matter insured, where loading therein or thereon is carried out
prior to attachment of this insurance or
by the Assured or their employees and they are privy to such unfitness at the time of loading.

5.2 Exclusion 5.1.1 above shall not apply where the contract of insurance has been assigned to the party claiming hereunder who has bought or agreed to buy the subject-matter insured in good faith under a binding contract.

5.3 The Insurers waive any breach of the implied warranties of seaworthiness of the ship and fitness of the ship to carry the subject-matter insured to destination.

**6.** In no case shall this insurance cover loss damage or expense caused by

6.1 war civil war revolution rebellion insurrection, or civil strife arising therefrom, or any hostile act by or against a belligerent power

6.2 capture seizure arrest restraint or detainment, and the consequences thereof or any attempt thereat
6.3 derelict mines torpedoes bombs or other derelict weapons of war.

**7.** In no case shall this insurance cover loss damage or expense
7.1 caused by strikers, locked-out workmen, or persons taking part in labour disturbances, riots or civil commotions
7.2 resulting from strikes, lock-outs, labour disturbances, riots or civil commotions
7.3 caused by any act of terrorism being an act of any person acting on behalf of, or in connection with, any organisation which carries out activities directed towards the overthrowing or influencing, by force or violence, of any government whether or not legally constituted
7.4 caused by any person acting from a political, ideological or religious motive.

**DURATION**

Transit Clause

**8.** 8.1 Subject to Clause 11 below, this insurance attaches from the time the subject-matter insured is first moved in the warehouse or at the place of storage (at the place named in the contract of insurance) for the purpose of the immediate loading into or onto the carrying vehicle or other conveyance for the commencement of transit,

continues during the ordinary course of transit

and terminates either

8.1.1 on completion of unloading from the carrying vehicle or other conveyance in or at the final warehouse or place of storage at the destination named in the contract of insurance,
8.1.2 on completion of unloading from the carrying vehicle or other conveyance in or at any other warehouse or place of storage, whether prior to or at the destination named in the contract of insurance, which the Assured or their employees elect to use either for storage other than in the ordinary course of transit or for allocation or distribution, or
8.1.3 when the Assured or their employees elect to use any carrying vehicle or other conveyance or any container for storage other than in the ordinary course of transit or
8.1.4 on the expiry of 60 days after completion of discharge overside of the subject-matter insured from the oversea vessel at the final port of discharge,

whichever shall first occur.

8.2 If, after discharge overside from the oversea vessel at the final port of discharge, but prior to termination of this insurance, the subject-matter insured is to be forwarded to a destination other than that to which it is insured, this insurance, whilst remaining subject to termination as provided in Clauses 8.1.1 to 8.1.4, shall not extend beyond the time the subject-matter insured is first moved for the purpose of the commencement of transit to such other destination.
8.3 This insurance shall remain in force (subject to termination as provided for in Clauses 8.1.1 to 8.1.4 above and to the provisions of Clause 9 below) during delay beyond the control of the Assured, any deviation, forced discharge, reshipment or transhipment and during any variation of the adventure arising from the exercise of a liberty granted to carriers under the contract of carriage.

Termination of Contract of Carriage

**9.** If owing to circumstances beyond the control of the Assured either the contract of carriage is terminated at a port or place other than the destination named therein or the transit is otherwise terminated before unloading of the subject-matter insured as provided for in Clause 8 above, then this insurance shall also terminate *unless prompt notice is given to the Insurers and continuation of cover is requested when this insurance shall remain in force, subject to an additional premium if required by the Insurers*, either

9.1 until the subject-matter insured is sold and delivered at such port or place, or, unless otherwise specially agreed, until the expiry of 60 days after arrival of the subject-matter insured at such port or place, whichever shall first occur,
or
9.2 if the subject-matter insured is forwarded within the said period of 60 days (or any agreed extension thereof) to the destination named in the contract of insurance or to any other destination, until terminated in accordance with the provisions of Clause 8 above.

Change of Voyage

**10.** 10.1 Where, after attachment of this insurance, the destination is changed by the Assured, *this must be notified promptly to Insurers for rates and terms to be agreed. Should a loss occur prior to such agreement being obtained cover may be provided but only if cover would have been available at a reasonable commercial market rate on reasonable market terms.*
10.2 Where the subject-matter insured commences the transit contemplated by this insurance (in accordance with Clause 8.1), but, without the knowledge of the Assured or their employees the ship sails for another destination, this insurance will nevertheless be deemed to have attached at commencement of such transit.

**CLAIMS**

Insurable Interest

**11.** 11.1 In order to recover under this insurance the Assured must have an insurable interest in the subject-matter insured at the time of the loss.
11.2 Subject to Clause 11.1 above, the Assured shall be entitled to recover for insured loss occurring during the period covered by this insurance, notwithstanding that the loss occurred before the

contract of insurance was concluded, unless the Assured were aware of the loss and the Insurers were not.

Forwarding Charges

**12.** Where, as a result of the operation of a risk covered by this insurance, the insured transit is terminated at a port or place other than that to which the subject-matter insured is covered under this insurance, the Insurers will reimburse the Assured for any extra charges properly and reasonably incurred in unloading storing and forwarding the subject-matter insured to the destination to which it is insured.

This Clause 12, which does not apply to general average or salvage charges, shall be subject to the exclusions contained in Clauses 4, 5, 6 and 7 above, and shall not include charges arising from the fault negligence insolvency or financial default of the Assured or their employees.

Constructive Total Loss

**13.** No claim for Constructive Total Loss shall be recoverable hereunder unless the subject-matter insured is reasonably abandoned either on account of its actual total loss appearing to be unavoidable or because the cost of recovering, reconditioning and forwarding the subject-matter insured to the destination to which it is insured would exceed its value on arrival.

Increased Value

**14.** 14.1 If any Increased Value insurance is effected by the Assured on the subject-matter insured under this insurance the agreed value of the subject-matter insured shall be deemed to be increased to the total amount insured under this insurance and all Increased Value insurances covering the loss, and liability under this insurance shall be in such proportion as the sum insured under this insurance bears to such total amount insured.

In the event of claim the Assured shall provide the Insurers with evidence of the amounts insured under all other insurances.

14.2 **Where this insurance is on Increased Value the following clause shall apply:**
The agreed value of the subject-matter insured shall be deemed to be equal to the total amount insured under the primary insurance and all Increased Value insurances covering the loss and effected on the subject-matter insured by the Assured, and liability under this insurance shall be in such proportion as the sum insured under this insurance bears to such total amount insured.

In the event of claim the Assured shall provide the Insurers with evidence of the amounts insured under all other insurances.

**BENEFIT OF INSURANCE**

**15.** This insurance

15.1 covers the Assured which includes the person claiming indemnity either as the person by or on whose behalf the contract of insurance was effected or as an assignee,

15.2 shall not extend to or otherwise benefit the carrier or other bailee.

**MINIMISING LOSSES**

Duty of Assured

**16.** It is the duty of the Assured and their employees and agents in respect of loss recoverable hereunder

16.1 to take such measures as may be reasonable for the purpose of averting or minimising such loss, and

16.2 to ensure that all rights against carriers, bailees or other third parties are properly preserved and exercised

and the Insurers will, in addition to any loss recoverable hereunder, reimburse the Assured for any charges properly and reasonably incurred in pursuance of these duties.

Waiver

**17.** Measures taken by the Assured or the Insurers with the object of saving, protecting or recovering the subject-matter insured shall not be considered as a waiver or acceptance of abandonment or otherwise prejudice the rights of either party.

**AVOIDANCE OF DELAY**

**18.** It is a condition of this insurance that the Assured shall act with reasonable despatch in all circumstances within their control.

**LAW AND PRACTICE**

**19.** This insurance is subject to English law and practice.

*NOTE:- Where a continuation of cover is requested under Clause 9, or a change of destination is notified under Clause 10, there is an obligation to give prompt notice to the Insurers and the right to such cover is dependent upon compliance with this obligation.*



**CL383**
**01/01/2009**

# APPENDIX 16

# INSTITUTE CARGO CLAUSES (C)

**RISKS COVERED**

Risks

1. This insurance covers, except as excluded by the provisions of Clauses 4, 5, 6 and 7 below,
   - 1.1 loss of or damage to the subject-matter insured reasonably attributable to
     - 1.1.1 fire or explosion
     - 1.1.2 vessel or craft being stranded grounded sunk or capsized
     - 1.1.3 overturning or derailment of land conveyance
     - 1.1.4 collision or contact of vessel craft or conveyance with any external object other than water
     - 1.1.5 discharge of cargo at a port of distress,
   - 1.2 loss of or damage to the subject-matter insured caused by
     - 1.2.1 general average sacrifice
     - 1.2.2 jettison.

General Average

2. This insurance covers general average and salvage charges, adjusted or determined according to the contract of carriage and/or the governing law and practice, incurred to avoid or in connection with the avoidance of loss from any cause except those excluded in Clauses 4, 5, 6 and 7 below.

"Both to Blame Collision Clause"

3. This insurance indemnifies the Assured, in respect of any risk insured herein, against liability incurred under any Both to Blame Collision Clause in the contract of carriage. In the event of any claim by carriers under the said Clause, the Assured agree to notify the Insurers who shall have the right, at their own cost and expense, to defend the Assured against such claim.

**EXCLUSIONS**

4. In no case shall this insurance cover
   - 4.1 loss damage or expense attributable to wilful misconduct of the Assured
   - 4.2 ordinary leakage, ordinary loss in weight or volume, or ordinary wear and tear of the subject-matter insured
   - 4.3 loss damage or expense caused by insufficiency or unsuitability of packing or preparation of the subject-matter insured to withstand the ordinary incidents of the insured transit where such packing or preparation is carried out by the Assured or their employees or prior to the attachment of this insurance (for the purpose of these Clauses "packing" shall be deemed to include stowage in a container and "employees" shall not include independent contractors)
   - 4.4 loss damage or expense caused by inherent vice or nature of the subject-matter insured
   - 4.5 loss damage or expense caused by delay, even though the delay be caused by a risk insured against (except expenses payable under Clause 2 above)
   - 4.6 loss damage or expense caused by insolvency or financial default of the owners managers charterers or operators of the vessel where, at the time of loading of the subject-matter insured on board the vessel, the Assured are aware, or in the ordinary course of business should be aware, that such insolvency or financial default could prevent the normal prosecution of the voyage

     This exclusion shall not apply where the contract of insurance has been assigned to the party claiming hereunder who has bought or agreed to buy the subject-matter insured in good faith under a binding contract
   - 4.7 deliberate damage to or deliberate destruction of the subject-matter insured or any part thereof by the wrongful act of any person or persons
   - 4.8 loss damage or expense directly or indirectly caused by or arising from the use of any weapon or device employing atomic or nuclear fission and/or fusion or other like reaction or radioactive force or matter.

5. 5.1 In no case shall this insurance cover loss damage or expense arising from
     - 5.1.1 unseaworthiness of vessel or craft or unfitness of vessel or craft for the safe carriage of the subject-matter insured, where the Assured are privy to such unseaworthiness or unfitness, at the time the subject-matter insured is loaded therein
     - 5.1.2 unfitness of container or conveyance for the safe carriage of the subject-matter insured, where loading therein or thereon is carried out

       prior to attachment of this insurance or

       by the Assured or their employees and they are privy to such unfitness at the time of loading.
   - 5.2 Exclusion 5.1.1 above shall not apply where the contract of insurance has been assigned to the party claiming hereunder who has bought or agreed to buy the subject-matter insured in good faith under a binding contract.
   - 5.3 The Insurers waive any breach of the implied warranties of seaworthiness of the ship and fitness of the ship to carry the subject-matter insured to destination.

6. In no case shall this insurance cover loss damage or expense caused by
   - 6.1 war civil war revolution rebellion insurrection, or civil strife arising therefrom, or any hostile act by or against a belligerent power
   - 6.2 capture seizure arrest restraint or detainment, and the consequences thereof or any attempt thereat
   - 6.3 derelict mines torpedoes bombs or other derelict weapons of war.

7. In no case shall this insurance cover loss damage or expense

7.1 caused by strikers, locked-out workmen, or persons taking part in labour disturbances, riots or civil commotions
7.2 resulting from strikes, lock-outs, labour disturbances, riots or civil commotions
7.3 caused by any act of terrorism being an act of any person acting on behalf of, or in connection with, any organisation which carries out activities directed towards the overthrowing or influencing, by force or violence, of any government whether or not legally constituted
7.4 caused by any person acting from a political, ideological or religious motive.

**DURATION**

Transit Clause

**8.** 8.1 Subject to Clause 11 below, this insurance attaches from the time the subject-matter insured is first moved in the warehouse or at the place of storage (at the place named in the contract of insurance) for the purpose of the immediate loading into or onto the carrying vehicle or other conveyance for the commencement of transit,

continues during the ordinary course of transit

and terminates either

8.1.1 on completion of unloading from the carrying vehicle or other conveyance in or at the final warehouse or place of storage at the destination named in the contract of insurance,
8.1.2 on completion of unloading from the carrying vehicle or other conveyance in or at any other warehouse or place of storage, whether prior to or at the destination named in the contract of insurance, which the Assured or their employees elect to use either for storage other than in the ordinary course of transit or for allocation or distribution, or
8.1.3 when the Assured or their employees elect to use any carrying vehicle or other conveyance or any container for storage other than in the ordinary course of transit or
8.1.4 on the expiry of 60 days after completion of discharge overside of the subject-matter insured from the oversea vessel at the final port of discharge,

whichever shall first occur.

8.2 If, after discharge overside from the oversea vessel at the final port of discharge, but prior to termination of this insurance, the subject-matter insured is to be forwarded to a destination other than that to which it is insured, this insurance, whilst remaining subject to termination as provided in Clauses 8.1.1 to 8.1.4, shall not extend beyond the time the subject-matter insured is first moved for the purpose of the commencement of transit to such other destination.
8.3 This insurance shall remain in force (subject to termination as provided for in Clauses 8.1.1 to 8.1.4 above and to the provisions of Clause 9 below) during delay beyond the control of the Assured, any deviation, forced discharge, reshipment or transhipment and during any variation of the adventure arising from the exercise of a liberty granted to carriers under the contract of carriage.

Termination of Contract of Carriage

**9.** If owing to circumstances beyond the control of the Assured either the contract of carriage is terminated at a port or place other than the destination named therein or the transit is otherwise terminated before unloading of the subject-matter insured as provided for in Clause 8 above, then this insurance shall also terminate *unless prompt notice is given to the Insurers and continuation of cover is requested when this insurance shall remain in force, subject to an additional premium if required by the Insurers*, either

9.1 until the subject-matter insured is sold and delivered at such port or place, or, unless otherwise specially agreed, until the expiry of 60 days after arrival of the subject-matter insured at such port or place, whichever shall first occur,
or
9.2 if the subject-matter insured is forwarded within the said period of 60 days (or any agreed extension thereof) to the destination named in the contract of insurance or to any other destination, until terminated in accordance with the provisions of Clause 8 above.

Change of Voyage

**10.** 10.1 Where, after attachment of this insurance, the destination is changed by the Assured, *this must be notified promptly to Insurers for rates and terms to be agreed. Should a loss occur prior to such agreement being obtained cover may be provided but only if cover would have been available at a reasonable commercial market rate on reasonable market terms.*

10.2 Where the subject-matter insured commences the transit contemplated by this insurance (in accordance with Clause 8.1), but, without the knowledge of the Assured or their employees the ship sails for another destination, this insurance will nevertheless be deemed to have attached at commencement of such transit.

**CLAIMS**

Insurable Interest

**11.** 11.1 In order to recover under this insurance the Assured must have an insurable interest in the subject-matter insured at the time of the loss.

11.2 Subject to Clause 11.1 above, the Assured shall be entitled to recover for insured loss occurring during the period covered by this insurance, notwithstanding that the loss occurred before the contract of insurance was concluded, unless the Assured were aware of the loss and the Insurers were not.

Forwarding Charges

**12.** Where, as a result of the operation of a risk covered by this insurance, the insured transit is terminated at a port or place other than that to which the subject-matter insured is covered under this insurance, the

Insurers will reimburse the Assured for any extra charges properly and reasonably incurred in unloading storing and forwarding the subject-matter insured to the destination to which it is insured.

This Clause 12, which does not apply to general average or salvage charges, shall be subject to the exclusions contained in Clauses 4, 5, 6 and 7 above, and shall not include charges arising from the fault negligence insolvency or financial default of the Assured or their employees.

Constructive Total Loss

**13.** No claim for Constructive Total Loss shall be recoverable hereunder unless the subject-matter insured is reasonably abandoned either on account of its actual total loss appearing to be unavoidable or because the cost of recovering, reconditioning and forwarding the subject-matter insured to the destination to which it is insured would exceed its value on arrival.

Increased Value

**14.** 14.1 If any Increased Value insurance is effected by the Assured on the subject-matter insured under this insurance the agreed value of the subject-matter insured shall be deemed to be increased to the total amount insured under this insurance and all Increased Value insurances covering the loss, and liability under this insurance shall be in such proportion as the sum insured under this insurance bears to such total amount insured.

In the event of claim the Assured shall provide the Insurers with evidence of the amounts insured under all other insurances.

14.2 **Where this insurance is on Increased Value the following clause shall apply:**
The agreed value of the subject-matter insured shall be deemed to be equal to the total amount insured under the primary insurance and all Increased Value insurances covering the loss and effected on the subject-matter insured by the Assured, and liability under this insurance shall be in such proportion as the sum insured under this insurance bears to such total amount insured.

In the event of claim the Assured shall provide the Insurers with evidence of the amounts insured under all other insurances.

**BENEFIT OF INSURANCE**

**15.** This insurance

15.1 covers the Assured which includes the person claiming indemnity either as the person by or on whose behalf the contract of insurance was effected or as an assignee,

15.2 shall not extend to or otherwise benefit the carrier or other bailee.

**MINIMISING LOSSES**

Duty of Assured

**16.** It is the duty of the Assured and their employees and agents in respect of loss recoverable hereunder

16.1 to take such measures as may be reasonable for the purpose of averting or minimising such loss, and

16.2 to ensure that all rights against carriers, bailees or other third parties are properly preserved and exercised

and the Insurers will, in addition to any loss recoverable hereunder, reimburse the Assured for any charges properly and reasonably incurred in pursuance of these duties.

Waiver

**17.** Measures taken by the Assured or the Insurers with the object of saving, protecting or recovering the subject-matter insured shall not be considered as a waiver or acceptance of abandonment or otherwise prejudice the rights of either party.

**AVOIDANCE OF DELAY**

**18.** It is a condition of this insurance that the Assured shall act with reasonable despatch in all circumstances within their control.

**LAW AND PRACTICE**

**19.** This insurance is subject to English law and practice.

*NOTE:- Where a continuation of cover is requested under Clause 9, or a change of destination is notified under Clause 10, there is an obligation to give prompt notice to the Insurers and the right to such cover is dependent upon compliance with this obligation.*



**CL384**
**01/01/2009**

# APPENDIX 17

# CONGEN BILL OF LADING

Revised 1994, 2007 (v2.0)

BIMCO

**CONGENBILL 2007**

**BILL OF LADING**

To be used with charter parties

**Page I**

| | | |
|---|---|---|
| Shipper | Bill of Lading No. | Reference No. |
| Consignee | Vessel | |
| Notify address | Port of loading | |
| | Port of discharge | |
| Shipper's description of goods<br><br>(of which on deck at shipper's risk; the Carrier not being responsible for loss or damage howsoever arising) | | Gross weight |

Freight payable as per CHARTER PARTY dated:

FREIGHT ADVANCE
Received on account of freight:

**SHIPPED** at the Port of Loading in apparent good order and condition on the Vessel for carriage to the Port of Discharge or so near thereto as the Vessel may safely get the goods specified above.

Weight, measure, quality, quantity, condition, contents and value unknown.

IN WITNESS whereof the Master or Agent of the said vessel has signed the number of Bills of Lading indicated below all of this tenor and date, any one of which being accomplished the others shall be void.

FOR CONDITIONS OF CARRIAGE SEE OVERLEAF.

| Date shipped on board | Place and date of issue | Number of original Bills of Lading |
|---|---|---|

Signature:

(i) ..........................................................................................Master
Master's name and signature

Or

(ii) ..........................................................................................as Agent for the Master
Agent's name and signature

Or

(iii) ..........................................................................................as Agent for the Owner*
Agent's name and signature

.......................................................................................... Owner
*if option (iii) filled in, state Owner's name above

Printed by BIMCO's *idea*

# CONGENBILL 2007

**BILL OF LADING**

To be used with charter parties

**Page 2**

**Conditions of Carriage**

**(1)** All terms and conditions, liberties and exceptions of the Charter Party, dated as overleaf, including the Law and Arbitration Clause/Dispute Resolution Clause, are herewith incorporated.

**(2) General Paramount Clause**

The International Convention for the Unification of Certain Rules of Law relating to Bills of Lading signed at Brussels on 25 August 1924 ("the Hague Rules") as amended by the Protocol signed at Brussels on 23 February 1968 ("the Hague-Visby Rules") and as enacted in the country of shipment shall apply to this Contract. When the Hague-Visby Rules are not enacted in the country of shipment, the corresponding legislation of the country of destination shall apply, irrespective of whether such legislation may only regulate outbound shipments.

When there is no enactment of the Hague-Visby Rules in either the country of shipment or in the country of destination, the Hague-Visby Rules shall apply to this Contract save where the Hague Rules as enacted in the country of shipment or if no such enactment is in place, the Hague Rules as enacted in the country of destination apply compulsorily to this Contract.

The Protocol signed at Brussels on 21 December 1979 ("the SDR Protocol 1979") shall apply where the Hague-Visby Rules apply, whether mandatorily or by this Contract.

The Carrier shall in no case be responsible for loss of or damage to cargo arising prior to loading, after discharging, or while the cargo is in the charge of another carrier, or with respect to deck cargo and live animals.

**(3) General Average**

General Average shall be adjusted, stated and settled according to York-Antwerp Rules 1994 in London unless another place is agreed in the Charter Party.

Cargo's contribution to General Average shall be paid to the Carrier even when such average is the result of a fault, neglect or error of the Master, Pilot or Crew.

**(4) New Jason Clause**

In the event of accident, danger, damage or disaster before or after the commencement of the voyage, resulting from any cause whatsoever, whether due to negligence or not, for which, or for the consequence of which, the Carrier is not responsible, by statute, contract or otherwise, the cargo, shippers, consignees or the owners of the cargo shall contribute with the Carrier in General Average to the payment of any sacrifices, losses or expenses of a General Average nature that may be made or incurred and shall pay salvage and special charges incurred in respect of the cargo. If a salving vessel is owned or operated by the Carrier, salvage shall be paid for as fully as if the said salving vessel or vessels belonged to strangers. Such deposit as the Carrier, or his agents, may deem sufficient to cover the estimated contribution of the goods and any salvage and special charges thereon shall, if required, be made by the cargo, shippers, consignees or owners of the goods to the Carrier before delivery.

**(5) Both-to-Blame Collision Clause**

If the Vessel comes into collision with another vessel as a result of the negligence of the other vessel and any act, neglect or default of the Master, Mariner, Pilot or the servants of the Carrier in the navigation or in the management of the Vessel, the owners of the cargo carried hereunder will indemnify the Carrier against all loss or liability to the other or non-carrying vessel or her owners in so far as such loss or liability represents loss of, or damage to, or any claim whatsoever of the owners of said cargo, paid or payable by the other or non-carrying vessel or her owners to the owners of said cargo and set-off, recouped or recovered by the other or non-carrying vessel or her owners as part of their claim against the carrying Vessel or the Carrier.
The foregoing provisions shall also apply where the owners, operators or those in charge of any vessel or vessels or objects other than, or in addition to, the colliding vessels or objects are at fault in respect of a collision or contact.

For particulars of cargo, freight,
destination, etc., see overleaf

# APPENDIX 18

## LETTER OF CREDIT

### IRREVOCABLE LETTER OF CREDIT

**Issue Date:** ________________

**Irrevocable Documentary Credit Number:** _____________

**Applicant:** _______________________________________
_______________________________________
_______________________________________

**Beneficiary:** Village of Lemont
418 Main Street
Lemont, Il 60439

**Amount:** _______________________

**Expiration:** _______________________

**Gentlemen:**

**We hereby establish our Irrevocable Letter of Credit in your favor for the account of the_____________________ (name), _____________________ (address) in the aggregate amount of _________ available by your draft drawn on site and marked "Drawn Under _____________", Letter of Credit Number _________, dated and accompanied by the following document:**

> **A signed statement by the Administrator or Engineer of the Village of Lemont certifying that any portion of the improvements on the __________ Subdivision, as specified in the plans and specification for the Subdivision known as ____________, as approved by the Village Engineer, have not been completed in accordance with said plans and specifications**

**If said improvements have not been installed in conformity with approved Plans and Village Ordinances, the Village is hereby granted authority to draw on this Irrevocable Letter of Credit for the purpose of completing said improvements, in accordance with the revisions herein and above set forth. The Irrevocable Letter of Credit shall be utilized to secure the installation of all improvements required under the Subdivision Control Ordinance of the Village of Lemont. This Irrevocable Letter of Credit shall not operate as a limitation on the obligation of the _______________ to install any improvement required by the Village of Lemont.**

**The principal amount of this Irrevocable Letter of Credit shall not be reduced for any improvements installed unless such reduction is approved by the Village Board. The Village may submit is sight drafts as herein and above provided without the consent of the ___________ or any other party. If within ten (10) days of the date such draft is presented in conformance with the terms of this Irrevocable Letter of Credit, we fail to honor same, we agree to pay all attorney's fees, court costs, and other expenses incurred by the Village enforcing the terms hereof.**

**We hereby agree that this Irrevocable Letter of Credit shall expire on __________ (two years minimum), as stated herein above; provided, however, that we shall notify the**

Village Administrator and Village Engineer by Certified Mail, return receipt requested, at least ninety (90) days prior to said expiration date that said Letter of Credit is about to expire. It is a condition of this Letter of Credit that it shall be automatically extended for additional periods of one (1) year, unless at least ninety (90) calendar days prior to the then relevant expiration date, we have advised you in writing by certified mail, return receipt requested, or hand delivery that we elect not to so extend. In that event, you may draw hereunder on or prior to the then relevant expiration date, up to the full amount then available hereunder against your sight draft(s) on us, bearing the number of this Letter of Credit. In no event shall this Irrevocable Letter of Credit or the obligations contained herein expire except upon prior written notice, it being expressly agreed that the obligations contained herein expire except upon prior written notice, it being expressly agreed that the above expiration date shall be extended as shall be required to comply with this notice provision.

____________________________________
(Signature of Bank Officer

____________________________________
(Officer's Title)

Subscribed and sworn to before me this _____ day of _______________, 2003.

____________________________________
Notary Public

This documentary credit is subject to the "Uniform Customs and Practice for Documentary Credits, the International Chamber of Commerce Publication No. 440 (Latest Revisions), except as herein and above modified.

G:\COMMUNITY DEVELOPMENT DEPT\LETTERS of CREDIT\LOC Template WP.wpd/lsc

# APPENDIX 19

# UCP600

## UCP 600 - Article 1

Application of UCP

The Uniform Customs and Practice for Documentary Credits, 2007 Revision, ICC Publication no. 600 ("UCP") are rules that apply to any documentary credit ("credit") (including, to the extent to which they may be applicable, any standby letter of credit) when the text of the credit expressly indicates that it is subject to these rules. They are binding on all parties thereto unless expressly modified or excluded by the credit.

## UCP 600 - Article 2

Definitions

For the purpose of these rules:

**Advising bank** means the bank that advises the credit at the request of the issuing bank.

**Applicant** means the party on whose request the credit is issued.

**Banking day** means a day on which a bank is regularly open at the place at which an act subject to these rules is to be performed.

**Beneficiary** means the party in whose favour a credit is issued.

**Complying presentation** means a presentation that is in accordance with the terms and conditions of the credit, the applicable provisions of these rules and international standard banking practice.

**Confirmation** means a definite undertaking of the confirming bank, in addition to that of the issuing bank, to honour or negotiate a complying presentation.

**Confirming bank** means the bank that adds its confirmation to a credit upon the issuing bank's authorization or request.

**Credit** means any arrangement, however named or described, that is irrevocable and thereby constitutes a definite undertaking of the issuing bank to honour a complying presentation.

**Honour means:**

**a.** to pay at sight if the credit is available by sight payment.

**b.** to incur a deferred payment undertaking and pay at maturity if the credit is available by deferred payment.

**c.** to accept a bill of exchange ("draft") drawn by the beneficiary and pay at maturity if the credit is available by acceptance.

**Issuing bank** means the bank that issues a credit at the request of an applicant or on its own behalf.

**Negotiation** means the purchase by the nominated bank of drafts (drawn on a bank other than the nominated bank) and/or documents under a complying presentation, by advancing or agreeing to advance funds to the beneficiary on or before the banking day on which reimbursement is due to the nominated bank.

**Nominated Bank** means the bank with which the credit is available or any bank in the case of a credit available with any bank.

**Presentation** means either the delivery of documents under a credit to the issuing bank or nominated bank or the documents so delivered.

**Presenter** means a beneficiary, bank or other party that makes a presentation.

## UCP 600 - Article 3

Interpretations

For the purpose of these rules:

Where applicable, words in the singular include the plural and in the plural include the singular.

A credit is irrevocable even if there is no indication to that effect.

A document may be signed by handwriting, facsimile signature, perforated signature, stamp, symbol or any other mechanical or electronic method of authentication.

A requirement for a document to be legalized, visaed, certified or similar will be satisfied by any signature, mark, stamp or label on the document which appears to satisfy that requirement.

Branches of a bank in different countries are considered to be separate banks.

Terms such as "first class", "well known", "qualified", "independent", "official", "competent" or "local" used to describe the issuer of a document allow any issuer except the beneficiary to issue that document.

Unless required to be used in a document, words such as "prompt", "immediately" or "as soon as possible" will be disregarded.

The expression "on or about" or similar will be interpreted as a stipulation that an event is to occur during a period of five calendar days before until five calendar days after the specified date, both start and end dates included.

The words "to", "until", "till", "from" and "between" when used to determine a period of shipment include the date or dates mentioned, and the words "before" and "after" exclude the date mentioned.

The words "from" and "after" when used to determine a maturity date exclude the date mentioned.

The terms "first half" and "second half" of a month shall be construed respectively as the 1st to the 15th and the 16th to the last day of the month, all dates inclusive.

The terms "beginning", "middle" and "end" of a month shall be construed respectively as the 1st to the 10th, the 11th to the 20th and the 21st to the last day of the month, all dates inclusive.

## UCP 600 - Article 4

Credits v. Contracts

**a.** A credit by its nature is a separate transaction from the sale or other contract on which it may be based. Banks are in no way concerned with or bound by such contract, even if any reference whatsoever to it is included in the credit. Consequently, the undertaking of a bank to honour, to negotiate or to fulfil any other obligation under the credit is not subject to claims or defences by the applicant resulting from its relationships with the issuing bank or the beneficiary.

A beneficiary can in no case avail itself of the contractual relationships existing between banks or between the applicant and the issuing bank.

**b.** An issuing bank should discourage any attempt by the applicant to include, as an integral part of the credit, copies of the underlying contract, proforma invoice and the like.

## UCP 600 - Article 5

Documents v. Goods, Services or Performance

Banks deal with documents and not with goods, services or performance to which the documents may relate.

## UCP 600 - Article 6

Availability, Expiry Date and Place for Presentation

**a.** A credit must state the bank with which it is available or whether it is available with any bank. A credit available with a nominated bank is also available with the issuing bank.

**b.** A credit must state whether it is available by sight payment, deferred payment, acceptance or negotiation.

**c.** A credit must not be issued available by a draft drawn on the applicant.

**d.**

**i.** A credit must state an expiry date for presentation. An expiry date stated for honour or negotiation will be deemed to be an expiry date for presentation.

**ii.** The place of the bank with which the credit is available is the place for presentation. The place for presentation under a credit available with any bank is that of any bank. A place for presentation other than that of the issuing bank is in addition to the place of the issuing bank.

**e.** Except as provided in sub-article 29 (a), a presentation by or on behalf of the beneficiary must be made on or before the expiry date.

## UCP 600 - Article 7

Issuing Bank Undertaking

**a.** Provided that the stipulated documents are presented to the nominated bank or to the issuing bank and that they constitute a complying presentation, the issuing bank must honour if the credit is available by:

**i.** sight payment, deferred payment or acceptance with the issuing bank;

**ii.** sight payment with a nominated bank and that nominated bank does not pay;

**iii.** deferred payment with a nominated bank and that nominated bank does not incur its deferred payment undertaking or, having incurred its deferred payment undertaking, does not pay at maturity;

**iv.** acceptance with a nominated bank and that nominated bank does not accept a draft drawn on it or, having accepted a draft drawn on it, does not pay at maturity;

**v.** negotiation with a nominated bank and that nominated bank does not negotiate.

**b.** An issuing bank is irrevocably bound to honour as of the time it issues the credit.

**c.** An issuing bank undertakes to reimburse a nominated bank that has honoured or negotiated a complying presentation and forwarded the documents to the issuing bank. Reimbursement for the amount of a complying presentation under a credit available by acceptance or deferred payment is due at maturity, whether or not the nominated bank prepaid or purchased before maturity. An issuing bank's undertaking to reimburse a nominated bank is independent of the issuing bank's undertaking to the beneficiary.

## UCP 600 - Article 8

Confirming Bank Undertaking

**a.** Provided that the stipulated documents are presented to the confirming bank or to any other nominated bank and that they constitute a complying presentation, the confirming bank must:

**i.** honour, if the credit is available by

**a.** sight payment, deferred payment or acceptance with the confirming bank;

**b.** sight payment with another nominated bank and that nominated bank does not pay;

**c.** deferred payment with another nominated bank and that nominated bank does not incur its deferred payment undertaking or, having incurred its deferred payment undertaking, does not pay at maturity;

**d.** acceptance with another nominated bank and that nominated bank does not accept a draft drawn on it or, having accepted a draft drawn on it, does not pay at maturity;

**e.** negotiation with another nominated bank and that nominated bank does not negotiate.

**ii.** negotiate, without recourse, if the credit is available by negotiation with the confirming bank.

**b.** A confirming bank is irrevocably bound to honour or negotiate as of the time it adds its confirmation to the credit.

**c.** A confirming bank undertakes to reimburse another nominated bank that has honoured or negotiated a complying presentation and forwarded the documents to the confirming bank. Reimbursement for the amount of a complying presentation under a credit available by acceptance or deferred payment is due at maturity, whether or not another nominated bank prepaid or purchased before maturity. A confirming bank's undertaking to reimburse another nominated bank is independent of the confirming bank's undertaking to the beneficiary.

**d.** If a bank is authorized or requested by the issuing bank to confirm a credit but is not prepared to do so, it must inform the issuing bank without delay and may advise the credit without confirmation.

## UCP 600 - Article 9

Advising of Credits and Amendments

**a.** A credit and any amendment may be advised to a beneficiary through an advising bank. An advising bank that is not a confirming bank advises the credit and any amendment without any undertaking to honour or negotiate.

**b.** By advising the credit or amendment, the advising bank signifies that it has satisfied itself as to the apparent authenticity of the credit or amendment and that the advice accurately reflects the terms and conditions of the credit or amendment received.

**c.** An advising bank may utilize the services of another bank ("second advising bank") to advise the credit and any amendment to the beneficiary. By advising the credit or amendment, the second advising bank signifies that it has satisfied itself as to the apparent authenticity of the advice it has received and that the advice accurately reflects the terms and conditions of the credit or amendment received.

**d.** A bank utilizing the services of an advising bank or second advising bank to advise a credit must use the same bank to advise any amendment thereto.

**e.** If a bank is requested to advise a credit or amendment but elects not to do so, it must so inform, without delay, the bank from which the credit, amendment or advice has been received.

**f.** If a bank is requested to advise a credit or amendment but cannot satisfy itself as to the apparent authenticity of the credit, the amendment or the advice, it must so inform, without delay, the bank from which the instructions appear to have been received. If the advising bank or second advising bank elects nonetheless to advise the credit or amendment, it must inform the beneficiary or second advising bank that it has not been able to satisfy itself as to the apparent authenticity of the credit, the amendment or the advice.

## UCP 600 - Article 10

Amendments

**a.** Except as otherwise provided by article 38, a credit can neither be amended nor cancelled without the agreement of the issuing bank, the confirming bank, if any, and the beneficiary.

**b.** An issuing bank is irrevocably bound by an amendment as of the time it issues the amendment. A confirming bank may extend its confirmation to an amendment and will be irrevocably bound as of the time it advises the amendment. A confirming bank may, however, choose to advise an amendment without extending its confirmation and, if so, it must inform the issuing bank without delay and inform the beneficiary in its advice.

**c.** The terms and conditions of the original credit (or a credit incorporating previously accepted amendments) will remain in force for the beneficiary until the beneficiary communicates its acceptance of the amendment to the bank that advised such amendment. The beneficiary should give notification of acceptance or rejection of an amendment. If the beneficiary fails to give such notification, a presentation that complies with the credit and to any not yet accepted amendment will be deemed to be notification of acceptance by the beneficiary of such amendment. As of that moment the credit will be amended.

**d.** A bank that advises an amendment should inform the bank from which it received the amendment of any notification of acceptance or rejection.

**e.** Partial acceptance of an amendment is not allowed and will be deemed to be notification of rejection of the amendment.

**f.** A provision in an amendment to the effect that the amendment shall enter into force unless rejected by the beneficiary within a certain time shall be disregarded.

## UCP 600 - Article 11

Teletransmitted and Pre-Advised Credits and Amendments

**a.** An authenticated teletransmission of a credit or amendment will be deemed to be the operative credit or amendment, and any subsequent mail confirmation shall be disregarded.

If a teletransmission states "full details to follow" (or words of similar effect), or states that the mail confirmation is to be the operative credit or amendment, then the teletransmission will not be deemed to be the operative credit or amendment. The issuing bank must then issue the operative credit or amendment without delay in terms not inconsistent with the teletransmission.

**b.** A preliminary advice of the issuance of a credit or amendment ("pre-advice") shall only be sent if the issuing bank is prepared to issue the operative credit or amendment. An issuing bank that sends a pre-advice is irrevocably committed to issue the operative credit or amendment, without delay, in terms not inconsistent with the pre-advice.

## UCP 600 - Article 12

Nomination

**a.** Unless a nominated bank is the confirming bank, an authorization to honour or negotiate does not impose any obligation on that nominated bank to honour or negotiate, except when expressly agreed to by that nominated bank and so communicated to the beneficiary.

**b.** By nominating a bank to accept a draft or incur a deferred payment undertaking, an issuing bank authorizes that nominated bank to prepay or purchase a draft accepted or a deferred payment undertaking incurred by that nominated bank.

**c.** Receipt or examination and forwarding of documents by a nominated bank that is not a confirming bank does not make that nominated bank liable to honour or negotiate, nor does it constitute honour or negotiation.

## UCP 600 - Article 13

Bank-to-Bank Reimbursement Arrangements

**a.** If a credit states that reimbursement is to be obtained by a nominated bank ("claiming bank") claiming on another party ("reimbursing bank"), the credit must state if the reimbursement is subject to the ICC rules for bank-to-bank reimbursements in effect on the date of issuance of the credit.

**b.** If a credit does not state that reimbursement is subject to the ICC rules for bank-to-bank reimbursements, the following apply:

**i.**An issuing bank must provide a reimbursing bank with a reimbursement authorization that conforms with the availability stated in the credit. The reimbursement authorization should not be subject to an expiry date.

**ii.**A claiming bank shall not be required to supply a reimbursing bank with a certificate of compliance with the terms and conditions of the credit.

**iii.**An issuing bank will be responsible for any loss of interest, together with any expenses incurred, if reimbursement is not provided on first demand by a reimbursing bank in accordance with the terms and conditions of the credit.

**iv.**A reimbursing bank's charges are for the account of the issuing bank. However, if the charges are for the account of the beneficiary, it is the responsibility of an issuing bank to so indicate in the credit and in the reimbursement authorization. If a reimbursing bank's charges are for the account of the beneficiary, they shall be deducted from the amount due to a claiming bank when reimbursement is made. If no reimbursement is made, the reimbursing bank's charges remain the obligation of the issuing bank.

**c.** An issuing bank is not relieved of any of its obligations to provide reimbursement if reimbursement is not made by a reimbursing bank on first demand.

## UCP 600 - Article 14

Standard for Examination of Documents

**a.** A nominated bank acting on its nomination, a confirming bank, if any, and the issuing bank must examine a presentation to determine, on the basis of the documents alone, whether or not the documents appear on their face to constitute a complying presentation.

**b.** A nominated bank acting on its nomination, a confirming bank, if any, and the issuing bank shall each have a maximum of five banking days following the day of presentation to determine if a presentation is complying. This period is not curtailed or otherwise affected by the occurrence on or after the date of presentation of any expiry date or last day for presentation.

**c.** A presentation including one or more original transport documents subject to articles 19, 20, 21, 22, 23, 24 or 25 must be made by or on behalf of the beneficiary not later than 21 calendar days after the date of shipment as described in these rules, but in any event not later than the expiry date of the credit.

**d.** Data in a document, when read in context with the credit, the document itself and international standard banking practice, need not be identical to, but must not conflict with, data in that document, any other stipulated document or the credit.

**e.** In documents other than the commercial invoice, the description of the goods, services or performance, if stated, may be in general terms not conflicting with their description in the credit.

**f.** If a credit requires presentation of a document other than a transport document, insurance document or commercial invoice, without stipulating by whom the document is to be issued or its data content, banks will accept the document as presented if its content appears to fulfil the function of the required document and otherwise complies with sub-article 14 (d).

**g.** A document presented but not required by the credit will be disregarded and may be returned to the presenter.

**h.** If a credit contains a condition without stipulating the document to indicate compliance with the condition, banks will deem such condition as not stated and will disregard it.

**i.** A document may be dated prior to the issuance date of the credit, but must not be dated later than its date of presentation.

**j.** When the addresses of the beneficiary and the applicant appear in any stipulated document, they need not be the same as those stated in the credit or in any other stipulated document, but must be within the same country as the respective addresses mentioned in the credit. Contact details (telefax, telephone, email and the like) stated as part of the beneficiary's and the applicant's address will be disregarded. However, when the address and contact details of the applicant appear as part of the consignee or notify party details on a transport document subject to articles 19, 20, 21, 22, 23, 24 or 25, they must be as stated in the credit.

**k.** The shipper or consignor of the goods indicated on any document need not be the beneficiary of the credit.

**l.** A transport document may be issued by any party other than a carrier, owner, master or charterer provided that the transport document meets the requirements of articles 19, 20, 21, 22, 23 or 24 of these rules.

## UCP 600 - Article 15

Complying Presentation

**a.** When an issuing bank determines that a presentation is complying, it must honour.

**b.** When a confirming bank determines that a presentation is complying, it must honour or negotiate and forward the documents to the issuing bank.

**c.** When a nominated bank determines that a presentation is complying and honours or negotiates, it must forward the documents to the confirming bank or issuing bank.

## UCP 600 - Article 16

Discrepant Documents, Waiver and Notice

**a.** When a nominated bank acting on its nomination, a confirming bank, if any, or the issuing bank determines that a presentation does not comply, it may refuse to honour or negotiate.

**b.** When an issuing bank determines that a presentation does not comply, it may in its sole judgement approach the applicant for a waiver of the discrepancies. This does not, however, extend the period mentioned in sub-article 14 (b).

**c.** When a nominated bank acting on its nomination, a confirming bank, if any, or the issuing bank decides to refuse to honour or negotiate, it must give a single notice to that effect to the presenter.

The notice must state:

**i.** that the bank is refusing to honour or negotiate; and

**ii.** each discrepancy in respect of which the bank refuses to honour or negotiate; and

**iii.**

a) that the bank is holding the documents pending further instructions from the presenter; or

b) that the issuing bank is holding the documents until it receives a waiver from the applicant and agrees to accept it, or receives further instructions from the presenter prior to agreeing to accept a waiver; or

c) that the bank is returning the documents; or

d) that the bank is acting in accordance with instructions previously received from the presenter.

**d.** The notice required in sub-article 16 (c) must be given by telecommunication or, if that is not possible, by other expeditious means no later than the close of the fifth banking day following the day of presentation.

**e.** A nominated bank acting on its nomination, a confirming bank, if any, or the issuing bank may, after providing notice required by sub-article 16 (c) (iii) (a) or (b), return the documents to the presenter at any time.

**f.** If an issuing bank or a confirming bank fails to act in accordance with the provisions of this article, it shall be precluded from claiming that the documents do not constitute a complying presentation.

**g.** When an issuing bank refuses to honour or a confirming bank refuses to honour or negotiate and has given notice to that effect in accordance with this article, it shall then be entitled to claim a refund, with interest, of any reimbursement made.

## UCP 600 - Article 17

Original Documents and Copies

**a.** At least one original of each document stipulated in the credit must be presented.

**b.** A bank shall treat as an original any document bearing an apparently original signature, mark, stamp, or label of the issuer of the document, unless the document itself indicates that it is not an original.

**c.** Unless a document indicates otherwise, a bank will also accept a document as original if it:

**i.** appears to be written, typed, perforated or stamped by the document issuer's hand; or

**ii.** appears to be on the document issuer's original stationery; or

**iii.** states that it is original, unless the statement appears not to apply to the document presented.

**d.** If a credit requires presentation of copies of documents, presentation of either originals or copies is permitted.

**e.** If a credit requires presentation of multiple documents by using terms such as "in duplicate", "in two fold" or "in two copies", this will be satisfied by the presentation of at least one original and the remaining number in copies, except when the document itself indicates otherwise.

## UCP 600 - Article 18

Commercial Invoice

**a.** A commercial invoice:

**i.** must appear to have been issued by the beneficiary (except as provided in article 38);

**ii.** must be made out in the name of the applicant (except as provided in sub-article 38 (g));

**iii.** must be made out in the same currency as the credit; and

**iv.** need not be signed.

**b.** A nominated bank acting on its nomination, a confirming bank, if any, or the issuing bank may accept a commercial invoice issued for an amount in excess of the amount permitted by the credit, and its decision will be binding upon all parties, provided the bank in question has not honoured or negotiated for an amount in excess of that permitted by the credit.

**c.** The description of the goods, services or performance in a commercial invoice must correspond with that appearing in the credit.

## UCP 600 - Article 19

Transport Document Covering at Least Two Different Modes of Transport

**a.** A transport document covering at least two different modes of transport (multimodal or combined transport document), however named, must appear to:

**i.** indicate the name of the carrier and be signed by:

- the carrier or a named agent for or on behalf of the carrier, or

- the master or a named agent for or on behalf of the master.

Any signature by the carrier, master or agent must be identified as that of the carrier, master or agent.

Any signature by an agent must indicate whether the agent has signed for or on behalf of the carrier or for or on behalf of the master.

**ii.** indicate that the goods have been dispatched, taken in charge or shipped on board at the place stated in the credit, by:

- pre-printed wording, or

- a stamp or notation indicating the date on which the goods have been dispatched, taken in charge or shipped on board.

The date of issuance of the transport document will be deemed to be the date of dispatch, taking in charge or shipped on board, and the date of shipment. However, if the transport document indicates, by stamp or notation, a date of dispatch, taking in charge or shipped on board, this date will be deemed to be the date of shipment.

**iii.** indicate the place of dispatch, taking in charge or shipment and the place of final destination stated in the credit, even if:

**a.** the transport document states, in addition, a different place of dispatch, taking in charge or shipment or place of final destination,

or

**b.** the transport document contains the indication "intended" or similar qualification in relation to the vessel, port of loading or port of discharge.

**iv.** be the sole original transport document or, if issued in more than one original, be the full set as indicated on the transport document.

**v.** contain terms and conditions of carriage or make reference to another source containing the terms and conditions of carriage (short form or blank back transport document). Contents of terms and conditions of carriage will not be examined.

**vi.** contain no indication that it is subject to a charter party.

**b.** For the purpose of this article, transhipment means unloading from one means of conveyance and reloading to another means of conveyance (whether or not in different modes of transport) during the carriage from the place of dispatch, taking in charge or shipment to the place of final destination stated in the credit.

**c.**

**i.** A transport document may indicate that the goods will or may be transhipped provided that the entire carriage is covered by one and the same transport document.

**ii.** A transport document indicating that transhipment will or may take place is acceptable, even if the credit prohibits transhipment.

## UCP 600 - Article 20

Bill of Lading

**a.**A bill of lading, however named, must appear to:

**i.** indicate the name of the carrier and be signed by:

- the carrier or a named agent for or on behalf of the carrier, or

- the master or a named agent for or on behalf of the master.

Any signature by the carrier, master or agent must be identified as that of the carrier, master or agent.

Any signature by an agent must indicate whether the agent has signed for or on behalf of the carrier or for or on behalf of the master.

**ii.** indicate that the goods have been shipped on board a named vessel at the port of loading stated in the credit by:

- pre-printed wording, or

- an on board notation indicating the date on which the goods have been shipped on board.

The date of issuance of the bill of lading will be deemed to be the date of shipment unless the bill of lading contains an on board notation indicating the date of shipment, in which case the date stated in the on board notation will be deemed to be the date of shipment.

If the bill of lading contains the indication "intended vessel" or similar qualification in relation to the name of the vessel, an on board notation indicating the date of shipment and the name of the actual vessel is required.

**iii.** indicate shipment from the port of loading to the port of discharge stated in the credit.

If the bill of lading does not indicate the port of loading stated in the credit as the port of loading, or if it contains the indication "intended" or similar qualification in relation to the port of loading, an on board notation indicating the port of loading as stated in the credit, the date of shipment and the name of the vessel is required. This provision applies even when loading on board or shipment on a named vessel is indicated by pre-printed wording on the bill of lading.

**iv.** be the sole original bill of lading or, if issued in more than one original, be the full set as indicated on the bill of lading.

**v.** contain terms and conditions of carriage or make reference to another source containing the terms and conditions of carriage (short form or blank back bill of lading). Contents of terms and conditions of carriage will not be examined.

**vi.** contain no indication that it is subject to a charter party.

**b.** For the purpose of this article, transhipment means unloading from one vessel and reloading to another vessel during the carriage from the port of loading to the port of discharge stated in the credit.

**c.**

**i.** A bill of lading may indicate that the goods will or may be transhipped provided that the entire carriage is covered by one and the same bill of lading.

**ii.** A bill of lading indicating that transhipment will or may take place is acceptable, even if the credit prohibits transhipment, if the goods have been shipped in a container, trailer or LASH barge as evidenced by the bill of lading.

**d.** Clauses in a bill of lading stating that the carrier reserves the right to tranship will be disregarded.

## UCP 600 - Article 21

Non-Negotiable Sea Waybill

**a.** A non-negotiable sea waybill, however named, must appear to:

**i.** indicate the name of the carrier and be signed by:

- the carrier or a named agent for or on behalf of the carrier, or

- the master or a named agent for or on behalf of the master.

Any signature by the carrier, master or agent must be identified as that of the carrier, master or agent.

Any signature by an agent must indicate whether the agent has signed for or on behalf of the carrier or for or on behalf of the master.

**ii.** indicate that the goods have been shipped on board a named vessel at the port of loading stated in the credit by:

- pre-printed wording, or

- an on board notation indicating the date on which the goods have been shipped on board.

The date of issuance of the non-negotiable sea waybill will be deemed to be the date of shipment unless the non-negotiable sea waybill contains an on board notation indicating the date of shipment, in which case the date stated in the on board notation will be deemed to be the date of shipment.

If the non-negotiable sea waybill contains the indication "intended vessel" or similar qualification in relation to the name of the vessel, an on board notation indicating the date of shipment and the name of the actual vessel is required.

**iii.** indicate shipment from the port of loading to the port of discharge stated in the credit.

If the non-negotiable sea waybill does not indicate the port of loading stated in the credit as the port of loading, or if it contains the indication "intended" or similar qualification in relation to the port of loading, an on board notation indicating the port of loading as stated in the credit, the date of shipment and the name of the vessel is required. This provision applies even when loading on board or shipment on a named vessel is indicated by pre-printed wording on the non-negotiable sea waybill.

**iv.** be the sole original non-negotiable sea waybill or, if issued in more than one original, be the full set as indicated on the non-negotiable sea waybill.

**v.** contain terms and conditions of carriage or make reference to another source containing the terms and conditions of carriage (short form or blank back non-negotiable sea waybill). Contents of terms and conditions of carriage will not be examined.

**vi.** contain no indication that it is subject to a charter party.

**b.** For the purpose of this article, transhipment means unloading from one vessel and reloading to another vessel during the carriage from the port of loading to the port of discharge stated in the credit.

**c.**

**i.** A non-negotiable sea waybill may indicate that the goods will or may be transhipped provided that the entire carriage is covered by one and the same non-negotiable sea waybill.

**ii.** A non-negotiable sea waybill indicating that transhipment will or may take place is acceptable, even if the credit prohibits transhipment, if the goods have been shipped in a container, trailer or LASH barge as evidenced by the non-negotiable sea waybill.

**d.** Clauses in a non-negotiable sea waybill stating that the carrier reserves the right to tranship will be disregarded.

## UCP 600 - Article 22

Charter Party Bill of Lading

**a.** A bill of lading, however named, containing an indication that it is subject to a charter party (charter party bill of lading), must appear to:

**i.** be signed by:

- the master or a named agent for or on behalf of the master, or

- the owner or a named agent for or on behalf of the owner, or

- the charterer or a named agent for or on behalf of the charterer.

Any signature by the master, owner, charterer or agent must be identified as that of the master, owner, charterer or agent.

Any signature by an agent must indicate whether the agent has signed for or on behalf of the master, owner or charterer.

An agent signing for or on behalf of the owner or charterer must indicate the name of the owner or charterer.

**ii.** indicate that the goods have been shipped on board a named vessel at the port of loading stated in the credit by:

- pre-printed wording, or

- an on board notation indicating the date on which the goods have been shipped on board.

The date of issuance of the charter party bill of lading will be deemed to be the date of shipment unless the charter party bill of lading contains an on board notation indicating the date of shipment, in which case the date stated in the on board notation will be deemed to be the date of shipment.

**iii.** indicate shipment from the port of loading to the port of discharge stated in the credit. The port of discharge may also be shown as a range of ports or a geographical area, as stated in the credit.

**iv.** be the sole original charter party bill of lading or, if issued in more than one original, be the full set as indicated on the charter party bill of lading.

**b.** A bank will not examine charter party contracts, even if they are required to be presented by the terms of the credit.

## UCP 600 - Article 23

Air Transport Document

**a.** An air transport document, however named, must appear to:

**i.** indicate the name of the carrier and be signed by:

- the carrier, or

- a named agent for or on behalf of the carrier.

Any signature by the carrier or agent must be identified as that of the carrier or agent.

Any signature by an agent must indicate that the agent has signed for or on behalf of the carrier.

**ii.**indicate that the goods have been accepted for carriage.

**iii.** indicate the date of issuance. This date will be deemed to be the date of shipment unless the air transport document contains a specific notation of the actual date of shipment, in which case the date stated in the notation will be deemed to be the date of shipment.

Any other information appearing on the air transport document relative to the flight number and date will not be considered in determining the date of shipment.

**iv.** indicate the airport of departure and the airport of destination stated in the credit.

**v.** be the original for consignor or shipper, even if the credit stipulates a full set of originals.

**vi.** contain terms and conditions of carriage or make reference to another source containing the terms and conditions of carriage. Contents of terms and conditions of carriage will not be examined.

**b.** For the purpose of this article, transhipment means unloading from one aircraft and reloading to another aircraft during the carriage from the airport of departure to the airport of destination stated in the credit.

**c.**

**i.** An air transport document may indicate that the goods will or may be transhipped, provided that the entire carriage is covered by one and the same air transport document.

**ii.** An air transport document indicating that transhipment will or may take place is acceptable, even if the credit prohibits transhipment.

## UCP 600 - Article 24

Road, Rail or Inland Waterway Transport Documents

**a.** A road, rail or inland waterway transport document, however named, must appear to:

**i.** indicate the name of the carrier and:

- be signed by the carrier or a named agent for or on behalf of the carrier, or

- indicate receipt of the goods by signature, stamp or notation by the carrier or a named agent for or on behalf of the carrier.

Any signature, stamp or notation of receipt of the goods by the carrier or agent must be identified as that of the carrier or agent.

Any signature, stamp or notation of receipt of the goods by the agent must indicate that the agent has signed or acted for or on behalf of the carrier.

If a rail transport document does not identify the carrier, any signature or stamp of the railway company will be accepted as evidence of the document being signed by the carrier.

**ii.** indicate the date of shipment or the date the goods have been received for shipment, dispatch or carriage at the place stated in the credit. Unless the transport document contains a dated reception stamp, an indication of the date of receipt or a date of shipment, the date of issuance of the transport document will be deemed to be the date of shipment.

**iii.** indicate the place of shipment and the place of destination stated in the credit.

**b.**

**i.** A road transport document must appear to be the original for consignor or shipper or bear no marking indicating for whom the document has been prepared.

**ii.** A rail transport document marked "duplicate" will be accepted as an original.

**iii.** A rail or inland waterway transport document will be accepted as an original whether marked as an original or not.

**c.** In the absence of an indication on the transport document as to the number of originals issued, the number presented will be deemed to constitute a full set.

**d.** For the purpose of this article, transhipment means unloading from one means of conveyance and reloading to another means of conveyance, within the same mode of transport, during the carriage from the place of shipment, dispatch or carriage to the place of destination stated in the credit.

**e.**

**i.** A road, rail or inland waterway transport document may indicate that the goods will or may be transhipped provided that the entire carriage is covered by one and the same transport document.

**ii.** A road, rail or inland waterway transport document indicating that transhipment will or may take place is acceptable, even if the credit prohibits transhipment.

## UCP 600 - Article 25

Courier Receipt, Post Receipt or Certificate of Posting

**a.** A courier receipt, however named, evidencing receipt of goods for transport, must appear to:

**i.** indicate the name of the courier service and be stamped or signed by the named courier service at the place from which the credit states the goods are to be shipped; and

**ii.** indicate a date of pick-up or of receipt or wording to this effect. This date will be deemed to be the date of shipment.

**b.** A requirement that courier charges are to be paid or prepaid may be satisfied by a transport document issued by a courier service evidencing that courier charges are for the account of a party other than the consignee.

**c.** A post receipt or certificate of posting, however named, evidencing receipt of goods for transport, must appear to be stamped or signed and dated at the place from which the credit states the goods are to be shipped. This date will be deemed to be the date of shipment.

## UCP 600 - Article 26

On Deck", "Shipper's Load and Count", "Said by Shipper to Contain" and Charges Additional to Freight

**a.** A transport document must not indicate that the goods are or will be loaded on deck. A clause on a transport document stating that the goods may be loaded on deck is acceptable.

**b.** A transport document bearing a clause such as "shipper's load and count" and "said by shipper to contain" is acceptable.

**c.** A transport document may bear a reference, by stamp or otherwise, to charges additional to the freight.

## UCP 600 - Article 27

Clean Transport Document

A bank will only accept a clean transport document. A clean transport document is one bearing no clause or notation expressly declaring a defective condition of the goods or their packaging. The word "clean" need not appear on a transport document, even if a credit has a requirement for that transport document to be "clean on board".

## UCP 600 - Article 28

Insurance Document and Coverage

**a.** An insurance document, such as an insurance policy, an insurance certificate or a declaration under an open cover, must appear to be issued and signed by an insurance company, an underwriter or their agents or their proxies.

Any signature by an agent or proxy must indicate whether the agent or proxy has signed for or on behalf of the insurance company or underwriter.

**b.** When the insurance document indicates that it has been issued in more than one original, all originals must be presented.

**c.** Cover notes will not be accepted.

**d.** An insurance policy is acceptable in lieu of an insurance certificate or a declaration under an open cover.

**e.** The date of the insurance document must be no later than the date of shipment, unless it appears from the insurance document that the cover is effective from a date not later than the date of shipment.

**f.**

**i.**The insurance document must indicate the amount of insurance coverage and be in the same currency as the credit.

**ii.** A requirement in the credit for insurance coverage to be for a percentage of the value of the goods, of the invoice value or similar is deemed to be the minimum amount of coverage required.

If there is no indication in the credit of the insurance coverage required, the amount of insurance coverage must be at least 110% of the CIF or CIP value of the goods.

When the CIF or CIP value cannot be determined from the documents, the amount of insurance coverage must be calculated on the basis of the amount for which honour or negotiation is requested or the gross value of the goods as shown on the invoice, whichever is greater.

**iii.** The insurance document must indicate that risks are covered at least between the place of taking in charge or shipment and the place of discharge or final destination as stated in the credit.

**g.** A credit should state the type of insurance required and, if any, the additional risks to be covered. An insurance document will be accepted without regard to any risks that are not covered if the credit uses imprecise terms such as "usual risks" or "customary risks".

**h.** When a credit requires insurance against "all risks" and an insurance document is presented containing any "all risks" notation or clause, whether or not bearing the heading "all risks", the insurance document will be accepted without regard to any risks stated to be excluded.

**i.** An insurance document may contain reference to any exclusion clause.

**j.** An insurance document may indicate that the cover is subject to a franchise or excess (deductible).

## UCP 600 - Article 29

**a.** If the expiry date of a credit or the last day for presentation falls on a day when the bank to which presentation is to be made is closed for reasons other than those referred to in article 36, the expiry date or the last day for presentation, as the case may be, will be extended to the first following banking day.

**b.** If presentation is made on the first following banking day, a nominated bank must provide the issuing bank or confirming bank with a statement on its covering schedule that the presentation was made within the time limits extended in accordance with sub-article 29 (a).

**c.** The latest date for shipment will not be extended as a result of sub-article 29 (a).

## UCP 600 - Article 30

Tolerance in Credit Amount, Quantity and Unit Prices

**a.** The words "about" or "approximately" used in connection with the amount of the credit or the quantity or the unit price stated in the credit are to be construed as allowing a tolerance not to exceed 10% more or 10% less than the amount, the quantity or the unit price to which they refer.

**b.** A tolerance not to exceed 5% more or 5% less than the quantity of the goods is allowed, provided the credit does not state the quantity in terms of a stipulated number of packing units or individual items and the total amount of the drawings does not exceed the amount of the credit.

**c.** Even when partial shipments are not allowed, a tolerance not to exceed 5% less than the amount of the credit is allowed, provided that the quantity of the goods, if stated in the credit, is shipped in full and a unit price, if stated in the credit, is not reduced or that sub-article 30 (b) is not applicable. This tolerance does not apply when the credit stipulates a specific tolerance or uses the expressions referred to in sub-article 30 (a).

## UCP 600 - Article 31

Partial Drawings or Shipments

**a.** Partial drawings or shipments are allowed.

**b.** A presentation consisting of more than one set of transport documents evidencing shipment commencing on the same means of conveyance and for the same journey, provided they indicate the same destination, will not be regarded as covering a partial shipment, even if they indicate different dates of shipment or different ports of loading, places of taking in charge or dispatch. If the presentation consists of more than one set of transport documents, the latest date of shipment as evidenced on any of the sets of transport documents will be regarded as the date of shipment.

A presentation consisting of one or more sets of transport documents evidencing shipment on more than one means of conveyance within the same mode of transport will be regarded as covering a partial shipment, even if the means of conveyance leave on the same day for the same destination.

**c.** A presentation consisting of more than one courier receipt, post receipt or certificate of posting will not be regarded as a partial shipment if the courier receipts, post receipts or certificates of posting appear to have been stamped or signed by the same courier or postal service at the same place and date and for the same destination.

## UCP 600 - Article 32

Instalment Drawings or Shipments

If a drawing or shipment by instalments within given periods is stipulated in the credit and any instalment is not drawn or shipped within the period allowed for that instalment, the credit ceases to be available for that and any subsequent instalment.

## UCP 600 - Article 33

Hours of Presentation

A bank has no obligation to accept a presentation outside of its banking hours.

## UCP 600 - Article 34

Disclaimer on Effectiveness of Documents

A bank assumes no liability or responsibility for the form, sufficiency, accuracy, genuineness, falsification or legal effect of any document, or for the general or particular conditions stipulated in a document or superimposed thereon; nor does it assume any liability or responsibility for the description, quantity, weight, quality, condition, packing, delivery, value or existence of the goods, services or other performance represented by any document, or for the good faith or acts or omissions, solvency, performance or standing of the consignor, the carrier, the forwarder, the consignee or the insurer of the goods or any other person.

## UCP 600 - Article 35

Disclaimer on Transmission and Translation

A bank assumes no liability or responsibility for the consequences arising out of delay, loss in transit, mutilation or other errors arising in the transmission of any messages or delivery of letters or documents, when such messages, letters or documents are transmitted or sent according to the requirements stated in the credit, or when the bank may have taken the initiative in the choice of the delivery service in the absence of such instructions in the credit.

If a nominated bank determines that a presentation is complying and forwards the documents to the issuing bank or confirming bank, whether or not the nominated bank has honoured or negotiated, an issuing bank or confirming bank must honour or negotiate, or reimburse that nominated bank, even when the documents have been lost in transit between the nominated bank and the issuing bank or confirming bank, or between the confirming bank and the issuing bank.

A bank assumes no liability or responsibility for errors in translation or interpretation of technical terms and may transmit credit terms without translating them.

## UCP 600 - Article 36

Force Majeure

A bank assumes no liability or responsibility for the consequences arising out of the interruption of its business by Acts of God, riots, civil commotions, insurrections, wars, acts of terrorism, or by any strikes or lockouts or any other causes beyond its control.

A bank will not, upon resumption of its business, honour or negotiate under a credit that expired during such interruption of its business.

## UCP 600 - Article 37

Disclaimer for Acts of an Instructed Party

**a.** A bank utilizing the services of another bank for the purpose of giving effect to the instructions of the applicant does so for the account and at the risk of the applicant.

**b.** An issuing bank or advising bank assumes no liability or responsibility should the instructions it transmits to another bank not be carried out, even if it has taken the initiative in the choice of that other bank.

**c.** A bank instructing another bank to perform services is liable for any commissions, fees, costs or expenses ("charges") incurred by that bank in connection with its instructions.

If a credit states that charges are for the account of the beneficiary and charges cannot be collected or deducted from proceeds, the issuing bank remains liable for payment of charges.

A credit or amendment should not stipulate that the advising to a beneficiary is conditional upon the receipt by the advising bank or second advising bank of its charges.

**d.** The applicant shall be bound by and liable to indemnify a bank against all obligations and responsibilities imposed by foreign laws and usages.

## UCP 600 - Article 38

Transferable Credits

**a.** A bank is under no obligation to transfer a credit except to the extent and in the manner expressly consented to by that bank.

**b.** For the purpose of this article:

Transferable credit means a credit that specifically states it is "transferable". A transferable credit may be made available in whole or in part to another beneficiary ("second beneficiary") at the request of the beneficiary ("first beneficiary").

Transferring bank means a nominated bank that transfers the credit or, in a credit available with any bank, a bank that is specifically authorized by the issuing bank to transfer and that transfers the credit. An issuing bank may be a transferring bank.

Transferred credit means a credit that has been made available by the transferring bank to a second beneficiary.

**c.** Unless otherwise agreed at the time of transfer, all charges (such as commissions, fees, costs or expenses) incurred in respect of a transfer must be paid by the first beneficiary.

**d.** A credit may be transferred in part to more than one second beneficiary provided partial drawings or shipments are allowed.

A transferred credit cannot be transferred at the request of a second beneficiary to any subsequent beneficiary. The first beneficiary is not considered to be a subsequent beneficiary.

**e.** Any request for transfer must indicate if and under what conditions amendments may be advised to the second beneficiary. The transferred credit must clearly indicate those conditions.

**f.** If a credit is transferred to more than one second beneficiary, rejection of an amendment by one or more second beneficiary does not invalidate the acceptance by any other second beneficiary, with respect to which the transferred credit will be amended accordingly. For any second beneficiary that rejected the amendment, the transferred credit will remain unamended.

**g.** The transferred credit must accurately reflect the terms and conditions of the credit, including confirmation, if any, with the exception of:

- the amount of the credit,

- any unit price stated therein,

- the expiry date,

- the period for presentation, or

- the latest shipment date or given period for shipment,

any or all of which may be reduced or curtailed.

The percentage for which insurance cover must be effected may be increased to provide the amount of cover stipulated in the credit or these articles.

The name of the first beneficiary may be substituted for that of the applicant in the credit.

If the name of the applicant is specifically required by the credit to appear in any document other than the invoice, such requirement must be reflected in the transferred credit.

**h.** The first beneficiary has the right to substitute its own invoice and draft, if any, for those of a second beneficiary for an amount not in excess of that stipulated in the credit, and upon such substitution the first beneficiary can draw under the credit for the difference, if any, between its invoice and the invoice of a second beneficiary.

**i.** If the first beneficiary is to present its own invoice and draft, if any, but fails to do so on first demand, or if the invoices presented by the first beneficiary create discrepancies that did not exist in the presentation made by the second beneficiary and the first beneficiary fails to correct them on first demand, the transferring bank has the right to present the documents as received from the second beneficiary to the issuing bank, without further responsibility to the first beneficiary.

**j.** The first beneficiary may, in its request for transfer, indicate that honour or negotiation is to be effected to a second beneficiary at the place to which the credit has been transferred, up to and including the expiry date of the credit. This is without prejudice to the right of the first beneficiary in accordance with sub-article 38 (h).

**k.** Presentation of documents by or on behalf of a second beneficiary must be made to the transferring bank.

## UCP 600 - Article 39

Assignment of Proceeds

The fact that a credit is not stated to be transferable shall not affect the right of the beneficiary to assign any proceeds to which it may be or may become entitled under the credit, in accordance with the provisions of applicable law. This article relates only to the assignment of proceeds and not to the assignment of the right to perform under the credit.

# Supplement for Electronic Presentation eUCP Version 1.1

## Article e1

### Scope of the eUCP

a. The Supplement to the Uniform Customs and Practice for Documentary Credits for Electronic Presentation ("eUCP") supplements the *Uniform Customs and Practice for Documentary Credits* (2007 Revision, ICC Publication No. 600) ("UCP") in order to accommodate presentation of electronic records alone or in combination with paper documents.

b. The eUCP shall apply as a supplement to the UCP where the credit indicates that it is subject to eUCP.

c. This version is Version 1.1. A credit must indicate the applicable version of the eUCP If it does not do so, it is subject to the version in effect on the date the credit is issued or, if made subject to eUCP by an amendment accepted by the beneficiary, on the date of that amendment.

## Article e2

### Relationship of the eUCP to the UCP

a. A credit subject to the eUCP ("eUCP credit") is also subject to the UCP without express incorporation of the UCP

b. Where the eUCP applies, its provisions shall prevail to the extent that they would produce a result different from the application of the UCP

c. If an eUCP credit allows the beneficiary to choose between presentation of paper documents or electronic records and it chooses to present only paper documents, the UCP alone shall apply to that presentation. If only paper documents are permitted under an eUCP credit, the UCP alone shall apply.

## Article e3

### Definitions

a. Where the following terms are used in the UCP, for the purposes of applying the UCP to an electronic record presented under an eUCP credit, the term:
   - i. appear on their face and the like shall apply to examination of the data content of an electronic record.
   - ii. document shall include an electronic record.
   - iii. place for presentation of electronic records means an electronic address.
   - iv. sign and the like shall include an electronic signature.
   - v. superimposed, notation or stamped means data content whose supplementary character is apparent in an electronic record.

b. The following terms used in the eUCP shall have the following meanings:
   - i. electronic record means
     - data created, generated, sent, communicated, received or stored by electronic means
     - that is capable of being authenticated as to the apparent identity of a sender and the apparent source of the data contained in it, and as to whether it has remained complete and unaltered, and
     - is capable of being examined for compliance with the terms and conditions of the eUCP credit.
   - ii. electronic signature means a data process attached to or logically associated with an electronic record and executed or adopted by a person in order to identify that person and to indicate that person's authentication of the electronic record.
   - iii. format means the data organization in which the electronic record is expressed or to which it refers.
   - iv. paper document means a document in a traditional paper form.
   - v. received means the time when an electronic record enters the information system of the applicable recipient in a form capable of being accepted by that system. Any acknowledgement of receipt does not imply acceptance or refusal of the electronic record under an eUCP credit.

## Article e4

### Format

An eUCP credit must specify the formats in which electronic records are to be presented. If the format of the electronic record is not so specified, it may be presented in any format.

## Article e5

### Presentation

a. An eUCP credit allowing presentation of:
   - i. electronic records must state a place for presentation of the electronic records.
   - ii. both electronic records and paper documents must also state a place for presentation of the paper documents.

b. Electronic records may be presented separately andneed not be presented at the same time.

c. If an eUCP credit allows for presentation of one or more electronic records, the beneficiary is responsible for providing a notice to the bank to which presentation is made signifying when the presentation is complete. The notice of completeness may be given as an electronic record or paper document and must identify the eUCP credit to which it relates. Presentation is deemed not to have been made if the beneficiary's notice is not received.

d. 
   - i. Each presentation of an electronic record and the presentation of paper documents under an eUCP credit must identify the eUCP credit under which it is presented.
   - ii. A presentation not so identified may be treated as not received.

e. If the bank to which presentation is to be made is open but its system is unable to receive a transmitted electronic record on the stipulated expiry date and/or the last day of the period of time after the date of shipment for presentation, as the case may be, the bank will be deemed to be closed and the date for presentation and/ or the expiry date shall be extended to the first following banking day on which such bank is able to receive an electronic record. If the only electronic record remaining to be presented is the notice of completeness, it may be given by telecommunications or by paper document and will be deemed timely, provided that it is sent before the bank is able to receive an electronic record.

f. An electronic record that cannot be authenticated is deemed not to have been presented.

## Article e6

### Examination

a. If an electronic record contains a hyperlink to an external system or a presentation indicates that the electronic record may be examined by reference to an external system, the electronic record at the hyperlink or the referenced system shall be deemed to be the electronic record to be examined. The failure of the indicated system to provide access to the required electronic record at the time of examination shall constitute a discrepancy.

b. The forwarding of electronic records by a nominated bank pursuant to its nomination signifies that it has satisfied itself as to the apparent authenticity of the electronic records.

c. The inability of the issuing bank, or confirming bank, if any, to examine an electronic record in a format required by the eUCP credit or, if no format is required, to examine it in the format presented is not a basis for refusal.

## Article e7

### Notice of Refusal

a. 
   - i. The time period for the examination of documents commences on the banking day following the banking day on which the beneficiary's notice of completeness is received.
   - ii. If the time for presentation of documents or the notice of completeness is extended, the time for the examination of documents commences on the first following banking day on which the bank to which presentation is to be made is able to receive the notice of completeness.

b. If an issuing bank, the confirming bank, if any, or a nominated bank acting on their behalf, provides a notice of refusal of a presentation which includes electronic records and does not receive instructions from the party to which notice of refusal is given within 30 calendar days from the date the notice of refusal is given for the disposition of the electronic records, the bank shall return any paper documents not previously returned to the presenter but may dispose of the electronic records in any manner deemed appropriate without any responsibility.

## Article e8

### Originals and Copies

Any requirement of the UCP or an eUCP credit for presentation of one or more originals or copies of an electronic record is satisfied by the presentation of one electronic record.

## Article e9

### Date of Issuance

Unless an electronic record contains a specific date of issuance, the date on which it appears to have been sent by the issuer is deemed to be the date of issuance. The date of receipt will be deemed to be the date it was sent if no other date is apparent.

## Article e10

### Transport

If an electronic record evidencing transport does not indicate a date of shipment or dispatch, the date of issuance of the electronic record will be deemed to be the date of shipment or dispatch. However, if the electronic record bears a notation that evidences the date of shipment or dispatch, the date of the notation will be deemed to be the date of shipment or dispatch. A notation showing additional data content need not be separately signed or otherwise authenticated.

## Article e11

### Corruption of an Electronic Record after Presentation

a. If an electronic record that has been received by the issuing bank, confirming bank, or another nominated bank appears to have been corrupted, the bank may inform the presenter and may request that the electronic record be re-presented.

b. If the bank requests that an electronic record be represented:
   - i. the time for examination is suspended and resumes when the presenter re-presents the electronic record; and
   - ii. if the nominated bank is not the confirming bank, it must provide the issuing bank and any confirming bank with notice of the request for re-presentation and inform it of the suspension; but
   - iii. if the same electronic record is not re-presented within thirty (30) calendar days, the bank may treat the electronic record as not presented, and
   - iv. any deadlines are not extended.

## Article e12

### Additional Disclaimer of Liability for Presentation of Electronic Records under eUCP

By satisfying itself as to the apparent authenticity of an electronic record, banks assume no liability for the identity of the sender, source of the information or its complete and unaltered character other than that which is apparent in the electronic record received by the use of a commercially acceptable data process for the receipt, authentication and identification of electronic records.

**ICC Business Bookstore**

**iccbooks.com**